1 AND 2 TIMOTHY, TITUS

THE NIV
APPLICATION
COMMENTARY

From biblical text . . . to contemporary life

THE NIV APPLICATION COMMENTARY SERIES

1 & 2 TIMOTHY, TITUS

THE NIV
APPLICATION
COMMENTARY

From biblical text . . . to contemporary life

WALTER L. LIEFELD

ZONDERVAN®

ZONDERVAN.com/
AUTHORTRACKER
follow your favorite authors

We want to hear from you. Please send your comments about this
book to us in care of zreview@zondervan.com. Thank you.

ZONDERVAN®

The NIV Application Commentary: 1 & 2 Timothy, Titus
Copyright © 1999 by Walter L. Liefeld

Requests for information should be addressed to:

Zondervan, *Grand Rapids, Michigan* 49530

Library of Congress Cataloging-in-Publication Data
Liefeld, Walter L.
    1 and 2 Timothy/Titus / Walter L. Liefeld.
    p. cm.—(NIV application commentary)
    Includes bibliographical references and indexes.
    ISBN-10: 0-310-50110-5
    ISBN-13: 978-0-310-50110-7
    1. Bible. N.T. Pastoral Epistles—Commentaries. I. Title. II. Title: First and second Timo-
thy/Titus. III. Series.
BS 2735.3.L54 1999
227'.83077—dc21   99–18861

Printed in the United States of America

09 10 11 12 13 14 • 18 17 16 15 14 13 12 11

To every pastor faithfully engaged

in preaching the Word

The NIV Application Commentary Series

When complete, the NIV Application Commentary
will include the following volumes:

Old Testament Volumes

Genesis, John H. Walton

Exodus, Peter Enns

Leviticus/Numbers, Roy Gane

Deuteronomy, Daniel I. Block

Joshua, Robert L. Hubbard Jr.

Judges/Ruth, K. Lawson Younger

1-2 Samuel, Bill T. Arnold

1-2 Kings, Gus Konkel

1-2 Chronicles, Andrew E. Hill

Ezra/Nehemiah, Douglas J. Green

Esther, Karen H. Jobes

Job, Dennis R. Magary

Psalms Volume 1, Gerald H. Wilson

Psalms Volume 2, Jamie A. Grant

Proverbs, Paul Koptak

Ecclesiastes/Song of Songs, Iain Provan

Isaiah, John N. Oswalt

Jeremiah/Lamentations, J. Andrew Dearman

Ezekiel, Iain M. Duguid

Daniel, Tremper Longman III

Hosea/Amos/Micah, Gary V. Smith

Jonah/Nahum/Habakkuk/Zephaniah,
    James Bruckner

Joel/Obadiah/Malachi, David W. Baker

Haggai/Zechariah, Mark J. Boda

New Testament Volumes

Matthew, Michael J. Wilkins

Mark, David E. Garland

Luke, Darrell L. Bock

John, Gary M. Burge

Acts, Ajith Fernando

Romans, Douglas J. Moo

1 Corinthians, Craig Blomberg

2 Corinthians, Scott Hafemann

Galatians, Scot McKnight

Ephesians, Klyne Snodgrass

Philippians, Frank Thielman

Colossians/Philemon, David E. Garland

1-2 Thessalonians, Michael W. Holmes

1-2 Timothy/Titus, Walter L. Liefeld

Hebrews, George H. Guthrie

James, David P. Nystrom

1 Peter, Scot McKnight

2 Peter/Jude, Douglas J. Moo

Letters of John, Gary M. Burge

Revelation, Craig S. Keener

To see which titles are available,
visit our web site at www.zondervan.com

Contents

NIV Application Commentary
Series Introduction

THE NIV APPLICATION COMMENTARY SERIES is unique. Most commentaries help us make the journey from the twentieth century back to the first century. They enable us to cross the barriers of time, culture, language, and geography that separate us from the biblical world. Yet they only offer a one-way ticket to the past and assume that we can somehow make the return journey on our own. Once they have explained the *original meaning* of a book or passage, these commentaries give us little or no help in exploring its *contemporary significance*. The information they offer is valuable, but the job is only half done.

Recently, a few commentaries have included some contemporary application as *one* of their goals. Yet that application is often sketchy or moralistic, and some volumes sound more like printed sermons than commentaries.

The primary goal of the NIV Application Commentary Series is to help you with the difficult but vital task of bringing an ancient message into a modern context. The series not only focuses on application as a finished product but also helps you think through the *process* of moving from the original meaning of a passage to its contemporary significance. These are commentaries, not popular expositions. They are works of reference, not devotional literature.

The format of the series is designed to achieve the goals of the series. Each passage is treated in three sections: *Original Meaning, Bridging Contexts,* and *Contemporary Significance.*

THIS SECTION HELPS you understand the meaning of the biblical text in its first-century context. All of the elements of traditional exegesis—in concise form—are discussed here. These include the historical, literary, and cultural context of the passage. The authors discuss matters related to grammar and syntax, and the meaning of biblical words. They also seek to explore the main ideas of the passage and how the biblical author develops those ideas.[1]

---

1. Please note that when the authors discuss words in the original biblical languages, the series uses the general rather than the scholarly method of transliteration.

After reading this section, you will understand the problems, questions, and concerns of the *original audience* and how the biblical author addressed those issues. This understanding is foundational to any legitimate application of the text today.

THIS SECTION BUILDS a bridge between the world of the Bible and the world of today, between the original context and the contemporary context, by focusing on both the timely and timeless aspects of the text.

God's Word is *timely*. The authors of Scripture spoke to specific situations, problems, and questions. Paul warned the Galatians about the consequences of circumcision and the dangers of trying to be justified by law (Gal. 5:2–5). The author of Hebrews tried to convince his readers that Christ is superior to Moses, the Aaronic priests, and the Old Testament sacrifices. John urged his readers to "test the spirits" of those who taught a form of incipient Gnosticism (1 John 4:1–6). In each of these cases, the timely nature of Scripture enables us to hear God's Word in situations that were *concrete* rather than abstract.

Yet the timely nature of Scripture also creates problems. Our situations, difficulties, and questions are not always directly related to those faced by the people in the Bible. Therefore, God's word to them does not always seem relevant to us. For example, when was the last time someone urged you to be circumcised, claiming that it was a necessary part of justification? How many people today care whether Christ is superior to the Aaronic priests? And how can a "test" designed to expose incipient Gnosticism be of any value in a modern culture?

Fortunately, Scripture is not only timely but *timeless*. Just as God spoke to the original audience, so he still speaks to us through the pages of Scripture. Because we share a common humanity with the people of the Bible, we discover a *universal dimension* in the problems they faced and the solutions God gave them. The timeless nature of Scripture enables it to speak with power in every time and in every culture.

Those who fail to recognize that Scripture is both timely and timeless run into a host of problems. For example, those who are intimidated by timely books such as Hebrews or Galatians might avoid reading them because they seem meaningless today. At the other extreme, those who are convinced of the timeless nature of Scripture, but who fail to discern its timely element, may "wax eloquent" about the Melchizedekian priesthood to a sleeping congregation.

The purpose of this section, therefore, is to help you discern what is time-less in the timely pages of Scripture—and what is not. For example, if Paul's primary concern is not circumcision (as he tells us in Gal. 5:6), what *is* he concerned about? If discussions about the Aaronic priesthood or Melchizedek seem irrelevant today, what is of abiding value in these passages? If people try to "test the spirits" today with a test designed for a specific first-century heresy, what other biblical test might be more appropriate?

Yet this section does not merely uncover that which is timeless in a passage but also helps you to see *how* it is uncovered. The author of the commentary seeks to take what is implicit in the text and make it explicit, to take a process that normally is intuitive and explain it in a logical, orderly fashion. How do we know that circumcision is not Paul's primary concern? What clues in the text or its context help us realize that Paul's real concern is at a deeper level?

Of course, those passages in which the historical distance between us and the original readers is greatest require a longer treatment. Conversely, those passages in which the historical distance is smaller or seemingly non-existent require less attention.

One final clarification. Because this section prepares the way for discussing the contemporary significance of the passage, there is not always a sharp distinction or a clear break between this section and the one that follows. Yet when both sections are read together, you should have a strong sense of moving from the world of the Bible to the world of today.

THIS SECTION ALLOWS the biblical message to speak with as much power today as it did when it was first written. How can you apply what you learned about Jerusalem, Ephesus, or Corinth to our present-day needs in Chicago, Los Angeles, or London? How can you take a message originally spoken in Greek and Aramaic and communicate it clearly in our own language? How can you take the eternal truths originally spoken in a different time and culture and apply them to the similar-yet-different needs of our culture?

In order to achieve these goals, this section gives you help in several key areas.

First, it helps you identify contemporary situations, problems, or questions that are truly comparable to those faced by the original audience. Because contemporary situations are seldom identical to those faced in the first century, you must seek situations that are analogous if your applications are to be relevant.

Second, this section explores a variety of contexts in which the passage might be applied today. You will look at personal applications, but you will also be encouraged to think beyond private concerns to the society and culture at large.

Third, this section will alert you to any problems or difficulties you might encounter in seeking to apply the passage. And if there are several legitimate ways to apply a passage (areas in which Christians disagree), the author will bring these to your attention and help you think through the issues involved.

In seeking to achieve these goals, the contributors to this series attempt to avoid two extremes. They avoid making such specific applications that the commentary might quickly become dated. They also avoid discussing the significance of the passage in such a general way that it fails to engage contemporary life and culture.

Above all, contributors to this series have made a diligent effort not to sound moralistic or preachy. The NIV Application Commentary Series does not seek to provide ready-made sermon materials but rather tools, ideas, and insights that will help you communicate God's Word with power. If we help you to achieve that goal, then we have fulfilled the purpose for this series.

The Editors

General Editor's Preface

How SHOULD WE DEAL with the plurality of non-Christian teachings and philosophies that characterize our culture and challenge the church? The apostle Paul faced the same challenge and in the Pastoral Letters offers an answer.

Paul begins, of course, by stating the obvious: Teach against them. But he does much more. As Walter Liefeld explains in the commentary that follows, the apostle recommends *how* to teach against them. Paul gives Timothy and Titus advice and counsel on methodology and attitude in counteracting false teachings, telling them both what *not to do* and what *to do*.

(1) As to what *not to do*, Paul warns against a great danger in dealing with non-Christian teachings. The danger seems at first glance a simple one: wasting time. Avoid godless chatter, he says, and focus on the really important things, such as the gospel of Jesus Christ. On one level this advice makes a great deal of sense. But since Paul does spend a great deal of time himself in the Pastorals and in his other letters warning against the dangers of false teachings, perhaps there is more here than a simple time-management seminar can cure.

What exactly is "godless chatter?" It is "secular and profane" talk that is "empty of real meaning." "Real meaning" for Paul is that which relates to the most real thing in the universe, God. Godless chatter is talk that doesn't have as either its content or goal the promotion of the gospel of Jesus Christ. In other words, what Paul is recommending is that our talk be "partisan" in the best sense of that word—that we never waste time in simple critique of false teaching, critique that doesn't go anywhere. No, Paul wants us always to talk in terms of the gospel.

(2) What keeps this partisanship from becoming mean-spirited, triumphalistic, and self-centered? Here is where Paul's advice about what *to do* comes in. When we talk about false teaching (by not wasting time talking about false teaching but by promoting the gospel), we should be awfully nice about it. You might say that we are to follow the law of love—which means we are to be clear, kind, and optimistic.

(a) Clarity is important to Paul because of the seriousness of the message. Elsewhere he says that good music is made up of notes distinctively sounded, for unless trumpets sound a clear call, no one will prepare for battle (1 Cor. 14:8). This is the theological version of Strunk and White's call for clear and simple writing. For Paul, however, it is not just a matter of clear communication (although that is an important part of it), but it is an actual reflection of the nature of the Incarnation: God did not just take on human flesh in Jesus Christ, but did so in such a way as to be effective in showing himself to human beings. No secret gnostic doctrine here!

(b) Kindness is also important. For Paul, this is not a soft, pablum-esque meekness in the face of false teachings. Kindness means a committed graciousness. Like clarity, Paul considers kindness a theological category—in this case, a human reflection, an imperfect imitation of God's grace toward all sinners. How can we show kindness to those who are threatening our faith through false teachings? Only by redistributing the kindness God showers on us toward others. We cannot find this kind of graciousness in ourselves.

(c) This leads to Paul's third methodological principle, optimism. What works in combating false teachings, Paul says, is not angry denunciation or pessimistic hand-wringing. Rather, what works is keeping the "hope that is within us" front and center in all that we do. Since we do not always feel optimistic and hopeful ourselves, this may mean that sometimes discretion is the better part of valor in combating false teachings. We need to be patient not just with the false teachers, but with ourselves.

The Pastoral Letters are aptly named—they are *pastoral* in the sense that they offer good, sound, practical advice on how to live out our calling as Christians in a world that is not often congenial to the radical demands of the gospel. Live by the law of love, Paul says. Be clear, kind, and optimistic. Then the false teachings will pale in significance next to the eternal truth of the good news of Jesus Christ.

Terry C. Muck

Author's Preface

THE PASTORAL LETTERS have encouraged and instructed me for many years, but never as much as during the writing of this commentary. Their complexity, including frequent repetition of topics and the intertwining of doctrine, instruction, and personal reminiscences add to the problems of dating and authorship. But it is perhaps these very characteristics that have drawn me to them the most. Having spent a lifetime in both theological education (teaching New Testament at Trinity Evangelical Divinity School) and ministry (InterVarsity Christian Fellowship, preaching, and pastoral ministry), I have found these letters not frustrating but true to life. In pastoral ministry, people and problems have a way of reappearing and reasserting themselves. Instructions from the Lord need to be heard again and again to keep us focused on the essentials. In teaching, doctrine needs to be clarified and reemphasized, and error needs to be discerned and dealt with repeatedly. In every situation temptations have a way of being new and old at the same time.

Given this dual perspective, it has been impossible for me to do the exegesis without thinking of its practical side, or to do the Bridging Contexts and Contemporary Significance sections without being aware of the need to be controlled by the text. In some ways I have found the exegesis more demanding but the "practical" sections more challenging. Sermon illustrations have always been hard for me to plan in advance; they always seem to wait to enter my mind until I am preaching! Perhaps there is some of that here, and if I occasionally fail to list sources on a topic. it is probably because the example comes out of my own observations and experience.

The personal nature of these letters, therefore, finds a parallel in the personal nature of my commentary and its preparation. That inevitably means that many people have had a part in it, not just in the research, writing, and editorial guidance, but in life. My father, who has been in heaven almost thirty years, wanted to be a missionary and, when that was not possible, became a medical doctor who devoted himself to Bible study, teaching, witnessing, and counseling. He was an example of the blend of doctrine and life enjoined in these Pastoral Letters. The early influence of my mother and the constant encouragement of my wife, Olive, can never be adequately expressed in writing. Beyond that, Olive provided both arduous typing and probing questions that improved the commentary immensely. The constant encouragement and challenge of my adult children, David, Beverly, and Holly, and their families all have had their part.

Author's Preface

If I were writing an extended preface, it should contain the names of all the students I have had—especially in my classes on the Pastoral Letters—and of all those who have encouraged me in the churches I have served. From among the latter group, Larry Smith was one among a number of cherished friends at Christ Church, Lake Forest, Illinois, who asked me as their pastor the tough questions of life. He went over the manuscript thoroughly and nudged me toward more difficult questions and more realistic answers of the sort that business men and women like himself were seeking. I also want to express appreciation for my faculty colleagues at Trinity, especially former Academic Dean Kenneth S. Kantzer, who devoted his time to us so that we could devote our time to teaching and writing and still have time for our students, families, and churches.

One of the joys of writing this commentary has been having the helpful editorial comments of my former student, Scot McKnight. His careful attention to my manuscript enhanced my appreciation for him even further. I am also indebted to the early editorial suggestions of Marianne Meye Thompson and another esteemed former student, Klyne Snodgrass. Terry Muck's written comments on the manuscript read like a conversation between friends on topics of joy. I recall the first conversation Jack Kuhatschek and I had about this commentary. His patience during the long time since then and his encouragement have helped carry me through personal delays. And any author is blessed to have a manuscript placed in the capable hands of Zondervan editor Verlyn Verbrugge.

Abbreviations

BAGD	W. Bauer, W. F. Arndt, F. W. Gingrich and F. W. Danker, eds. *A Greek-English Lexicon of the New Testament and Other Early Literature*. Chicago: Chicago Univ. Press, 1979.
DPL	*Dictionary of Paul and His Letters*. Gerald F. Hawthorne, Ralph P. Martin and Daniel G. Reid, eds. Downers Grove, Ill.: Inter-Varsity, 1993.
EDNT	*Exegetical Dictionary of the New Testament*. Horst Balz and Gerhard Schneider, eds. 3 volumes. Grand Rapids: Eerdmans, 1990–1993.
EDT	*Evangelical Dictionary of Theology*. Walter A. Elvell, ed. Grand Rapids: Baker, 1984.
EEC	*Encyclopedia of Early Christianity*. Everett Ferguson, ed. New York: Garland, 1990.
EvQ	*Evangelical Quarterly*
ICC	International Critical Commentary
ISBE	*International Standard Bible Encyclopedia*
JBL	*Journal of Biblical Literature*
JETS	*Journal of the Evangelical Theological Society*
JSNT	*Journal for the Study of the New Testament*
JSNTSup	Journal for the Study of the New Testament Supplement Series
JTS	*Journal of Theological Studies*
KJV	King James Version
LSJ	Henry G. Liddell and Robert Scott. *A Greek-English Lexicon*. Rev. ed. by Henry Stuart Jones. Oxford: Clarendon, 1968.
LXX	Septuagint
NASB	New American Standard Bible
NIDNTT	*New International Dictionary of the New Testament Theology*. Colin Brown, ed. 4 volumes. Grand Rapids: Zondervan, 1975–1986.
NIV	New International Version
NKJV	New King James Version
NLT	New Living Translation
NRSV	New Revised Standard Version
NTS	*New Testament Studies*

Abbreviations

REB	Revised English Bible
RestQ	*Restoration Quarterly*
SBL	Society of Biblical Literature
SBLDS	Society of Biblical Literature Dissertation Series
TDNT	*Theological Dictionary of the New Testament.* G. Kittel, G. Friedrich, eds.; trans. G. W. Bromiley. 9 volumes. Grand Rapids: Eerdmans, 1964–1974.
TynB	*Tyndale Bulletin*
UBS	United Bible Societies

Introduction

MOST OF THE OTHER COMMENTARIES in this series have a separate unit in the Introduction on contemporary significance. The present introduction will depart somewhat from that usual form by blending data with significance. After making observations on the nature of these letters, we will deal with such traditional issues as background, doctrine, and authorship from the dual perspective of both the original recipients and the modern reader. It will, therefore, be useful to read this introduction in its entirety rather than merely consulting individual topics, such as authorship, separately. The section on the recipients, for example, is intended to provide a useful approach to that vexing problem of authorship, which, in turn, relates to the strong emphasis in these letters on integrity.

The Nature of the Pastoral Letters

AS FAR AS we know, D. N. Berdot, writing in 1703, was the first to use the term *pastoral* to describe the letters as a group. Half a century later, P. Anton used the term for his commentary on these letters.[1] The reason for the description is clear: They were addressed to individuals commissioned to care for churches with specific needs. This is especially true for 1 Timothy and Titus, with 2 Timothy being more personal than ecclesiastical.

But is the term *pastoral* appropriate for these letters? The task assigned to Timothy and Titus, who may be described as "envoys" or "apostolic delegates," was to address problems that required an apostolic authority. The nature of the care to be given had more to do with combating false teaching than with the day-to-day shepherding of the flock. Their aim was to establish stable leadership within the churches rather than to serve as pastors themselves among the flock on a long-term basis. Yet pastoral concern, gifts, and personal qualities were needed during this period of stress, both in the two apostolic delegates and in the elders they sought to establish firmly in the churches. Paul had previously exhorted the Ephesian elders to be "shepherds of the church of God" (Acts 20:28). Such pastoral qualities are needed today, and the term *pastoral*, though not completely appropriate, has value. What then was the relationship of Timothy and Titus to Paul? What was their commission?

---

1. *Exegetische Abhandlung der Pastoralbriefe S. Pauli* (Halle, 1753–55), cited, along with Berdot, in Knight, *The Pastoral Epistles*, 3.

The Relationship of Timothy and Titus to the Author

THE AUTHOR CALLS Timothy his "true son in the faith" (1 Tim. 1:2) and "my dear son" (2 Tim. 1:2), and he calls Titus "my true son in our common faith" (Titus 1:4). In spite of the indications of mutual experiences between these men and Paul, many scholars claim that these expressions of endearing relationship are constructions in a pseudonymous letter to fictitious recipients. However, taken together with the other references to them in the letters, the reader naturally assumes a real and intimate relationship. Moreover, the references to the relationship of these two men with Paul in his earlier letters and (in the case of Timothy) in the book of Acts are important to make any sense of the literature.

Timothy may have heard Paul during the latter's first missionary journey, and perhaps he was converted at that time. The first specific mention of Timothy is in Acts 16:1–5, where he joins Paul in his second missionary journey. The young man had Paul's confidence, and while at times Timothy was sent on individual missions (1 Thess. 3:1–6), the two often worked closely together (see Acts 18:5; 19:22; cf. also the references to Timothy as a coauthor in 2 Cor. 1:1; Phil. 1:1; Col. 1:1; 1 Thess. 1:1; 2 Thess. 1:1). Within Paul's letters there is further evidence of Timothy's service with Paul (1 Cor. 4:17; 16:10–11; cf. also Rom. 16:21, where Paul calls him "my fellow worker"). Of course within the Pastoral Letters Paul speaks warmly of Timothy, and we will observe these instances in the course of the commentary.

Titus seems to have been a troubleshooter for Paul. The correspondence and sequence of visits between Paul and the Corinthians, including the probability of additional letters not recorded in the New Testament, is difficult to trace. It is clear, however, that Titus played an important role in representing Paul at Corinth. His name occurs in 2 Corinthians 2:12–13 and 7:5–7, 13–15, as well as in several verses concerning the sensitive matter of the collection (8:5–6, 16–19). Paul commended Titus for his difficult work in 12:14–18. Also, Titus went with Paul to Jerusalem on the significant visit described in Galatians 2:1–5. It is clear from the letter to Titus that he had been given yet another difficult assignment when Paul left him in Crete. During the period described in the Pastoral Letters Paul asked Titus to visit him at Nicopolis (Titus 3:12). Finally, at the end of what is most likely the last of the Pastoral Letters to be written, Titus was on his way to Dalmatia, probably on another assignment for Paul (2 Tim. 4:10).

The preceding summary shows us two things in particular. (1) It is difficult to isolate the personal references to Timothy and Titus from the rest of the Pastoral correspondence and to separate that correspondence from what we might call an ongoing "real time" relationship between the two men and

Paul. This observation does not in itself constitute a proof that the letters were written by the apostle Paul himself or that they were actually sent to the named recipients. What it does indicate is that if the historical Paul and the historical Timothy and Titus are not the author and recipients, we move away not only from history towards fiction, but also away from a natural, legitimate understanding of the text.

(2) Assuming historical reality here, we learn that to deal with intricate problems and hostile people in Ephesus and Crete Paul chose two men who were experienced, close companions, although with perhaps less maturity, social standing, and honor than the leaders of the churches. This indicates something of Paul's principles in choosing people for leadership.

The situations Timothy and Titus faced were more serious than may at first appear. False teaching was already progressing aggressively in Ephesus. The use of the present tense in the compound verb "to teach false doctrines" (1 Tim. 1:3) indicates that this activity was already underway and not merely a cloud on the horizon. The mention of "myths and endless genealogies" in 1:4 suggests a complex and esoteric heresy.

The nature of the false teaching will be addressed in the commentary itself, but here we observe that it involved an inappropriate application of Judaistic elements (see the mention of "the law" in 1:7–11). The teachings of two named heretics (the term *heretic* does not seem to be too strong, given the evidence), Hymenaeus and Alexander, either contained blasphemy or were spoken in a blasphemous way (1:20); this required handing them over to Satan. The words "in later times some will abandon the faith and follow deceiving spirits and things taught by demons" show that the false teachings were not simply human speculations, but demonic lies (4:1). The teachers themselves were not merely misled but were "hypocritical liars" (4:2). There was also an ascetic dimension to the false teaching: "They forbid people to marry and order them to abstain from certain foods" (4:3). After reading about demonic teachings and lies, we may think that "godless myths and old wives' tales" (4:7) are not as serious in comparison. However, the fact that they stand in contrast to being "godly" shows that they were insidious. A further reference to the false teachings in 6:3–10 shows that financial greed was also a factor (6:6–10).

By the time of 2 Timothy the activities of the false teachers may seem to have fallen into the background. However, 2 Timothy 2:17–18 provides us with a significant clue about at least one important facet of the false teaching. Hymenaeus and Philetus had "wandered away from the truth" and said "that the resurrection has already taken place." This may not at first seem serious, but Paul says that by teaching this "they destroy the faith of some." This teaching has sometimes been termed *over-realized eschatology*. As people with some interest in the law and Jewish teachings, these false teachers probably were familiar with the idea of the two ages, the present age and the age to come. They also knew of Jesus' teaching about the inauguration of the coming kingdom. Apparently they disregarded or disputed the eschatological teachings of Jesus and of Paul about events yet future.

Many scholars have concluded that some people in the Corinthian church had taught a similar though not identical teaching: Christians were already experiencing so much of the reality of the future age that they could disregard some of the claims of life around them, thereby becoming proud of a superior spirituality. This over-realized eschatology of the Corinthians expressed itself in asceticism and spiritual pride. But the error of the heretics at Ephesus seems to have been somewhat different. While those at Corinth were apparently saying that there is no resurrection (1 Cor. 15:12), Hymenaeus and Philetus were saying that the resurrection was past. This means that they had to deny a good deal of orthodox teaching, and they denied it strongly enough to destroy some people's faith.

Another indication of the false teaching and the serious circumstances that faced Timothy at Ephesus is found in 2 Timothy 3:6–9. The false teachers victimized women who lacked sober self-discipline and who were swayed by sinful desires. A curious comment on these women is that they were "always learning but never able to acknowledge the truth" (3:7). Therefore these women were open to exploitation on more than one level. Along with other clues in the Pastoral Letters, this passage has suggested to some scholars that there was something about these women (if not women in general, as some have claimed) that made them especially vulnerable to false teaching. Given this situation, the prominence of the goddess cult at Ephesus, and significant social changes in the role and perception of women (especially in the incipient ideas that would later merge together in Gnosticism), the interpreter of the Pastoral Letters must consider these elements as reasons for the limitations Paul puts on women especially in 1 Timothy 2:9–15.

But one must not rush to unwise conclusions in this matter. The issues here are complex, and their resolution is important.[2] The approach used in this commentary is to draw primarily on the material within the Pastoral Letters for an understanding of the situation in the Ephesian church, allowing such external background data as we have to inform but not determine the interpretation. It would be inappropriate to ignore the social and religious background, especially with regard to women, but conditions for women were not

---

2. See commentary on 1 Timothy 2:12 for an assessment of the evidence and for bibliography pertaining to this background.

uniform throughout the Roman empire and their circumstances in Ephesus may have been overstated by some scholars. Nevertheless, we must be realistic and acknowledge that the circumstances of and perceptions about women in contemporary North America are considerably different from what one would find anywhere in the first-century world. Our application of the text must be done carefully.

In the face of the false teachings, Timothy and Titus were given authority by Paul as apostolic delegates. The unique authority of the apostle was thereby extended through the ministry of these two men to the churches at Ephesus and Crete. As noted above, their ministry cannot be equated with that of the modern pastor. They were sent to deal with specific circumstances in the name of the apostle. That is, they went under the command of Paul and were commissioned to apply his commands to the circumstances in these churches (see esp. comments on 1 Timothy 1:3–5; 4:1).

The fact that Paul's words in 1 Timothy 4:13, "Devote yourself to the public reading of Scripture, to preaching and to teaching," are prefaced by "until I come" implies that this commission was not a long-term one but rather for a limited period in order to accomplish the necessary goals. Put another way, as apostolic delegates, Timothy and Titus had more personal authority than those in church ministry today can claim, for we stand under the authority of the Bible. At the same time their ministry was more focused than that of the typical pastor today, though that focus did not exclude other ministries, such as evangelism (2 Tim. 4:5).

It is important to understand the implications of this unique role of Timothy and Titus as apostolic delegates. (1) Their ministry constituted an extension of Paul's strong authority, and that fact is an integral part of the instructions in all three letters.

(2) To recognize the limited focus of their task keeps us from an indiscriminate, inappropriate application of the texts relevant to their ministry to ministries of a different nature in the church today.

(3) Since the content of these three pastoral letters was so closely linked to the mission of these apostolic delegates "in real time," unless we lightly dismiss these circumstances and the actual extension of apostolic authority through them, we cannot exclude the role of Paul in the composition of the letters. If we assume that the names Timothy and Titus merely stand for ideal figures or for "Rev. Everypastor," attempts to restore the actual situation and authorship of the letters are doomed at the start.

This reconstruction, in turn, is related to the narrative in Acts 20:17–38. In this address to the Ephesian elders, Paul predicted that "savage wolves" would invade the flock and that other dissidents would arise "even from your own number." The letters to Timothy allude to circumstances that are in accordance with this prediction. If the naming of Timothy and Titus and of Paul is a complete fiction, this connection is lost.

Assuming the historical Timothy and Titus as the actual recipients of letters from Paul as thus described still leaves problems to be addressed—specifically the difficulty of tracing the itineraries of Paul and of Timothy and Titus. The postulation of missionary travels on the part of Paul and these two associates after the conclusion of Acts does not provide us with a full picture. In a possible reconstruction of Paul's further missionary travels, perhaps eastward and then westward towards Spain (experiencing another arrest in the process), he apparently revisited Ephesus with Timothy. How long this visit was cannot be estimated, but it was long enough for Paul to realize that the predictions he made to the Ephesian elders in Acts 20 about invading wolves and insidious false teachers within the church were unfortunately being fulfilled. They were serious enough to require a visit by someone working under and with Paul's authority to counter and correct.

For some reason Paul then decided to proceed north and east from Ephesus back to Macedonia (cf. 1 Tim. 1:3). Paul must have recognized that even though Timothy was still relatively young, he had the wisdom and maturity to deal with the problems in the Ephesian church. Thus, when he "went into Macedonia" he "urged" Timothy to remain in Ephesus in order to "command certain men not to teach false doctrines any longer" (1:3).

It is impossible to determine whether Paul and Titus visited Crete before the visit with Timothy to Ephesus or after the visit to Macedonia. The wording of Titus 1:5, "I left you in Crete," is most naturally understood as indicating that Paul was with Titus in Crete, leaving him there as Paul moved on. Reconstruction of an itinerary after that would most likely have Titus leaving Crete and joining Paul at Nicopolis (Titus 3:12). Perhaps Paul then went to Spain and, while in the western part of the Roman empire, was arrested and imprisoned again. At some point Paul sent Titus to Dalmatia (2 Tim. 4:10).[3]

Authorship and the Ethical Teaching of the Pastoral Letters

HAVING CONSIDERED THE identity of the recipients, with some implications for authorship, we now must probe the matter of authorship further. Since

---

3. It must be emphasized that this reconstruction is based on the assumption of further missionary activity by Paul after the close of Acts. J. van Bruggen has given careful attention to the possibility that the writing of the Pastoral Letters and the attendant circumstances took place during the period covered by Acts; see his *Die geschichtliche Einordnung der Pastoralbriefe* (Wuppertal: Brockhaus, 1981).

this introduction includes concerns regarding practical implications of these matters, it is necessary to inquire about the relationship between authorship and the ethical nature of these letters. Is it possible to avoid the shadow of deception if Timothy and Titus are only part of a literary fiction, figures in a book by an unknown, pseudonymous author?

The term *literary fiction* might seem strong, but it is not intended to be prejudicial. Pseudonymity was accepted in the first century, but apparently not, as will be noted, in Christian literature. In the case of the Pastoral Letters it would be what Bassler calls (approvingly) a "double pseudonymity," referring to both author and the named recipients.[4] There are, however, several other options that include the retention of some measure of integrity in the relationship of author and recipients.[5]

(1) One option is that the sections containing personal comments about Paul and his two associates are genuine fragments of earlier correspondence. This has the advantage of taking those sections at face value and perhaps justifying the use of Paul's name as the author of the letters. It has the disadvantage of failing to explain all of the stylistic, linguistic, and theological differences between the letters as a whole and Paul's accepted writings. It changes the nature of the correspondence as literary units. Further, it still requires a late date for the finished product, with other consequent problems. It also requires fitting the fragments into actual periods in Paul's life and travels.

(2) Perhaps Paul used an amanuensis, a secretary, to whom he gave unusual liberty that amounted to the secretary's recasting Paul's thoughts in his own style and vocabulary. It is less likely, however, that even given that freedom, such a person would also develop the distinctive theology we find in the letters. This matter will be discussed further below. The most likely candidate for the role of amanuensis is Luke. It is easy to look at the distinctive vocabulary and find terms that an urbane physician (assuming that tradition about Luke) would have used, such as "healthy" or "sound" as a description of orthodox teachings.

(3) Another option, a mirror image of the preceding one, is that Paul wrote the Pastoral Letters with his own hand without secretarial help, though

---

4. Bassler, *I Timothy, 2 Timothy, Titus*, 24.

5. In place of repeated references to various sources for the arguments and evidences concerning authorship, this footnote will provide several suggestions for useful works (see bibliography). A. T. Hanson has a vigorous introduction of fifty-one pages, in which he argues against Pauline authorship. Equally vigorous (and just three pages longer) is George Knight's introduction, which contains a scholarly, well-researched defense of Pauline authorship. The treatments by Bassler (against) and in Towner's commentary (for) are more concise and very useful. An excellent article by E. Ellis, "Pastoral Letters," supporting Pauline authorship is easily accessible in *DPL*, 658–66.

he dictated the *other* letters commonly ascribed to him. This seems highly unlikely, but most now acknowledge that Paul had coauthors and probably secretaries as he wrote those letters. His comment about writing large letters with his own hand (Gal. 6:11) probably refers to just those concluding lines. It is certainly possible that in his final travels Paul did not have ready access to a secretary or that he wrote with haste and urgency, especially since he was writing to personal friends rather than to churches. Nevertheless, the stylistic evidence of all the letters attributed to Paul does not fit this theory.

(4) Possibly the letters were actually written by someone other than Paul, probably after his death, but there are reasons why Paul may legitimately be considered the true author. They are not pseudonymous in the usual sense, for they were not ascribed to Paul in order that the actual writer might claim Paul's authority falsely for his own purposes or might honor Paul's name by using a literary fiction. Rather, they contained Paul's real instructions to Timothy and Titus, and they conveyed the actual theological truths Paul was teaching at the end of his life. They were intended simply to preserve all this in a form (and with edited content) that communicated well to the churches and applied to their needs as they emerged from their loss of Paul's continuing presence. On this construction the letters are not a literary fiction. Timothy and Titus were the true objects of Paul's concerns, but the historical setting of the actual setting was later and the style and language were inevitably different from Paul's own writing.

(5) The option held by most evangelicals and some others is that Paul wrote the letters himself, with the occasional aid of a secretary (hence the stylistic differences). Much of the change in theological emphasis was due to the nature of the circumstances, especially the content of the false teaching in Ephesians and at Crete. The absence of typical Pauline themes may be attributed (a) to his having adequately dealt with these themes previously and (b) to different topics in the false teachings he was now confronting. This option also makes allowance for theological development in Paul's mind, along with the privilege of selectivity of choosing topics and vocabulary he had not used before. He may also have drawn on some of the ideas and vocabulary of Luke (such as the word "sound," i.e., healthy) whether or not Luke was involved in the writing. This view values the Pastoral Letters as not only containing what Paul was *likely* to teach or was *reported* to have taught, but what he in fact *did* teach.

Several factors are important in deciding the authorship of these letters. The external evidence has often been discussed. The facts themselves are clear, and their significance tends to be tilted by the position of the interpreter. Polycarp, who died around A.D. 135 (and who wrote on this subject some twenty years earlier) and Clement of Rome (who wrote to the Corinthians around A.D. 96) made apparent allusions to the Pastoral Letters, as did Justin Martyr, writing around A.D. 140. The heretic Marcion (mid-second century), who judged the acceptability of Christian writings on the basis of their usefulness for his teachings, rejected their authenticity.[6]

The first mention of the Pastorals as written by Paul is around A.D. 180 (Irenaeus, *Against Heresies* 2.14.7; 3.3.3). They were mentioned in the Muratorian Canon (a list of accepted biblical writings compiled around A.D. 170–180). The most serious problem regarding authorship is their omission from the Chester Beatty Papyrus (p^{46}), probably written around A.D. 200 (though this was not a complete collection). One further testimony from the early church, often overlooked, is the statement by the bishop of Antioch, writing some undetermined time before his death around A.D. 211, that pseudepigraphic writings in the name of an apostle are to be rejected. Against modern theories of authorship that consider the Pastorals to be pseudepigraphic, claiming that ancient people easily accepted such writings, such a testimony is significant.

Among other factors that would need prolonged attention in a more detailed survey are recent studies in literary style and the appearance in the Pastoral Letters of Hellenistic moral conventions. Regarding style, the reader of one or another statistical survey cannot help but be impressed with the amount and apparent weight of convincing arguments. This approach includes vocabulary and grammatical factors in the attempt to quantify style and target authorship. Yet studies over the years have often failed to answer each other's alleged facts and arguments. Also the statistical methodology used (such as the selection of data to examine) has sometimes been inadequate or simply wrong. Earlier studies did not have the advantage of more sophisticated computer programming, though even the most advanced techniques are only as good as the information fed to them.

One of the most recent studies on the subject is D. L. Mealand's compilation of surveys and charts, which indicate that a methodology that accurately isolates such materials as the Johannine letters, Hebrews, and 1 and 2 Peter from the major Pauline letters also puts the Pastorals in a separate group.[7] Evaluation of this study must take note that Ephesians and Colossians are also markedly different from Paul's major letters and that "minor" Pauline works (such as Philippians) also show some differences as well.[8]

---

6. Tertullian records this fact in his *Against Marcion* 5.21.

7. D. L. Mealand, "The Extent of the Pauline Corpus: A Multivariate Approach," *JSNT* 59 (1995): 266-86.

8. Assessment of the methodology and validity of this approach must also note that, contrary to contemporary views of the Petrine letters that postulate different authors, they are actually grouped together stylistically.

Introduction

Only certain portions of the major Pauline letters were used in this study in contrast to the proportionately large units of all the Pastorals in the attempt to collect representative samples that were of approximately equal size for meaningful analysis. The greatest weakness in this approach is that sections within the Pastorals were not divided so that possible "fragments" (such as the personal comments to Timothy and Titus and sections exhibiting Hellenistic moral conventions) could be compared with each other. In spite of challenges to the methodology and samples used, the fact that a variety of studies have revealed differences that seem to have relevance to the issue of authorship cannot be ignored. Painstaking analysis must continue.[9]

The appearance of moral conventions familiar from Hellenistic writing is also relevant to the issue of authorship, but it has significance beyond that. In the course of her commentary, Bassler cites "the exhortation to 'fight the good fight' [which] echoes the philosophical moral discourse of the period," the terminology and ideas of "godliness" (*eusebeia*) and "dignity" (*semnotes*), the provision for parents as a religious duty, the calling to be free from distractions (applied in the writings of Epictetus to Cynic philosophers and in 2 Tim. 2 to the good soldier), and the importance (in 2 Tim. 2) of struggling for virtue as a moral "athlete" and the "rhetorical device of presenting the opponents as a negative foil."[10]

Such examples, of course, do not prove a late date for the Pastorals. Epictetus, for example, was born around the time Paul was preaching and writing, close enough for both to have shared in the same world of ideas. Nor are such allusions unknown in the accepted Pauline letters. The relevance is rather that the Pastoral Letters seem to have more concern than do the early Pauline writings for surpassing the expectations of Hellenistic moralists. But such concerns and reminders of conventional morality are not inconsistent with the Paul we already know.

The strong emphasis on ethics in the Pastoral Letters is also relevant to the issue of authorship. It would be strange indeed if an author who intended to teach such standards would himself go beyond honesty and truth by attempting to deceive the readership into thinking that not he but Paul was the author. If these letters convey only what Paul was *likely* to teach, but not what he, in fact, *did* teach, however noble that author's motives may have been, it seems impossible to put any confidence in such a person as an ethical or moral teacher.

---

9. See I. H. Marshall, "Recent Study of the Pastoral Epistles," 11–12, for a survey of contributions on language and style.

10. Bassler, *I Timothy, 2 Timothy, Titus*, 46, 51, 84, 95, 140, 162.

Theology and Ethics

THERE ARE A number of specific elements of doctrine that are either *absent from* or uniquely *characteristic of* these letters in comparison with earlier Pauline works. Elements *absent* from the other letters include justification and the "in Christ" formula in its unique Pauline sense. Uniquely prominent elements *characteristic* of the Pastorals include the references to God as Savior and the epiphany theme. Themes such as "the faith" and "truth" as the essence of the Christian message occur in 1 Timothy 1:19; 2:4; 3:9; 4:1, 3, 6; 5:8; 6:10, 12; 2 Timothy 2:25; 3:7–8; 4:7; Titus 1:1, 13. Another theme is "sound" doctrine (teaching, instruction, or faith) in 1 Timothy 1:10; 6:3; 2 Timothy 1:13; 4:3; Titus 1:9, 13; 2:1–2. These receive attention at appropriate places in the commentary, as does the repeated appearance of the phrase "trustworthy saying" (or "faithful/true saying," KJV) in 1 Timothy 1:15; 3:1; 4:9; 2 Timothy 2:11; Titus 3:8 and the idea of a "deposit" committed or entrusted to Paul and his delegates (1 Tim. 6:20; 2 Tim. 1:14).

God as Savior. One of the most obvious theological distinctives in the Pastoral Letters is their repeated designation of God as Savior. Whereas the earlier Pauline letters and Paul's messages in Acts attribute characteristics of deity, divine prerogatives (such as the role of Savior), and even the title *kyrios* ("Lord") to *Christ*, the Pastorals attribute salvation directly to *God*, with Christ as Mediator.

This is not, however, to the detriment of Christ. The new emphasis on the epiphany (i.e., the appearance) of Christ counters such an idea. In this trio of letters, which appeals to Christians to live morally impeccable lives in the pagan world around them, Paul, a "teacher of the true faith to the *Gentiles*" (1 Tim. 2:7), exalts the *one true God*, "who wants *all* [people] to be saved and to come to a knowledge of the truth" (1 Tim. 2:3–4, italics added). His reference in 2 Timothy 4:1 to both "God and . . . Christ Jesus, who will judge the living and the dead," recalls Paul's words to the council in pagan Athens. But this God not only brings judgment; he also brings grace and the opportunity of salvation to all (Titus 2:11). This verse also contains the idea of epiphany, to which we shall return. Thus, "the kindness and love of God our Savior appeared" (Titus 3:4, another epiphany saying). God did not do this because of our works, but because of his mercy, through the agency of the Holy Spirit and "through Jesus Christ our Savior" (vv. 5–6).

The saving work of Christ is thus not separated from or subordinated to the saving work of God, but is proclaimed in the context of the love of God for the entire world (see comments on 1 Tim. 2:1–7 for the place of prayer in this grand scheme of God's universal concern). There is nothing in all this that is incompatible with Pauline theology as we know it from Acts or the apostle's earlier letters. This theme is understandable in the context of the Pastorals as they address the household of God, scattered in their various house church settings, seeking to be a testimony to the world around them.

The epiphany passages and the deity of Christ. The great "mystery of godliness" (or "mystery of [our] religion") is basically an epiphany, a manifestation of Christ that includes vindication and acceptance (1 Tim. 3:16; see comments). While the Pastoral Letters are not triumphalistic—that is, they do not emphatically proclaim the success of God's kingdom—there is nevertheless a strong sense of vindication: In the midst of unbelief, God has made his salvation known. Isaiah had longed to see God "rend the heavens and come down ... to make your name known to your enemies" (Isa. 64:1–2). He reported God's proclamation, "Arise, shine, for your light has come" (60:1), predicted that nations would come to God's light (v. 3), and recorded God's own words, "I revealed myself to those who did not ask for me" (65:1). Whether or not the Pastoral Letters specifically allude to such verses, we can see the common theme that God has now manifested his salvation to all people (Titus 2:11).

These letters, while directed to problems in the churches, are also (can we say mainly?) concerned with the missionary task of the church. In this respect they have a dual focus: (1) the revelation of Christ and the salvation he accomplished by God through Christ, and (2) the obligation of the church and its leaders to reflect this revelation not only in their message but in their manner of life, in order to "make the teaching about God our Savior attractive" (Titus 2:10).

The idea of appearing (represented not only by *epiphaino*, but also by *epiphaneia* and *phaneroo*) occurs at several places in the letters with different points of reference. (1) It signifies the first coming of Christ. First Timothy 3:16 does not specify Christ by name or title, but uses the pronoun "he" (or, in some manuscripts, "God"), clearly referring to Christ. In two other verses Christ is referred to by metonymy, using the word "grace." Second Timothy 1:10 says, for example, that God's grace "has now been revealed through the appearing of our Savior, Christ Jesus, who has destroyed death and has brought life and immortality to light through the gospel." According to Titus 2:11, "the grace of God that brings salvation has appeared to all [people]."

(2) God's word was revealed through Paul's preaching. "At his appointed season he brought his word to light [*phaneroo*] through the preaching entrusted to me by the command of God our Savior" (Titus 1:3).

(3) The second coming of Christ, the *parousia*, is called an epiphany in the Pastoral Letters. We are to "keep this command without spot or blame until the appearing of our Lord Jesus Christ" (1 Tim. 6:14). Paul gives a charge "in the presence of God and of Christ Jesus, who will judge the living and the

dead, and in view of his appearing and his kingdom" (2 Tim. 4:1). That apostle has fought the good fight and says: "Now there is in store for me the crown of righteousness, which the Lord, the righteous Judge, will award to me on that day—and not only to me, but also to all who have longed for his appearing" (2 Tim. 4:8). Also we wait for "the blessed hope—the glorious appearing of our great God and Savior, Jesus Christ" (Titus 2:13). Other passages in the Pastorals certainly uphold the deity of Christ, but the passage just cited is especially important in its wording.[11]

Ecclesiology. Although not much is said in the Pastorals regarding church *organization*, great emphasis is placed on church *leadership*. The most perplexing aspect of this, often debated, is the relation between "the overseer" and "elders." The former word, *episkopos*, occurs only in the singular and only with the definite article (1 Tim. 3:2; Titus 1:7). Other considerations aside, this appears to indicate an individual rather than a group. The word *presbyteroi*, "elders," occurs (apart from 1 Tim. 5:1; Titus 2:2, where the word means "older men") in 1 Timothy 5:17 ("the elders who direct the affairs of the church well"), in 5:19 ("do not entertain an accusation against an elder"), and in Titus 1:5 ("appoint elders in every town"). Except for 1 Timothy 5:19, this word is in the plural in the Pastorals.

A detailed discussion is not possible here, but it may be useful to offer a summary. Several options (not all mutually exclusive) are possible. (1) The Pastoral Letters were written so long after Paul's death that there was already a trend towards the monoepiscopate. The occurrence of "the overseer" marks the early stages of that development. In this case, while the KJV word "bishop" is anachronistic, it points in that direction. The use of the term *episkopos* is not, on this view, a directive of Paul, but shows the influence of the changing ecclesiology of the church.

(2) The term *episkopos* is adapted from its common use in Hellenistic literature, where it can indicate a public official or other responsible person. Paul was well acquainted with this usage and thought it appropriate, perhaps using it to describe a particular aspect of church leadership, such as governance, though not a particular office.

(3) Elders were common in Jewish leadership and in churches that were somewhat patterned after the synagogues. Readers would assume this Jewish background and shape their ecclesiological understanding accordingly.

(4) A natural assumption on the basis of the preceding view—and one that has been common among scholars for some time—is that the genuine Paul

---

11. See the commentary, esp. the reference there to the exegetical discussion in Murray J. Harris, *Jesus As God: The New Testament Use of* Theos *in Reference to Jesus* (Grand Rapids: Baker, 1992).

encouraged the expression of charismatic gifts by the people rather than dominance by elders. Whether charismatic ministry was incompatible with having official leaders in the church has been heavily debated. In any case, some claim the Pastorals represent a blending of views in a more organized church, one that must have taken shape after Paul's time. Along these lines, *episkopos* and *presbyteros* are commonly thought to be alternate terms referring to the same leaders.

We may pause to note that one major reason for thinking that the terms are applied to the same group of leaders is that both terms occur (along with "shepherds") in the account of Paul's address to the church leaders of Ephesus (Acts 20:17–38, esp. vv. 17, 28). Moreover, Paul's use of the terms *episkopoi* and *diakonoi* but not *presbyteroi* in the salutation of Philippians suggests that he easily used the one term as a synonym for the other. This view is strengthened by the appearance of "the overseer" in a passage about elders (Titus 1:7).

(5) Another view has been proposed recently.[12] Eldership in Judaism and the early church was not an official position but a status of honor, usually accorded to older men. It would have been appropriate to describe leaders of household churches this way because they were, at least for the most part, the most honored family member of the household itself. At Lystra, Paul and Barnabas pointed out (*cheirotoneo*) those honored leaders who should be recognized as such by the church (Acts 14:23). This was neither an election nor the appointment of officers of the church. Paul did this *kat' ekklesian*, "church by church" or "in each church." As time went on, there were several churches in many cities and, therefore, a number of elders functioning in "every town" (*kata polin*)—hence the instructions using that term in Titus 1:5. The use of the singular "overseer" with the article indicates an individual who, unlike the honorific elders, was an official leader of a group of churches. This was a step towards monoepiscopal polity.

Without interacting with the whole proposal, we should note that this requires taking elders in an honorific, nonofficial sense in the phrase "apostles and elders" in Acts 15:2, 4, 6, 22–23; 16:4, which is possible but debatable. To view elders as honored household church leaders who received recognition and obedience without being elected or appointed to what we would call "office" may be closer to the truth than viewing them as elected officials who were honored and obeyed only because, and during the time that, they occupied a stated office in the church.

There is a subtle but substantial difference here. The former of these two ways of viewing elders accords better with the fact that there is no Greek

---

12. R. Alistair Campbell, *The Elders: Seniority Within Earliest Christianity* (Edinburgh: T. & T. Clark, 1994).

word for "office" in the Pastoral Letters. Such a view does not in any way detract from the presence of elders as the authoritative leaders of the church. That authority is clear in 1 Timothy 5:17: "the elders who direct the affairs of the church well." Thus, although the Pastorals were written at a time when leadership structure was still in a state of development, the church did not lack authority. Campbell's attempt to preserve the honorific status of elders while explaining the term *episkopos* as designating an elder who has special supervisory status is commendable, even if there still exist vagaries in his reconstruction. The early evidence is, after all, spotty and inconclusive.

It can be seen from the preceding that the matter of ecclesiology is related to the matter of date and authorship. One of the major reasons offered for postulating a late date, well after the death of Paul, is that the structure of elders was already in view. The use of the term *episkopos* fortifies this theory. But it can also be argued that (1) elders were already in place in most churches, with Crete being an exception; (2) there had been a rapid spread of false teaching in these two churches; (3) this acceleration of error is not impossible, given the parallel earlier (doctrinally worse) situation at Galatia, where Paul was "perplexed" at their desertion (Gal. 4:20); and (4) to deal with false teaching in part by strengthening the authoritative leadership, now including those called *episkopoi*, was an early response of the sort that resulted in the rise of the monarchical episcopate. There is no reason why all of this could not have taken place in Paul's lifetime.

Ethical and moral teachings. Perhaps the most unique feature of the Pastoral Letters is the repeated insistence on ethical and moral integrity. There is a deep concern that the two apostolic delegates, the church leaders, and everyday Christians live morally above reproach. This is not merely one theme among many or a theme reserved for the second "practical" half of a letter, but one that is inextricably connected to sound teaching, woven into the fabric of the whole corpus. Christians are not only to live lives of inner holiness; they are to live in such a way publicly as to demonstrate the moral superiority of the Christian way.

It is possible that Paul's concern that the battle with false teachers had severe ethical overtones was heightened over the several years following his earlier Roman imprisonment. He may have broadened in his experience, he may have listened more intently to advisors such as Luke, and he may have realized more keenly that it was necessary to surpass the moral expectations of ethically minded Jews and Gentiles. The opponents at Ephesus and on Crete were vulnerable to criticism, and it was important to take the high road in controversy. Their behavior may have become much worse than anything Paul had encountered before.

All this is connected with the important social elements of honor and shame. In the ancient world shame was not simply a matter of having done wrong and becoming ashamed of that action. It was a matter of public approval or disapproval of certain customs and habits as well as actions.[13] In the Pastoral Letters the elders were to be worthy of honor and respect outside as well as inside the church.[14]

But it is more than the use of specific words for *honor* and *shame* that signals the idea. Dignity (*semnotetos*) was important for elders, so their children should view them this way (1 Tim. 3:4). Deacons and their wives were to have that quality also (3:8, 11, where the adjective *semnos* is used, which also carries the idea of solemnity), as were older men and Titus himself (Titus 2:2, 7). Slaves were to consider their masters "worthy of full respect [*time*], so that God's name and our teaching may not be slandered" (1 Tim. 6:1). Blamelessness in the community was important for overseers (3:2), and those who were responsible for enrolling a widow on the "list" had to be observant of her behavior so that they themselves might not be open to blame (5:7, see comments). These concerns, shared with Hellenistic moralists, are strongly represented in the Pastorals and also appear in other letters traditionally attributed to Paul. Forms of the household codes occur in Ephesians 5:21–6:9 and Colossians 3:18–4:1, and the avoidance of shame is significant in 1 Corinthians 11:2–16.

These examples show the importance of Christians adhering to standards of morality that will not bring blame on themselves, the church, and their Savior. The reasons for appropriate behavior in Titus 2 make this abundantly clear: (1) "so that no one will malign the word of God" (v. 5; "malign" here translates the Greek word *blasphemeo*, "blaspheme"), (2) "so that those who oppose you may be ashamed because they have nothing bad to say about us" (v. 8), and (3) "so that in every way they will make the teaching about God our Savior attractive" (v. 10, where the Greek word *kosmeo*, translated "make ... attractive," means "adorn, decorate").

The ethical and moral concerns are interwoven with doctrine. For that reason it is impossible to cite here one or two major sections where this is done. The relevant passages will unfold and receive comment as they occur. This interweaving is itself significant. It reflects Paul's picture of the ideal Christian leader, whose doctrinal teaching is blended with personal integrity, in contrast to teachers, whose corrupt doctrine is accompanied by corrupt morals.

---

13. Some relevant verses in the earlier Pauline letters are Rom. 9:3; 10:11; 13:7; 1 Cor. 1:26–29; 4:10; 11:6–7, 14–15; 12:23–24, 26; 14:35; 2 Cor. 4:2; 6:8; 8:23; 2 Thess. 3:1.
14. See 1 Tim. 3:7; 5:17.

Other Characteristics of the Pastoral Letters

IN ADDITION TO its theological emphases, the Pastoral Letters display several other unique characteristics. Some are linguistic, such as the use of "sound" or "healthy" to describe doctrine (see relevant places in the commentary). It also is one of the bits of language evidence often cited in discussions about authorship (see above). Two more deserve special attention.

The alternation of blocks of material. Instead of the familiar twofold division of doctrine and practice (e.g., Rom. 1–11 and 12–16), the Pastorals move frequently between exhortation, doctrine, and example. This pattern appears in each letter. For example, after the introduction, 1 Timothy 1 has a block of instruction (vv. 3–7), then the reason for this instruction (vv. 8–11), followed by a personal testimony (vv. 12–14), next a "trustworthy saying" and testimony and doxology (vv. 15–17), and then another block of instruction (vv. 18–20). Second Timothy 2 has instructions (vv. 1–7), the foundation for these (vv. 8–13), and further instructions (vv. 14–26). Titus 3 comprises instructions (vv. 1–2), foundation (including narrative and trustworthy saying, vv. 3–8), further instructions (vv. 9–11), and the conclusion (vv. 12–15).

The fact that it is different from the style we are used to seeing in the letters traditionally attributed to Paul not only has bearing on authorship and composition but on the study and teaching of the contents. The reader must make careful observation of all the transitions along with conjunctions and other vocabulary of transition and the topic and purpose of each section.[15]

Methods of argumentation. These letters also contain repeated maneuvers of defense (maintaining the faith) and of offense (opposing false teachers and their teachings). The word "faith," especially when accompanied by the definite article, often means doctrine. It is not always clear when it refers to doctrine rather than personal faith, but some examples are 1 Timothy 3:9; 4:6; 5:8; 6:10, 12, 21; 2 Timothy 4:7; Titus 1:13; 2:2. One of the most noteworthy feature of the Pastorals is the repeated "trustworthy" or "faithful" saying (1 Tim. 1:15; 3:1; 4:9; 2 Tim. 2:11; Titus 3:8; see comments in the commentary).[16]

Paul not only defends the faith, he vigorously attacks error. That in itself is not unique. What is especially noteworthy is the attitude he recommends that Timothy and Titus have towards the false teachers and the way they are to deal with controversy. At the opening of 1 Timothy, Paul sets out the problem of false teaching and the need to stop it (1:3–4, 6–7, 19–20). Within

---

15. Peter G. Bush ("A Note on the Structure of 1 Timothy," *NTS* 36 [1990]: 152–56) proposes an analysis of 1 Timothy that fits the blocks of that letter into an inclusio structure (between 1:12–20 and 6:11–16, 20, 21a).

16. See Knight, *The Faithful Sayings in the Pastoral Letters.*

this section he tells Timothy to "fight the good fight," but does not enlarge on that language. Paul's description of the false teachers and their errors continues in 4:1–2, after which he counsels Timothy to point out error and truth and to have nothing to do with "godless myths and old wives' tales" (vv. 6–7). The heavy language about "quarrels about words that result in envy, strife, malicious talk," and so forth (6:4–5), is followed by instructions to Timothy to "turn away from godless chatter" and falsehoods (v. 20).

Among the examples in 2 Timothy are the counsel to "warn [the heretics] before God against quarreling about words," but, on Timothy's part, to "avoid godless chatter" (2 Tim. 2:14, 16). After strong words about Hymenaeus and Philetus (vv. 17–18), the advice to Timothy is, "Don't have anything to do with foolish and stupid arguments, because you know they produce quarrels. And the Lord's servant must not quarrel" (vv. 23–24). Instead, Timothy is to be kind and use gentle instruction, hoping for their repentance and escape from Satan (vv. 25–26).

Titus likewise is to "avoid foolish controversies ... arguments and quarrels ... because these are unprofitable and useless" (Titus 3:9). Paul makes it clear that the "divisive person" is "warped and sinful" (vv. 10–11). The contrast is thus clear. The false teachers are evil; the Lord's servants must not use their methods but must be clear, kind, and optimistic.

Vocabulary of command. The present commentary will take special note of the terminology of command. This is not "authority" such as the Lord has or as Jesus gave to his disciples over demons, disease, and "all the power of the enemy" (not over people, Luke 10:19; see Matt. 10:1; Mark 3:15; 6:7; Luke 9:1). The Gospels use the Greek word for authority (*exousia*) forty-four times. It occurs only once in the Pastorals, referring to secular authority. Elsewhere in these letters the English word "authority" occurs in the NIV in 1 Timothy 2:15, where it translates the rare word *authenteo* (see comments), and in Titus 2:15, where it translates the noun *epitage* ("command"). Nevertheless, the command vocabulary in the Pastoral Letters is strong and variable and refers mainly to the specific orders and instructions Paul gave Timothy and Titus, which they, in turn, are to pass on to the churches (see esp. comments on 1 Tim. 1:1, 3; Titus 1:3).

Sound teaching and sound living: The importance of integrity. Returning to the idea of "soundness," we note that "sound teaching" occurs frequently along with other combinations with *hygiaino* and *hygies*, words for being healthy (1 Tim. 1:10; 6:3; 2 Tim. 1:13; 4:3; Titus 1:9, 13; 2:1–2, 8). For Paul, this is not simply a clever pictorial idiom. His concern is for a sound faith that expresses itself in sound living. It is as though he was increasingly disgusted with the "slurry" of falsehood in teaching and living, the filthy mixture of corrupted doctrine and morals that he found in his theological opponents. He realized that what was needed desperately was not only truth in word but truth in the lives of teachers and other church leaders. *What characterizes the Pastoral Letters most is not doctrine but doctrine blended with holy living.*

Perhaps 1 Timothy 4:16 expresses this theme most succinctly: "Watch your life and doctrine closely. Persevere in them, because if you do, you will save both yourself and your hearers." By this startling use of "save," Paul indicates that Christians hold the key to the salvation of others by living such morally superior lives that they demonstrate the reality of the gospel. Life and doctrine are the winning combination.

This concern for sound teaching and godly living has a missionary goal, but it is also a means of honoring God. This is especially apparent in 1 Timothy, where:

- "sound doctrine" conforms to the "glorious gospel of the blessed God" (1:10–11)
- God displayed his patience in his dealing with Paul (1:16)
- "good deeds [are] appropriate for women who profess to worship God" (2:10)
- it is "in God's household" that people should conduct themselves well (3:15)
- we should give thanks for "everything God created" (4:4)
- to care properly for widows is a religious act "pleasing to God" (5:4)
- "in the sight of God" believers should display a holy reverence (5:21)
- slaves should respect their masters "so that God's name . . . may not be slandered" (6:1)

All this accords with the doxologies that characterize the Pastoral Letters (1 Tim. 1:17; 6:15–16; 2 Tim. 4:18).

A recognition of the theocentric nature of the Pastoral Letters reveals by contrast the inadequacy of the *christliche Bürgerlichkeit* ("Christian citizenship")[17] theme that is commonly attributed to these letters. Even the recognition that the household concept is a major element in the Pastorals fails to give sufficient place to the theme of sound teaching plus godly living plus doxology. As seen in the reference to "the glorious gospel" quoted above from 1 Timothy 1:11, God's salvation is basic to all this. Towner calls salvation the "centerpoint of the message."[18] The blend of faith and godly character appears early in the letters, in 1 Timothy 1:5: "The goal of this command is love,

---

17. A term often used after Dibelius.

18. Towner, *The Goal of Our Instruction*, 75–119. Towner's work is a masterful correction of how scholars have commonly misconstrued the theology and purpose of the Pastorals, especially the idea of *"christliche Bürgerlichkeit."*

which comes from a *pure heart* and a *good conscience* and a *sincere faith,"* which is partially repeated in 1:19, "holding on to *faith* and a *good conscience"* (italics added). When we grasp the importance of this and apply it, we have begun to understand the Pastoral Letters. They were written not only by Paul the theologian or Paul the churchman, but by Paul the missionary.

Procedure in the Commentary

I CLOSE WITH one final note. Because the style of the Pastoral Letters is to alternate blocks of material and within these to repeat topics and the relevant vocabulary, a commentator has to make decisions as to where and how best to deal with them without excess repetition. The most natural way is to discuss a topic fully at the point of first mention. But this does not serve well the reader who may be working on a later passage pertaining to that topic and only consults the commentary at that place. The procedure followed here, therefore, is to deal with the topics or vocabulary as thoroughly as seems appropriate at first mention. This, along with the desire to establish exegetical integrity, especially with regard to crucial issues that appear only in 1 Timothy, has resulted in an overbalance of comments on that book. I have attempted to indicate in later passages where earlier comments on a given subject may be found, but the reader is encouraged to find all relevant passages on a topic and to range over all the sections (including the Bridging Contexts and Contemporary Significance sections) that may touch on any item of interest.

Outline

1 Timothy

A. Salutation (1:1–2)

B. Timothy's Commission from Paul (1:3–20)
  1. The Problem of False Teachers (1:3–7)
  2. The Issue of the Law and Its Use (1:8–11)
  3. The Lord's Grace and Call to Paul (1:12–17)
  4. Reaffirmation of Timothy's Mission (1:18–20)

C. Demeanor in the Church That Will Further Its Outreach (2:1–15)
  1. Demeanor in Prayer (2:1–8)
  2. Demeanor of Women While Learning (2:9–15)

D. The Importance of Respected Leadership in the Church (3:1–13)
  1. Demeanor Expected of Elders (3:1–7)
  2. Demeanor Expected of Deacons and Their Female Associates (3:8–13)

E. Godliness (3:14–16)
  1. Godliness in the Church (3:14–15)
  2. The "Mystery of Godliness" (3:16)

F. Further Specifics As to Timothy's Assignment (4:1–16)
  1. Errors He Must Correct (4:1–10)
  2. Timothy's Own Life and Ministry (4:11–16)

G. Social Relationships in the Church (5:1–6:2)
  1. Timothy's Relationships Across Age and Gender Lines (5:1–2)
  2. Caring for Widows (5:3–16)
  3. Honoring Elders (5:17–20)
  4. Various Instructions (5:21–25)
  5. Slaves and Masters (6:1–2)

H. Strong Comments About False Teachers and Greed (6:3–10)

I. Concluding Charge to Timothy (6:11–21)

Outline

2 Timothy

A. Salutation (1:1–2)
B. Personal Encouragement (1:3–14)
  1. Reminder of Timothy's Spiritual Heritage (1:3–7)
  2. Reason for Being Faithful (1:8–12)
  3. Command Regarding Sound Teaching (1:13–14)
C. Paul's Circumstances (1:15–18)
  1. Deserted By Friends (1:15)
  2. Helped By Onesiphorus (1:16–18)
D. Exhortation (2:1–26)
  1. Encouragement Regarding Endurance (2:1–7)
  2. Reasons for Endurance (2:8–13)
  3. Specific Instructions Regarding Controversy (2:14–26)
    a. Destructive Argumentation (2:14–18)
    b. True and False Members of the Household (2:19–21)
      i.   Identification (2:19)
      ii. Separation (2:20–21)
    c. Instruction Towards Repentance (2:22–26)
E. The Coming of Terrible Times (3:1–13)
  1. List of Vices (3:1–5)
  2. The Victimization of Women (3:6–9)
  3. Persecution (3:10–13)
F. The Power of Scripture (3:14–17)
G. Paul's Final Charge to Timothy (4:1–8)
  1. Preaching and Other Ministries (4:1–5)
  2. Paul's Personal Reflections (4:6–8)
H. Conclusion (4:9–22)
  1. Paul's Circumstances (4:9–18)
  2. Greetings to and from Friends (4:19–21)
  3. Benediction (4:22)

Titus

A. **Opening** (1:1–4)
  1. Introduction (1:1–3)
  2. Salutation (1:4)
B. **The Need for Elders in the Churches of Crete** (1:5–16)
  1. Initial Directions (1:5)
  2. Qualifications for Elders (1:6–9)
  3. The Special Problems Among the People of Crete (1:10–16)
C. **Ethical Teachings** (2:1–15)
  1. Inclusio A:[1] The Norm for Ethical Teaching (2:1)
  2. Teaching Older Men (2:2)
  3. Teaching Older Women (2:3)
  4. Older Women Teaching the Younger Women (2:4–5)
  5. Teaching Young Men (2:6–8)
  6. Teaching Slaves (2:9–10)
  7. The Foundation for Ethical Instruction (2:11–14)
  8. Inclusio B: Restatement of Titus' Responsibility for Ethical Teaching (2:15)
D. **The Importance of Doing Good** (3:1–11)
  1. General Statement (3:1–2)
  2. The Positive Effects of God's Saving Grace (3:3–8)
  3. The Wisdom of Avoiding Controversies (3:9–11)
E. **Concluding Personal Remarks** (3:12–15)

---

1. Note that Part C is bracketed in 2:1 and 2:15 by the device of an *inclusio*, the use of similar wording at the beginning and ending of a section to indicate its unity of content.

Annotated Bibliography

Recent Commentaries Most Useful for Bible Teaching and Preaching

Fee, Gordon. *1 and 2 Timothy, Titus*. New International Biblical Commentary. Peabody, Mass.: Hendrickson, 1984. A commentary on the English (NIV) text that includes transliterations of the Greek where useful. It demonstrates fresh, careful exegesis. The commentary is readable, with detailed treatment of exegetical issues handled in separate notes.

Knight, George W. *The Pastoral Epistles*. New International Greek Testament Commentary. Grand Rapids: Eerdmans, 1992. The most detailed commentary of recent times by a scholar who has long specialized in the Pastoral Epistles. Knight had already gained recognition for his work on the "faithful sayings."

Stott, John. *Guard the Truth: The Message of 1 Timothy & Titus*. Downers Grove, Ill.: InterVarsity, 1996. Stott's ability to be erudite, practical, and devotional on the same page makes this a highly desirable commentary on these two letters. Those who have heard Stott preach an expository sermon will appreciate seeing that style in print.

Towner, Philip H. *1–2 Timothy & Titus*. The IVP New Testament Commentary Series. Downers Grove, Ill.: InterVarsity, 1994. Highly readable and an excellent combination of exposition and application. Towner drew on his own doctoral study of the Pastorals, later revised and published as *The Goal of Our Instruction* (see below).

Other Recent Commentaries Significant for Scholarship

Bassler, Jouette M. *1 Timothy, 2 Timothy, Titus*. Abingdon New Testament Commentaries. Nashville: Abingdon, 1996. Up-to-date. Draws on a broad spectrum of historical and sociological data. Analyzes the text in literary units rather than verse by verse. Intended primarily for theological students, but does not incorporate the Greek text.

Dibelius, Martin, and Hans Conzelmann. *The Pastoral Epistles*. Hermeneia. Philadelphia: Fortress, 1972. As with other volumes in this series, this represents the best critical German scholarship. It is of little help to preachers but is of great importance for scholars.

Hanson, A. T. *The Pastoral Epistles.* New Century Bible Commentary. Grand Rapids: Eerdmans, 1982. Always worth consulting when one wants a scholarly yet competently presented study from the perspective of one who holds to a post-Pauline date and authorship, probably after A.D. 90.

Kelly, J. N. D. *The Pastoral Epistles.* Harper's New Testament Commentaries. New York: Harper & Row, 1963. This is one of the commentaries written by eminent scholars for the Harper series (among them C. K. Barrett on Romans and G. B. Caird on Revelation). It is one of the best commentaries available on the Pastorals. Kelly argues well for Pauline authorship.

Older Important Commentaries

Calvin, John. *Commentaries on the Epistles to Timothy, Titus, and Philemon.* Ed. John Pringel. Grand Rapids: Eerdmans, 1948. The author needs no introduction. This particular sample of his commentaries reflects his thoughtful (and strong) views on church polity.

Ellicott, Chas. J. *A Commentary on the Epistles of St. Paul,* vol. 2. Philadelphia: Smith, English, & Co., 1868. One of the classical nineteenth-century commentators. It is based on the Greek text, devoting a full page of commentary to every few lines of the text.

Lock, Walter. *The Pastoral Epistles.* The International Critical Commentary. Edinburgh: T. & T. Clark, 1924. A lesser known but worthy volume in the old but distinguished International Commentary Series. It is based on the Greek text with concise comments that make frequent reference to primary as well as secondary sources.

Scott, E. F. *The Pastoral Epistles.* The Moffatt New Testament Commentary. London: Hodder & Stoughton, 1936. It is a running commentary on the English text, unencumbered by pedantic discussions. Scott was a professor at Union Theological Seminary New York.

Other Relevant Monographs

Donelson, L. R. *Pseudepigraphy and Ethical Arguments in the Pastoral Epistles.* Tübingen: Mohr/Siebeck, 1986.

Kidd, Reggie M. *Wealth and Beneficence in the Pastoral Epistles: A "Bourgeois" Form of Early Christianity?* SBLDS 122. Atlanta: Scholars, 1990.

Knight, George W. *The Faithful Sayings in the Pastoral Letters.* Kampen: Kok, 1968; reprinted, Grand Rapids, 1979.

Marshall, I. Howard. "Recent Study of the Pastoral Epistles." *Themelios,* 23/1 (1997): 3–29.

Moule, C. F. D. *Essays in New Testament Interpretation.* Cambridge: Cambridge Univ. Press, 1982. Pages 113–32, "The Problem of the Pastoral Epistles: A Reappraisal."

Annotated Bibliography

Prior, Michael. *Paul the Letter Writer and the Second Letter to Timothy*. JSNTSup 23. Sheffield: Sheffield Academic Press, 1989.

Towner, Philip H. *The Goal of Our Instruction: The Structure of Theology and Ethics in the Pastoral Epistles*. JSNTSup 34. Sheffield: Sheffield Academic Press, 1989.

Verner, David C. *The Household of God: The Social World of the Pastoral Epistles*. SBLDS 71. Chico, Calif.: Scholars, 1983.

Young, Frances. *The Theology of the Pastoral Letters*. Cambridge: Cambridge Univ. Press, 1994

1 Timothy 1:1–2

P AUL, AN APOSTLE of Christ Jesus by the command of
God our Savior and of Christ Jesus our hope,
²To Timothy my true son in the faith:
Grace, mercy and peace from God the Father and Christ
Jesus our Lord.

THE OPENING LINES of letters at the time of the
New Testament followed a conventional style,
which included the names of both sender and
recipient, with some kind words concerning the
latter and solicitous wishes for his or her well-being.[1]

The Sender and His Authority (1:1a)

PAUL'S IDENTIFICATION OF himself as "an apostle of Christ Jesus" is similar to
the way he identifies himself in every other letter except Philippians and 1
and 2 Thessalonians. In Galatians, where he was preparing to make some
strong authoritative declarations about what the true gospel is and what it
means, he enlarged on the implications of his unique apostleship (Gal. 1:1–
2). Here, where he is going to address false teaching, he uses the unusual
phrase "by the command of God our Savior." We know from several passages that Paul understood his being an apostle as a calling (cf. Rom. 1:1) "by
the will of God" (1 Cor. 1:1; 2 Cor. 1:1; Eph. 1:1), but this is the only salutation in a letter where he attributes his ministry to God's "command." The
strong word used here (*epitage*) occurs again in 1:5, 18; 4:11; 5:7; 6:13, 17; Titus
1:3; 2:15.[2]

Distinctive Elements About God and Jesus (1:1b)

PAUL CALLS GOD "our Savior." We are so used to thinking of Jesus as our Savior that the use of that term to describe God arrests our attention. The phrase
"God our Savior" occurs only five times in the entire Old Testament (1 Chron.

---

1. On the form of letters in the New Testament period see S. K. Stowers, *Letter Writing
in Greco-Roman Antiquity* (Philadelphia: Westminster, 1986); P. T. O'Brien, "Letters, Letter
Forms," *DPL*, 550–53.

2. See comments on 1:3, on the other passages, and esp. in the Bridging Contexts section for Titus 1:3.

16:35; Ps. 65:5; 68:19; 79:9; 85:4) and only six times in the New Testament, of which five are in the Pastoral Letters (here; 1 Tim 2:3; Titus 1:3; 2:10; 3:4; Jude 25). In Titus 1:3 the phrase occurs in the salutation, as here, where it is also linked with the word "command."

It is striking to realize that although the word "salvation" appears forty-six times in the New Testament and the word "save" 107 times, "Savior" occurs only twenty-four times. In Paul's letters it occurs only twice outside of the Pastorals (Eph. 5:23; Phil. 3:20), but ten times within them (1 Tim. 1:1; 2:3; 4:10; 2 Tim. 1:10; Titus 1:3, 4; 2:10, 13; 3:4, 6). Almost half of the appearances of this word in the New Testament, therefore, are in the Pastoral Letters. Such words give Paul's opening words to Timothy (and also those to Titus) a weight of authority and majesty. The God who brought about the salvation of Israel time and time again has the authority to command Paul regarding the preservation of the true faith.

Paul goes on to describe Christ Jesus as "our hope." This phrase does not occur anywhere else, nor does the phrase "God our hope," but certainly the idea does. For example, "May your unfailing love rest upon us, O LORD, even as we put our hope in you" (Ps. 33:22). Three texts in Titus have the word "hope": "the hope of eternal life" (1:2; 3:7), and "the blessed hope—the glorious appearing of our great God and Savior, Jesus Christ" (2:13). Significantly, the words "God" and "Savior" reappear in that phrase in connection with Jesus Christ.

The Recipient (1:2a)

TIMOTHY IS PAUL'S "true son in the faith." The word for "true" (*gnesios*) is different from the more common one (*alethes*), which means true as opposed to false. The present word means "genuine" as opposed to illegitimate or fake. The word could be used of a child born within a legitimate marriage, and the implication in the figurative statement here refers to the quality of Timothy's relationship to Paul. Paul had met this young man in Lystra; Acts 16:1 describes him as a "disciple," with a Jewish mother and Gentile father. Second Timothy 1:5 refers to Timothy's "sincere faith," which "first lived" in his grandmother and mother, Lois and Eunice. From his infancy Timothy had known the Scriptures, through which he had come to "salvation through faith in Christ Jesus" (3:15).

This repeated terminology about faith and the identification of his believing mother provides a background for Paul's reference to Timothy as his "true son in the faith." Timothy's mother provided the environment of Jewish faith in which he had grown up; Paul provided the nurture of his Christian faith. Since he is called a "disciple" at the outset of the Acts 16 narrative, he probably had become a Christian before Paul's arrival, possibly through Paul's earlier ministry in Lystra (Acts 14:8–20). Paul also had a part in the conferral of a spiritual endowment on Timothy (1 Tim. 4:14; 2 Tim. 1:6).

The other extant Pauline letters are to churches (and, at Philippi, to their leaders), not to individuals. Outside the Pastoral Letters only Philemon, which is clearly personal, is addressed to an individual. This fact gives the impression that the early churches had a plural leadership and that Timothy and Titus are addressed individually only because they have a special mission as "apostolate delegates" (i.e., sent by the apostle as his authorized representatives). These letters are probably not only for their personal reading but function as public documents attesting the authority bestowed on these two delegates.

Kind Wishes (1:2b)

IT WAS CUSTOMARY for letters in the first century to convey kind wishes for the continued well-being of the recipients. Paul uses some Christian terms for this purpose, but also uses common terminology with a Christian meaning. Here he expresses these thoughts with the words "grace, mercy and peace." Those who spoke Greek would normally greet a friend with the word *chaire.* The word for "grace," *charis,* has a similar sound.

Paul's third greeting, *eirene* (from which we derive our word irenic), means "peace." This word recalls the Hebrew greeting *shalom,* which connotes wholeness and well-being as well as peace.

In addition to these usual two words of greeting in Paul's letters, 1 and 2 Timothy add "mercy" (cf. also 2 John 3). This word can shade towards the idea of pity or compassion. It recalls the Hebrew *ḥesed,* with its overtones of mercy and kindness to those within God's covenant. The terms *grace* and *mercy* imply that those who receive those benefits have a need they cannot fulfill themselves.

In most of his letters, Paul indicates, as here, that these beneficial favors come "from God the Father and Christ Jesus our Lord." This is not to deny the fact that the Holy Spirit gives gifts, but it simply attributes generosity to God as Father (James 1:17) and adds the name of Christ, who conveys God's grace to us.

 BRIDGING CONTEXTS IS always important, but because opening greetings seem so familiar, we may not realize that they also require attention. It is helpful to read such a text as these first two verses carefully, as though for the first time.

Apostle. Since communication requires shared points of reference, mention of a concept, event, person, or object is meaningless unless the reader or hearer has some knowledge of the subject. If we, for example, received a letter from an unknown person who identified him or herself as "the

Chancellor," we would need to know the significance of that word in the sender's vocabulary. Is this from the honorary head of some American university, from the prime minister of a foreign country, or perhaps from a British government official? In a similar manner, we cannot simply assume that a contemporary reader of Paul's letters knows what the term *apostle* means, especially how this word was used in a different culture and a different language nearly two thousand years ago.

Even if such a person knew that messengers, such as official envoys, were called *apostles* in ancient Greek, that person might not know the special use of the term for Jesus' apostles and for a few others, such as Paul. In the Jewish world later reflected in the Mishnah, the term *shaliach* denoted a person who was sent on a mission and was to be received as though he was the sender himself (*m. Ber.* 5:5). In the New Testament, the qualifications for being chosen to take over the "apostolic ministry" abandoned by Judas Iscariot included the stipulation that the candidate had been with the Lord Jesus during his ministry and had witnessed his resurrection (Acts 1:21–26). Paul's vision of the risen Lord and God's choice of him thus qualified him to serve as an apostle. Therefore, he calls himself "an apostle of Christ Jesus." Translators rendering this for some cultures may need to employ some culture-specific term both to express the meaning of apostleship and to explain why Paul functioned under a "command."[3]

God and Christ. The relationship between God and Christ is difficult to understand and explain. In verse 1 the command comes from both God and Christ Jesus. To those who have a non-Trinitarian monotheistic view of God, the term *God* excludes Christ. To those who have a polytheistic religion, Christ can also be a god, but the two persons (in Christian terms, the Father and the Son) would be considered different gods. The biblical view is that there is only one being who is God and that he exists in three persons. Christ, therefore, is God as to his *nature* and the Son as to his *person*. Many attempts have been made to illustrate the Trinity, but endeavors to do so from the material world fail because God is not material, but spirit in essence. Likewise, what is illogical or impossible in human experience does not determine what is logical or possible for God.[4]

Paul calls God "our Savior." During the Hellenistic period, when religious aspects of Greek culture blended with the Roman, the term *savior* was applied

---

3. The literature on the term *apostle* is immense. For a useful summary with bibliography, which, though dated, contains literature from an important period of discussion on its meaning, see D. Müller and C. Brown, "Apostle," *NIDNTT*, 1:126–37. For a more recent treatment, see P. W. Barnett, "Apostle," *DPL*, 45–51.

4. For a superb study of passages where Christ is called "God," see Murray J. Harris, *Jesus As God: The New Testament Use of* Theos *in Reference to Jesus* (Grand Rapids: Baker, 1992).

to various mythical figures. In no case, however, was there a divine being who brought people into relationship with himself by personally removing the guilt of sin. The New Testament understanding of salvation is in accord with that of the Old Testament, not derived from the Greco-Roman world.[5] God is the Savior in both spiritual and human spheres. In understanding the significance of this concept in the pluralistic world of today, we need to maintain the distinctiveness of Christian salvation.

Of course this distinctiveness includes the truth that Christ, who is Immanuel ("God with us"), died to be our Savior. His death and resurrection bring forgiveness and eternal life. Therefore, when Paul calls Christ Jesus "our hope," he is going beyond the ideas held in the various cultures of his day. As he says in 2 Timothy 1:10, Christ "destroyed death and has brought life and immortality to light through the gospel."

THE NEED FOR **clarity and authority.** The biblical hope just mentioned often tends to be replaced by a subjective, fuzzy optimism about a future life. When we invite people to the Christian hope, we must do so with a clear explanation as to how the Christian message offers the only basis for hope. We must also proclaim this truth, as other truths, with biblical authority. This authority is an important theme in the Pastoral Letters. Unless the original reader had some awareness that this apostleship gave Paul authority to declare what was (or was not) orthodox teaching, Timothy's attempt to repudiate false doctrine could seem overbearing.

That would especially be the case for anyone today who has a democratic, pluralistic worldview. On occasion, citizens will grant extraordinary authority to a ruler, such as happened in Belarus while I was writing this, in reaction to what many considered an ineffective democratic arrangement after years of monolithic communist rule. But in most countries today where there is a choice, totalitarianism is rejected. Likewise, to many people the idea of a mere human being claiming authority derived from God, such as happens in various cults, seems medieval or even worse. But we must not hesitate to state that what Paul speaks in his letters, he speaks with divine backing.

Furthermore, the whole idea of a coherent universe in which truth can be known objectively and a universe governed by exclusive divine authority is contrary to the postmodern worldview. By its very nature, 1 Timothy 1:1

---

5. For Old and New Testament teaching about salvation, see Liefeld, "Salvation," *ISBE*, 4:287–95.

would be unacceptable to postmoderns. Therefore, not only do the elements in this verse require some definition, but the assumptions in it require some agreement before its implications can be accepted.

What significance does the fact that this letter was addressed to Timothy have for us? When we attempt to apply Scripture to contemporary life, it is sometimes helpful for us to identify with the nature and circumstances of biblical characters. Usually when we study narratives, it is easy to find events and personalities that are familiar to us. But there are not many readers who can identify with a young man who is called "son" by the outstanding Christian figure of his day and is given the difficult mission of correcting false teaching and countering false teachers. Yet there are aspects of his life and mission that are relevant to many of us. We need, of course, to assemble the various bits of information we have about him and his relationship with Paul from Acts and the two letters Paul wrote him. We can draw some conclusions about his personality (e.g., see 2 Tim. 1:6–8) and his youthfulness (1 Tim. 4:12).

Moreover, the reference to Timothy and his mission will, along with subsequent passages, serve to alert us to the formidable but necessary task to keep the church doctrinally pure. Once elders are in place, this is their job (see Acts 20:17–35 for Paul's charge to the elders of this very church at Ephesus; also see 1 Tim. 3:1–7 for the requirements of an overseer). But elders need to be instructed so that they will be prepared. The instructional sequence illustrated here in the relationship between Paul and Timothy and specified in 2 Timothy 2:2 can and should still be employed.

The Christian vocabulary. Like the word "hope" in verse 1, the words "grace, mercy and peace" in verse 2, properly understood, have an important place in contemporary Christian vocabulary. But they need clarification today. The problem with the term *grace* is that it is, on the one hand, so content specific in Christian use that it often fails to communicate to those who are not theologically literate, while on the other hand it has become such a common term with the nearly universal use of the hymn "Amazing Grace" that it tends to lose much of its inherent content. To read "grace be with you" to a person who knows nothing of Christianity can be as meaningless as hearing "the Force be with you" is to someone who does not know the American *Star Wars* vocabulary. The meaning of "grace," therefore, is not merely that God gives us free salvation. It is also more than "God's Riches At Christ's Expense," though there is truth in that acronym. The ancient Greek usage of that word implies an inability on the part of the recipient that requires the help of someone else. We need grace because we have no other option.[6]

---

6. Philip Yancey's *What's So Amazing About Grace* (Grand Rapids: Zondervan, 1997) also tells us of our need to extend grace to others.

The middle term, *mercy*, seems (and theologically is) ego-deflating. Who wants to be in the position of needing mercy? And yet faithful churchgoers, in particular those in liturgical church services, acknowledge that need in saying the *Kyrie Eleison*, "Lord, have mercy." The key to understanding the importance of this concept is to have a healthy sense of one's own sin and need. That will bring about an appreciation for mercy.

The last term, *peace*, has become so diluted in its many applications today that it cannot be assumed people understand it specifically as the peace with God that has been brought about by being reconciled to God through the death of Christ on the cross. We should not hesitate to let other people know that they are out of sorts with God and that they need reconciliation.

1 Timothy 1:3–7

A S I URGED you when I went into Macedonia, stay there in Ephesus so that you may command certain men not to teach false doctrines any longer ⁴nor to devote themselves to myths and endless genealogies. These promote controversies rather than God's work—which is by faith. ⁵The goal of this command is love, which comes from a pure heart and a good conscience and a sincere faith. ⁶Some have wandered away from these and turned to meaningless talk. ⁷They want to be teachers of the law, but they do not know what they are talking about or what they so confidently affirm.

Original Meaning

IT WAS NO ordinary mission that Timothy was called to, in contrast to the time when Paul had sent him to Thessalonica "to strengthen and encourage you in your faith" (1 Thess. 3:2). Apparently Timothy was already at Ephesus when it becomes clear to Paul that conditions are critically unhealthy there because of false teaching by immoral persons. Paul therefore has to "urge" Timothy (v. 3) to "stay" there for a specific purpose: to command these false teachers to stop. He had originally urged Timothy to do this on a previous occasion as Paul was heading to Macedonia, and he is now reinforcing that charge.[1]

The verb to urge (*parakaleo*) has a warm, personal feel (though strong) in contrast to the impersonal and imperatival overtones of the following verb of command. Paul gives Timothy the authority to require the false teachers to desist from spreading error. The verb he uses in verse 3 for "command" (*parangello*) occurs thirty-two times in the New Testament (mainly in the Gospels and Acts), five of which are in 1 Timothy. This letter also has two out of the five New Testament occurrences of the noun form (*parangelia*). The verbal form of another word that means command (*epitasso*) is not used at all in the Pastoral Letters, but three of seven occurrences of the noun form (*epitage*) are in these letters (we have already met

---

1. Paul's actual sentence structure is "As I urged you to stay . . ."; there is no main verb in the sentence. There are several ways to express what he meant: (1) "As I urged you, . . . stay" (NIV); (2) "I urge you, as I did . . . [earlier], to remain" (NRSV); (3) "I urged you to stay" (NLT); or (4) possibly, "I want you to stay, as I urged you to. . . ."

one of them in 1:1). This indicates how important the idea of authority is in the Pastoral Letters.

In some translations, the Greek words in the *parangell-* group are rendered by English words that have a lighter connotation than commanding, such as merely instructing or directing. It is helpful to study the accounts of Jesus' feeding of the multitudes. In the feeding of the four thousand, Jesus gives directions to the crowd with the word *parangello*, whereas different verbs, *keleuo* and *epitasso*, occur in the similar instructions to the five thousand. Since these accounts are similar verbally and since *keleuo* and *epitasso* generally have the strong connotation of "command," we can assume that the other verb, *parangello*, also carries that ring of authority.[2] Note also the use of *parangello* in the commands the authorities gave to the apostles to desist from preaching in the name of Jesus (Acts 4:18; 5:28, 40). All this, far from being mere statistics, cautions us to give proper weight to the authority that Timothy is to exercise at Ephesus.[3]

The word translated "teach false doctrines" (*heterodidaskaleo*) reappears in 6:3. That context shows that it is not merely something "different" (as in the NRSV), as the etymology of this word ("teach [something] different") might by itself imply. Since in chapter 6 this verb is set in contrast to "the sound instruction of our Lord Jesus Christ" and to "godly teaching," we know that what is not "sound" is not only different; it is false. In Galatians 1:6–8 Paul says that the "different gospel" that people were turning to was "really no gospel at all" and that anyone who preached another "gospel" should be "eternally condemned." To weaken *heterodidaskaleo* is to undervalue Paul's strong teachings about truth and error.

The word "nor" at the beginning of verse 4 does not introduce something additional to the false teachings, but identifies specific aspects of those teachings. "To devote oneself to something" means here to pay or give attention to it. One can be overly attracted to something intellectually without

---

2. See Matt. 15:35; Mark 8:6 (Gk. *parangello*), NIV "he told" (the crowd of 4,000 is told to sit down to be fed); Matt. 14:19 (Gk. *keleuo*), NIV "he directed" (the 5,000); Mark 6:39 (Gk. *epitasso*), NIV "Jesus directed" (the 5,000).

3. The NIV has "command certain men not to teach false doctrines," NLT has "stop those who are teaching wrong doctrine," NRSV has "instruct certain people not to teach any different doctrine." Notice how the NIV has the strongest wording ("command ... false"), the NLT a moderate wording ("stop ... wrong"), and the NRSV the weakest wording: "instruct ... different." The paraphrase in *The Message* hardly communicates the seriousness either of the command or of the error: "Stay right there on top of things so that the teaching stays on track." The erroneous impression this gives is that the teaching at Ephesus was sound, "on track," and that the teachers did not need any corrective command from Timothy, as long as he could "stay on top of things."

necessarily giving it personal devotion. In this case "myths" and "genealogies" hold some kind of fascination for the false teachers and their followers. While folk myths may have value as referring to ways in which a society has expressed the origin of certain customs or beliefs, the kind of myth referred to in the New Testament is profane (i.e., not sacred, 1 Tim. 4:7), contrary to truth (2 Tim. 4:4; Titus 1:14), and slyly concocted, without a true basis or a noble tradition (2 Peter 1:16).

The fact that "genealogies" are linked with "myths" here, which in turn are called "Jewish" in Titus 1:14, and with "quarrels about the law" in Titus 3:9 suggests that these are genealogies found in sacred Jewish writings (perhaps including Genesis). Some have looked to the heresy of Gnosticism as the referent, with its lists of cosmic figures. This is anachronistic, since Gnosticism as a system appeared later. But it did incorporate some elements of Judaism, and it is often difficult to trace origins of various aspects of Gnostic thought. The Jewish context of the references to genealogies in the Pastoral Letters requires putting any developing Gnostic ideas as secondary at best.[4] But it is not necessary to identify the source or nature of the "myths" and "endless genealogies" precisely to realize their detrimental effect on Christian thought, which, in this context, is the important point.

That effect is to "promote controversies," the latter word (*ekzetesis*) being unique in the Greek New Testament. It is an extension of a word meaning investigation, controversy, or discussion. The NIV "controversies" captures that extended meaning but does not express the basic idea of intellectual speculation.[5] In 1 Timothy 6:4 a related word (*zetesis*) is paired with "quarrels about words" and in Titus 3:9 with "arguments and quarrels." Therefore, "controversial speculations" may express the nuance best.

That which ought to be promoted instead of controversial speculation is "God's work [*oikonomia*]." Paul uses this word for God's plan and work, especially (though not exclusively) administered as a stewardship by Paul (cf.

---

4. Among the sources of information and opinion on the matter are F. Büchsel, "γενεαλο-γία," *TDNT*, 1:663–65; "γενεαλογία," BAGD, 153; Fee, *1 and 2 Timothy, Titus*, 41–42; Knight, *Pastoral Epistles*, 73–74; Kelly, *Pastoral Epistles*, 44–45. Towner, referring to Philo (*Moses* 2.46–47) and the Dead Sea Scrolls (1QS 3:13–15), says that these "make it clear that the term itself was a reference not just to lists of family names and descendants but also to edifying stories about significant Old Testament figures" (*1–2 Timothy & Titus*, 45–46). Given the uncertainty of the meaning of the word as used here, it is better to keep the literal "endless genealogies" (NIV, NRSV) rather than creating such paraphrases as "spiritual pedigrees" (NLT) or "fanciful family trees" (*The Message*).

5. The NRSV has simply "that promote speculations," NLT has a paraphrase that includes the expression "endless speculation," and *The Message* reduces the clause to "that digress into silliness."

1 Cor. 9:17; Eph. 3:2, 9; Col. 1:25).[6] This work is in contrast to controversial speculation, probably in part because it is effective and unifying but specifically here because it is "by faith." One should think and act out of a confidence in what God is doing. False teaching, spawning endless detrimental discussions, is the concern of this letter. It arises from disbelief in what God has revealed. Thus, the rejection of faith is not a mere addendum to the sentence, but a major factor in the deterioration of the Ephesian church.

Faith is a basic term in the Christian vocabulary, as is *love*. Paul goes on to cite love as "the goal of this command." The recognition of purpose is important in this letter. In verse 3 Paul has told Timothy to stay in Ephesus for the purpose of commanding certain people to refrain from false teaching; this is in the first place the command that should lead to love. Note that the verb "command" in verse 3 and the noun "command" in verse 5 have the same linguistic root.

Yet since Christian love would seem to be the goal of a greater command than merely one that opposes false teaching, perhaps we should look further for its referent. The mention of "the law" in verse 7 and the major subject of verses 8–11 suggest the possibility that it is also the Old Testament law, specifically the law of Moses, that Paul refers to as the command that leads to love. Note Romans 13:10, where Paul says that "love is the fulfillment of the law." Nevertheless, he nowhere else uses the word *parangelia* ("command" in this verse) to refer to the law. Furthermore, in 1 Timothy 1:18 Paul refers to "this instruction," using this same Greek word. Thus we may conclude that the "command" referred to in verse 5 is Paul's *whole* instruction to Timothy, which, in turn is consistent with God's law when properly applied.

Several further observations bear this out. (1) The word "this" in the phrase "this command" represents the Greek definite article used as a demonstrative pronoun, and so it points to a topic *in the context*. (2) The command not to teach false doctrines has application *beyond* that local situation. God's revealed Word (and that includes the Old Testament laws) must not be skewed by false teachings. (3) In the further use of the word *epangelia* in verse 18 ("instruction"), there is also a reference to a goal, this time introduced by "so that."

The "goal of this command," like the fulfillment of the law (Rom. 13:8–10), is "love." The solidity of the love Paul speaks about in verse 5, in contrast to mere feeling, is established by the fact that it requires an integrity of

---

6. Knight has a helpful discussion of *oikonomia*, referring to J. Reumann, "OIKONOMIA-Terms in Paul in Comparison With Lucan *Heilsgeschicte*," NTS 13 (1966–67): 147–67.

character to exist: "a pure heart and a good conscience and a sincere faith" (v. 5). As the introduction of all three aspects by a single preposition "from" (*ek*) indicates, they belong together; they are not separate, disparate characteristics. The Greek word for conscience, *syneidesis*, occurs thirty times in the New Testament, six of them in the Pastoral Letters.[7]

Paul pursues this matter of integrity further by stating in verse 6 that some people had "deviated from these" (NRSV, i.e., the virtues of v. 5). The NIV "wandered" can be misunderstood to imply a casualness; the verb used here (*astocheo*) means to miss the mark, deviate, or deliberately depart from something.[8] The heretics turned *away* from Christian character *to* empty, "meaningless" talk, a striking contrast between steadfast doing or being and vacuous speaking. The word "meaningless" contains the idea of futility, but in Titus 1:10 Paul classes "mere talkers" (a different form of the same root term, *matios*) with the rebellious and deceivers, so the idea of emptiness is not neutral but negative. The root term can be translated by such words as "useless, futile, empty, fruitless." In the Pastoral Letters it appears in Titus 3:9, where it describes controversies and quarrels.[9] Second Peter 2:18 says that heretics "mouth empty, boastful words" (NRSV, "speak bombastic nonsense") and appeal to the low, lustful nature of people who have just escaped from people living in error. The use of this kind of terminology in 1 Timothy underlines the danger facing the church at Ephesus if the false teachers are allowed to continue unchecked.

It is ironic that the same people whose speech is empty "want to be teachers" (v. 7) and that those who repudiate love, a pure heart, a good conscience, and sincere faith want to be teachers "of the law." The irony continues in verse 7 with the statement that they do not comprehend either what they are talking about or what they are asserting with great confidence. The word translated "teachers of the law" occurs in Luke 5:17, and it describes the great

---

7. See Towner, *1–2 Timothy & Titus*, 47; see also J. M. Gundry-Volf, "Conscience," *DPL*, 153–56, for the understanding of conscience throughout Paul's letters. Unlike readers in our modern Western culture, Paul's readers would have thought in corporate terms of honor and shame rather than in terms of individual conscience. In that culture one sensed the opinion of the group. This does not dilute Paul's emphasis on individual responsibility. In addition to 1:5, the other occurrences in the Pastorals are 1 Tim. 1:19 ("holding on to faith and a good conscience"); 3:9 ("they must keep hold of the deep truths of the faith with a clear conscience"); 4:2 (the false doctrines at Ephesus "come through hypocritical liars, whose consciences have been seared as with a hot iron"); 2 Tim. 1:3 ("I thank God, whom I serve . . . with a clear conscience"); and Titus 1:15 ("to those who are corrupted and do not believe . . . both their minds and consciences are corrupted").

8. Another word Paul uses in the Pastoral Letters is *planao* (see 1 Tim. 3:13; Titus 3:3), to wander or deceive, which has a significant history in ancient religious controversies.

9. See also Acts 14:15; 1 Cor. 3:20; 15:17; James 1:26; 1 Peter 1:18; and related forms in Rom. 1:21; 8:20; 2 Peter 2:18.

teacher Gamaliel in Acts 5:34. The implication from that and from the context here is that these people wanted to be recognized authorities in the Old Testament, perhaps especially regarding case law applying to the Ten Commandments. Such teachers would have the heady experience of telling people what they ought or ought not to do in specific "cases" or instances. Luke 12:13 provides an example of the status they may have sought, where Jesus is approached as an authority on the law by someone who says, "Teacher, tell my brother to divide the inheritance with me."

FAITH, TRUTH, AND love. Given the importance of right doctrine in this passage, one might have expected that the goal of the command in 1:5 would be doctrinal correctness. Instead it is *love.* This is not a sentimental turn in Paul's instructions; love in Scripture is not weak emotion. Love is "as strong as death, its jealousy unyielding as the grave. It burns like blazing fire, like a mighty flame" (Song 8:6). Theologically, "love is the fulfillment of the law" (Rom. 13:10) and the heart of the two great commandments (loving God and loving one's neighbor, Matt. 22:36–39). Love is the divinely appointed, intentional object of God's law. It is also the motivating force in God's sending of his Son (John 3:16), in our Lord's death for us (Gal. 2:20), and in our sacrificial service to him (2 Cor. 5:14).[10]

Love (v. 5) issues from having one's heart purified and from a "good conscience." These in turn are possible only to those who have "a sincere faith." And where these three—the pure heart, the good conscience, and a sincere faith—exist together in their wholeness, the result is love. Jesus showed one aspect of this relationship when he said that a person "who has been forgiven little loves little" (Luke 7:47).

In contrast to the false teachers, Timothy should hold on to *both* "sincere faith" and "a good conscience." The word "sincere" that modifies faith adds force to the importance of a clear conscience. When Paul refers to faith as "sincere," he is not dealing with the question of whether one has faith or not (i.e., is a believer or an unbeliever), nor is he concerned with whether one has little or great faith.[11] It is rather a matter of whether faith is genuine or

---

10. The Pastoral Letters refer to love in 1 Tim. 1:14; 2:15; 4:12; 6:10, 11; 2 Tim. 1:7, 13; 2:22; 3:3, 10; Titus 2:2, 4; 3:4, 15.

11. See Jesus' comments on "little faith" in Matt. 6:30; 8:26; 14:31; 16:8; 17:20; Luke 12:28. Jesus uses this expression to describe not so much an amount of faith measured on a broad scale as much as a lack of faith in a given situation; if the disciples had even a tiny particle of faith they could move mountains.

hypocritical, well-intentioned or postured. Once more he is dealing with one's character. Paradoxically those whose consciences are corrupt are the very ones who are practicing asceticism (1 Tim. 4:2–5) and no doubt congratulating themselves on their righteousness. Sincerity and having a good conscience, therefore, are both marks of the integrity that must characterize the servant of the Lord.

The expression "pure heart" (v. 5) immediately calls to mind Jesus' beatitude, "Blessed are the pure in heart, for they will see God." The heart represents the total inner person in both Old and New Testaments. It appears frequently in the Psalms and Proverbs.[12] In 2 Timothy 2:22 Paul counsels Timothy: "Flee the evil desires of youth, and pursue righteousness, faith, love and peace, along with those who call on the Lord out of a pure heart." That verse and the present one have the words "love" and "faith" in common as well as "pure heart." In addition, the words "a good conscience" and "faith" occur both here and near the end of the chapter (v. 19).[13]

An important theme. This is the first occurrence in the Pastoral Letters of the blend of beliefs and character, of orthodoxy and orthopraxy, sound doctrine and moral living, that will be developed as a major theme in the Pastoral Letters. The integrity of the Lord's servant is both important in itself and in contrast to the lives of the false teachers, who, like their teachings, are despicable. The fact that there are references in these letters to vices and virtues that are similar to conventional moral standards in the first century does not detract from their authenticity, but rather shows their relevance. Servants of the Lord, including elders and deacons and their families, must not live on a moral level below that of their neighbors. Gentiles also had morals, in spite of some of the gross things they practiced, and they were quick to criticize inconsistent Christians and dismiss their teachings.

In this connection, when Paul tells Timothy clearly and forcibly that heresy is not to be tolerated, he makes it clear that the most important characteristic of the heretics here is their provocation of controversy.[14] Note the contrast to this characteristic, love, the goal of the command (v. 5). If, there-

---

12. A few examples: "I praise you, O LORD, with all my heart" (Ps. 9:1; cf. 111:1); "my heart rejoices" (13:5; cf. 16:9; 28:7); "my heart fails" (40:12; cf. 73:26), "my heart is steadfast" (57:7; cf. 108:1; 112:7); "apply your heart to understanding" (Prov. 2:2; cf. 2:10; 23:15); "create in me a pure heart, O God" (Ps. 51:10).

13. See also 4:2 and comments.

14. The Greek word *hairesis* does not appear in the Pastoral Letters. *Heresy* and *heretic* are used in this commentary because (1) it has (over the course of time) the meaning of choice, a philosophic system, a sect, a faction, dissension; and (2) it has also come to mean doctrinal error. It therefore appropriately describes the destructive situation that was happening at Ephesus.

fore, Timothy undertakes his commission to wipe out heresy as a license to vent his anger (as some bellicose defenders of the faith have done throughout history), he will be *like* the false teachers in *attitude,* forgetting the "goal."

Of the three expressions discussed in verse 5, "a pure heart and a good conscience and a sincere faith," the middle one, "a good conscience" is probably generally least understood. Conscience is an innate God-given ability to make moral judgments. It does not tell us what is right or wrong, but, on the basis of what we have been taught, it discerns whether or not a particular moral option accords with that knowledge. We are responsible to make decisions according to conscience. If there is doubt about the rightness of a particular behavior, Romans 14:23 directs us not to follow it. Such action is not based on faith, and "everything that does not come from faith is sin."

This reality shows that even Christians who follow their consciences faithfully may differ in their behavior, since the basis (standards they have adopted and with reference to which their consciences function) may differ from one another. No one's conscience is infallible. Even those who do not know God's law have a conscience and are morally responsible (Rom. 2:12–16), but their moral judgments may be flawed. Sincerity and a good conscience are important characteristics for the Lord's servant. Such qualities may seem too weak or fuzzy to be prime requirements at times when (as has happened in notorious periods of church history) error has been rampant. At such times the battle lines have been drawn and the indomitable zeal of a crusader seems to be the most important qualification for leaders. But that is precisely why we need the Pastoral Letters—to set our priorities straight.

HOW TO ADDRESS error. The message of the Pastoral Letters for us today is not only how to identify a particular kind of heresy. The message is also (and perhaps even more important in some circumstances), the *way* such deviations are to be addressed. It will become increasingly clear in the study of the Pastorals that *how* the sound teacher should confront heresy shares the spotlight with *what* heresies to confront. A major application of the Pastoral Letters today—and it can be argued that it is the distinguishing one in that corpus—is not simply maintaining correct doctrine, much less insisting on some form of church organization that we may discern in those letters, but the importance of *the integrity of doctrine and life.*

When Paul was on his missionary journeys, he had occasion to meet and to hear about itinerant pagan preachers, such as philosophic missionaries and cultic practitioners, who were making a living off their naive supporters and converts. We have ample evidence from those days that the reputations of some of these wandering preachers revealed a slurry of bad teaching and evil living.[15] But even in Christianity, as churches were being established and Paul's span of control became too broad to be effective, he increasingly observed instances of such a mixture in the lives of teachers within the churches. He observed ungodliness that was coupled with corrupted and corrupting teaching (1 Tim. 1:18–20; 4:1–2; 2 Tim. 2:16–17; 3:1–9; Titus 1:10–14). Therefore, Paul urged not just pure doctrine or just a pure life, but a *blend* of these to counter the evil slurry of impure doctrine and impure life. The doctrine he called for was not only correct, but "sound." A sound, or healthy, doctrine produces moral, healthy living. This blend is not only important in Christians and especially in Christian teachers, but is, in itself, a testimony to the truth of the message.[16]

Identifying error. The foregoing does not minimize the contemporary task of confronting doctrinal error. What do the Pastorals teach us about doing this? In order to apply New Testament passages that warn against doctrinal deviation to our own circumstances, it is helpful to understand as fully as possible the biblical background. This can be a frustrating task in the Pastorals, however, since they do not present the heresy cohesively. This is not a defect since, as noted in connection with the terms in the salutation, the recipients had information that later readers do not. They could put the pieces together.

Yet there are a number of hints throughout the letters as to what constituted the areas of disagreement. As we have seen already, in 1:3 Paul mentions "false doctrines," so we know that it was not just a matter of practices or opinions but truth that was at stake. He refers to "myths and endless genealogies," but these terms are somewhat obscure, so they do not help us greatly to discern the nature of the error. We also know that there is something about the law that these people have misunderstood, because apparently they are not using it "properly" (v. 8). Further bits of information will be discovered in later passages of the Pastorals. But even if we are unable to paint as accurate and as colorful a picture as we would like of these deviations from truth, are we at a complete loss? Does that mean that we cannot extract from a passage such as 1:3–7 anything that is concrete enough to help us discern doctrinal deviation today? On the contrary, there are several ways in which we can apply the text.

---

15. *Slurry* is a term used in mining and metallurgy for a mixture of particles such as clay, cement, and coal in a liquid. I use it as descriptive of the mixture of impure doctrine and deeds.

16. The passages where Paul emphasizes this "blend," the integrity of doctrine and life, are 1 Tim. 1:5, 19; 2:8–15; 3:2–13, 15–16; 4:2, 6–7, 11–12, 15–16; 5:5–6, 8, 10; 6:1–2, 6–10, 11–12; 2 Tim. 2:19–22; Titus 2:1–10; 3:8 (see also Introduction).

(1) Even though we may not be able to identify a specific contemporary error corresponding to what was in Paul's mind as he wrote, we can usually discern enough of the shape of things in the churches of the first century to be able to flesh out a corresponding potential problem in our own situation. The proper use of the law, for example, has been a matter of debate for many centuries, and there are legitimate differences among branches of Christianity. But if we encounter a strong legalistic attitude or its opposite, libertarianism, we can probe for a doctrinal assumption that may lie behind this erroneous abuse of the law.

(2) Another approach is to note the presence of any hindrances to normal growth in our church (or fellowship of churches). One hindrance may be controversy, as in the church at Ephesus (1:4). This does not mean that controversy always indicates heresy, for even orthodox theologians and church leaders can let their personal agendas and sinful motives propel them into controversies. But controversy can also arise from underlying differences in basic doctrinal assumptions, especially if one or the other embraces ideas that are incompatible with orthodoxy. Another clue that a doctrinal virus may be present is if God's work is not going forward by faith (cf. again v. 4). While monetary interests and personal "empire building" can displace faith, so can aberrant doctrine. There can be an erosion of dependence on God, with the consequent subtle shifting of the ground underneath a newly planted church or missionary work.

I recall that when I was a young boy, there was a group of churches united in their doctrine and opposed to what was then called modernism. One church in that fellowship, however, did not seem to have the strength or make the progress of the others. One wise Christian detected a serious flaw in the preaching of the pastor of that church. The fundamentals of the faith were not being clearly proclaimed. It was not long before that pastor left and joined an institution that had no commitment to what we today would call evangelical faith. For many, that pastor's move came as a complete surprise. But it was not so to those who had discerned that the cause, for the weakness in "God's work" was at heart doctrinal.

(3) It might seem, given the history of confrontations between so-called modernists and fundamentalists, and more recently between liberals and evangelicals, that it would be harder today than formerly for those whose doctrine is not sound to escape being detected and called into account. Today also we have the advantage of a number of excellent, theologically sound seminaries whose faculties and alumni are well equipped to identify heresy and deal with it. Nevertheless, there are reasons for a widespread and dangerous ignorance concerning the Bible and doctrine. (a) One reason is the lack of references in the public schools to Bible facts and church history.

(b) Another is the diminishing of family Bible reading and instruction, due in part to the disappearance of the family evening dinner hour.

(c) Moreover, the preoccupation of pastors with administrative duties, community-related events, and counseling often means less time for study.

(d) It is also possible for preachers to be so intent on reaching the unchurched or the younger generation that doctrinal preaching suffers. It is now widely recognized that newer generations have difficulty in following extended nonrelational sermons, and that contemporary sermons often, in the sincere process of adaptation to this audience, are doctrinally thin. Unless some provision is made for doctrinal instruction, both Christians and seekers may lack the foundation needed to deal knowledgeably with doctrinal issues. Cult members coming to the door are often better trained in stating their beliefs than the Christians they visit are grounded in biblical truth. It is possible for people to hear modern equivalents of "myths and endless genealogies" and not know how to deal with them. And when teachers "confidently affirm" (v. 7) doctrinal matters—whether about the law or other topics more current today—the average person has little idea that those teachers "do not know what they are talking about."

Addressing relativism. Another contemporary problem is that in contrast to a dogmatic stand for theological purity, discussions about religious and ethical topics often include relativistic terms like *pluralism* and *values*. Christian teachings are often assessed as having only proportionate worth. Eclecticism is a way of looking at religion and beliefs in which one is not committed to any one religious organization or belief system, but instead chooses aspects of these at will. Any teaching or ethical yardstick that is personally appealing is considered valid. Thus many Catholics today accept traditional Catholic teachings about Mary but dismiss Catholic teachings on birth control. Religious authority and theological absolutism are dismissed.

The term *values* seems harmless and even good, but it can be a poor substitute for *morals*. Differing value systems claim equal status with moral absolutes. In various cultures around the world and over the years, Christian missionaries have had to decide how to acknowledge genuine values in the beliefs and practices of the people they are seeking to reach, without compromising either the gospel itself or the moral standards and the doctrine they are commissioned to bring.

1 Timothy 1:8–11

W̄E KNOW THAT the law is good if one uses it properly. [9]We also know that law is made not for the righteous but for lawbreakers and rebels, the ungodly and sinful, the unholy and irreligious; for those who kill their fathers or mothers, for murderers, [10]for adulterers and perverts, for slave traders and liars and perjurers—and for whatever else is contrary to the sound doctrine [11]that conforms to the glorious gospel of the blessed God, which he entrusted to me.

Original Meaning

IN A PLAY on words, Paul says the law (*nomos*) must be used legitimately (*nomimos*). Proper use, of course, requires an understanding of its purpose. There has been much theological discussion on this matter and especially on the function of the law in the lives of those who have been saved by grace.

Paul speaks to this issue at length in more than one place, but reference may be most profitably made, besides the present passage, to Galatians 5:13–26. There the law is summarized "in a single command: 'Love your neighbor as yourself.'" This assumes, of course, the love of God as the "greatest" commandment (Matt. 22:37–38). The Galatians passage goes on to show that the "acts of the sinful nature" (lit., "flesh") must be replaced by the "fruit of the Spirit [which] is love, joy, peace, patience, kindness, goodness, faithfulness, gentleness and self-control. Against such things there is no law" (Gal. 5:22–23). Here in 1 Timothy 1 Paul describes those whose actions are contrary to that law, not now in personal debauchery as in Galatians 5:19–21, but in opposition to God (1 Tim. 1:9a) and in hostility to human beings (vv. 9b–10a). Such people love neither God nor neighbor.

Verse 9 establishes a principle that the law[1] has been made[2] not for the righteous but for "lawbreakers and rebels." Those who resist doing what is

---

1. The word "law" (*nomos*) is anarthrous in the Greek text of verse 9. That is, it lacks the definite article "the." This does not make the word indefinite, however, as though it referred to law in general. Even when the article does not occur, a context may make it clear that the law of Moses is in mind, as in Romans 2:14, where Paul says the Gentiles do not have "law," and in Galatians 3:17, where he says "law" came four hundred years after Abraham. Usually when Paul refers to law he means the law of Moses.

2. "Made" (*keitai*) has a legal sense here. The word can also be rendered "given, exist, be valid" (BAGD, 426).

right need to be confronted by a standard that clarifies what they are doing is wrong. Paul wrote, "I felt fine when I did not understand what the law demanded. But when I learned the truth, I realized I had broken the law and was a sinner, doomed to die" (Rom. 7:9, NLT). If Paul, who was already committed to that law, needed to be confronted in that manner, how much more those whose sins are listed in the following section.

It has often been pointed out that the list of sins in verses 9–10 not only recall the so-called "vice lists" found in ancient moralistic writings, but follow topics in the Ten Commandments (Deut. 5:6–21):[3]

1 Timothy 1:9–10	10 Commandments (Deut. 5:6–21)
lawbreakers and rebels, the ungodly and sinful, the unholy and irreligious	You shall have no other gods before me
those who kill their fathers or mothers	Honor your father and your mother
for murderers	You shall not murder
for adulterers and perverts	You shall not commit adultery
for slave traders	You shall not steal
and liars and perjurers	You shall not give false testimony against your neighbor

Most of the comparisons are self-explanatory. The description of those who do not honor God includes various aspects of disrespect. The word translated "adulterers" (1 Tim. 1:10) has a broad meaning and was understood (as was the seventh commandment) as applying to various acts of sexual immorality. Nevertheless the Hebrew na'ap in Deuteronomy 5:18 specifically meant adultery (another word, zana, was used for fornication in general), and at the time of the New Testament, although the Greek word porneia was broadly used for sexual immorality, it could (depending on the context) refer specifically to adultery. Pornoi, used here, is appropriately translated "adulterers" in the NIV. The NIV "perverts" is an interpretation of the Greek arsenokoi, male homosexuals (NRSV "sodomites"; NLT "homosexuals"). Slave trading may seem to be an unusual example of stealing, but it was understandable and all too common in that society (see also Ex. 21:16; Deut. 24:7).

Verse 10 uses the rhetorical method of going from the particular to the general. After listing the sins that require judgment and correction by the law,

---

3. Young shows that this list reflects the Decalogue and also fits into the "Hellenistic-Jewish bridge culture" in the Pastorals (*Theology of the Pastoral Letters*, 24–28).

Paul generalizes, "and whatever else is contrary to the sound doctrine." There are several significant points in verses 10–11:

(1) What is contrary to the Old Testament law is also contrary to Christian doctrine.

(2) True doctrine is called "sound" or healthy. This word is a medical term (see below) and may be a clue to some participation or influence by Luke in the writing of the Pastoral Letters (see Introduction).

(3) The sound doctrine in turn "conforms to the glorious gospel." The first teaching that the non-Christians heard through the preaching of the gospel and the subsequent instruction they received through the teaching of doctrine were consistent with each other.

(4) This gospel comes from the "blessed God." This emphasizes both its truth and its immense importance.

(5) That gospel was entrusted to Paul, a fact that expresses both Paul's authority and his responsibility in communicating it.

The expression "sound teaching" occurs only in the Pastoral Letters. "Sound" represents the participle of the verb *hygiaino*, "to be healthy," used as an adjective.[4] It is combined with "words," "doctrine," or "in the faith." In each case, it is used to describe true belief. Usually the immediate context shows that it is true belief in contrast to false teaching. The verb alone, in its literal sense of being healthy, is found elsewhere in the New Testament only in Luke and 3 John.

This is a vivid figurative expression, specially employed in the Pastoral Letters to describe teaching that is not "sick," but wholesome and resistant to the disease of error.[5] The false teachers, by contrast, had an "unhealthy [*nosos*, sick] interest" in quarrels (1 Tim. 6:4). The sins that counter the Ten Commandments, listed in 1:9–10, are "contrary to" this sound doctrine. To show that those sins are not merely lapses or mistakes, Paul chooses a word (*antikeita*, "set over against, opposed to, antithetical to") that seems to be a play on the word *keitai* ("made or given") in the phrase "the law is made" (v. 9).

There is a further implication in the vocabulary of verses 10–11. The unsound, sick, and false doctrine has a formidable opponent, the "glorious gospel of the blessed God." The noun "glory" (used here adjectivally in the

---

4. Occurrences of the verb in the Pastoral Letters in addition to 1:10 are 6:3; 2 Tim. 1:13; 4:3; Titus 1:9, 13; 2:1–2.

5. For an alternative viewpoint that draws on Greek and Hellenistic occurrences where the word means "rational" or "reasonable" rather than "sound" and is used to counter Pauline authorship of the Pastoral Letters, see Dibelius and Conzelmann, *Pastoral Epistles*, 24–25. The problem with their presentation is their methodology, not the literary or linguistic resources they cite.

genitive case) appears also in 1:17 (where honor and glory are ascribed to God); in 3:16 (Christ was "taken up in glory"); in 2 Timothy 2:10 (regarding obtaining "salvation that is in Christ Jesus, with eternal glory"); in 4:18 (where glory is again ascribed to God); and in Titus 2:13 (the "glorious appearing [or manifestation of the glory, NRSV] of our great God and Savior, Jesus Christ"). In discussing whether the phrase here should be understood as (1) "the glorious gospel of the blessed God" (which follows the Semitic idiom familiar to the writer), or (2) "the gospel of the [or, which tells the] glory of the blessed God," Knight rightly consults 1 Corinthians 4:4, where parallel wording appears, usually translated "the gospel of the glory of Christ."[6] Rendering (2) is therefore appropriate here.[7]

Bridging Contexts

CHRISTIANS AND THE **Old Testament law.** Theologians have long argued over the function of the Old Testament law for New Testament believers. Is it to be discarded as inappropriate for this dispensation? Is it only useful insofar as it shows human sinfulness? Should it be taught as a standard for Christian life? Should Christians seek to bring society into conformation with that law?[8]

This paragraph does not rule out any one of these uses and so does not answer those questions directly, but it does provide some essential principles. Verses 8–11 make three points. (1) They contrast the knowledge that "well informed Christians"[9] have ("we know," v. 8) with the ignorance of the false

---

6. Peterson's paraphrase in *The Message* gives the Corinthians wording a happy contemporary twist, "the Message that shines with Christ." It is unfortunate, however, that in 1 Tim. 1:11 the significant terminology about glory is obscured in that paraphrase by the mere word "great." (In the previous verse the important key phrase "sound doctrine" does not appear at all, apparently spoken for by the word "truth" in a compressed summary of vv. 10–11.) This illustrates the difficulty one faces in the commendable attempt to contemporize biblical terms for those to whom they are unfamiliar.

7. In this connection, NRSV and NLT join in correcting NIV in Titus 2:13 from "glorious appearing" to "manifestation of the glory [of Christ]" and "wonderful event when the glory [of Christ] will be revealed," respectively. *The Message* has "the glorious day when [Christ] appears," applying the idea of glory to the time rather than to Christ. See my comments on that passage.

8. The Old Testament Law, the Torah, has been applied and misapplied in many ways, partly because of some exegetical uncertainties. Jesus addressed the matter of the law in the Sermon on the Mount, especially in Matt. 5:17–48 and in his examples "You have heard ... but I tell you." The exact significance of this is still debated. Paul said that Christ is the "end" of the law. "End" here represents the Greek *telos*, which can mean both goal and discontinuance, but which of these Paul means or emphasizes is also debated.

9. Kelly, *The Pastoral Epistles*, 48.

teachers, who misuse the law. (2) They teach that although Timothy has to oppose those who want to be teachers of the law, the law itself must be affirmed, for it is good (v. 8; cf. Rom. 7:12). (3) They provide important insights for the readers as to the proper objects of the law's teachings (1 Tim. 1:9–10).

The immediate concern of this passage is not the same as those we have today, such as the possible role of the Old Testament law in the realm of secular society, the extent to which that law should function as a basis of Christian life in the present age, or the function of the law in salvation history. There is instead a particular concern, a problem that these letters are addressing. Apparently the heretics were making a stringent application of the law to achieve their own purposes in the church. In ways we no longer fully understand, they were applying the law to the "righteous" by trying to force it into a doctrinal or ethical role it was not intended to have. The same apostle (assuming Pauline authorship) who wrote that love is the fulfillment of the law in a context that urges giving respect, honor, and revenue to those who deserve them (Rom. 13:7–8), could hardly now be ruling out such an application as one of its proper functions.

There must be a specific reason, though unclear to us, why Paul not only says that the law is for sinners but identifies by category the particular sinners who need to be exposed to its condemning light. The law apparently functions as a kind of vice list familiar to the Ephesian believers and to the false teachers. This suggests that one legitimate use of the law is to point out sin in whatever form it may take in a given culture. What arrests the reader is that after mentioning slave traders, liars, and other such sinners as those against whom the law should be directed, he then brings it to bear on the teachings of those very people who were misusing it ("and whatever else is contrary to the sound doctrine"). The false teachers found that their gun had been turned around to point at themselves.

The standard of truth. Sometimes otherwise logical persons have difficulty in drawing obvious logical conclusions and acting on them. The standard of truth in this passage is "sound doctrine *that conforms to* the glorious gospel" (italics added). Any teaching that does not conform to the "glorious gospel" is clearly not sound doctrine and should be abandoned. Otherwise, for what may be personal, political, or sentimental reasons, we allow the nose of heresy to slip under the tent flap of our study class, youth program, or the church itself. The reason why one might choose to overlook that a teaching does not "conform" to the gospel may be deliberate, or it may be lack of good teaching, in which case the leadership of the church is to blame. Paul implies that any teaching, not only about the law but about any basic element of doctrine, that does not clearly conform with the essential gospel should be declared false.

THE OLD TESTAMENT **law today.** Few Christians today will be involved in deep discussions of the Old Testament law. There are two ways, however, in which the circumstances of this paragraph may bear strongly on typical experiences of Christians today. (1) Christians may, perhaps without realizing it, be criticized for behavior or actions on the basis of an overzealous application of the law. This is not necessarily legalism in the sense of the Judaizing activities of Paul's day, but it is a legalism that forgets the law of love. This happens when there is a focus on one or another *detail* of behavior or of a theological *opinion*[10] while ignoring certain whole principles. Jesus spoke of those who "give a tenth of your spices . . . but you have neglected the more important matters of the law—justice, mercy and faithfulness. You should have practiced the latter, without neglecting the former" (Matt. 23:23). This obviously is not antinomian, but it is a revision of perspective.

(2) The other way in which this passage has relevance for today's Christian concerns the failure to discern what does and does not conform or correspond to the truth of the gospel. Over the past decades the opening lines used by cult representatives as they do their missionary work from door to door have changed. These lines are more likely now to appeal to the religious consciousness of the person being visited or to commonly accepted "family values" (much as the old door-to-door salesman would get the people to say "yes" as often as possible before coming to the sales pitch itself). It is becoming harder and harder to discern what does and what does not conform to the gospel.

On distinguishing truth from error. As noted earlier, some Christians may be unprepared to discern the difference because of insufficient biblical and doctrinal teaching in many churches today. If one makes a comparison between two radically different church cultures—that, for example, of the 1930s with that of the 1990s—the situation may become more clear. In the earlier period, religious literacy was high. Those who were won to Christ in the various evangelistic meetings both in and out of church were often already well aware of the truth of the gospel even before their conversion. They knew more of the Bible than most people do today and they knew something of doctrine. The fact that people today who have not been previously educated in Christian theology and Bible are coming to Christ is, of course, a matter for thanksgiving. The fact that they have been so ill taught is not.

---

10. I like to call these "doctoids," on the analogy of unimportant "factoids."

We need to put extra effort into seeing that new Christians are given the background that they lack as quickly as possible, so that they will be able to tell the difference between "the gospel" and heresy and thereby successfully resist the latter. We need also to include enough biblical doctrine in our preaching (and worship) to provide a foundation for seekers on which to ground their faith when the time of their conversion arrives.

There may, however, also be parts of sermons, commentaries, articles, and even hymns *within* the truly Christian orbit that, while not heretical statements, do not conform to the gospel. Is it true that angels have wings and harps of gold? And is it true that "still through the cloven skies they come / With peaceful wings unfurled"? We sing that every Christmas in "It Came Upon a Midnight Clear." I see no harm in it, *if* we sing it symbolically, but we should recognize its poetic embellishment.

I once heard a worship leader say that we "worship with (sic) the Father" and heard him pray that we might be "exalted above the Lord." These were, I presume, merely slips of the tongue, but they illustrate the need for precision in public worship. In the hymn "Joyful, Joyful We Adore Thee" we sing, "Thou the Father, Christ our Brother—all who live in love are Thine." If we sing this with the context of Hebrews 2:11–12, 17 and 1 John 4:7 in mind, all is well; but there is no doubt that many have sung it with the presuppositions of liberal theology in mind, and thus with a meaning that did not conform to the gospel.

These observations may seem pedantic, but truth requires precision. We need to ask further, however, whether when we detect outright heresy, we should attack the motives or those who teach error. Paul did this openly in the Pastoral Letters. Perhaps we should distinguish between outright immorality and hostility to the gospel on the one hand and private thoughts on the other, which, while apparently improper, are best left to God to judge.

Often the choice reflects the personality of the person who makes the judgment—either reticent to speak out or aggressively censorious. In today's climate the latter attitude quickly loses a respectful hearing. If the goal of the command is love and requires a pure heart (1:5), we need to examine our own motives when declaring the sins and errors of others. We also need to keep in mind that the moral judgments expressed in the Pastoral Letters have been written under the inspiration of the Holy Spirit and therefore are accurate in their assessment of the motives of the heretics—something we cannot claim.

1 Timothy 1:12–17

I THANK CHRIST Jesus our Lord, who has given me strength, that he considered me faithful, appointing me to his service. ¹³Even though I was once a blasphemer and a persecutor and a violent man, I was shown mercy because I acted in ignorance and unbelief. ¹⁴The grace of our Lord was poured out on me abundantly, along with the faith and love that are in Christ Jesus.

¹⁵Here is a trustworthy saying that deserves full acceptance: Christ Jesus came into the world to save sinners—of whom I am the worst. ¹⁶But for that very reason I was shown mercy so that in me, the worst of sinners, Christ Jesus might display his unlimited patience as an example for those who would believe on him and receive eternal life. ¹⁷Now to the King eternal, immortal, invisible, the only God, be honor and glory for ever and ever. Amen.

Original Meaning

PAUL MOVES FROM gratitude to Christ the Lord in verse 12 to praise to God the King in verse 18, which forms a climax to the section. Between these verses he moves from the particular (Paul the blasphemer was shown mercy, vv. 13–14) to the general (Christ came to save sinners, v. 15), and then to the particular again (Paul the sinner was shown mercy, vv. 15b–16).

God's Gracious Commission to Paul (1:12–14)

PAUL'S GRATITUDE IS to the One who gave him strength. In Philippians 4:13, he had expansively declared, "I can do everything through him who gives me strength"; and later in the Pastoral Letters he writes of a specific instance in which the Lord gave him strength when he had to face his accusers alone (2 Tim. 4:16–17). The apostle also encouraged Timothy to "be strong in the grace that is in Christ Jesus" (2 Tim. 2:1). The idea in this exhortation to strength is not to brute force but to moral strength and confirmation for service. But while the strength comes from God, faithfulness is required of Paul. "Now it is required that those who have been given a trust must prove faithful" (1 Cor. 4:2). This faithfulness is not a virtue that earns Paul a commission, but is a requirement for God's "service" (*diakonia*, 1 Tim. 1:12).

The word *diakonia* appears thirty-four times in the New Testament, and the verb *diakoneo* ("serve") thirty-seven times. First Corinthians 12:5 informs us that "there are different kinds of service, but the same Lord." Throughout the New Testament many different kinds of service are mentioned without confining service (or "ministry") to some special order or office. In Acts 6:2, 4 waiting on tables (i.e., providing food for needy widows) and the apostolic teaching of the Word of God are both called "service." In Paul's case his service, as unique as his conversion, is to be the great apostle to the Gentiles.

Verses 13–14 form an interesting contrast to Paul's testimony in Philippians 3:4–6, where he portrays himself as formerly being proud of his accomplishments. There he cited his persecution of the church as an evidence of zeal and described himself "as for legalistic righteousness, faultless." He did immediately follow those words with the demurral, "Whatever was to my profit I now consider loss for the sake of Christ" (v. 7), but that is mild compared to his strong self-condemnation here in 1 Timothy 1:13: "once a blasphemer and a persecutor and a violent man."

Blasphemy is the defamation of God's name, a horrendous act and attitude punishable by death in Old Testament times (Lev. 24:16). Its seriousness is also clear in 1 Timothy 1:20, where Paul says he has handed two individuals "over to Satan to be taught not to blaspheme."[1] Here in verse 13 Paul links blasphemy with persecution and violence, as he did in his "testimony" to King Agrippa (Acts 26:9–11), telling how he not only imprisoned many of the Christians and agreed to their death (see Acts 8:1), but also tried to force them to blaspheme.

Paul's explanation to Timothy as to why God had mercy on him is because he acted "in ignorance and unbelief." That does not mean that God automatically forgives anyone who acts without knowledge in their non-Christian days, but it does express the sovereign mercy of God in reaching out to Saul of Tarsus, who sought to honor him by trying to wipe out the Christians when *he* thought *they* were blaspheming.

Verse 14, where "grace" now joins the "mercy" mentioned in verse 13, echoes Ephesians 2:4–5, where, after describing the state of those dead in sins, Paul writes: "But ... God, who is rich in mercy, made us alive with Christ ... it is by grace you have been saved." And like Ephesians, where Paul uses superlatives (e.g., *hyperballo* and *hyperekperissou*, Eph. 1:19; 2:7; 3:19–20), he says in 1 Timothy 1:14 that this grace was "poured out on me abundantly" (*hyperpleonazo*).

---

1. Further insight into what was considered to be blasphemy comes from the words of those who were about to stone Jesus to death: "because you, a mere man, claim to be God" (John 10:33). See also T. Rees, "Blaspheme; Blasphemy," *ISBE*, 1:521–22.

It is striking that faith and love, which in verse 5 formed the goal of Paul's command to Timothy, reappear here in a somewhat different role, qualities that are "in Christ Jesus." If "faith" is understood as "faithfulness" (as *pistis* may indeed mean), this may refer to qualities Christ possesses. If, as is more likely, it is belief in contrast to Paul's former unbelief (v. 13), it refers to faith as accessible from its source, Christ Jesus. Faith and love, like grace, are abundantly bestowed by God. This also is reminiscent of Ephesians 2, especially the familiar "by grace you have been saved, through faith—and this is not from yourselves, it is the gift of God" (2:8–9), where the salvation God gives seems to include the gift of faith itself, though the grammar is not clear in that regard.

God's Mercy to Paul (1:15–16)

VERSE 15 BEGINS with *pistos*, an adjective related to the noun *pistis* immediately above. Sometimes translated "faithful" ("This is a faithful saying," KJV), it means here that which can be trusted; thus the NIV has "here is a trustworthy saying."[2] The phrase occurs several other times in the Pastoral Letters (3:1; 4:9; 2 Tim 2:11; Titus 3:8). Two of the passages in 1 Timothy add the words "that deserves full acceptance."[3]

This trustworthy saying contains the essence of the Christian message: "Christ Jesus came into the world to save sinners." Paul combines the title "Christ" ("Anointed One"), which by now had become a proper name, with the human name of Jesus. The order, as noted above, is common in the Pastoral Letters. The expression "came into the world" implies, but does not require, preexistence. (One can speak of a puppy coming into the world.) However, such passages as Philippians 2:5–8 and Colossians 1:15–17 certainly indicate that Paul held to the preexistence of the Son of God.

The purpose of Christ's coming, "to save sinners," has been welcomed by two millennia of human beings who, conscious of their guilt before God, have gratefully accepted the redeeming events of the incarnation and saving death of the Lord Jesus as accomplished for them as sinners. Moreover, in this passage two extremes are cited of those for whom Christ came. One is the group of sinners described in verses 9–10; the other is Paul himself, who, in spite of all his righteous deeds, calls himself "the worst" of sinners.

These two extremes illustrate the terminology of Romans 5. In 5:8 the apostle writes, "While we were still sinners, Christ died for us," and goes on

---

2. The NLT's "this is a true saying" undervalues the strength of the word. Something can be true without calling for dependence. *The Message* nicely expresses the phrase idiomatically in reverse order: "Here's a word you can take to heart and depend on."

3. For a detailed study of the "faithful sayings" see Knight, *The Faithful Sayings.*

to describe sinners as "powerless," "ungodly," and "enemies" (5:6, 10). He not only counts himself here among that group, but puts himself the lowest place because of his active persecution of not only Christians but also the Lord himself (as was made clear to Paul when, at his conversion, the voice from heaven said, "I am Jesus, whom you are persecuting," Acts 9:5).

It was not only as an act of kindness that God showed Paul mercy, true and wonderful as that is. Verse 16 explains that he was a showcase for God's "unlimited patience." In a sense all those who are forgiven sinners display God's mercy and patience. What God did for us stands "to the praise of his glorious grace" (Eph. 1:6). The church itself, in its wonderful blending of Jew and Gentile as one, displays the "manifold wisdom of God ... to the rulers and authorities in the heavenly realms" (Eph. 3:10). But Paul sees himself (emphatic *ego,* "I myself," at the end of 1 Tim. 1:15) as a prototype of all hostile, sinful rebels against God, whom God tolerates while patiently waiting for their conversion.[4]

The result of this faith is "eternal life." We know from 6:12 that this is a future life we can "take hold" of now. John 5:24 tells us that the believer *"has eternal life"* and *"has crossed over* [Greek perfect tense] *from death to life"* (italics added). It is the life of God in which we participate, which is more than an endless extension of life.

Doxology (1:17)

VERSE 17 BRINGS this moving testimony to a climax. It is a doxology[5] honoring God as (1) the King, (2) beyond the limitation of time, (3) incapable of dying, (4) invisible, and (5) existing alone as God.

---

4. The word "worst" in verses 15 and 16 is literally "first" and can also be translated "foremost" (see NRSV). The NIV cleverly uses the negative word "worst" to express its meaning in the context of both verses. *The Message* has a felicitous paraphrase: "I'm proof—Public Sinner Number One—of someone who could never have made it apart from sheer mercy. And now he shows me off—evidence of his endless patience—to those who are right on the edge of trusting him forever." The words "are right on the edge of" chooses one possible meaning of *mellonton* to describe an action that is about to happen, but that implies that in each case the example of Paul comes into play just before conversion. It is acceptably translated "would" in NIV and NRSV, but neither of these translations brings out the nuance of destiny, something impending, which is often an important part of its meaning. The point is that for those who in the future are going (*mellonton*) to believe, Paul serves as an encouraging example.

5. A doxology is a statement with creedal content, sometimes in hymnic form, celebrating the praiseworthy attributes of God. The Greek word for glory, used later in this verse, is *doxa,* from which "doxology" is derived. What one seems to be and what people think of that individual (both ideas are in the related Greek verb *dokeo*) become that person's reputation. God's reputation is his glory. We do not add to what God is by our praise, but we do "glorify" him; that is, we enhance his reputation.

As early as Genesis 21:33, in Psalm 10:16, in Isaiah 26:4, and on through the New Testament (see Rom. 16:26), God is acknowledged as eternal. The expression here is literally "King of the ages."⁶ This characteristic of God is true of the Son (Heb. 1:8–12), who is the same "yesterday and today and forever" (Heb. 13:8), the "First and the Last ... the Living One," who is "alive for ever and ever" (Rev. 1:17–18). God is immortal; he cannot die or see corruption in any form (Rom. 1:23). The difference between God's eternality and his immortality is that the first describes him as existing from untold ages past and into the limitless future, while the second describes his nature as incapable of ever experiencing corruption. God is also revered as the One who cannot be seen (1 Tim. 6:16).

All of the characteristics of God cited in this doxology accord with Old Testament descriptions. In a pagan world "gods" were worshiped in the form of visible, humanly created idols, but the true God is unseen. Indeed, he is "the only God" (see also 1 Tim. 6:15, "the blessed and only Ruler," and Rom. 16:27, "the only wise God"). Honor and glory belong to him alone.

Bridging Contexts

VERSES 3–11 HAVE vigorously established the importance of steadfastly maintaining the truth of the gospel, which in turn reaffirms the truth of the Old Testament law. False teachers at Ephesus have already both introduced error and dabbled in controversial speculations, and they need to be stopped. Paul has also declared his right to authorize Timothy to counter this encroachment on the church at Ephesus. But Paul is not just being militant. He is conscious of a divine commission. He has been given an assignment, a trust. Specifically he has been entrusted with the very gospel (v. 11) that transformed him from being its opponent to its exponent. He cannot go on further in setting out Timothy's duties without expressing his overwhelming gratitude for God's grace to himself.

Readers who are used to the linear writing of Paul in his earlier letters as he presented theological affirmations and their implications in two major blocks may be surprised at the frequent intrusions of personal comments in the Pastoral Letters. If the heresies at Ephesus are as serious as verses 1–11 seem to indicate, it seems strange that Paul interrupts his treatise to speak about his own past sins and present mission. When, however, these letters are seen as personal communications that were intended to show Timothy and Titus how to combine doctrinal rectitude with personal ministry and

---

6. For a discussion of the meaning of this terminology see Kittel in *TDNT*, 1:200–202. See also 1:469; 2:77.

character, the reason for this becomes clear. Paul's personal example is important to Timothy.

What is given to Timothy as a reminder is also, of course, to be passed on to the Ephesian church as a reintroduction of the one who had so powerfully preached the gospel there. Unlike other situations in which Paul felt compelled to affirm his calling (e.g., 2 Cor. 10:1–11:15; Gal. 1:11–2:10), his words here are not defensive or counteroffensive. They express gratitude and awe that God has saved him and entrusted him with the gospel. It may seem like a strange digression at this point, but it is both understandable from Paul's point of view and beneficial to us.

There is, however, another reason for the insertion of this paragraph. Verse 11 concludes with reference to "the glorious gospel of the blessed God, which he entrusted to me." It is the gospel itself that leads to Paul's testimony, and he wants to explain why he has been entrusted with it. The Greek word order in verse 11 at the end of the preceding section reinforces this connection. That verse ends with the emphatic word "I" (*ego*). We might paraphrase it: "The gospel . . . with which *I myself* was entrusted."

The idea of a trust[7] recurs in 6:20; 2 Timothy 1:12, 14; Titus 1:3; it is important in the Pastoral Letters as a consequence of vested authority. In 1 Corinthians 9:16 Paul writes, "Yet when I preach the gospel, I cannot boast, for I am compelled to preach. Woe to me if I do not preach the gospel!" The context of that chapter is Paul's assertion of his rights as an apostle and the surrender of advantages he may have gained from his apostleship. While he may choose not to accept the advantages, he cannot decline the responsibility.

CHRISTIAN CHARACTER AS a witness. Throughout the Pastoral Letters, as we will continue to observe, Paul emphasizes the character of the servant of God. That applies to him as the writer, to Timothy, the immediate recipient, and to the church leaders, and it extends to us. Although a preacher cannot constantly speak of himself, his salvation, and his responsibility to preach the gospel, neither should we omit the personal side of our experience with God. Just as the blend of sound teaching and personal integrity is important in these letters, so is the blend of proclamation and testimony in our ministry. We will revisit and further explore this theme frequently.

Personal experience speaks loudly today. While it is unfortunate that exposition is not as welcome as it used to be and while it should not be surrendered

---

7. Sometimes conveyed by a form of the verb *pisteuo*, sometimes by the noun *paratheke*.

on that account, it must be accompanied by testimony. Personally I have found it effective to weave the testimony of others into my sermons and, in fact, I wish I had done so more often. In addition to hearing outstanding testimonies of recent converts, congregations can benefit greatly from hearing the testimonies of the preacher's spouse, of elders and deacons and their families, of the ministers of worship and music, of the youth leaders, of Sunday school teachers, and of others.

One powerful effect of testimonies was experienced in a series of men's breakfasts in Lake County, Illinois, which a small group of us started several years ago. Modeled on a similar outreach in California, these are called "Straight Talk Breakfasts." The main speaker is usually a business or sports figure—once it was an astronaut—who gives his personal testimony and applies it in an evangelistic appeal. Prior to that talk, another person, often a man from the immediate locality, gives his testimony. These have attracted as many as nine hundred or more attendees, with many after each breakfast indicating on a "score card" that they have placed their faith in Christ. In this way thousands of men who would never have come to listen to a sermon are able to hear stories of business failure, moral failure, or marital failure with which they can identify, admissions of inner guilt and unfilled aspirations, and then testimonies of peace and reconciliation with the Lord through the death and resurrection of Christ.

So it is that Paul does not merely stand on his credentials but shows that he himself is a sinner saved by God's grace and has received this great trust humbly. The Lord Jesus once said that the person who has been forgiven much loves much (Luke 7:47). One way that Paul can assure the reader of God's love is to show how much he personally has been forgiven.

The blessings of God's grace are so extensive that we may tend to forget that we are saved not only for our own benefit but for the glory of God. This is made outstandingly clear in Ephesians 1:6, 12, 14; 2:6–10. Thus, Paul is conscious here in 1 Timothy 1:16 of the fact that he is to be a display of God's mercy.

A doxology. Appropriately Paul concludes with a doxology in 1:17. It is not trite to remind ourselves that our lives should be one continuous doxology, a life lived in praise of God.

1 Timothy 1:18–20

TIMOTHY, MY SON, I give you this instruction in keeping with the prophecies once made about you, so that by following them you may fight the good fight, ¹⁹holding on to faith and a good conscience. Some have rejected these and so have shipwrecked their faith. ²⁰Among them are Hymenaeus and Alexander, whom I have handed over to Satan to be taught not to blaspheme.

Original Meaning

THE INTERPLAY OF vocabulary between the opening and closing verses of this chapter is striking. Paul calls Timothy "my son" in verses 2 and 18. In verse 3 he tells Timothy what to command (*parangello*) the false teachers; in verse 18 Paul uses the noun form of the same verb (*parangelia*, translated "instruction"), but this time he commands Timothy himself. In verse 3 Paul mentions his prior urging of Timothy to stay at Ephesus; in verse 18 he mentions prior "prophecies" about Timothy. The apostle does not mean prophecies related to Ephesus; rather, he wants Timothy's ministry there to be consistent with the prophecies made about him as well as with Paul's urgings. These prophecies pertain somehow to the fight he will wage there, something not mentioned in the earlier section.

The next words, "faith and a good conscience" (v. 19), pick up, in reverse order, "a good conscience and a sincere faith" from verse 5 (see comments there). The structure of the phrases that follow (though not all the words in them) are also similar: "Some have wandered away from these" (v. 6) and "some have rejected these" (v. 19). Finally, verse 7 refers to some of the heretics without naming them, while verse 20 cites two heretics by name. There is, therefore, something of a long, complex *inclusio* in these two sections, marking out chapter 1 as a literary unit.

Knight observes that the word "give" in verse 18 (*paratithemai*) carries the idea of entrusting something to someone else, often with the idea of subsequent transmission to yet another person.[1] The instruction or command thus given is passed from Paul to Timothy and applied to the Ephesians. Timothy's

---

1. Knight, *Pastoral Epistles*, 107–8, referring to BAGD, 623; it can have this meaning when used in the middle voice (see also Luke 12:48; 2 Tim. 2:2).

authority in Ephesus is specifically delegated to him as one whom we call, with good reason, an apostolic delegate.

We do not know what "the prophecies" were, but 4:14 mentions a prophetic message as the agency of the gift Timothy received at the laying on of hands (see comments there). That "gift" is not identified, but the purpose of the "instruction" and "prophecies" in 1:18 are for the purpose of his fighting well, so the gift is probably not of a ministry as such but of the means to carry out that ministry. Since the ministry was to involve confrontation and conflict in the process of giving corrective teaching, the gift may have been, or included, the power, love, and self-discipline mentioned in 2 Timothy 1:7.

The word translated "these" in verse 19 (a relative pronoun in Greek), referring to what the heretics have rejected, is feminine gender singular and therefore in agreement with both *syneidesin* ("conscience") and *pistin* ("faith"), which precede it. The NIV understands this word as referring to both concepts and pluralizes it ("these"). The NRSV chooses the second word and uses the paraphrase "by rejecting conscience." It actually may, be extension, refer to the blend of a pure heart, good conscience, and sincere faith that produce the love that is the goal of the command (cf. 1:5). This would point up the contrast between the bad mixture of heresy and personal evil that characterizes the false teachers and the blend of sound doctrine and godly life that is to characterize Timothy.

Regardless of our understanding of the referent for the relative pronoun, it is by an attitude of rejection that "some . . . have shipwrecked their faith." Paul uses the definite article with "faith," which, as elsewhere in the Pastoral Letters, can refer to the body of faith, that is, essential Christian doctrine. If so, the heretics would not have shipwrecked it, but rather have suffered shipwreck *concerning* (*peri*) that faith. The verb used here means to suffer, not cause, shipwreck. Nevertheless, since faith was just mentioned in the verse with the probable meaning of one's own faith or trust, the definite article can have a possessive sense. The heretics then have suffered shipwreck with regard to their own personal faith.[2]

Hymenaeus reappears in 2 Timothy 2:17. Alexander may be the same person who tried to speak during the uproar when Paul was at Ephesus (Acts 19:33). Acts mentions him as though he were known to the readers, which would have been the case if he were known in the Ephesian church (see also 2 Tim. 4:14 and comments).[3]

---

2. BAGD, 644 (sub *peri* [1e]).

3. See also F. F. Bruce, *The Acts of the Apostles: Greek Text With Introduction and Commentary*, 3d rev. (Grand Rapids: Eerdmans, 1990), 419.

THIS CLOSING SECTION gives chapter 1 a tight integrity. The opening greetings are followed by the statement of the need for Timothy's presence in Ephesus, which specifies his main duty there. The problems he will face include the teaching of those with a defective view of the law. This leads to a discussion about the law that, in turn, segues, via a mention of the gospel, into Paul's testimony. It now remains for the initial statement of Timothy's assignment to Ephesus to be enlarged by a transformation into a charge, which is the function of this final section.

The reference to prophecy here is significant. Timothy had the benefit of both clear words of instruction from Paul and prophetic direction that he was to follow. This shows that the Pastoral Letters, in spite of the ecclesiastical structure evident, are not in conflict with the charismatic nature of the church's ministry as seen in the Corinthian letters (e.g., 1 Cor. 11:4–5, 7–11; 14:1–40). It also shows that Paul's own instruction to Timothy was consistent with the prophetic word. This presumably relieved Timothy of the type of inner struggle that earlier must have taken place in Paul when his friends begged him to change his plans because of the prophetic word of Agabus, which, while not commanding Paul to stop his journey to Jerusalem, gave him reason to reconsider his intentions (Acts 21:10–14).

Christian ministry is more than proclamation; it is combat. The names change, but people like Hymenaeus and Alexander have managed to infiltrate groups of professing Christians down through the ages. The very expressions "shipwrecked" and "handed over to Satan to be taught not to blaspheme" hammer home the seriousness of heresy. And in this paragraph about resisting heresy Paul picks up the words from earlier in the chapter, "faith and a good conscience." The repetition of expressions in his instructions to Timothy that combine sound religious faith and integrity of character is not only a major distinctive of the Pastoral Letters but the final legacy of Paul to all Christians who would succeed Timothy in the service of their Lord.

It is not clear what it means to hand someone over to Satan. It appears to be a much stronger action than the one prescribed in 2 Thessalonians 3:14–15, not to associate with someone "in order that he may feel ashamed." The language is close to that in 1 Corinthians 5:5, where an immoral man is to be "handed over [*paradidomi*, as here in 1 Timothy] to Satan." In 1 Timothy the purpose is correction; in 1 Corinthians it was to save the person's spirit by destroying the "flesh," which could, as in the NIV, mean destroying the sinful nature or, perhaps more likely, afflicting the incestuous man physically. The function of Satan may be as the prince of this world (John 12:31; 14:30; 16:11), in which the excommunicated member now lives, exposed to evil without the protection of church fellowship. These two men must learn not to blaspheme. Since they are already in the church, their blaspheming is more serious than Paul's (1 Tim. 1:13), who acted in ignorance.

TIMOTHY'S CALL. TIMOTHY had the certainty of God's direction for him through both the prophetic word he had received and Paul's specific instructions. Prior to his designation as Paul's delegate to Ephesus, he had the assurance of God's leading into "missionary" work from the very fact that Paul had chosen him (Acts 16:1–5).

Many Christians who are open to special ministries would like to know with certainty whether God is calling them. Several major issues call for investigation prior to anything near a conclusive discussion of this question. One main issue is whether God calls people in the New Testament period in the same manner and to the same extent as he called prophets in Old Testament times. If there is a specific "call" defined in the New Testament, we need to discern (1) what ministries require such a call, which is too large a question to discuss here, and (2) what the nature of a call is. Should there be an inner sense or feeling that one is called, and if so, how does one avoid subjectivism? Is a perceived need or specific spiritual gifting part of a call?

It should be observed that instances of what we might term as a *call to ministry* are infrequent in the New Testament. The following are notable: Jesus' call of his disciples (see esp. Mark 3:14–15; Luke 5:1–11 for details of their assignment), the Great Commission (Matt. 28:16–20), Peter's commission (John 21:15–19), the commission to the disciples in Acts 1:8 by the risen Lord, the conversion of Paul on the road to Damascus and his subsequent direction through Ananias in Damascus (9:1–19), the commissioning of Paul and Barnabas for their first missionary journey (13:1–3), and Paul's dream of a "man of Macedonia" (16:9–10). Apart from these, there is no example of a call as we usually think of it in the New Testament except for Timothy's experience.

What Timothy had was the communication of God's will to him *through other Christians.* Paul was one of these intermediaries (1) when he selected Timothy at Lystra in Acts 16, (2) when he sent him to Macedonia (1 Thess. 3:2–5), and (3) when he instructed him to stay in Ephesus (1 Tim. 1:3). Also we know that a prophetic word was given when hands were laid on Timothy by Paul and by the elders (see 1 Tim. 4:14; 2 Tim. 1:6). And if the prophecy referred to in 1 Timothy 1:18 was given on an occasion different from the laying on of hands, that would be yet another instance of other Christians' conveying God's direction to him. In all of this we may assume that believers at Ephesus joined in the commendation of Timothy.

Calling in the New Testament. These instances of calling in the New Testament can be grouped according to the means God used: (1) the audible voice of Jesus, (2) the unique conversion of Paul, (3) the dream about Macedonia, and (4) God's call through other Christians. Even Paul's own specific commission came not only from the voice in heaven but through another believer, Ananias (Acts 9:15–16).[4] This means that apart from the call to Macedonia, there is no instance of a call to ministry that was not either directly from Jesus prior to his ascension or through other believers. All of the above underscores the importance of the Christian community in whatever we might define as a "call" and requires great care if all that an individual has is some sense of inner direction without the confirmation of other Christians.

In Timothy's case he had solid grounds for knowing the ministry God wanted him to accomplish. While we have the inner leading of the Spirit in daily life (Rom. 8:14), we must not disregard the Christian community, the church, to give us direction and to confirm—or call into question—what we may believe is the ministry God is calling us to fulfill.[5]

There is a strong contrast between Timothy, who was drawn close to God and his people through hearing the "prophecies" and through Paul's instruction, and Hymenaeus and Alexander, who were handed over to Satan. One was accepted, the others were rejected. Whatever "handed over to Satan" may have involved, it certainly included separation from the church fellowship. A friend of mine once read an account about his great-grandfather, who was disciplined because he had "fallen horribly." Quaint as that may seem, it was probably much closer to the way Christians in the first century looked at sin and put someone out of fellowship than are our practices today. To be barred from the warm fellowship of the house church and exposed to the influence of the one who is the "prince" of that pagan, ungodly world must have seemed fearsome at that time.

Postmodernism and the need for discernment. The message of the last paragraph—and of 1 Timothy 1 as a whole—is that while truth is to be celebrated, error must be discerned and corrected. This is a difficult assignment for the contemporary Christian. The very nature of pluralism and postmodernism makes this unpopular. Postmodernism has been with us for some decades now, not only in philosophy, theology, and literature, but also in art,

---

4. Apparently it was through Ananias that Paul was told what he "must do" (Acts 9:6).

5. This whole matter of calling and confirmation by the church is also relevant to the passages on Timothy's receiving the laying on of hands; thus this discussion will be continued in the comments on 1 Tim. 4:14; 2 Tim. 1:6.

music, and architecture. Old norms and standards, the depiction of form and reality and structure of any sort, have long been out of fashion.[6]

Recently laypeople have become more aware of deconstruction as it has become more pronounced and as its effects on biblical study and theology have become more obvious.[7] A postmodernist will deconstruct traditional sacred writings and their teachings. Ascribing univocal meaning to, say, a piece of literature or art, with the assertion that this is what the author or artist "meant," is unacceptable in many quarters today. One may only approach art and literature from his or her own perspective; in postmodernism any construction of a "worldview" is considered illegitimate. Nothing has universal truth, value, or meaning.

While such developments as the waning of Newtonian physics are twentieth-century developments, the rejection of authority and absolutes is not confined to our contemporary society. From the words of the serpent, "Did God really say . . . ?" (Gen. 3:1), to the false prophets and foreign priests in the time of Elijah, to the false teachers Timothy confronted at Ephesus, the person who declares "God's truth" has been considered narrowminded and unacceptable. However, that person must make sure that "God's truth" is indeed just that and not some individual and idiosyncratic interpretation of the biblical text.

In grappling with such issues, we often find ourselves grappling with people as well. Within the church, the "combat" metaphor colors relationships as well as dialogues. We must remember that Paul's references to combat may be with respect to personal diligence (2 Tim. 4:7). But such terminology does not necessarily imply that personal antagonism against those who hold different doctrines is advisable. As the Pastoral Letters unfold, we will see the importance of patient, gentle wooing of false teach-

---

6. Some helpful works on postmoderism are David S. Dockery, ed., *The Challenge of Postmodernism: An Evangelical Engagement* (Wheaton: Victor, 1995); Jimmy Long, *Generating Hope: A Strategy for Reaching the Postmodern Generation* (Downers Grove, Ill.: InterVarsity, 1997); Dennis McCallum, ed., *The Death of Truth* (Minneapolis: Bethany, 1996).

7. The process of deconstruction disentangles or takes apart the language of a text, thereby separating it from any validation of objective truth, including philosophic and theological affirmations. Without going into this complex topic here, we can acknowledge that our human ideas do indeed intrude into the reading of a text and into our attempt to understand truth, and that our ideas are often subjective and to a greater or lesser degree fallible. The facts of human sinfulness and of the distortion and partiality of our perceptions do not, however, mean that God's truth cannot be comprehended at all. Acts 17:22–31; Rom. 1:18–20; 2 Tim. 3:14–17; and 1 Corinthians 1 are among the pertinent Scriptures. For a comprehensive treatment of these and relevant issues see Kevin J. Vanhoozer, *Is There a Meaning in This Text?* (Grand Rapids: Zondervan, 1998). On deconstruction see Grant R. Osborne, *The Hermeneutical Spiral* (Downers Grove, Ill.: InterVarsity, 1991), 380–86.

ers back to truth as well as of sharp rebuke of those whose rebellion is destroying the church.

The relevant texts are an integral part of these letters and cannot be merely lifted out of their contexts for citation or applied indiscriminately to a contemporary situation we may be facing. The Pastoral Letters need to be applied in the whole, not just in part. If we do not do this, we will be in danger of either tolerating what we should not or alienating those we seek to win.

1 Timothy 2:1–7

I URGE, THEN, first of all, that requests, prayers, intercession
and thanksgiving be made for everyone—[2]for kings and all
those in authority, that we may live peaceful and quiet
lives in all godliness and holiness. [3]This is good, and pleases
God our Savior, [4]who wants all men to be saved and to come
to a knowledge of the truth. [5]For there is one God and one
mediator between God and men, the man Christ Jesus, [6]who
gave himself as a ransom for all men—the testimony given in
its proper time. [7]And for this purpose I was appointed a herald
and an apostle—I am telling the truth, I am not lying—and a
teacher of the true faith to the Gentiles.

Original Meaning

FROM A DISCUSSION of Timothy's general ministry in Ephesus relative to the heretics, Paul moves to the topic of prayer. The purpose of this passage is to encourage prayer for an orderly society in which the gospel will be able to reach everyone.

Prayer for Rulers (2:1–4)

"THE KEYWORD OF this section . . . is universality."[1] The instruction is given "first of *all*" that prayer is to "be made for *everyone*—for . . . *all* those in authority," in order that we may live "in *all* godliness and holiness," which will please God, who "wants *all* . . . to be saved," since "Christ Jesus . . . gave himself as a ransom for *all*" (italics added).

The syntax is tight. Verse 1 begins with the inferential *oun*, "therefore," which connects this with what precedes (thereby making it unlikely that this is an extract from an early church manual). The question is often asked whether "therefore" relates to the immediately preceding section (1:18–20) or to something earlier. Since, as we noted in the previous section, the first chapter is an enclosed unit, with the opening verses restated in the closing, it is most likely that Paul is referring back to the entire section following the opening greetings. He has been establishing not only the need to oppose heresy, but stating his own commission and passion for the gospel.

1. Lock, *Pastoral Epistles*, 24.

In order for that gospel to gain the response it should, several things are necessary, as set forth in chapters 2 and 3: prayer for the kind of circumstances that will move the gospel forward (2:1–7), appropriate behavior during prayer and learning (2:8–15), the selection of overseers and deacons whose lives are consistent with the gospel (3:1–13), and corporate conduct appropriate to the "mystery of godliness" (3:14–16). Chapter 4 resumes the personal instructions to Timothy about maintaining doctrinal and personal purity in a church attacked by heresy.

This present section (2:1–7) begins with the words, "I urge," similar to 1:3 ("as I urged"). After his important statement of the reason for the letter in 1:4–20, Paul now continues his instructions to Timothy. He hovers between commanding and urging, with the two merging together just as do his apostleship and his fatherly relationship with Timothy. "First of all" indicates an order of precedence, which can also imply an order of importance.

Paul uses several words for prayer in verse 1, as he does elsewhere.[2] While such a listing can be redundant, it is more likely that Paul is expressing the breadth of prayer in its various aspects, each of which is relevant here. One might have expected that Paul would begin with the most general word, but instead he starts with *deeseis* ("requests"), perhaps because he is mainly concerned here with a focused request. He immediately follows with *proseuchas*, the more general word for prayers. Next he urges *enteuxeis* ("intercessions"; the NIV uses the singular as more idiomatic in a collective sense); this is the nature of the initial prayer here, offering petitions on behalf of the rulers. Finally he mentions *eucharistias* ("thanksgivings," again singular in the NIV), which he already indicated in Philippians 4:6 should accompany requests. The thanksgivings are for the rulers, for whom we not only pray but are thankful, a remarkable concept in the age of the Roman emperors. The plural form extends to the words for "kings," which would include even the likes of Nero, and for "those in authority," modified by the word "all," thereby including local authorities as well as imperial.

The tight syntactical construction proceeds with the word "that" (middle of v. 2), which introduces the intended result of the prayers. Paul's desire for a quiet life does not mean that he simply seeks personal tranquillity for Christians.[3] His goal and all-consuming passion is that the gospel might freely

---

2. A prime example is Phil. 4:6. On prayer in its various forms see W. Liefeld, "Prayer," *ISBE*, 4:938–39.

3. Nor is the teaching here to be understood as "good citizenship," as Dibelius and Conzelmann understand it (*Pastoral Epistles*, Excursus: "The Ideal of Good Christian Citizenship," 39–41). Towner critiques this interpretation convincingly in *The Goal of Our Instruction*.

penetrate society, which will be forwarded most effectively in a peaceful context. But it is not only so that the messengers of the gospel may be unhindered; it is that their "peaceful and quiet lives" will be carried out in the manner Paul repeatedly prescribes for Timothy: "in all godliness and holiness."

Ten of the fifteen times that "godliness" (*eusebeia*) occurs in the New Testament are in the Pastoral Letters. Its next occurrence is describing the "mystery" in 3:16, and then it appears in 4:7, 8; 6:3, 5, 6, 11; 2 Timothy 3:5; Titus 1:1. It was a term well known by Paul's non-Christian contemporaries (much as "religion" and "religious" are today). "Holiness" (or "dignity," *semnotes*) and its adjectival cognate, *semnos* ("worthy of respect"), occur in 1 Timothy 2:2; 3:4, 8, 11; Titus 2:2, 7. Together, these references emphasize the great importance of God's servants—which especially includes Timothy and elders and deacons—having a good reputation in the world. Later Paul writes Titus that the lives of Christians should affirm to onlookers the validity and attractiveness of the gospel (Titus 2:5, 8, 10; see comments).

In the present passage Paul emphasizes that Christians in general must be *fully* characterized by the twin virtues of godliness and holiness. The implication, amply supported throughout these Letters, is that as the world sees the Christian character of believers, not only will the gospel go forward in an orderly, peaceful society, but also it will be recognized as genuine.[4]

The verses that follow support this interpretation. The word "who" at the beginning of verse 4 carries the implied sense, as often, of "because."[5] God is pleased with these prayers for *everyone* (v. 1), because he is the God who wants *everyone* to be saved (v. 4). To this end, good government and quiet lives are also "good" and pleasing to God (v. 3). This passage is not dealing with questions of election or universalism, but it does bring such matters to mind. What God wants is that all people be saved. This is not the same as willing them into salvation regardless of whether they respond positively or not to Jesus, which would be contrary to the whole direction of Scripture on the need for personal response. It may be comprehensive rather than universal, meaning that God wants people to be saved whoever and wherever they are.[6]

"To be saved" and "to come to a knowledge of the truth" are not different but overlapping experiences. This terminology was familiar to Paul's Hel-

---

4. Fee recognizes this connection between the godly life and the attractiveness of the gospel to unbelievers. He points out the similarity of 1 Thess. 4:11–12, "Make it your ambition to lead a quiet life . . . so that your daily life may win the respect of outsiders" (Fee, *1 and 2 Timothy, Titus*, 63).

5. By way of example, we might say, "Michael, who likes good food, would especially appreciate this restaurant." The clause introduced by "who" does not merely identify Michael, but gives the reason why he would appreciate what the restaurant serves.

6. See Titus 2:11 and commentary for a possible parallel use of "all people."

lenistic contemporaries, but with different meanings. The gods were thought to save their adherents from different forces of evil. Salvation was also thought to be experienced through initiation into the mystery religions.[7] Knowledge of the truth could be merely cognitive, but in the developing Gnostic systems the terms came to have further nuances.[8] Here, however, it has more of a Hebraic sense. Salvation is the active work of God, who has compassion and strength to rescue. The truth is to be grasped, appropriated, and allowed to change our behavior. Given that sense, it is appropriate that the phrase "knowledge of the truth" occurs further in the Pastorals in 2 Timothy 2:25; 3:7; Titus 1:1.

Basis for This Prayer (2:5–7)

GOD'S CONCERN FOR people is comprehensive, and his being the "one God" (v. 5) is both exclusive and inclusive. It is *exclusive* in the sense that there is no other God, a truth that is not stressed here but is implicit and explicit throughout Scripture. He is the only God, with no competitors other than in the imagination of pagan idolaters. But *inclusively*, he wants to be accepted as the God and Savior of all people.[9]

This being the case, it is both logical and right that there is only one Mediator. Old and New Testaments show the need for mediation between the holy God and sinful people. Jesus Christ is prophet, priest, and king. Especially in his priestly role, being both divine and human, and offering himself as the sacrifice, he is the only true Mediator.[10] He gave himself as a "ransom," that is, he released us from bondage. In our contemporary circumstances we think of paying a ransom in money, but Jesus did not, as is sometimes thought, pay a ransom price to Satan. The ransom was that he gave himself up in death (Mark 10:45).[11] He did this "for" (*hyper*, i.e., "on behalf of") all people.

The preposition *hyper* can indicate also substitution ("instead of"). In his article on "Prepositions and Theology in the Greek New Testament,"[12] Murray Harris notes that *hyper*, unlike *anti*, could simultaneously express both representation and substitution. In our passage the idea of substitution is already suggested in the word "ransom" (*antilytron*). The preposition *hyper* is

---

7. See M. Slusser, "Salvation," *Encyclopedia of Early Christianity*, Everett Ferguson, ed. (New York: Garland, 1990), esp. 825.

8. See Carl F. H. Henry and R. K. Harrison, "Know, Knowledge," *ISBE*, 3:48–50.

9. On the topic of salvation and of God as Savior in the Pastoral Letters see Frances Young, *The Theology of the Pastoral Letters*, for bibliography.

10. See R. S. Wallace, "Mediation," *ISBE*, 3:299–305.

11. Leon Morris, *The Atonement: Its Meaning and Significance* (Leichester, England: Inter-Varity Press, 1983), 116–19.

12. See *NIDNTT*, 3:1196–97.

followed by the comprehensive word "all" (modifying the generic *anthropon*, "people"), which emphasizes once again the widespread extent of God's saving work, accomplished through Christ.

The next phrase has perplexed exegetes. It literally translates, "the witness [or testimony] in [or at] the proper [or right] time." The following are among the possible interpretations of this phrase: (1) Since it is not connected to the preceding by a conjunction, it can be viewed as an appositional phrase to "who gave himself as a ransom for all." In this case Jesus' death as a ransom is a testimony to God's saving work on behalf of all people, and it took place at just the right time. (2) But Paul may instead be referring indirectly to his own preaching as a testimony now being given.[13] Whatever the case, Paul refers once more to his own commission as a "herald" as well as an "apostle" (v. 7), and he affirms this solemnly.

PRAYERS FOR RULERS. If Paul's testimony in 1:12–17 seems to enter on the scene unexpectedly, so does his request for prayer in 2:1–7, concluding with another affirmation of his calling. Although the Greek word for "therefore" (v. 1) can be used as a transitional word without logical emphasis, there does seem to be a deliberate connection here with the preceding paragraphs. This is not the sort of prayer request that Paul usually makes. Think, for example, of his request following the passage about the Christian's armor in Ephesians 6, where the apostle asks for prayer for himself and for his own boldness in proclaiming the message. Throughout the New Testament are various appeals for prayer having to do with the gospel, healing, boldness in preaching, and so on. The request in this passage is, uniquely, for people in authority. While it is not only for kings, the use of that word gives focus to the request. We are not merely to pray for the gospel or for God's power on behalf of the preacher and witness, but for the very officials whose decisions can affect the environment in which the gospel is to operate.

The breadth of the activity (prayers, intercession, and thanksgiving) and the number of those for whom it is to be made ("everyone—for kings and all those in authority") shows that this is serious business. This world and its governments are the arena of God's activity. While it is true that the gospel flourishes under tyranny, as seen in many places under the Communists, that is by no means the ideal to be sought after. But neither is the immediate goal simply to "live peaceful and quiet lives." Beyond that it is to live "in all god-

---

13. For other possibilities and citations, see Lock, *Pastoral Epistles*, 28, Dibelius and Conzelmann, *Pastoral Epistles*, 41–42, Knight, *Pastoral Epistles*, 123.

liness and holiness." And even beyond this, by implication the goal is for people to be saved (v. 4).

Christian witness and pluralism. Paul comes around again to his own goal in life, his calling, to be a "herald and an apostle" (v. 7). He is sweeping in the way he expresses himself in this paragraph. His excitement and sense of responsibility are transparent. We are not only to *pray* for "everyone" (lit., "all people"), but should realize that God wants all people *to be saved*. To this end the plurality of rulers to be prayed for and the plurality of people whom God wants to be saved and to come to the knowledge of the truth stand in contrast with the fact that there is just "one God and one mediator between God and men." In our pluralistic age we may tend to say "there are many ways to God," but it would be more proper to say "there are many ways to Christ but only one way to God, and that is through Christ."

When arguing over whether it is right that there is only one way to God, it is sometimes forgotten that it is God himself who has provided that way so that all people might indeed by saved. Pluralism is not to be confused with universalism, though the two usually come to the same conclusion. Universalism is the assertion that everyone will be saved regardless of their response to the gospel. Pluralism is the assertion that no one religion is right but that all have value. Today pluraism often takes an aggressive stance, in that the only belief that pluralists consider to be invalid is the belief that one's religion alone is correct. Therefore—ironically and irrationally—the pluralistic ideal falters in that it refuses to recognize the validity of such a position. The challenge of pluralism is perhaps best met not by merely repeating exclusivistic claims, but by emphasizing a true kind of inclusivism in the comprehensive biblical sense. That is, the gospel is for all people in all cultures. The key to the application of this passage in all cultural contexts is its comprehensiveness.[14]

Those who take the purpose of the Pastoral Letters largely to be providing instructions for church order need to inquire as to why this section does

---

14. Much has been written recently on pluralism. I especially recommend D. A. Carson, *The Gagging of God: Christianity Confronts Pluralism* (Grand Rapids: Zondervan, 1996); D. L. Okholm and T. R. Phillips, *More Than One Way? Four Views on Salvation in a Pluralistic World* (Grand Rapids: Zondervan, 1995). On Christianity and other world religions see also Carl E. Braaten, *No Other Gospel! Christianity Among the World's Religions* (Minneapolis: Fortress, 1992); Daniel B. Clendenin, *Many Gods, Many Lords: Christianity Encounters World Religions* (Grand Rapids: Baker, 1995); Ajith Fernando, *The Supremacy of Christ* (Wheaton: Crossway, 1995); Lesslie Newbigin, *The Gospel in a Pluralist Society* (Grand Rapids: Eerdmans, 1989); Edward Rommen and Harold Netland, eds., *Christianity and the Religions* (Pasadena: William Carey Library, 1995); Kevin J. Vanhoozer, ed., *The Trinity in a Pluralistic Age* (Grand Rapids: Eerdmans, 1997). For discussions that include the perspectives of other religions, see Kenneth Cragg, *The Christ and the Faiths* (Philadelphia: Westminster, 1986); Hans Küng, Josef van Ess, Heinrich von Stietencron, and Heinz Bechert, *Christianity and World Religions* (Maryknoll, N.Y.: Orbis, 1986).

not deal with broader aspects of prayer in the service of worship.[15] Instead, the instructions here are narrowly focused to accomplish the goals mentioned above. We can extrapolate the following guidelines. Prayer is a normal and, one may conclude, a major part of the church's spiritual ministry. It should be purposeful, not haphazard. The good of the church and the community (probably extensible to the nation) is to be kept in mind, with the broad acceptance of the gospel a larger goal.

OUR MESSAGE TO those without Christ. One of the most perplexing questions that theologians and others have addressed over the centuries is the fate of those who do not believe in Christ or who have never even heard of Christ. While such a complex question cannot be satisfactorily addressed in this brief discussion, it is good to have questions like these in mind when we come across passages that may contribute to their answer.

Perhaps the key word here is the Greek *thelo* (translated "wants" in NIV and NLT in v. 4; NRSV has "desires"). Its range of meaning reaches from the desire for something to be done to willing something to be done. A similar verb, though not an exact synonym, *boulomai*, appears in 2 Peter 3:9: "The Lord is not slow in keeping his promise, as some understand slowness. He is patient with you, not *wanting* anyone to perish, but everyone to come to repentance" (emphasis added). All three of the translations just cited translate *boulomai* as "want" here. Both *thelo* and *boulomai* can refer to a desire to do something or, in a stronger sense, a definite purpose or plan to do something.[16] At the very least these two passages show that God takes no pleasure in people dying without salvation. Neither one of them, however, teaches that God will save people irrespective of their own stance toward Christ.

When preaching the gospel it is difficult today to keep from alienating people who have a contemporary aversion to any exclusive religious claims. As far as truth is concerned, we are convinced that Christ is the only way. But *how* we declare this in today's world can move people toward or away from our gospel. Without weakness or compromise we must declare the narrow way, but in doing so we must stress that there *is* a way, a wonderful way. It is important that we show the love of God in *providing* that way (John

---

15. Scott, *Pastoral Epistles*, 19.

16. In the former sense see Matt. 20:21; Acts 17:20; 19:30; Phil. 1:12; in the stronger sense see Matt. 1:19; Acts 5:28; 7:39; Col. 1:27. But even in such citations there can be an overlap of meanings.

3:16) and the grace of Christ in becoming that way through his sacrifice on the cross.

There *is* a ransom. Our message is not gloom or doom but the open way made by the Mediator, the man Christ Jesus. The way in which we say there is only one mediator can communicate either a negative connotation—every other religion is wrong and we are proudly and dogmatically right—or a positive connotation—God wants all to be saved, and we humbly and happily proclaim that way and the means for everyone who comes to him.

As for anyone who has not learned enough about God, sin, and salvation to make a meaningful decision, I believe we can agree with Abraham's rhetorical question, "Will not the Judge of all the earth do right?" (Gen. 18:25). No matter how much God—or we—desire to see any individual saved, there is only one way that God accomplishes that. It is a wonderful way, through Christ, "who gave himself as a ransom for all [people]."[17]

Our mission and attitudes. Paul offers a statement of clear purpose for his life in verse 7: "and for this purpose I was appointed a herald and an apostle." The Greek expression translated "for this purpose" is *eis ho*, "toward which." This is one case where we can take for ourselves at least one part of the apostolic mission of Paul, which was to proclaim the gospel and to be "a teacher of the true faith." Whatever one's opinion as to how God will deal with those who have never heard the gospel, it is incumbent on us to see that everybody possible within our range of human relationships does come to know the gospel of Christ.

Paul's exhortation to pray for "those in authority" stands opposed to the tendency of some Christians to criticize or ridicule them. The pastor of one megachurch in the Chicago area rightly admonished the congregation when they hissed at a mention of President Clinton. This paragraph in 1 Timothy should cause all of us to review our attitudes to leaders. Although a weekly sentence in the pastoral prayer about those in authority can be mere rote, it is better than no prayer at all. To pray for a leader, as is done in some liturgical churches, using the words "your servant" and his or her first name, reminds us of the humanity of that leader, who needs God's direction.

---

17. On the issue of the destiny of those who reject Christ and the question of those who have never heard the gospel, see William V. Crockett and James G. Sigountos, eds., *Through No Fault of Their Own? The Fate of Those Who Have Never Heard* (Grand Rapids: Baker, 1991); Millard J. Erickson, *How Shall They Be Saved? The Destiny of Those Who Do Not Hear of Jesus* (Grand Rapids: Baker, 1996); Gabriel Fackre, Ronald H. Nash, and John Sanders, *What About Those Who Have Never Heard?* (Downers Grove, Ill.: InterVarsity, 1995); Ronald H. Nash, *Is Jesus the Only Savior?* (Grand Rapids: Zondervan, 1994); Clark H. Pinnock, *A Wideness in God's Mercy: The Finality of Jesus Christ in a World of Religions* (Grand Rapids: Zondervan, 1992); Clark H. Pinnock and Robert C. Brow, *Unbounded Love* (Downers Grove, Ill.: InterVarsity, 1994). See also footnote 14, above.

1 Timothy 2:8–15

I WANT MEN everywhere to lift up holy hands in prayer, without anger or disputing.
⁹I also want women to dress modestly, with decency and
propriety, not with braided hair or gold or pearls or expensive
clothes, ¹⁰but with good deeds, appropriate for women who
profess to worship God.
¹¹A woman should learn in quietness and full submission.
¹²I do not permit a woman to teach or to have authority over
a man; she must be silent. ¹³For Adam was formed first, then
Eve. ¹⁴And Adam was not the one deceived; it was the woman
who was deceived and became a sinner.
¹⁵But women will be saved through childbearing—if they
continue in faith, love and holiness with propriety.

Original Meaning

PAUL HAS already given instructions concerning the *content* of prayer. What follows here
relates to the *manner* of praying. Content has to
do with theology; manner has to do with attitude and appearance.

Attitude and Behavior of Men in the Christian Church (2:8)

THE USE OF *oun* ("therefore") in this verse, while it may be simply an idiomatic
nonessential indication of transition (omitted by NIV), does suggest that content affects attitude. Those who have been instructed to pray for people in
authority for the sake of peaceful and quiet lives should themselves pray
without argumentation. "I want" can indicate a strong preference, though
not as strong as "I urge" (2:1) or "I do not permit" (v. 12) and certainly not
equal to "[God] wants" (v. 4). Although it is not a command, the word used
here (*boulomai*) can express what the individual strongly wants, expects, or
even intends to happen.

The word translated "men" (pl. of *aner*) usually means males, though there
are examples in classical Greek rhetoric of its use to include women. Here,
however, it clearly stands in contrast with "women" in verse 9. This policy is
in accordance with public prayer in the Jewish synagogue, though women

did pray in gatherings of Christians (1 Cor. 11:5).[1] "Everywhere" is reminiscent of "as in all the congregations of the saints" in 1 Corinthians 14:33, where the subject is the role of women in public meetings. This fact should caution us against any assumption that Paul's instructions in our passage apply only to the church at Ephesus.[2] To lift up "holy hands" does not put emphasis on the hands themselves (as washed and ritually pure). Such would go against Jesus' teachings (Matt. 15:1–2, 10–11). Rather, it is assumed that men will pray in the customary Jewish manner, with hands uplifted; thus, these hands should belong to men whose lives are consistent with God's holiness.

The Bible teaches that there are controllable factors affecting the efficacy of our prayer. These are mainly relational—both our relationship with God (hidden sin, "planned" sin, lack of trust) and our relationship with other people ("forgive us our debts, as we also have forgiven our debtors," a condition that Jesus singles out for further comment after the Lord's Prayer in Matt. 6:12, 14–15).[3] In 1 Timothy 2:8 "anger" and "disputing" are inconsistent with the life of holiness that God requires of those who pray publicly, but they are also counter to effective praying.

Attitude and Behavior of Women in the Christian Church (2:9–10)

THESE VERSES HAVE been differently interpreted depending on how one evaluates the significance of syntax and word order. The main issues are the omission of "to pray" in verse 9 and the syntactical role of "to dress," which seems to replace prayer in the previous clause.

In the following structure the syntactical elements are listed in the order in which they occur in the order of the Greek text.

SYNTACTICAL ELEMENT	VERSE 8	VERSE 9
Main verb	I want	[understood]
Infinitive object of main verb	**to pray**	
Accusative of reference ("subject" of the infinitive)	the men	women

---

1. For early paintings depicting women at prayer, see the illustrations on pp. 57 and 93 and the comments on p. 92 in Ruth A. Tucker and Walter L. Liefeld, *Daughters of the Church: Women and Ministry From New Testament Times to the Present* (Grand Rapids: Zondervan, 1987).

2. Lit., "everywhere" translates "in every place [*topos*]." For a discussion of *topos* in 1 Timothy 2:8 see E. Ferguson, "τόπος in 1 Timothy 2:8," *RestQ* 33 (1991): 65–73.

3. See Walter L. Liefeld, "Lord's Prayer," *ISBE*, 4:162.

SYNTACTICAL ELEMENT	VERSE 8	VERSE 9
Adverbial modifiers		
place	in every place	
manner	lifting holy hands,	in tasteful attire
	without anger or disputing	with decency and propriety
Infinitive object of the unexpressed main verb, "I want"		**to dress**
Further adverbial modifiers		not with braided hair ... but with good deeds

The question we face is whether Paul (1) intends to imply that the women do *not* pray (publicly) and that *instead of* praying their ministry is to dress modestly, or (2) expects the reader to infer that women *do* also pray (perhaps implied by *hosautos*, "also" in NIV; lit., "likewise"), and that *while* praying they are to be modestly dressed. The reason Paul puts the first expressed verb in the second clause (*kosmein*, "to dress") into the infinitive form is for grammatical correctness (since he omits the verb "to pray," which would have been in the infinitive). It corresponds in the sequence of thought, but not in syntax, to the participle *epairontas* ("to lift up [holy hands]") in verse 8. If Paul had intended to state clearly that the counterpart to men's prayer was women's modest dress, we must ask why he did not put the verb "to dress" up front in the unoccupied position in verse 9 that corresponds to the infinitive "to pray" in verse 8.

It will be helpful to recall that there are basically two types of information communicated in a Greek sentence. One is what might be called "message" or "content" information; the other is "structure" information. The first is that which we learn from word meanings (i.e., lexical or semantic meaning). This includes the meaning of nouns, verbs, adjectives, adverbs, prepositions, conjunctions, prefixes, suffixes, and so on. Structure information is what we learn from the relative placement of words, the case endings of nouns, the relationship between verb and indirect object, and so forth. Structure usually depends on syntax, but structural meaning is also found in word order (which may be independent of syntax).[4] Both types of information combine in a clause or sentence to produce a semantic whole.

---

4. An example of striking word order is the placement of *akolutos* as the climactic last word in Acts (though he was imprisoned, Paul "taught about the Lord Jesus boldly and *without hindrance*" [lit. trans.]).

To analyze 2:9 in terms of *message* information, we note the absence of any verb meaning "to pray." Further, in terms of *structure* information two facts are worth noting. (1) According to the *syntax*, "to dress" is the only expressed infinitive object of the understood verb "I want." (2) According to the *word order* it can be understood that Paul *assumes* women's prayer (suggested by the "likewise") and proceeds to describe how women should dress when they are praying. He then goes beyond the circumstance of prayer to comment on the function of good works as an appropriate substitute for expensive clothing. The interpreter must choose (1) or (2); either is possible.

A major reason, external to this passage, for doubting that Paul is exclud-ing women from praying in church meetings is that his instructions in 1 Corinthians 11:2–16 on women's head-covering is based on the fact that women did pray and prophesy (v. 5). Any doubt that Paul had the regular church meeting in mind is erased by the fact that this passage and the fol-lowing one (11:17–34) on the Lord's Supper "when you come together as a church" (v. 18) are not only placed together but are linked structurally by the similar phrases "I praise you" (v. 2) and "I have no praise for you" (v. 17). The Eucharist was mentioned in the preceding chapter (10:14–22), so the church service was already in mind when Paul wrote chapter 11.

It is possible, of course, that Paul had a different kind of prayer in mind here in 1 Timothy from that in 1 Corinthians, but that is hard to imagine since there is nothing in the circumstances to indicate such a difference. In both 1 Corinthians and 1 Timothy there is a concern for appearance (head-covering in one, modest dress in the other), suggesting that both meetings are public. Whatever the case may be as to women praying, it is clear that the main goal of the instruction in 1 Timothy 2:8–10 is not to command the *act* of prayer (the specific command to pray having already been given in vv. 1–2) but the *demeanor* of both men and women *while* praying and wor-shiping (see below on v. 10).

It is clear by now in this sequence of thought that Paul is dealing with expressions of morality in connection with the religious practices of men and women. He insists that their outward appearance should not be in con-flict with their inner character. In verses 9–10 the example is that women's inner piety should be expressed in good deeds. In ancient Greece, and to some extent still in Paul's day, lavish dress, hair style, and jewelry were con-sidered inconsistent with moral uprightness and true piety. Thus, Christian women were to dress "modestly."

The description of the clothing, hairstyle, and jewelry suggests two rea-sons why they were improper. (1) One is inordinate expense. The mention of gold speaks for itself, and the adjective used to describe the inappropri-ate clothing is "expensive." (2) The other is traditional association with immoral behavior.[5] "With decency" is not the antithesis of extravagance, but has to do with ancient concepts of shame and honor. The noun used here (*aidos*) can mean reverence, self-respect, or shame. One could have a sense of shame not because of doing something immoral but as a commendable modest attitude. The word "propriety" (perhaps better translated "modesty") accords with this as another factor in Christian women's being moderate in their appearance. In sum, they are to avoid what exudes wealth and what suggests immorality.

Such external appearance may seem inconsequential to us, but it was not so in the ancient world. While it was not a doctrinal matter from a Christian standpoint, what one wore did communicate something to morally sensitive Jews and pagans. Note how the antithesis to wearing ostentatious and expensive clothing and jewelry is not only modesty but also "good deeds" (v. 10). In this context, good deeds are important not only for the help they bring to individuals, but especially for what they demonstrate about Christianity.

Paul emphasizes good deeds in the Pastoral Letters.[6] While some deeds are to be done modestly in private (cf. Jesus' words in Matt. 6:16–18), Jesus did teach that our light should shine before others so that they "may see your good deeds and praise your Father in heaven" (5:16). Several references to good deeds in the Pastoral Letters specifically mention public awareness of them. A widow, for example, must be "well known for her good deeds" in order to be put on the list for support (1 Tim. 5:10). Good deeds are "obvious" and "cannot be hidden" (1 Tim. 5:25). Titus 2:7 says that young men should show themselves as a "model of good works" (NRSV) so that opponents will be ashamed since they will then have nothing bad to say about Christians.

It is debatable whether the "worship" in which women participated (v. 10) was limited to acts of worship in the church, which, as we have just suggested, could include public prayer. The implication of the NIV translation, "women who profess to worship God," can be taken to be that while these women professed the *object* of their worship to be God, it is indeed the *act* of worshiping that is in view, presumably in the church service. This implication does not, of course, exclude worship in daily life. The word for "worship" here is *theosebeia*, which refers to piety in general, not necessarily to acts of worship. It can connote church worship, however, as the word does in Epistle to Diognetus 4:5. There it refers to the practice of religion that in Christianity does not require the use of visible accouterments, as it does in pagan worship.

---

5. Cynthia L. Thompson, "'Cosmetics': The Social Power of Clichés." This is a paper delivered at the AAR/SBL annual meeting, as far as I know never published.

6. See 1 Tim. 3:1; 5:10(2x), 25; 6:18; 2 Tim. 2:21; 3:17; Titus 1:16; 2:7, 14; 3:1, 8, 14.

Special Instructions About Women Learning (2:11–15)

THE NEXT SECTION continues this same theme. Verse 11 begins, in the Greek text, with the words, "woman in quietness."[7] The same word for quietness also concludes verse 12, forming what is called an *inclusio,* an identical or similar word or phrase to mark the beginning and ending of a section of literature. This device shows how important Paul considered the attitude of quietness in learning to be for women.

What stands in contrast to this quietness is teaching and exercising authority over a man (v. 12). The contrasting expressions are separated in the middle of verse 12 by the strong adversative *alla* ("but, however," not trans. in NIV). While the structure does not require it, the attitude of quietness in verses 11–12 can be understood as ruling out teaching and the attitude of submission as ruling out exercising authority. This would not have been surprising to either Jews or Greeks, since neither culture permitted women to teach.[8] While in some parts of the Roman empire a more permissive attitude existed, in general the prevailing attitudes toward women would have been favorable to Paul's approach. This fact will require attention in the application of the text to our day. An additional factor in the interpretation of the quietness and submission of women in learning is that this attitude was also expected of male students studying under a rabbi, who, *after* ordination, *would* be both teaching and exercising authority.

There is a considerable body of literature on the meaning of verse 12.[9] Among the issues that have entered the discussion are: the meaning of "I do not permit," the meaning of the words "teach" and "have authority," the

---

7. Some translate the Greek word *hesychia* with the word "silence," but the corresponding adjective, *hesuchion,* just above in verse 2, clearly means "quiet" (in the phrase "quiet lives"). In verse 11, since it could mean either silence or quietness, the meaning that is consistent with its usage earlier in the chapter should at least be given preference. This is especially so, given the integrity of this chapter around the topic of Christian demeanor.

8. Sigountos and Shank, "Public Roles for Women in the Pauline Church," *JETS* 26 (1983): 289–92.

9. Representative recent works include Douglas J. Moo, "What Does It Mean Not to Teach or Have Authority Over Men?" in *Recovering Biblical Manhood and Womanhood,* John Piper and Wayne Grudem, eds. (Wheaton: Crossway, 1991), 179–93; Richard Clark Kroeger and Catherine Clark Kroeger, *I Suffer Not a Woman: Rethinking 1 Timothy 2:11–15 in Light of Ancient Evidence* (Grand Rapids: Baker, 1992); Craig S. Keener, *Paul, Women and Wives* (Peabody, Mass.: Hendrickson, 1992), 101–32; Andrew C. Perriman, "What Eve Did, What Women Shouldn't Do: The Meaning of αὐθεντέω in 1 Timothy 2:12," *TynBul* 44 (1993): 129–42; Andreas J. Köstenberger, Thomas R. Schreiner, and H. Scott Baldwin, eds., *Women in the Church: A Fresh Analysis of 1 Timothy 2:9–15* (Grand Rapids: Baker, 1995), and Rebecca Merrill Groothuis, *Good News for Women* (Grand Rapids: Baker, 1997), 209–29.

---

reason for the references to Adam and Eve, and the bearing, if any, of verse 15 on verse 12.

(1) Proper understanding of Paul's introductory words, "I do not permit," requires three separate decisions. (a) Is this a prohibition? In English "I do not permit" does not sound as strong as "I forbid." However, permission and non-permission were strong expressions with which Jewish readers especially would have been familiar.

(b) Does the use of the present tense mean Paul was intending only a temporary prohibition? Can it be paraphrased "I am not now permitting," with the implication that he may permit it in the future but does not at the present time for some temporary reason? That may be the case, though it seems more likely a normal narrative use of the present indicative expressing a simple fact. The point is not the tense but the mood.

(c) Therefore, why does Paul use this indicative form rather than making it a command by using an imperative? There can be little doubt that the reason he is telling Timothy what he does not permit is so that Timothy will follow the same practice. But read from the viewpoint of later generations, how significant is it that Paul does not issue a command such as, "Do not permit women to teach" or "Women must not teach or have authority?" Theologically it may be significant to observe that the Holy Spirit could have led Paul to use an imperative construction that might be interpreted as binding the church to follow that practice for all time, but instead led Paul to use a construction that describes his practice without making it permanently binding.[10]

(2) As to the meaning of "teach," given the use of the word and its cognates in the Pastoral Letters, it probably refers to the authoritative communication of "the faith," that is, the apostolic doctrine, with the witness to Jesus and his teachings at its core.[11] As noted above, women teachers were not acceptable in either Greek or Jewish societies. Also, women did not count as witnesses (reflected in the fact that Paul did not mention the women at the tomb in his list of witnesses in 1 Cor. 15:3–8). It would have been counterproductive to allow women to teach and proclaim the apostolic witness to Christ.

To "have authority" is not as clear in its meaning. The Greek verb *authenteo* and its related forms are rare in Greek literature, and the word only appears here in the New Testament. Its use changed over the centuries, including both dreadful, obnoxious ways of imposing one's will on others and more moderate

---

10. Even an imperative can be understood as operational only in relevant circumstances, as with the familiar "greet one another with a holy kiss." That action, like teaching, had cultural significance.

11. See especially *didasko* in 1 Tim. 4:11; 6:2; 2 Tim. 2:2; *didache* in 2 Tim. 4:2, and *didaskalia* in 1 Tim. 1:10; 4:6, 13, 16; 5:17; 6:1, 3; 2 Tim. 3:10, 16; 4:3; Titus 1:9; 2:1, 7, 10.

expressions of taking and wielding authority. The exegete's task is to discern what people in Paul's day and circumstances would have understood by it. The matter is complicated by the fact that words do not suddenly and irreversibly change their meaning, but do so gradually and sometimes with reversion to earlier implications. It is significant that in the give and take of research, the most recent substantial study (and a study, it should be noted, by a proponent of the view that restricts women) offers "to control, dominate, compel, influence, assume authority over, or flout the authority of" as possible meanings, with the context needed for final decision.[12]

It may be concluded from the grammatical relationship between the two words *didaskein* ("to teach") and *authentein* ("to have authority"), joined by *oude* ("nor"; "or" in NIV), that since *didaskein* is viewed as a positive activity in the Pastoral Letters, so also is *authentein*.[13] Understanding *authentein* in a *positive* sense, however, does not rule out its having a *strong* sense. What is sometimes overlooked in discussions on the meaning of *authenteo* is that Paul chose this rare verb over *exousiazo*, which is a member of the common word group relating to authority.[14] The exegete of 1 Timothy 2:12 must ask why, if Paul was writing about authority in the usual sense, he chose a most unusual word that had a history of very strong meanings.

Given all the above, it may be doubted that the assumption of authority Paul forbids is the same as a shared participation in the corporate decisions of a body of elders chosen by the congregation. Finally, it should be noted that the clause in verse 12 specifically limits its prohibition of a teaching and having authority to exercising these over a man (or, as some suggest, over a woman's own husband) and does not rule out, even in those circumstances, any other ministry for women.

(3) As for the allusions to Adam and Eve (vv. 13–14), Paul appeals to the order of God's creation of man and woman: "Adam was formed first." This phrase recalls 1 Corinthians 11:8, "For man did not come from woman, but woman from man." Paul goes on in 1 Timothy 2:14 to appeal to the deception of Eve, a verse that recalls 2 Corinthians 11:3: "I am afraid that just as

---

12. H. Scott Baldwin, *Women in the Church: A Fresh Analysis of 1 Timothy 2:9–15*, in A. J. Köstenberger, T. R. Schreiner, and H. S. Baldwin, eds. (Grand Rapids: Baker, 1995), 65–80. Kroeger and Kroeger's *I Suffer Not a Woman* has been heavily criticized, and with some justification (see R. W. Yarbrough, "*I Suffer Not a Woman*: A Review Essay," *Presbyterion* 18 [1992]: 25–33. Nevertheless, it provides data in support of a strong sense of *authenteo* that need (with caveats about possible anachronisms and confusion of different universes of discourses) to be given consideration.

13. Köstenberger in Köstenberger, Schreiner, and Baldwin, eds., *Women in the Church*, 103.

14. Interestingly, and significantly for biblical gender studies, the verb *exousiazo* does occur in 1 Cor. 7:4, where Paul says that sexually a husband and wife have reciprocal authority over one another's bodies.

Eve was deceived by the serpent's cunning, your minds may somehow be led astray from your sincere and pure devotion to Christ." This cautions the exegete to recognize that the application of these Old Testament allusions is broader than just the passage before us. The one in 1 Corinthians uses the priority of Adam's existence to support women's wearing of head-coverings; the one in 2 Corinthians shows that all Christians (including men) can be deceived just as Eve was.

This fact, plus Paul's note in our passage that Eve "became a sinner" (lit., "came to be in transgression") shows that his point is not just that women are more easily deceived than men, as has sometimes been asserted. The main verbal affirmation is "became a sinner," with "having been deceived" expressed by a circumstantial participle showing concurrent action. For centuries both before and after Christ, Eve was derided as the sinner who plunged the human race into misery. In this passage a parallelism puts the focus on Adam with regard to his creation and the fact that he was not the one deceived.

> Adam was formed first,
>> then Eve.
> [And] Adam was not deceived,
>> but the woman
>>> having been deceived
>> became a sinner.

The implications of this passage will be discussed more fully in the Bridging Contexts section, but two further observations should be made here. (a) The word "for" (*gar*) that introduces verses 13–14 can indicate either the grounds for the foregoing statement or provide an explanation for it. That is, the circumstances cited from Genesis can either *require* the restriction of women or *explain* it, in this case by an analogy. Some consider that to be a significant difference. On the latter reading, Paul does not maintain that Eve's sin necessarily leads to the restrictions he makes, but rather that he makes these because her deception has led others to think that any woman is open to deception and therefore untrustworthy as a teacher or leader.

(b) A further observation is that it has become common for those who restrict women to interpret the Fall as a result of the insubordination of woman to man. This not only requires interpreting the elements of the creation narrative as portraying woman as subordinate *before* the Fall, but also reads something into the account of the Fall that is not there. It also produces an inner contradiction, for being insubordinate is not the same as being deceived. The biblical reference in both Genesis and 1 Timothy is to Eve's deception, not to insubordination.

(4) Verse 15 has been the object of much study and hypothesizing. Among the points to be noted are: (a) The subject of the main clause is singular, "she," indicated by the verb ending (no subject is named). It is usually, but not always, assumed that it refers to any woman who fulfills the conditions in the verse. The main verb is "will be saved" (future passive) and assumes the fulfillment of the condition that begins "if they continue" (see [c] below).

(b) The meaning of "saved" is debated. The word can mean to be rescued from some danger or disease. It is translated "healed" several times in the Gospels, mainly in connection with one incident (Matt. 9:21, 22[2x], and parallels, but see also Mark 6:56; 10:52; Acts 4:9; 14:9). Normally in Paul's writings being saved refers to salvation from sin and judgment (though that is at issue in Phil. 2:12, "continue to work out your salvation with fear and trembling"). At times some human being has opened the way for a person to be saved (1 Cor. 7:16; 1 Tim. 4:6). Nevertheless, it is conceivable that it has some other, or extended, meaning here.

(c) On the face of it, the woman's being saved seems to be on the basis of works since it is dependent on her fulfilling the condition of "continu[ing] in faith, love and holiness with propriety."

(d) One other factor is that there is a prepositional phrase modifying "saved," and that is *dia tes teknogonias* ("through childbearing," or, lit., "through the childbirth"). The phrase can mean (i) saved "through the [ordeal of] childbearing" (in which case "salvation" reverts to its broader meaning of preservation or rescue); (ii) saved "through the [means of] childbearing" (in which case it appears to clash with the doctrine of salvation by grace alone); or (iii) saved "through [*both* through the ordeal of and by means of] bearing children."[15] (iv) A fourth possibility, however, takes special note of the fact that the genitive object of that preposition, *teknogonias*, has the article (i.e., "the childbirth"). This occurrence of the article makes it possible that a particular instance of childbirth is in mind, usually understood to be the birth of Christ.

This fourth option is the most natural meaning, given both the context in 1 Timothy and the related context of Genesis. In both 1 Timothy and Genesis the mention of Eve's transgression is followed by a reference to childbearing (actually there are *two* such references in the Genesis passage). In Genesis 3:15–16, following the account of the fall of Adam and Eve, there is the promise of her victorious offspring: "And I will put enmity between you and the woman, and between your offspring and hers; he will crush your head, and you will strike his heel"; and the prediction of pain in childbirth for the woman: "To the woman he said, 'I will greatly increase your pains in

---

15. This *double entendre* is proposed by Murray Harris, "Prepositions & Theology in the Greek New Testament," *NIDNTT*, 3:1177).

childbearing; with pain you will give birth to children."' Salvation by the birth of a (particular) child and the need for salvation through the pain of childbirth are thus alluded to in both Genesis and 1 Timothy.[16]

It may also be significant in this connection that the next words in Genesis are about the new domination of woman by her husband as a result of the Fall. "Your desire will be for your husband, and he will rule over you."[17] We can portray the two texts as follows:

1 Timothy 2:12–15	The woman gives place to the **man**
	Adam was formed first
	Eve was deceived and sinned
	woman will be saved through the **childbirth**.
	If they continue in faith, etc.
Genesis 3:1–20	**Adam** was formed first
	Eve was deceived and sinned
	her **offspring's** heel will be struck by the serpent's offspring
	her **offspring** will crush the head of the offspring of the serpent
	Woman would have pain in **childbirth**
	The **man** would rule over the woman.

This diagram helps us see that the reference to the childbirth in 1 Timothy 2 corresponds to the reference to Eve's offspring in Genesis 3. It also points up the prediction that follows in the Genesis passage about the man's ruling over the woman. The fact that man's rule over the woman is a result of the Fall raises the question as to whether Paul had this in mind also, even though he only specifically mentions Eve's part in the Fall. If so, there is a further question: Just as we try to relieve women's pain in childbirth, should we alleviate the sometimes aggressive and oppressive control men tend to seek over women? At the very least, men who seek leadership in marriage and in the church should recognize and temper the male tendency to dominate.

---

16. Ignatius and others gave honor to the virgin Mary through whose act of childbearing (a different Greek word was used) our salvation was made possible.

17. One common view of the New Testament passages about women is that the domination of man over woman ended for Christians at the cross and should not be perpetuated by negative interpretations of problematic passages like the one under consideration. That is not for discussion here, except to point out the need for exegetes to take seriously the effect of the Fall and redemption in gender relations.

That does not solve all the problems, however. The use of "the child-bearing" is a rather obscure way of referring to the birth of Christ. Neither Mary nor Christ are named here, and elsewhere Scripture emphasizes the death, not the birth of Christ, as the means of salvation. Also the protasis, "if they continue . . . ," does not seem related to the coming of Christ and still stands as a condition of women's salvation.

(e) That brings us to the next problem, that there is an unusual change from the singular form of the first verb ("she shall be saved") to the plural form of the next verb ("if they continue"). This may possibly, but not necessarily, be explained as a shift from the specific to the general. The final clause has a familiar ring in the literature of the Pastorals. In these letters "faith" (*pistis*) occurs thirty-three times, "love" (*agape*) ten times, and "propriety" (*sophrosyne*) once (2:9), with related words from the same root appearing eight times. "Holiness" (*hagiasmos*) does not appear elsewhere in these letters, though the idea of godliness is frequent (including 2:2). These are not "good works" but qualities that mark a believer. This forms an appropriate conclusion to this particular chapter with its emphasis on the demeanor expected of Christians in this world.

In conclusion, we may propose, then, that verse 15 fits in well with verse 14 with its reference to Eve as showing that the Seed of the woman made salvation possible. It accords with the need for women to avoid the seductive false teachers and to ignore their teachings against marriage (1 Tim. 4:3) and instead to live normal lives, bearing children (if "the childbirth" has a primary or even secondary reference to that). This does not demean women or confine them to the home, for Paul has already taught—indeed ordered—that women learn (v. 11).[18]

THE NEED FOR careful interpretation. This section, especially verses 12–15, has probably received more attention in recent years than any other passage of similar length. It has been explored and perhaps exploited by those concerned with gender roles in the

---

18. There is much literature on this verse. To select a few recent works with varying viewpoints we will mention Andreas Köstenberger, "Saved Through Childbearing?" *CBMW News* 2 (1997): 1–6 (an abridgment of an earlier article); Douglas J. Moo, "What Does It Mean Not to Teach or Have Authority Over Men?" in *Recovering Biblical Manhood and Womanhood*, 192; S. E. Porter, "What Does It Mean to be 'Saved by Childbirth' (1 Timothy 2.15)?" *JSNT* 49 (1993): 87–102. Köstenberger sees "saved" as being kept safe from being deceived, that is, kept safe from Satan. Moo sees childbearing as a metonymy for the woman's whole ministry at home. Porter takes "saved" in its Pauline theological sense and holds that childbearing refers not to Jesus' birth of the virgin but to a woman having children. She must, however, continue in the qualities indicated.

church. The approaches have been as varied as the concerns. Before venturing specific suggestions for application (see Contemporary Significance) one should consider the problems involved in moving from the text in its ecclesiastical, historical, and social background to its meaning beyond those immediate circumstances.

Although one must avoid generalizations and be aware of modifications and nuances in exegetical and hermeneutical findings, two major approaches can be identified. One approach views the text as a major piece in a continuum of biblical teaching that women, while equal to men in worth, are intended from the beginning to be subordinate to them. The other is that any subordination of women is contrary to God's ideal, was caused by the fall of Adam and Eve, was reversed in the church through the sacrifice of Christ, but has been perpetuated by erroneous interpretations of Scripture.

Modifications of these positions include various views on the relationship of Adam and Eve prior to the Fall, the possible reasons for the all-male priesthood and Jesus' all male apostolate, examples of ministering women in Old and New Testaments, the positive view Jesus had of women, the nature of the husband-wife relationship described in Ephesians 5:22–33, the positive attitudes Paul had to his women associates, the significance of Acts 18:24–26; Romans 16:1–15; 1 Corinthians 11:2–16; 14:33–35; Galatians 3:28, and the possible role of cultural factors.

However relevant those biblical passages and cultural factors may be and whatever the position and image of women in Ephesus may have been in the first century, we need look no further than the Pastorals themselves for circumstances that are important in bridging contexts. Second Timothy 3:6–7 informs us about vulnerable women who were being victimized—women "always learning but never able to acknowledge the truth." Without need for elaborate theories, this circumstance should alert us to problems that deeply affected at least some women in the Ephesian church and their fitness to learn, let alone teach. The interpreter should exercise care in the application of 1 Timothy 2:12 in churches that do not have problems of such severity. It is important to ask whether the low level of women's education, and especially of religious education, is relevant not only to the command for them to learn but also to the restriction on their ministry.[19]

To restate matters from another perspective and in the form of a question: Does the New Testament see women as gifted by God, enabled by the Spirit, and called to minister without limitations because of their gender, unless there are specific, circumstantial contraindications; or does it see women as being limited from engaging in certain ministries that are reserved for men?

---

19. See the comments in the Bridging Contexts section of 2 Timothy 3:6–7.

The matter has been clouded by the adoption of inadequate and perhaps misleading nomenclature. "Egalitarian" is adopted by some, but opponents claim that they also hold to equality—although, it must be observed, many women feel that they are not considered equal as long as they are restricted from particular ministries. "Complementarian" has been adopted by others, but it can be argued that in the church and increasingly in society it is widely recognized that men and women do complement each other. Neither term is adequate or accurate; neither belongs exclusively to the people who use it.

As regards positions concerning the passage in view, it is perhaps best to be strictly objective and say that (1) some hold a "restrictive" position, believing that Paul restricts women in all circumstances and cultures from teaching men or having authority over them, while (2) others are "nonrestrictive," in the sense they hold that for one reason or another what Paul says he does not permit (and even the meaning of the practices not permitted is disputed) should not be considered restrictive at all times and in all places. It would be unfortunate if the debate prevents us from seeing the broad teachings of the passage about prayer, modesty, good deeds, the command for women to learn, and the moral qualities described in verse 15.

The importance of context. The topics in 1 Timothy 2:8–15—men lifting up holy hands in prayer, women worshiping in modest clothing without expensive jewelry and modish hairstyles, and women not teaching or assuming authority over a man—may seem unconnected. Further, some issues (e.g., jewelry) may seem of no spiritual consequence in many quarters today. Yet others may seem of immense ecclesiastical importance (e.g., women's ministry). It would be inadvisable to attempt the process of application without first understanding the relationship of these topics to each other.

The common thread to all these areas is that they are related to *public behavior* and that this behavior is linked with living "peaceful and quiet lives in all godliness and holiness" (v. 2), which, in turn, relates to the church's outreach to the non-Christian world (vv. 3–7). If this commentary is correct in seeing the interrelationship of belief and behavior as a major distinctive of the Pastoral Letters, the present passage is an important example of that. We saw in chapter 1 the need not only for faith but also for a good conscience on the part of a Christian leader, and we will note in chapter 3 the importance of public reputation on the part of elders. Here in chapter 2, while there is a private side to worship, it is the open side of the church at worship that is under consideration. Paul is far more concerned about church behavior than he is about church order. That concern ultimately has to do with missionary strategy.

Christians today tend to look back, with some justification, at pagans in the Greco-Roman world as godless and immoral. Both Jewish and Christian writers of the Hellenistic period wrote of the deficiencies of paganism, and many of us see that world only through their eyes. It is true that many of their practices were morally reprehensible. But there were also some aspects of ancient personal and public life that came under the enlightened scrutiny of pagan moral philosophers. To some degree these aspects were important more as a means of keeping order than of personal piety. Nevertheless, there were standards that Christians were not to appear to fall below in their own lives and in their public behavior lest God's reputation be sullied. This is a major consideration in the Pastoral Letters.

One well-known example of ancient standards was the assortment of "household codes," that is, lists of duties and relationships that were traditionally observed within families and in external society in ancient Greece (see Introduction). While it is not held here that these existed in well-defined forms in the New Testament period or that they were a significant formative factor in the teachings of the Pastoral Letters, we must not ignore the fact that deviation from reasonable norms of interpersonal behavior would have been noted against the Christians.

This reality is made clear especially in Titus 2 (italics added below):

- verses 4–5: "Then they [older women] can train the younger women to love their husbands and children, to be self-controlled and pure, to be busy at home, to be kind, and to be subject to their husbands, *so that no one will malign the word of God.*"
- verses 6–8: "Similarly, encourage the young men to be self-controlled. In everything set them an example by doing what is good. In your teaching show integrity, seriousness and soundness of speech that cannot be condemned, *so that those who oppose you may be ashamed because they have nothing bad to say about us.*"
- verses 9–10: "Teach slaves to be subject to their masters in everything, to try to please them, not to talk back to them, and not to steal from them, but to show that they can be fully trusted, *so that in every way they will make the teaching about God our Savior attractive.*"

We must be sure that our appropriation of biblical ethical teachings accords with their original purposes in the biblical contexts. The principles here are confirmed in 1 Peter 2:11–12 (note the sequence of thought in 2:13–3:7). With Christ as our example we are *all* to have appropriate submission and respect (including the respect of husbands for wives in 3:7).

Understanding ethical principles. It is important to realize two complementary facts. (1) Ethical practices and commands taught in Scripture are theologically grounded, even though they may apply to passing circumstances. Some examples are instructions regarding the tabernacle in the desert after the Exodus (based on the holiness of God), the rejection of endless repetition of verbiage in pagan prayers to which Jesus referred (based on God's Fatherhood), and decisions concerning the eating of meat offered to idols (based on the nonexistence of other gods).

(2) Nevertheless, the same theological truths that call for a particular response or set of practices in one circumstance may call for *different* responses and practices in other circumstances in order to be meaningful. One Old Testament example of this is the series of commands in Leviticus 19 that are based on the holiness of God. These include not only commands against such sins as stealing and lying, but also the decree not to wear "clothing woven of two kinds of material" (v. 19). These instructions may belong to the law of Moses that is no longer binding, but God is still holy, and we need to find substitute ways of proclaiming this same truth in our lives. New Testament examples include women's wearing of head-coverings (1 Cor. 11) and foot-washing (John 13). The theological ground for head-coverings is considerable (among them the headship of Christ and the order of creation), as is that for foot-washing (Jesus is Lord and Teacher). The fact that Christians have disagreed about how these practices are to be reproduced in contemporary culture shows that some thought needs to be given to such matters. There are various ways to express biblical gender relationships and the Lordship of Christ.

It is sometimes difficult for readers of Scripture today to perceive the reasons for certain practices, especially those that are not usually followed in one's own culture. Even detailed exegetical scholarship may miss nuances. The larger context, both of the text and of the society addressed, is important. Sometimes biblical practices are meaningful in one situation and not in another. In fact, they may seem strange and even turn people away if they are repeated in another situation than their original context. Clearly the necessary procedure is to determine the theological basis, the reason for any accompanying biblical text, the purpose of the practice, and the changing circumstances that may require a substitute practice to accomplish the same purpose and express the same theological truths.

This is not a matter of interpreting Scripture by culture, which can relativize God's Word. Rather, Scripture stands over and often against its contemporary culture. Obviously we will be better able to apply Scripture in our situation if we understand how it was intended to be applied to its own. Culture, then, is not a control, but a target. Discernment of what biblical practices should be transferred unchanged and repeated in an identical manner in our very different culture is sharpened by an accurate understanding of the original cultural target, *if* (that word is important here) it can be determined. This may help us also determine the functional reasons why certain commands and practices were put in Scripture, where they dealt with real life situations.

The difficulty in assessing background data. In making these observations it must be acknowledged that it is perhaps more difficult to bridge contexts with regard to this passage than for any other passage in the Pastoral Letters. Some have observed that hermeneutically it is especially difficult here to incorporate the two horizons—the horizon of the reader in its original setting (the context of the passage in its cultural background as well as its textual setting) and the horizon of the modern reader.

Several scholars have recently addressed the background issues.[20] S. M. Baugh's article is the most detailed and latest word on the background in Ephesus. Whether it is also the last word remains to be seen. The influence of the Artemis cult may indeed have had some effect on the women in the Ephesian church. There is disagreement as to whether the Ephesian Artemis was a stronger sexual figure than other similar female deities in the Roman empire, but there is no question that throughout the empire converts to Christianity had acquaintance with such figures. The hermeneutical question is whether this should be a major factor in the interpretation of the text before us. For those who think the text restricts women in all places at all times it means little. For those who think Paul was addressing a serious circumstance in the Ephesian church of women being unduly influenced by false teachers with their myths and distorted doctrines it is significant.

The question of contemporary influences on interpretation. The horizon of the modern reader is different, of course, but the question here is whether proponents of one side or another have shaded their hermeneutics to adapt to their own culture. It is common for some today to charge those holding a nonrestrictive position with yielding to feminist trends and influence.[21] Unfortunately the larger picture of women in the early church, the varying fortunes of women in ministry throughout the ages of church history, and the facts that women's ministry is not new, that family breakdown is not exclusively the responsibility of women's freedom, and that Christians have often championed such causes as women's right to vote, to attend college, and to have equal pay for equal work—much of this has tended to be for-

---

20. See esp. Sharon Hodgkin Gritz, *Paul, Women Teachers, and the Mother Goddess at Ephesus* (Lanham, Md.: Univ. Press of America, 1991); Kroeger, and Kroeger, *I Suffer Not a Woman*, esp. 47–58, 127–70, 193–211; and S. M. Baugh, "A Foreign World: Ephesus in the First Century," in Köstenberger, Schreiner, and Baldwin, eds., *Women in the Church*, 13–52, which critiques the Kroegers' work heavily.

21. R. W. Yarbrough is convinced that it has influenced those who take a nonrestrictive view of the text ("The Hermeneutics of 1 Timothy 2:9–15," in Köstenberger, Schreiner, and Baldwin, eds., *Women in the Church*, 155–96).

gotten.[22] So has the negative influence of views about male leadership on generations of sermons and commentaries. We *all* need to beware of unbiblical influence.

Specific issues. Also overlooked in much of the discussion is the fact that verse 12 contains no command. There is no imperative addressed to Timothy, to the women, or to the churches about women teaching or having authority (see the Original Meaning section). Nevertheless, such practices had significance. Just as the church avoided shame in husband-wife relationships in Paul's day by having women wear head-coverings, a common practice then (see 1 Cor. 11:2–16), so women expressed quietness and submission in the church by refraining from teaching and exercising authority over men.

Paul does, however, use the imperative in verse 11: "A woman should learn (*manthaneto*) in quietness and full submission." (Note: To translate this "Let ... learn" [NRSV, NASB, KJV] can lead the English reader to think it is permissive rather than imperative.) The verb is in the third person singular since Paul is giving the command for women indirectly through Timothy. The modifying words are important, "in quietness and full submission." It is unfortunate that in the present-day discussions far more attention is given to the limits Paul sets than to the imperative for women to learn.

The relevance of 1 Corinthians 11:2–16. One of the strongest arguments offered for maintaining Paul's restrictions permanently and universally is his allusion to the Genesis record. It is important to compare this with the way Paul uses biblical and theological facts in 1 Corinthians. It is clear that in 1 Corinthians 11 Paul is concerned about honor and shame in public worship (such words as dishonor, disgrace, and glory are significant there). It was important that women express a proper attitude to their husbands by keeping their heads appropriately covered, possibly done by wearing one's hair modestly bound up. Paul employs a barrage of biblical allusions to support his instruction about women's heads: (1) The head of every man is Christ; (2) man is the head of woman; (3) the head of Christ is God; (4) man is the image and glory of God; (5) woman is the glory of man; (6) man did not come from woman but woman from man; (7) man was not created for woman but woman for man; and (8) the angels are to be considered.

We see that there is a much *greater* biblical and theological support offered in 1 Corinthians for a practice about women's head-coverings that is largely *discarded* in today's churches than is offered in 1 Timothy regarding women's teaching and authority; yet women are widely *restricted* today on the basis of

---

22. See Ruth Tucker and Walter Liefeld, *Daughters of the Church*, which is a historical survey of women and ministry over the course of church history. This historical perspective is often overlooked in the debate.

this latter passage. If it is reasonably argued that there are other ways women today should observe the eight truths in 1 Corinthians 11 than by wearing head-coverings, it is certainly also reasonable for women to observe the two truths in 1 Timothy by other means than refraining from teaching and exercising authority. The application section will address this.

We should also note that following Paul's strong argumentation pertaining to the relationship between man and woman in 1 Corinthians 11:3–10, he writes: "In the Lord, however, woman is not independent of man, nor is man independent of woman. For as woman came from man, so also man is born of woman. But everything comes from God" (vv. 11–12). That is, having explained why the demeanor of a woman when speaking publicly in the assembly was important by referring to the Old Testament, he then shows that spiritually, "in the Lord," things are different. He affirms the mutual interdependence of men and women and states that although man came first in the creation, woman comes first (giving birth to males) in succeeding generations. And God is the ultimate source of life, so chronological order is less important.

Since the bearing of the Old Testament on male-female relationships in the Lord is modified somewhat in 1 Corinthians, there is a legitimate question as to whether the reference in 1 Timothy to Eve's deception, at a time when there was almost universal condemnation of Eve (especially by many rabbis) and when women's ability to teach was therefore widely discounted, is as relevant to women's ministry in other circumstances as might be thought.

THE SPIRITUAL BENEFITS of proper attitudes. The church today can realize significant spiritual benefit from the appropriation of this passage. The chapter began with a call to prayer, with the ultimate purpose of fulfilling God's desire for all people "to be saved and to come to a knowledge of the truth" (2:4). We may assume not only that this purpose is valid for today, but also that the rest of the chapter is consistent with it. It is possible to concentrate so narrowly on what men and women may or may not do that we lose the significance of the passage as a whole. Since the call to prayer includes the *way* Christians should pray and is followed by further instructions to both men and women on how to live and learn, we should confidently pursue attitudes and practices that honor God and draw others to him.

There are so many incidents today of people with allegedly moral agendas expressing unwarranted anger and committing other offenses (one thinks immediately of bombing of abortion clinics and demonstrations of white supremacy) that being able to raise holy hands (v. 8) is immensely important. And while Christian women today make use of cosmetics and stylish attire without cause for criticism, there is still something to be said for the limitation of expenditures on clothing and for the consideration of modesty as well. This also relates to our testimony in the world. If verses 11–15 are applied only to church order within the four walls of a building, something of the purpose of this chapter is lost.

It is, of course, difficult to prescribe the application of verses 11–15 because of the vast difference in interpretation. But the modest attitude promoted in these verses can forward the witness of the church outside of those walls. This can stand in contrast to the harshness that still characterizes some male-female relationships as well as to some of the strident calls one used to hear, especially in the mid-twentieth century, from so-called radical feminists. This passage need not be construed as consigning all women to household chores and child-bearing in order to find in it a modern call to faith, love, holiness, and modesty.[23]

Theology, morality, and custom. We must also observe the specific restriction that Paul placed on women in its context. This chapter is a unit, and such seemingly different matters as cosmetics and teaching are related to each other. What we might consider today to be matters of little consequence, such as cosmetics and jewelry, apparently had great moral importance in the ancient world. What we might consider a *theological* matter today, such as whether a woman teaches a man, may have had more significance then as a *custom* that communicated a *moral* message. But this custom has little *moral* significance today. Note that even after all the biblical and theological truths that Paul refers to in connection with women's hair in 1 Corinthians 11:2–16, at the end of the passage he calls what he advocates a "custom" (*synetheia*, NIV "practice"). We should seek ways in which women can communicate the kind of relationship to their husbands described in Ephesians 5 and the kind of honorable public attitude displayed in 1 Corinthians 11 through means that are meaningful and do not alienate the very people we seek to reach.

The importance of consistency. In doing this it is crucial that we avoid inconsistencies. I know of a missionary who concluded her talk to the women (in the basement of a church that forbade women to preach or teach men), only to find that the men had been listening in the adjoining kitchen. Another church interviewed a missionary rather than let her speak on her own, then played a tape of a well-known woman speaker at a missionary conference. In another instance, some mission executives who would not allow a woman

---

23. "Modesty" (NRSV, NLT) is perhaps a better translation of *sophrosyne* than the NIV's "propriety."

to speak in their church went to hear her in another church. A congregation that showed a film of a woman who founded and led a church in a foreign country would nevertheless not allow women even to read Scripture publicly. A teenager once asked why it was all right for her to lead in prayer at the young people's meeting downstairs but not in a church service upstairs.

In addition to avoiding inconsistencies it is wise to avoid legalism and dogmatism. (In modern terms we might add "micro-managing.") One hears discussions over the age at which a boy must stop learning the Bible from a woman teacher. One has also seen an extensive, detailed list of what ministries a woman may or may not do. Such attempts to establish precise rules can tend either to trivialize the issues or to be rigidly legalistic.

Paul's restriction on women's teaching made good sense in a world that refused to give women teachers a hearing. In his day the New Testament had not yet been completed and circulated, so people were dependent on the authoritative spoken word. Today when anyone teaches the Bible to a church class of men and women, that person is not a lone authority, but may at any time be challenged or corrected by anyone with an open Bible. In the pulpit neither male nor female preachers have authority in themselves; the authority is in the Word of God they proclaim and under which they stand.

In the first century Paul was willing to become all things to all people in order to save some (1 Cor. 9:22). Would not the apostle think it inappropriate for us to forbid a female college president from teaching a Bible class composed of university students—men and women—when such restriction could "stumble" people and cause them to turn from the gospel? A different kind of question often being asked today is whether it is right for a church to be deprived of the spiritual gift of leadership God may have given a woman when she is limited to using that gift in the women's group.

These are real situations that raise legitimate questions. If, on the one hand, Paul's restrictions *were* intended to keep women from doing missionary teaching of men today, from leading a mixed Bible study, or from serving among a group of elders, those restrictions must not be ignored. If, on the other hand, Paul would have valued missionary principles such as not hindering people from the gospel as primary, and if he considered secondary such practices as head-coverings and restricting the teaching of a mixed group to males, we need to be consistent in that regard. No doubt thoughtful readers will see strong points on each side.

Asking the right questions. To test whether this passage requires that women must be restricted from any teaching of men or from any participation in church leadership, we may ask the following questions:

1. Does the use of the verb *authenteo* in this context restrict women from authority of *any* sort, or is a stronger meaning of controlling, domi-

nating, or assuming authority on one's own in view here, narrowing the scope of restriction?

2. If a woman teaches a mixed group today, does that imply the same authority that the teaching of the early apostolic traditions about Christ had in the first century?

3. Would a woman's teaching men or being part of a leadership team to which men are accountable violate moral standards of decency today as it would have in Paul's day?

4. Was Paul's description of his apostolic practice ("I do not permit") a command for all time and circumstances, even though it was not expressed as an imperative?

5. As we address our biblically illiterate society, is it meaningful to reflect Adam's chronological priority and Eve's deception by forbidding women from teaching men and from participating in leadership?

6. If we require women to refrain from teaching or participating in leadership, should we, for the sake of hermeneutical consistency with Paul's instructions about head-coverings in 1 Corinthians 11 (given the eight biblical and theological reasons for that practice), also require that practice today?

Applying the answers. If our answer to *any* of these questions is uncertain or raises a legitimate doubt about restricting women, we may well hesitate to prevent them from the full exercise of their Spirit-given gifts in the church. The very fact that it is difficult to assign a specific contemporary significance to this passage, especially verse 12, makes it necessary to face the hard issues just outlined and not continue any practice that we may have wrongly assumed is biblical. These questions are listed to encourage us to work diligently on the answers and to respect those who decide matters differently.

We have seen that there are two opposing sides on these matters. At the risk of over-simplification, it may be useful to summarize these two viewpoints. (1) There is no legitimate way to avoid concluding from verses 11–15 that Paul did not allow women either to teach men or to have any kind of authority over them. Further, this prohibition was not confined to the socio-religious conditions at Ephesus. Thus, any attempts to adjust it for Western or other contemporary cultures are futile and wrong. (2) Paul's statement was directed to specific circumstances at Ephesus and in the Ephesian church, such as the prominence of women in pagan religion and the victimization of women in the church. It is wrong to apply it without adjustment to other circumstances.

The strength of (1) is its focus on the words and grammar of the text. Its weakness is its failure to pay sufficient attention to the larger context or take fully into account the problems of application. The strength of (2) is its awareness that the letter was written to address specific circumstances that are different from our own. Its weakness is in overemphasizing the background, perhaps to the point of distortion, and (in the arguments of some) straining the text.

(3) There is, however, a possible third approach. The vocabulary, grammar, and structure of this section *and* its context in chapter 2 are seen as one unit. It deals with the importance of leading "peaceful and quiet lives in all godliness and holiness" (v. 2), not only as a blessing for Christians but in reaching non-Christians (vv. 3–7). This accords with the tone and the goals of the whole Pastoral corpus. Paul intends for Timothy to follow his practice of restricting women, while carefully avoiding putting it into a command for all times and places. The instructions are not limited to the conditions at Ephesus but apply to the whole ancient culture, Jewish and pagan, that regarded it as immoral for women to transcend certain public restrictions. Paul had a missionary purpose, as in 1 Corinthians 9:20, where he "became like one under the law . . . so as to win those under the law." According to this approach to the passage, the application should facilitate the fulfillment of Paul's missionary purpose in our own social context rather than repeat the same restrictions that were appropriate then but can be a hindrance to conversions now.

However this issue may be settled, the ideals of this passage, beginning with prayer and including peaceful holiness on the part of men and modesty on the part of women, should be pursued by Christians today. Also men should not justify abuse or harsh domination of women, as they sometimes have done. Women should not neglect their pursuit of the gracious qualities taught in verses 9–15, as they also sometimes have done. *And no church should split over these issues.* To incite dissension is to sink to the level of the false teachers whom the Pastoral Letters so strongly condemn. "Make every effort to keep the unity of the Spirit through the bond of peace" (Eph. 4:3).

1 Timothy 3:1-7

HERE IS A trustworthy saying: If anyone sets his heart on being an overseer, he desires a noble task. ²Now the overseer must be above reproach, the husband of but one wife, temperate, self-controlled, respectable, hospitable, able to teach, ³not given to drunkenness, not violent but gentle, not quarrelsome, not a lover of money. ⁴He must manage his own family well and see that his children obey him with proper respect. ⁵(If anyone does not know how to manage his own family, how can he take care of God's church?) ⁶He must not be a recent convert, or he may become conceited and fall under the same judgment as the devil. ⁷He must also have a good reputation with outsiders, so that he will not fall into disgrace and into the devil's trap.

THE CHURCH AT Ephesus was troubled by men who taught error and, in at least some cases, lived immorally. Christians, especially women, were harassed and in need of help. In chapter 1 Paul urged Timothy both to teach truth and to live a life appropriate to his teachings. In chapter 2 he stressed the importance of conduct that befits God's truth on the part of both men and women. Now Paul takes another step to address the problem of false teachers by ensuring that the church has leaders who are morally qualified and "above reproach." This chapter will come to a climax with the exposition of the "mystery of godliness" in verses 14–16.

Paul's approach to the problems at Crete was similar: He wrote Titus to appoint elders (Titus 1:5–9). At Ephesus elders were already in place (Acts 20:17), but apparently some tightening of qualifications was needed. The text of 1 Timothy does not say whether any of the false teachers were elders or deacons, but there is no hint in the list of qualifications that there were doctrinal errors among the recognized leadership. In fact, it is surprising that the qualifications only touch obliquely on doctrine; the emphasis is almost entirely on moral integrity.

Before he lists the qualifications for overseers, Paul affirms the importance of their work. "Here is a trustworthy saying" (v. 1) may refer to an important saying that circulated among the early churches or may mean simply "You can depend on this" (see comments on 1:15; see also 4:9; 2 Tim. 2:11; Titus 3:8). Either way, this phrase introduces an important assertion.[1] Those who desire to serve in this way are to be encouraged, perhaps as those who build the church with valuable materials as in 1 Corinthians 3:12–14, a task that is indeed "noble."

The word Paul uses here for church leadership is *episkope*. It is hard to translate; "overseership" might be the best literal rendering. It describes the work or position of an overseer.[2] Whether the term *bishop* should be employed is linked with the historical question of whether the bishopric was a post-New Testament development. Within the New Testament the word occurs in Luke 19:44 and 1 Peter 2:12, where it refers to God's visitation and to his coming to oversee the world and, by implication, to bring judgment: It is the "time of God's coming to you" (Luke; cf. Peter's "the day he visits us"). The same Greek word occurs in the Septuagint (LXX) translation of Job 31:14 to signify God's future "examination" of Job. In Job 10:12 it refers to God's protection or care. From the idea of care comes that of responsibility, and a person who has responsibility for something is "in charge" of it, as Aaron's son Eliezer was of the whole tabernacle (Num. 4:16).

A well-known use of the word is in Acts 1:20, which quotes Psalm 109:8: "Let another take his *episkope*." This refers to Judas and his responsibility as an apostle. The implication is that there was an opening in the ranks of the apostles to be filled, so the word "office" may be appropriate in this case. (The difference between "office" and "function" is that office refers to a designated position that exists even if there is no incumbent at the moment.) *Episkope* need not, however, always imply an office.

It is noteworthy that here in 1 Timothy 3:1 Paul defines being an overseer in terms of function ("a noble task"), not of status or office. He is not encouraging people to seek status but responsibility. Whether this responsibility is *also* an "office" depends partly on the meaning we assign to that word.[3] We should observe that no word corresponding to "office" accompa-

---

1. Some have proposed that the "faithful saying" in this passage refers to the preceding verse (2:15) about women, but that verse does not seem to be the kind of statement, either in form or in content, that would be quoted as a weighty dictum.

2. Translations include "office of a bishop" (KJV), "position of a bishop" (NKJV), "office of overseer" (NASB), "office of bishop" (NRSV), "leadership" (REB), "leadership in the church" (*The Message*), "an elder" (NLT), along with the NIV's "being an overseer."

3. There has been much discussion on the various types of leadership and authority (including the status of holding an "office") that exist in society, especially since the work of Max Weber. See especially Bengt Holmberg, *Paul and Power* (Philadelphia: Fortress Press, 1978) for a stimulating analysis of these issues with regard to the Pauline churches. In New Testament circles, there has been a long running discussion about two kinds of leadership, charismatic and official. Some have thought these virtually mutually exclusive, with the

nies *episkope* in the Greek text here. But whatever way that issue is decided, *episkope* does describe a position of special responsibility and leadership, as the accompanying qualifications imply.

There has been much uncertainty as to whether the term *overseer* is synonymous with *elder* (see discussion in the Introduction). In Acts 14:23 Paul and Barnabas appointed "elders" in each church they had established thus far. In 20:17 those whom Paul summoned from Ephesus are called "elders," but in verse 28 he said that the Holy Spirit had made them "overseers" to shepherd the church. Obviously, "elders" and "overseers" refer to the same group in this passage. It has been argued that this use of two words could suggest that while a church may appoint elders, only the Spirit makes them overseers, but such a distinction does not seem to be the point here in 1 Timothy. Likewise, the idea that "elder" refers to the *person* while "overseer" refers to the *work* is questionable. It is precarious to identify any direct categorization of duties in the early church based on such distinctions.

Elders, of course, were well known in Judaism from the time of Moses to second-temple Judaism. There is no passage in the New Testament that radically differentiates the role of Christian elders from the Jewish ones. The word *episkopos* was used in the secular world to describe various kinds of responsible leadership, largely civic or financial. In Titus 1, Paul clearly refers to the same group as "elders" (v. 5) and "overseers" (v.7). Since the overseers "shepherd" the church (Acts 20:28), it is reasonable to call them also *pastors* (from the Latin word for shepherd), though this does not limit the work of pastoring to a body of overseers.

It also seems clear that the overseers are the same people who "work hard among you, who are over you in the Lord and who admonish you" (1 Thess. 5:12), and who are the "leaders" in Hebrews 13:7 "who spoke the word of God to you." In Hebrews 13:17 the author commands the readers, "Obey your leaders and submit to their authority. They keep watch [lit., are on guard] over you as those [there is no Greek word behind the NIV "men"] who must give an account. Obey them so that their work will be a joy, not a burden, for that

---

Corinthians church being an example of charismatic leadership and the (allegedly later) Pastorals reflecting the official. Others have noted that there is organization discernible in 1 Corinthians 12 and charismatic activity in the Pastorals (endowment of a spiritual gift at the laying on of hands, 1 Tim. 4:14; 2 Tim. 1:6). Probably these two types of leadership were overlapping. For a useful summary and conclusion see Ronald Y. K. Fung, "Charismatic versus Organized Ministry?", *EvQ* 52 (1980); 195–214. The KJV employs the word "office" in several contexts where it does not occur in the Greek text (Luke 1:8–9; Rom. 12:4; 1 Tim. 3:1; Heb. 7:5). The influence of that version over the centuries has led generations of readers to suppose that a formal office existed in each of these cases. That circumstance makes it unfortunately easy to think primarily in terms of office rather than of function in the present passage.

would be of no advantage to you."[4] The New Testament listing of spiritual gifts and spiritually gifted persons includes those who take "leadership" (Rom. 12:8) and have "gifts of administration" (1 Cor. 12:28).

In verses 2–7 Paul sets out some significant moral requirements for the overseers. His concern that overseers be "above reproach" will be paralleled in 5:7 regarding widows, where a form of the same Greek word appears (NIV, "[not] open to blame"), and in 6:14. The meaning of this is spelled out in the following instructions, which do not describe a person totally without sin, but one morally careful and responsible. Later in the Pastorals Paul will issue moral instructions to people in three social classes and buttress each with a reference to the importance of avoiding blame and enhancing the gospel (Titus 2:5, 8, 10).

The first way for an overseer to be "above reproach" is faithfulness to his wife. As is often observed, the expression used here literally translates "man [or husband] of one woman [or wife]," but this needs careful interpretation. Does it mean "husband of but one wife" (NIV), "husband of one wife" (NASB), "married only once" (NRSV), or something like "committed to his wife" (*The Message*) or "faithful to his wife" (NLT)? The same expression occurs below in verse 12, where each of the translations cited uses the same terminology as here. The converse phrase occurs in 5:9, "woman [or wife] of one man [or husband]," which NIV does not translate by a phrase corresponding to the one used here, but rather by "faithful to her husband."[5]

The terminology in verse 2 is equivalent to a Latin word that in its feminine form, *univira*, referred to a Roman woman, typically one of the noble Roman matrons. It is sometimes found as a tribute on tombstones, where it implies that the woman so honored her husband that she did not remarry. However, as divorce increased in the Roman empire, matrons were no longer assumed to have been married only once and so other terms came into use to describe their good character. Conversely, *univira*, still implying only one marriage, came to be used for women in lower social classes.[6] These developments made the term widely available for use and thus serviceable for the

---

4. See also 1 Peter 5:1–2, where Peter (calling himself a "fellow elder") addresses church elders and encourages them not only in terms of their ministry ("be shepherds of God's flock that is under your care, serving as overseers"), but also in terms of their character ("not because you must, but because you are willing, as God wants you to be; not greedy for money, but eager to serve").

5. The NLT has this terminology of faithfulness in all three passages; NASB has "husband of only one wife" in 3:12 and "wife of one man" in 5:9; KJV has "husband of one wife" or equivalent phrase in each place; NRSV translates the idiom "married only once" consistently.

6. Majorie Lightman and William Zeisel, "*Univira*: An Example of Continuity and Change in Roman Society," *Church History* 46 (1977): 25–26.

new and growing Christian church. Eventually the church used it to designate those who were celibate after widowhood.[7]

It could be concluded from the secular background that Paul has used this
phraseology to mean marriage only once. However, we must keep in mind
that purity of character is the main concern of this passage and that its secular counterpart was employed as a means of honoring the character of the
person. Faithfulness and honor could be expressed by refraining from a second marriage after a spouse's death. Paul, rather than being legalistic as to
whether an elder was married more than once, has chosen a phrase here
indicating a standard of marriage that would earn respectability in the society within which the early church functioned. Commitment and faithfulness would speak more meaningfully to that society than just whether a man
or woman had remarried after being widowed.[8]

The word "temperate" (*nephalios*) need not refer only to the use of wine;
its meaning must be determined by context. In verse 11, where it refers to
the deacons' wives or deaconesses, it occurs between "not malicious talkers"
and "trustworthy in everything." It also occurs in Titus 2:2, where in a description of "older men" the list begins with *nephalios* and goes on to such general
virtues as "worthy of respect" and "self-controlled." The next section,
addressed to older women, does not have the word "temperate," but it specifies one area of temperance, not being "addicted to much wine." This does
not imply that women are more likely than men to be alcoholic, but is one
of several illustrations that apply to both. Here in 1 Timothy 3, the word
"drunkenness" appears separately in verse 3. Perhaps it is listed separately
because it is not implied by "temperate" in verse 2, or it may explain what that
word means.

Similarly, "self-controlled" (v. 2) is followed by "not violent" in verse 3. The
latter may be implied by the former, though "self-controlled" has a broader
application. It is probably best to recognize these various terms as expressing a selection of virtues similar to those in moralistic secular writings and
commonly understood to represent a character that is commendable in the
public eye.

"Respectable" (v. 2) enforces the fact that the overseer must have a good
reputation.

Being "hospitable" was important in the first century because of the miserable travel conditions often encountered. Considerate people would be
hospitable to visitors. The word implies far more than having friends over for

---

7. Ibid., 30–32.

8. See the discussion along similar lines but with an application to widows in the comments on 5:9.

dinner. The instructions for widows in 5:10 also include hospitality (cf. also Rom. 12:13; Heb. 13:2; 1 Peter 4:9).

The phrase "able to teach" (representing one Greek word, *didaktikon*) refers to ability, not knowledge (cf. 2 Tim. 2:24, where, following a reference to heretics, Paul turns to the *manner* in which Timothy is to refute them and the *ability* he must have to do that). Even though teaching the truth was important at Ephesus because of the spread of false doctrine, the stress is on ability rather than on correct doctrine, which is undoubtedly assumed.[9]

The wording "not given to drunkenness" (v. 3) by implication allows moderate use of alcoholic beverages (cf. 5:23). The point, however, goes beyond advice regarding moderation. Along with the following words, "not violent . . . not quarrelsome" and "not a lover of money," it mandates behavior opposite to the grossly offensive habits of the false teachers and other ungodly people. These expressions function to describe the character required of overseers by way of contrast. Once again, the later instructions in 2 Timothy 2:23–24 are similar: "Don't have anything to do with foolish and stupid arguments, because you know they produce quarrels. And the Lord's servant must not quarrel; instead, he must be kind to everyone, able to teach, not resentful." The manner of argumentation and the attitude toward money that characterize true or false teachers are such important topics that Paul will return to them with emphasis in 1 Timothy 6:3–10.

The next qualification, "he must manage his own family well" (v. 4), is not only more extended, but also includes an explanation. The parallel between managing one's family and caring for the church requires careful attention. It is important to see where the point of comparison lies. There is one common element in this parallel: the ability of the overseer to guide and to care for those who are his responsibility. The elements that differ are (1) the people to whom the overseer needs to relate (family and church), and (2) the words used to describe his leadership (managing and taking care of).

The more extended households in first-century society, which included children, other relatives, and slaves, required strong household management skills. In the parallel sociological unit, the church, the leadership skill cited is to "take care of," not to "manage." This does not mean that there is no caring involved in management or that there is no managing involved in caring. But disaster may await the church whose leaders see themselves primarily as managers. We know from Hebrews 13:17 that church leaders were to be obeyed. Using a different word for leader, that text says, "Obey your lead-

---

9. By contrast, the section about elders in Titus 1:9 does not have the adjective *didaktikos* but deals instead with the doctrinal integrity of the elder in a different environment of false doctrine.

ers and submit to their authority." But this emphasis is different from the present passage, where Paul stresses not authority but the caring side of leadership. Even at home the father should not discharge his duty just by giving orders. The children must not only "obey" their father; they must have "proper respect" for him. Once again the accent is on the elders' character.

The same observation can be made with regard to verse 6, "He must not be a recent convert." The warning is not against doctrinal immaturity, serious as that would be, but against the danger of a character flaw, "conceit." The false teachers were "conceited," among other things (2 Tim. 3:4), but here the conceit comes from spiritual immaturity, not from moral depravity. Nevertheless, the consequence of conceit is somber: Such people "fall under the same judgment as the devil."

This judgment may seem severe, because to "become conceited" (*typhoo*) probably does not strike us today as serious or culpable. Yet the same verb appears in Paul's description of the last days, which include such sinful attitudes as "boastful, proud, abusive . . . treacherous, rash, conceited" (2 Tim. 3:2–4). As Proverbs 21:4 asserts, "Haughty eyes and a proud heart . . . are sin."[10]

Verse 7 underlines the importance, noted above, of "a good reputation with outsiders," in order to avoid "disgrace." But Paul also keeps in mind here the lurking danger of Satan. Even the more mature overseers (Paul is no longer speaking of recent converts) must beware of falling "into the devil's trap." Paul is deeply conscious of the malevolent intentions of Satan: "Be self-controlled and alert. Your enemy the devil prowls around like a roaring lion looking for someone to devour" (1 Peter 5:8).

THE NEED FOR **leadership**. The selection of leaders was of crucial importance to Paul. There may have been considerable fluidity as to the form leadership took in the early churches, and even as to the terminology. It is difficult to define the terms *elder* and *overseer*, as used in the New Testament, as distinct categories of leadership. In spite of differences in nomenclature and background, they seem to have overlapped in person and duty.

---

10. Some see here an allusion to the ruler of Tyre in Ezek. 28:1–19, where some of terminology sounds as though it is really describing Satan (as in vv. 12–14, "you were the model of perfection . . . you were in Eden . . . you were anointed as a guardian cherub"). The point of comparison is Paul's terminology here regarding conceit and falling under "the same judgment as the devil." Ezekiel reports God's judgment, "In the pride of your heart you say, 'I am a god'" (v. 2), and "you have come to a horrible end and will be no more" (v. 19).

What is most important to grasp is the need for recognized, authoritative church leadership. It is authoritative with regard to conveying the apostles' teachings and with regard to the discipline of those who do not conform to them. The need for such leadership is seen in the fact that Paul and Barnabas appointed elders with amazing rapidity on the return trip of the first missionary journey (Acts 14:23), though it meant appointing people who were within the early months of their faith. Initially the selection was made by Paul and Barnabas, but the apostle Paul could not do this everywhere himself. Some provision had to be made for continuation beyond his personal presence of godly leadership in all the churches.

The deteriorating circumstances at Ephesus (and Crete) made such a provision necessary.[11] The activities of doctrinally and morally deficient teachers there made the need for qualified elders obvious. As time went on and there were no longer any apostles to appoint elders, the guidelines here and in Titus provided direction. Thus, the situation at Ephesus and Crete providentially resulted in the availability of divinely inspired instructions suitable for many different churches around the world from then till now. Whether the resultant leadership is continued through a tradition of apostolic succession or not, the messages here and in Titus 1 are essential for the continuity of doctrinally sound churches.

The need for *qualified* leaders. The inclusion of the "trustworthy saying" in 1 Timothy 3:1 also underscores the importance of having qualified leaders. It is directed to those who are cautiously debating whether to be publicly available for the work. Not only should the church be looking for people who are qualified, but those with potential should be developing within themselves the qualities that will one day qualify them for the work. It is not enough for a church to hunt at the last moment for people to elect as elders at an annual meeting. It is a long-term, ongoing process. Early on in a Christian's life one should be growing spiritually and using the Spirit's gifts for the good of the church, with the possibility, humbly considered, of special ministry such as elderhood. Although this passage does not say so, elders and other mature Christians should be encouraging younger believers to seek God's leading in this direction.

Paul's choice of the description "noble" for the task leads us to ask in what way it deserves that adjective. We do not use this word much today. It conveys a sense of dignity that few value. Instead, during a job search we tend to look for work that is fulfilling, satisfying, financially rewarding, enjoy-

---

11. Later on, the increasing threat of heresies in the early church occasioned both the further clarification of doctrine and the establishment of a single leader over the others, to whom was given the official title of *bishop*.

able, and perhaps needed in society, but without thought as to whether it is *noble*. The Greek word is a common one that in most contexts means simply "good," but in such a special context has this lofty nuance, which it often had in Greek literature.

It is sometimes noted that most of the qualities required in elders are urged elsewhere in Scripture for Christians at large. Thus, the specifications of being the husband of one wife and not being a drunkard do not imply that Christians who are not elders *can* be polygamous or frequently intoxicated. A biblical perspective is that elders should exemplify Christian character as a model for others. Being an elder is not a right but a privilege for responsible people.

Interpreters do not agree on whether the phrase "husband of but one wife" by implication excludes women. It can be viewed in one of two ways. Either (1) the phrase was intended by the author to exclude women from eldership, or (2) it merely assumes the common circumstance that Jewish elders were male. If (1) is the case, it can be construed (a) to bar women for all time, or (b) to bar them under the conditions of Paul's day, but (lacking an explicit prohibition) not for all time. If (2) is the case, the possibility of women elders may simply have been so slim in those days that male-oriented language was natural but not intended to be exclusive.

It should be mentioned that there is some evidence of women elders (both Jewish and Christian) by the second century. Some of the claims have been exaggerated or difficult to prove, but the evidence cannot be ruled out entirely. Whether or not women ought to be elders along with men will depend partly on one's interpretation and application of various relevant Scriptures on women's ministry (including 1 Tim. 2:12) and partly on the kind of ministries that elders perform in a given church. Even some who hold that 2:12 excludes women from authority over men think eldership is open to women because (1) the authority the elders have in their church is corporate and not a matter of one individual ruling over others in the congregation, and (2) the shepherding ministry of the eldership is one in which all benefit from the presence of women.

Overseers and elders. We have assumed that elders and overseers in biblical times were identical, but we must keep in mind that the duties of leadership were multiple (see 1 Tim. 5:17). This may imply that there were subgroups. There was clearly a plurality of leadership (possibly within each house church, but certainly within a city) and a plurality of leadership bodies. There may have been three clearly defined groups (elders, overseers, and deacons), with the groups having overlapping functions. The overseer may have been an elder who had a significant span of authority. There may have been just one ruling body plus the deacons, with their individual members having different functions. In that case, it is possible, though it is doubtful, that some may have been known as elders and some as overseers, depending on their work.

It is noteworthy that when Paul lists several ministries in Ephesians 4:11 (apostles, prophets, evangelists, pastors, and teachers), he does not assign the title *overseer* or *elder* to any of them individually or as a group. In Romans 12:3–8 and 1 Corinthians 12:28–30 various gifted ministries are named, without indicating that the utilization of these was the particular province of elders or overseers. Those passages include the ministry of leadership (Rom. 12:8; 1 Cor. 12:28). Returning to 1 Timothy, there seem to be differing functions among the elders: "The elders who direct the affairs of the church well are worthy of double honor, especially those whose work is preaching and teaching" (1 Tim. 5:17). It is possible that "especially" here has the sense "I mean" (see comments on that passage), but otherwise Paul is recognizing a specialized ministry among the elders, with some, but not all, concentrating on teaching and preaching.

We conclude, then, that (1) there was a body of leaders in each city, possibly in each house church in a city; (2) its members were known as elders or overseers, the terms possibly varying with the social situation or with function; (3) within each group were different responsibilities, including leadership (ruling, but "not lording it over" the church, 1 Peter 5:3), preaching and teaching (1 Tim. 5:17), standing guard, and shepherding; and (4) the Spirit also distributed some of the same gifts that were requisite for these ministries to other believers who were not elders or overseers.[12]

OVERSEERS (OR ELDERS) **as pastors.** We tend today to assess leadership with a corporate mentality. Eldership can be thus seen as an achievement, as a reward, or as an opportunity for advancement. It is all too easy to assume that the elder's duties are parallel to those of board membership in a corporation. This can lead to a perception of elders' meetings basically as a time for decision-making, with the executive (the CEO, as the pastor may be conceived) carrying out the directives of the board. In this scenario, it is possible for elders to consider pastoral concern and care to be outside of their sphere of responsibility and to belong instead to that of the pastor.

---

12. We do not know the extent to which the early Pauline and non-Pauline churches were uniform in their practice. Therefore a subsidiary question (which we cannot discuss here) is whether church structure was less developed and more flexible in the Corinthian church than in the churches addressed in the Pastorals.

That is a common and serious misconception. It is corrected by Paul's instructions to the Ephesian elders in Acts 20:28 ("be shepherds") and Peter's to elders in 1 Peter 5:2 ("be shepherds of God's flock that is under your care"). The examples of shepherding (the good shepherd in Psalm 23 and John 10 and our "Chief Shepherd" in 1 Peter 5:4) also serve as correctives. As churches today take new organizational shapes and the "pastor" may become less and less involved personally with individual needs in the congregation, pastoral concern can shift to those even further removed from what should be the spiritual leadership of the elders. Therefore, the pastoral ministry of elders is vital and crucial today.

This raises the question of whether it is necessary to have an official group called "elders" who perform the identical functions of New Testament elders. Of course, denominations have for years differed in the designated names for leadership positions and in whether the pastorate is in itself equivalent to the eldership of a church. Some large churches have brought the members of the pastoral staff and "lay" leaders together in a leadership council (perhaps including women), with only some members responsible for the more traditional ministries of elders while others are involved more intensively in visitation, worship and music, evangelism, disciplining, and so on. It can reasonably be argued that such a leadership council can more effectively cover the larger responsibilities typical of many contemporary churches.

Two paradoxes. One of the paradoxes in church history is that provisions in Scripture that were intended, at least in part, to promote unity have sometimes resulted in the opposite. The Eucharist or communion, for example, in which the bread, in addition to its primary meaning, symbolizes the united body of believers, has instead been an occasion of disagreement and division. The same is true of baptism. So it is with elders, whose function includes keeping the sheep safely together. It is unfortunate that denominations have even separated from each other over the form of church government. Churches are also dividing over the issue of women elders.

Another paradox that can affect individual churches severely is that those in leadership, who should be people of character devoted to nurturing the flock, sometimes dominate it instead and demolish the aspirations of other spiritually gifted people. Authoritarian leaders have caused much damage in some house church movements and in some megachurches, as well as in churches of all sizes. Some of the denominational splits and divisions throughout church history have resulted from leadership that lacked the qualities set out so plainly in 1 Timothy 3. Scandals that rock churches can arise from neglect of the warnings against such behavior as marital infidelity, temper, quarrels, and greed. It is easy for a person who becomes heady with power to ignore the moral restrictions to which "ordinary" Christians are subject.

Is there a clear biblical order? Church leaders for centuries have been pre-occupied with determining which church order best represents biblical teaching and example. Conclusions in the area range from indifference or passive satisfaction with one's denominational practice to restless probing and experimentation. Every new missionary enterprise has had to grapple with the question as new churches were established. The same has been true of the rapid growth of independent churches in the later part of the twentieth century. The familiar example of trying to establish the shape of an elephant by feeling its various parts can be applied to trying to determine the structure of the New Testament church simply by "feeling" the various Scriptures that touch on it. We must both find the broad features that New Testament churches had in common and recognize that variations do not necessarily compromise these features.

First Corinthians 12, which stresses the charismatic work of God's Spirit in distributing gifts to the Lord's people, does not deal with, and therefore does not exclude, structure in church government. When we do look at passages that deal with that subject, we see leadership by elders. Recall again Paul and Barnabas's appointment of elders as they revisited their churches (Acts 14:23). Before his final trip to Jerusalem, Paul met with the elders from Ephesus at Troas (20:13–38). It appears from Titus 1:5 that the proper establishment of a church was not accomplished until elders were put in place. While this does not mean that there was no room for individual leadership (we find that being exercised at the Jerusalem Council in Acts 15:13–21), the selection of leaders to deal with financial matters in Acts 6:3–6 was by the congregation, and Paul directed the entire congregation to make a decision in 1 Corinthians 5:4–5.

Plural leadership. These passages allow the conclusion that the early church usually had plural leadership. No doubt it was common that in a city with several house churches each small group had perhaps one main leader and also functioned under the plural leadership of elders in the city. Questions of structure and government are, however, too vast to consider here, and that is not the main subject of 1 Timothy 3. Nowhere does the New Testament give a complete manual on church structure. The emphasis here is on the qualifications for eldership, and the main ingredient in these qualifications, in the context of the situation in Ephesus, is Christian character.

Moral leadership. One of the remarkable social changes that will be remembered as marking the end of the twentieth century in America is that from the permissiveness of the 1960s we seemed to move to a new accountability for moral standards, particularly among public officials. Several striking examples occurred in the military. At one point even the appointment of the Joint Chief of Staff became a moral issue. The public seemed to require a higher moral standard among their elected officials than they required of themselves. Yet the recent toleration of President Clinton's admitted moral failure indicates that a leader's moral life is now considered less significant.

First Timothy 3:1–13 sets forth a standard of behavior that, while not different from that which all Christians should live by, is to be more rigorously monitored among elders and deacons. The only qualifications besides those regarding morality, family responsibility, and reputation in the community are those relating to teaching and doctrine. Elders should be "able to teach" (v. 2), and deacons must "keep hold of the deep truths of the faith with a clear conscience" (v. 9). Even these requirements are set without a break in the midst of behavioral requirements, and the deacons are not only to understand truth but hold it "with a clear conscience" (cf. 1:5, 19).

Appointing overseers. In view of these qualifications, how can a church determine who should serve as overseers or elders? It might be easier if the main qualifications were skill in leadership as demonstrated by success in business and powerful public speaking, for these would be obvious. No doubt in many churches elders and deacons have been chosen because of such prominence. But how does a church find those who have the less obvious spiritual and moral characteristics?

I know of one church that tried to avoid the pitfalls of a popular election by stressing the importance of recognizing those on whom God had put his approval, using the following means. On the Sunday before the annual meeting, the sermon was devoted to the nature of leadership in the church and the kind of people whom God chooses for that leadership. The qualifications for elders and deacons were clearly laid out. When the congregation came to the annual meeting, they were given an unusual ballot. At the top were words from the Pastoral Letters on the qualifications for elders and deacons. The congregation was asked to think of people who met those qualifications, whose lives reflected the values in 1 Timothy 3 and Titus 1.

From among those who were thus deemed worthy by these criteria they were to list names as they thought appropriate in response to one or more of three questions that followed. One question was (as best as I can remember it), "Whom do you respect enough to follow and obey as an elder?" The next question, "From whom have you learned the Word of God? Who has taught you Scripture and doctrine privately or publicly?" A final question was, "To whom would you go if you needed counseling in your spiritual life? Who has ministered to you in a pastoral way?" Different names could be entered with respect to the different questions.

The advantage of doing this is obvious. It focuses on the life and ministry of elders rather than on the popularity of well-known church figures. It also helps one to avoid simply choosing friends. In the church I have just referred to were some healthy surprises when this was done. Naturally, no one procedure will be appropriate in all churches. Inevitably as a church grows it becomes harder and harder for people to know who would best function as an elder.

The same church just mentioned addressed this latter problem at a later stage in its history in two ways. Prior to an annual meeting the congregation was invited to send nominations to the elders, who then considered these, added any proposals of their own, and made the "nominations" known to the congregation. After the congregation responded, if a person who was not chosen as an elder was nevertheless mentioned by a significant number of people, that individual was interviewed by the elders and, if there seemed to be potential, was invited to attend the elders' meetings for one year as an "elder in training." (They were excused from the meeting when confidential issues were discussed.) By the next annual meeting the reputation of that gifted person was usually strong enough to bring a majority response from the congregation. This avoided some of the problems that arise when nominations are accepted from the floor, which makes it difficult to screen any whose qualifications are questionable without embarrassment to a proposed nominee or to the nominator.

This system was not perfect, of course, and required further modification, but it is worth mentioning to provide ideas that may be useful as we attempt to rescue the sacred matter of identifying the elders of God's choice from the hazards of a political process. A modified procedure could be followed for deacons.

Can a divorced person be an overseer or elder? In the attempt to apply this passage about elders to the church today, the matter of remarriage after divorce enters more often than the question of remarriage after bereavement. Positions may vary as widely from each other as the following: (1) A person who has been divorced cannot be an elder even if not remarried, because divorce indicates some failure in the relationship. (2) Those who have remarried after divorce are ruled out simply because they have been married more than once. This position is usually taken more strongly regarding someone whose former spouse remains unmarried. (3) Such a person may be an elder if the divorce occurred before conversion. (4) Such a person may become an elder if fault lies with the former spouse, especially if that spouse committed adultery or committed abusive or perverted acts. (5) Such a person may be an elder only after making earnest attempts at reconciliation. (6) Divorce in itself does not prevent service as an elder. (7) Those who have been divorced and remarried may serve because God forgives and heals, and perhaps also because such persons can effectively counsel others because of their experience.

The issue is too complex for a full and responsible treatment here, but the following observations may be useful. (1) On the one hand, conversion makes a difference because the person is new in God's sight. On the other hand, marriage is a social, not just a Christian relationship, and while the person may be renewed, the circumstances have not changed and one or two families may continue to be adversely affected.

(2) On the one hand, even if the proposed elder was converted and even if major fault lay with the former spouse, divorce may indicate some personal flaw, lack of wisdom, or other characteristic in the proposed elder that needs counseling and healing. On the other hand, such consideration should apply to any elder candidate, because avoidance of divorce does not guarantee that the individual, the marriage, and the family are healthy.

(3) In today's complex society, blame is often hard to determine, and the state of a former spouse is likewise sometimes elusive. If the question is not only whether the former spouse has remarried but has had relations with another person, the whole matter becomes very cloudy.

(4) Is the ideal that an elder has had a perfect marriage and is an outstanding example, or has he had an imperfect marital experience, perhaps even because of former sin, and can therefore identify with and be a help to others in the church likewise troubled?

It is possible to be legalistic in such matters, and one does not want to legislate regarding internal church decisions on the pages of a commentary. This much, however, can be suggested: The standard that an elder should be "blameless" surely refers to one's present life. Paul himself writes of his former sins as forgiven, so that he could be an apostle. At the same time, sometimes a divorce and remarriage produce continuing effects that can hinder the testimony and work of an elder. Some matters may need to be cleared up before considering such a person for eldership. An elder who has gone through sin and forgiveness, divorce and remarriage, may indeed be a more wise and understanding counselor. At the same time, one does not have to be an elder to provide counseling

Whether or not a person has been divorced is not the major issue. That issue is whether the individual's life and care of his family now exemplify Christianity. It needs to be said too that there are times when a person's life is complex enough that one of the many other opportunities for ministry should be pursued rather than eldership. However, the testimony of a godly person who has survived a divorce clearly brought about by the former spouse, especially before conversion, may be a strong example of God's grace.

One further question is whether a person who has *never* been married can be an elder. Since in New Testament times an elder would have probably been a married male, it is not strange that the wording of the qualifications reflects that reality. It is true that a person who has never been married lacks experience that can be valuable in counseling, but that person may, through celibacy, have demonstrated a valuable self-discipline. Singleness need not be considered a barrier to eldership. The text does not make such a statement but deals rather with character and purity of sexual relationship.

Children. The matter of an elder candidate whose children are not only unbelievers but are living in disrespectful rebellion is difficult. This calls into question whether there are flaws in parenting that may render an elder unqualified to care for the church. A parent is not necessarily responsible for the fact that a son or daughter has not yet become a Christian; that is an individual decision that not even a parent can control. The parent may, nevertheless, have been so unfair and inconsistent that the child has recoiled against adopting the same faith. Family relations are so complex today that instances of parental abuse, or of "false memory syndrome" on the part of one who claims to have experienced child abuse, make it even more difficult to determine whether an elder candidate should receive sympathy or be rejected. Once again, it is vital that an elder be respected by children and in the community.

The importance today of having elders who are capable teachers. The nature and influence of postmodernism adds to the importance of the qualifications for elders. When the *statement* of Christian truths (even the apologetic defense of the faith) gains little response from today's "pagans," the *demonstrated reality* of truth in the lives of those who represent the church becomes all the more important. We Christians know that truth *is* important and that Scripture contains the saving gospel, but in order to communicate it to our world we must prove that it is genuine through its effectiveness in our lives.

With the combination of scandals about preachers and the critical pronouncements against the "gospel truth" popularized by the media in recent decades, this has become all the more crucial. Elders need to know and respond to these circumstances by more diligent study of God's Word and its doctrines, by sharpening their teaching skills, by understanding the times, and by applying the truth in their lives as well as in their teaching. It is no longer enough (if it ever was) for preachers and professors simply to address such issues. Others, especially those who have responsibility for the oversight of the church, need to give their minds, hearts, and lives to this task of living in the present world.

It may seem that, given the recent history of confrontations between so-called liberals and evangelicals or, in the early decades of the 1900s, between modernists and fundamentalists, that it would be harder today than formerly for those whose doctrine is not sound to escape being called into account. We also have the advantage of a number of excellent, theologically sound seminaries whose faculties, alumnae, and alumni are well equipped to identify heresy and deal with it. Nevertheless, it is still possible for churches to reduce the amount and intensity of their doctrinal preaching to the point where congregations are not able to deal knowledgeably with doctrinal issues. It is therefore urgent that elders be well taught, alert, and "able to teach."

Elders are also needed to keep an even hand in the assessment of trends in today's evangelical world. Differences of opinion on some important doctrines are growing even among evangelicals. While one hopes that pastors are well apprised of these matters, some may not be. And pastors who are theologically alert should make sure that elders also, if not formally educated in theology, are at least well taught on basic biblical and theological topics.

At the same time, because of the ease with which individual Christian opinion-makers can accrue, through publishing and various other media, a popularity and a perceived authority in matters that may lie beyond their expertise, elders must be aware of the influences on the congregation from outside the church. It is also possible for such opinion-makers to usurp the doctrinal authority of the local church. They can also unjustly diminish the reputation and consequently the ministry of leaders with whom they disagree, even where the issue may not be one of essential doctrine. In recent years matters in such diverse fields as political opinion, women's ministry, Bible translation, and church music have been addressed publicly and sometimes divisively and without sufficient knowledge. Elders can protect the flock of God from such detrimental influences as well as from heresy.

The message of the Pastoral Letters for us today is not only identification of a particular kind of heresy, whether it deals with myths or genealogies, the misuse of the law, or other deviations, but also—perhaps even more important in some circumstances—with the *way* such deviations are to be addressed. It will become increasingly clear in the study of the Pastorals that *how* the sound teacher confronts heresy shares the spotlight with what heresies to confront.

1 Timothy 3:8-13

𝕴

DEACONS, LIKEWISE, ARE to be men worthy of respect, sincere, not indulging in much wine, and not pursuing dishonest gain. ⁹They must keep hold of the deep truths of the faith with a clear conscience. ¹⁰They must first be tested; and then if there is nothing against them, let them serve as deacons.

¹¹In the same way, their wives are to be women worthy of respect, not malicious talkers but temperate and trustworthy in everything.

¹²A deacon must be the husband of but one wife and must manage his children and his household well. ¹³Those who have served well gain an excellent standing and great assurance in their faith in Christ Jesus.

PAUL BEGINS THIS section on deacons without any definition or description of their duties. We must conclude that they were well known both to the sender and to the recipient of this letter. The linguistic group of Greek words beginning *diakon-* was familiar enough so that anyone hearing it would know it referred to someone in a serving capacity. But nowhere in the New Testament is there a description of how they came into being as a recognized group or what their duties were.

The seven men who were appointed to care for the financial needs of a specific group of widows (Acts 6:1–6) may well be the forerunners of deacons. It is possible that as the church grew and needs increased that threatened to distract leaders from the ministry of the Word and prayer (as with the apostles in Acts 6), those who were appointed to meet those needs came to be called *deacons*. One problem with this scenario is that the qualifications for the men in Acts 6:3 ("full of the Spirit and wisdom") are not the same as those Paul mentions here. Since, however, there was undoubtedly a need in the developing church for people to function together in specific areas of service, and since there was an available word ("deacon") to describe such a group, it is not surprising that by the time of the Pastoral Letters this term was already in use. The word was dignified enough for Paul to have used it of himself and his associates as those who were servants (*diakonoi*) of the gospel (1 Cor. 3:5; Eph. 3:7) and of the new covenant (2 Cor. 3:6). Nevertheless, there were also separate groups called elders or overseers and deacons, and so the present passage goes on to give instructions for the latter.

Paul's concern with the demeanor and public reputation of church leaders continues with the deacons as "men worthy of respect." The word "men" is not in the Greek text; it is assumed from the gender of the noun *diakonos*. However, it should be noted that at the time of Paul there was no feminine form of that word.[1]"Worthy of respect" translates *semnos*, a word that describes a person of dignity, who both gives and receives appropriate respect. These two aspects of giving and receiving allow the use of the cognate noun *semnotes* to refer to the respectful attitude required of an overseer's children in 3:5. The same word appears in 2:4: ". . . quiet lives in all godliness and holiness [NRSV, dignity]." Since non-Christians, perhaps even "kings" and "those in authority" may take note of how the Christians are living, another possible translation, "integrity," may fit well in that context. The terminology here portrays a person who can be depended on to act with transparent integrity.

The next description, "sincere," further supports this. This word applies to someone whose speech does not betray conflicting dispositions toward others (lit., "not double-tongued," NRSV).

Like the overseer (3:3), the deacon must exercise moderation in drinking and in regard to money. The word *aischrokerdes*, translated "pursuing dishonest gain" (NIV), includes the idea of shame (*aischro-*). This accords with the recurring theme in the Pastorals of a reputation that will not bring shame on the gospel.

It may seem strange that there is a reference to doctrine ("the deep truths of the faith," v. 9) in connection with deacons, but not in the qualifications for overseers. The reason may be that this is taken for granted in elders but might not be thought of as important for deacons. By translating the Greek *mysterion* as "deep truths" rather than as "mystery," the NIV avoids a possible misunderstanding that there is some arcane doctrine that only certain people can grasp, but the NLT's "revealed truths" does this better. God's *mysterion* is his sovereign work throughout history, which he reveals stage by stage. For example, the mystery of the kingdom includes the truths that good and evil coexist until God's time for judgment (Matt. 13:1–52), that during the period when Israel is hardened, God shows mercy to Gentiles (Rom. 11:25–27), and

---

1. The unavailability of the feminine form of *diakonos* may provide the solution of the problem concerning Phoebe in Romans 16:1. While the verbal form means *serve* in general, the noun form in the New Testament usually indicates a position that is more than just *servant*. We cannot assume that since the form is masculine in 16:1 and since Phoebe was a women, it cannot mean "deacon" there and must be translated "servant." If the writer wanted to say she was a deacon, there was no other way to do it than to use the masculine form.

that in the church Jew and Gentile are brought together into one body (Eph. 3:2–6). Christ is the center of God's mystery (Col. 1:25–27).

Here the expanded phrase "mystery of the faith" (lit. trans.) expresses the broad body of essential truths. This accords with the meaning of the word "faith" characteristic of the Pastoral Letters: the truth that all believers should hold. Deacons must "keep hold" (with tenacious conviction) of these important doctrines "with a clear conscience." This is yet one more occasion where Paul insists on the personal integrity of those who lead and serve the church. But their own conscience is not sufficient; they "must first be tested" to be sure there is no occasion for blame before beginning their service as deacons.

Verse 11 interrupts the instructions about deacons with some directions concerning women. The word *gyne* can mean either "woman" or "wife," so it is impossible to tell whether these were the wives of the deacons or women who were serving as deacons. They are identified separately from the deacons addressed in verses 8–10 by the word translated "in the same way." On the one hand, since this verse occurs within the instructions for deacons, the behavior of their wives may be intended as part of their qualifications. If the *gynai* were women deacons, one might have expected them to be addressed separately from the passage. On the other hand, verse 11 could be a summary of verses 8–10 applied now to women deacons and inserted here before the next statement about being the husband of one wife, which would not apply to them.

It may also be that at first the women who served as deacons were the wives of deacons, so it would have been natural for them to be addressed within the section applying to their husbands. It seems strange that there are no similar instructions within the section on overseers. One would think that the character of their wives was at least as important as that of the wives of deacons. But if women were at that time serving as deacons but not as elders, and if those women were at first the wives of the deacons, the picture becomes clear.

Verse 12 about the deacons' family relationships corresponds to 3:2b, 4–5 about overseers (see comments), reinforcing the importance of marital fidelity and a strong family. The translation "have served" (v. 13) may imply some duration of service already, though this is not a necessary inference from the aorist tense of the participle, which can express action without reference to time. The descriptive words "excellent standing" and "great assurance in their faith in Christ Jesus" reveal what a noble task serving is. The "standing" (*bathmos*) can be moral, "a vantage ground for influence,"[2] but this word came later to be used for a position or rank in the church hierarchy. The

---

2. Lock, *Pastoral Epistles*, 41.

word "Christ" is used with, and precedes "Jesus," as it does almost every time in the Pastorals. It is striking that faithful service on the part of deacons strengthens their own "assurance [or boldness] in their faith."

MODELS OF SERVICE. The first direct mention of a group in the early church whose function was to care for others is in Acts 6:1–6.[3] They were to "wait on tables" to provide for the Greek-speaking widows, who had been neglected in the distribution of food. Their service was clearly not merely being "waiters," even though the immediate need was food, but also attending to the material needs of the widows. The group appointed to do this in Acts 6 is not identified by any title, but their work was certainly similar to what deacons would do.

Humanitarian service was carried out in various ways in the Hellenistic world. There were associations of people with like interests who cared for one another and reached out in times of need. It was natural that Christians, who were organized into identifiable social groups, would need to have some provision for responsibility in meeting human needs. These needs, however, extended beyond the material. If in the secular and Jewish communities there was dignity in serving other members of their group, this was also true in Christianity.

Moreover, the term *diakonos* had applied at times in Greek literature to those who were messengers. Whether the fact that Stephen, one of the seven men who were appointed in Acts 6, was also a messenger—in his case, an evangelist—has significance in this regard is hard to say, given the absence of the word *diakonos* in Acts 6. Paul describes himself as a "servant" of the gospel (Eph. 3:7; Col. 1:23), of the new covenant (2 Cor. 3:6), and of the church (Col. 1:25). While both witnessing and caring for others are the concern of all Christians, the specialization that is necessary in the functioning of the human body is required also for the functioning of the church, the body of Christ. Therefore it has been necessary for churches across the ages and the continents to make provision for the type of ministries carried out in the early church by deacons.

Abilities to help people and to provide administrative leadership are sandwiched in between the charismatic gifts of healing and tongues in the list of those whom "God has appointed" in 1 Corinthians 12:28, but they are the only gifts listed in verses 27–28 that are not repeated in verses 29–30 (beginning

---

3. Prior to this were the women who served the needs of Jesus and his disciples (Luke 8:1–3).

with "Are all apostles . . ."). Is this because these were abilities that *were* given to all, and so did not belong among the limited groups in those latter verses? Another possibility is that they were people whom God appointed, but whose work did not require a charismatic gift, only the will to serve.

Wherever the church exists, the models of leadership and service presented in 1 Timothy 3 are important. Those who assume fiscal responsibility in any form and for any purpose also assume a position of high visibility and accountability. Whether they are managing church funds internally or extending the church's help to those outside, their personal integrity is crucial. Any trace of greed (v. 8) is fatal among those who handle money, abuse of alcohol raises the question of dependability, and being "double-tongued" will torpedo any claim of honesty. Such leaders should also represent well the doctrinal convictions of the church, and must do so "with a clear conscience" (v. 9).

Difficulties in defining deacons. Given the facts that (1) there is no specific description of the duties of deacons in the New Testament, (2) the "Seven" in Acts 6 are not called "deacons" even though they served the church, and (3) there is a paucity of specific groups called "deacons" in the social background of the New Testament, it is hard to shape the "bridge" between contexts. We do know that the elders ruled, taught, and cared for the flock and that the deacons, by definition, performed services. We also noted that the apostle Paul considered himself and his associates to be servants of the gospel and of the new covenant, but such usage does not clarify the corporate function of those called *deacons*. Note too that Paul functioned like a deacon when he collected money for the needy in Jerusalem while on his missionary travels (2 Cor. 8:1–15).

Acts 14:23 tells us that Paul and Barnabas appointed elders, but the text does not mention deacons. At Philippi Paul does address both "overseers and deacons," along with the entire body of Christians (Phil. 1:1). Their omission from Acts 14 and the absence of deacons from the instructions to leaders in Titus 1:5–9 could lead one to infer either (1) that deacons were simply to be appointed as needed and did not exist as a standing committee in every church, or (2) that the elders, not the deacons, were the main leadership group, so that specific mention of the deacons depended on the circumstances. From Philippians and the parallel instructions to both elders and deacons here in 1 Timothy 3, it could be inferred that both groups had some leadership status in common, even if their duties were different.

It is appropriate to question whether church polity was still in flux at this time and, if so, whether there were still open options. The Scriptures seem to teach that the church should always recognize a body of leaders and teachers, whether or not they are called elders, and also should make provision for the care of individual and corporate needs, financial and whatever else may be appropriate. These people need not be called deacons, but they should always be present to serve.

The status and distinctive role of deacons could be helped if we had a greater knowledge of similar groups in the social background. The associations mentioned above were committed to meeting needs, but it is difficult to find an exact parallel to what was going on in the church. There were *diakonoi* in Hellenistic religions, where their function was to serve the various gods and goddesses. Jewish synagogues had a servant known as a *hazzan*, who served as caretaker of the building; but more important he was the attendant (Gk. *hyperetes*, Luke 4:20) who took care of the sacred scrolls of Scripture and taught Scripture in the children's schools. Whether this figure was a significant element in the concept of the Christian deacons is hard to determine.[4]

As time went on, the role of deacons became more defined. When Ignatius went to Rome in A.D. 107/108, a deacon went with him,[5] and we know that by this time the threefold office of bishops, presbyters, and deacons was taking shape. The deacons came to have an important role in collecting gifts for distribution to needy persons. However, over the centuries their importance tended to be reduced to the first step in holy orders, though Calvin and others attempted to restore a more significant ministry to them.

Naturally the need for a group devoted to service will vary with the kinds of service required by economic and other circumstances, including the availability of help from governmental sources. Care of the church building and other facilities will depend on the size and complexity of the facilities. Certainly some of the deacons' functions have to be carried out by paid employees, but if volunteer acts of mercy cease, the spirit of the early deacons in a caring community is gone.

SERVANT LEADERSHIP. THE term *servant leadership* came into prominence around the 1980s. In some management quarters it brought a needed corrective. It has proved to be a difficult ideal to bring into the corporate world, but is it really much easier in the church than in secular society? Christians certainly respect the example of Christ and have other fine models in Scripture and church history, but as long as we human beings have an innate desire for approval and even prominence, we will find it difficult to conform to the models.

---

4. See also 1 Cor. 4:1. The word appears frequently in the New Testament for guards and other Jewish officials.

5. Ignatius, *Philadelphians* 11.1.

One tricky thing about servant leadership is that by definition it implies a leadership position to begin with, and the church can accommodate only so many leaders. However, if we think of leadership as any ministry in which one person guides and develops the spirit of another, it can apply to even the most humble relationships. In the church, therefore, a person may be a servant leader either (1) by exercising leadership with a servant attitude, or (2) by serving in such a way as to lead by godly example. Either way, servanthood must characterize Christians, whether or not they serve publicly. "Ministry" should not be a prerogative or opportunity for dominance but a service, as the word *diakonos* makes clear (cf. 1 Peter 5:2–3).

Varieties of the ministry of deacons. The diaconate today signifies various things, including the first level in the episcopal hierarchy and what is in effect the ruling body in Baptist churches. Since the central element in the ministry of deacons is not leadership but service, the serving aspect is easily minimized in popular understanding. What the church needs, and what the surrounding community needs, is love enacted in the name of Christ.

There is, in fact, an agency serving in various areas of the country that has incorporated that ideal in its name: "Love INC" (INC = In the Name of Christ). I have been able to refer people with various real or perceived needs to this group. They are able to discern, by interview and sometimes by cross-checking the files of other local agencies, who can be helped in a genuine immediate need, who can best be served by financial counseling, job opportunities, and so on, and who wants a handout for selfish reasons. In one church I have served, there is a board of deacons to manage the facilities and handle other needs; there is also a "St. James Society" (from James 1:27), which helps people in various situations of need confidentially; and Love INC is also available. Neither Love INC nor the St. James Society are called "deacons," but they can do much of the work of deacons externally and internally.[6]

In many churches today, a "Deacon Board" is needed to deal with building repairs, salaries, fund-raising, and other aspects of church finances. In that they operate in areas of material need, they embody some of the ministries probably carried out by New Testament deacons. It is easy, however, for such a board to lose the "heart" of their calling, even though fixing a leaky roof is of service to God's people and even though they may forward money to many needy individuals through their benevolent fund.

Goals. To fulfill the goals of the early deacons, three things are necessary. (1) Churches must take initiative to seek men and women who have the moral and spiritual integrity described in 1 Timothy 3. (2) Such people need

---

6. There are, of course, other parachurch and world organizations dealing with major needs that no local organization can possibly handle.

to have the vision, heart, and will to serve, already demonstrating this before their public appointment in acts of practical kindness. They should *be* deacons before they are *named* deacons. (3) The church should make this an intentional ministry on behalf of the whole body. It should be visible to the community at large, so that the community may not only *experience* but also *perceive* the loving ministry of the church. It is true that the left hand should not know what the right is doing and that it is wrong to "trumpet" one's giving (Matt. 6:2–4). At the same time Jesus said, "Let your light shine before [people], that they may see your good deeds and praise your Father in heaven" (5:16).

What, then, is the difference between being a servant and being a deacon? The key may be found in Romans 12 and 1 Corinthians 12. Just as there is a group of recognized leaders called *elders*, while at the same time these passages refer to individuals gifted and serving as leaders, so there is a group of recognized leaders called *deacons*, while there is also a reference in Romans 12:7 to serving (where the word *diakonia* is used). One can be an active servant without being a deacon. Just as one does not have to be an elder in order to lead others spiritually, neither does one have to be a deacon in order to serve others helpfully (cf. 1 Cor. 12:28).

Yet there is need in the church to have people selected as deacons and be given a charge to act responsibly on behalf of the whole church. They care for people in practical as well as spiritual ways, handle the financial affairs of the church without greed or deceit, and provide the facilities needed by the church. This goes beyond just an individual, personal ministry. It is a corporate commitment of deacons, appointed and accountable to the church. Although the teaching of Jesus about light and good deeds quoted above is a word to all Christians, deacons have the special privilege of fulfilling this on behalf of the whole congregation.

1 Timothy 3:14–16

※

ALTHOUGH I HOPE to come to you soon, I am writing you these instructions so that, ¹⁵if I am delayed, you will know how people ought to conduct themselves in God's household, which is the church of the living God, the pillar and foundation of the truth. ¹⁶Beyond all question, the mystery of godliness is great:

> He appeared in a body,
> was vindicated by the Spirit,
> was seen by angels,
> was preached among the nations,
> was believed on in the world,
> was taken up in glory.

BOTH THE FIRST personal singular reference in verses 14–15 and the description of personal circumstances ("I hope to come ... [but] ... if I am delayed ...") lead the reader to assume that the writer is Paul. If this were constructed by some follower of Paul, it would have been either a tour de force or outright deception to make it appear as if Paul were writing it himself.[1] Concern over this possible delay providentially caused Paul not only to write the instructions in this chapter, but, in that connection, to affirm the importance of the church and to append the creedal statement in verse 16.

The purpose of this letter is mainly to deal with false teaching and teachers, but in the need for truth and personal integrity it is also concerned with church relationships as God's "household." Paul emphasizes this by concluding the section on overseers and deacons with a statement of his purpose, "that ... you will know how people ought to conduct themselves in God's household ... the church," in which the household terminology appears again (see also 3:4–5, 12).

But the passage goes on to emphasize doctrine: "the church of the living God, the pillar and foundation of the truth." This wording calls to mind the

---

1. For a position opposite to the above, see the descriptive language in Bassler's commentary referring to "the letter's fictional situation.... The resulting scenario provides an ideal pretext for introducing the letter's exhortations ..." (*1 Timothy, 2 Timothy, Titus*, 72).

truth of Peter's great confession, "You are the Christ, the Son of the living God," and Jesus' response, "on this rock [i.e., the *foundation*] I will build my church" (Matt. 16:16, 18).[2] The words "pillar" and "foundation" may be intended to recall the solid structure of God's house, the temple, in the Old Testament.

The introduction to Paul's great creedal statement in verse 16 begins with an affirmation, "beyond all question." While this could apply to the reliability of the creed, grammatically it refers to the description "great" in the predicate nominative position. No one can disagree that the creed is indeed great, so that is what lies "beyond all question." If the reliability of the creed itself were in view, Paul would probably have used instead the familiar phrase, "Here is a trustworthy saying." His point here is the magnificence of the revealed truth called "the mystery of godliness."

The word "mystery" (*mysterion*; see comments on 3:9) describes God's revelation of his sovereign work throughout history. In this context Paul may be thinking of Christ as the center of the mystery (cf. Col. 1:25–27). Christ was not known until his revelation through the Incarnation and further stages of his experience (e.g., "declared with power to be the Son of God by his resurrection from the dead"). "Godliness" (*eusebeia*; see also comments on this word in 2:2) is a broad term used in Greek literature to mean religion or personal piety. Christ is the source of the Christian religion and of our spiritual life (cf. 1 Cor. 1:30). Therefore "the mystery of godliness" is Christ himself, revealed and vindicated.

The hymnic form of this remarkable statement calls for an analysis of its structure.[3] While that structure is obviously less important than the content, to study it helps the reader to focus carefully on content and its points of emphasis. Among the possibilities are the following:

(1) Chronological

He appeared in a body,	Jesus' incarnation
was vindicated by the Spirit,	Jesus' earthly life

---

2. See also "how you turned to God from idols to serve the *living* and *true God*" (1 Thess. 1:9), and "no one can lay any *foundation* other than the one already laid, which is Jesus Christ" (1 Cor. 3:11, italics added).

3. The origin of the hymn is unknown. It is assumed to be a hymn because of its structure, though it is not clear whether it was a hymn (or fragment of a hymn) that Paul incorporated or whether he composed it himself. We accept it as part of Scripture in its canonical context. The fact that the first word in the original text probably was "who" (given an "A" rating in the UBS text on the basis of extensive early manuscript support) rather than "God" is usually thought to indicate a hymn, though opinions are changing on Phil. 2:5–11 in that regard.

was seen by angels,	Jesus' resurrection
was preached among the nations,	missionary proclamation
was believed on in the world,	response to this proclamation
was taken up in glory.	Jesus' acceptance and in glorification in heaven

The obvious problem here is that chronologically the last phrase would seem to belong earlier in the sequence. Also, there is sufficient ambiguity in the creed (the meaning of "vindicated [or justified] by the Spirit" and the time when he "was seen by angels") that it is hard to make a firm determination of the chronology. The vindication by the Spirit could have taken place at the resurrection (cf. 1 Peter 3:18, "made alive by the Spirit"), and Jesus could have been "seen by angels" at his ascension. But the word in the last phrase for "taken up" refers in Acts 1:2 to the ascension and also appears in Luke 9:51, almost certainly an allusion to the ascension. How can this have been preceded by the missionary proclamation and the nations' response to it?

(2) Alternating

Earthly	*Heavenly*
He appeared in a body.	. . . . .was vindicated by the Spirit,
Heavenly	*Earthly*
was seen by angels.	. . . . .was preached among the nations,
Earthly	*Heavenly*
was believed on in the world.	. . . . .was taken up in glory.

This scheme gives more attention to the literary structure and is consistent within itself. Its bipolar structure causes the reader (and speaker) to focus on the two loci of the revelation of Christ.

(3) Emphatic

The reappearance near the middle of each line of the Greek suffix -*the* (to indicate the third singular aorist passive form) draws attention to the verbs. Each verb expresses a kind of vindication, manifestation, or attestation. This is embedded in the actual structure of the Greek text and stands whatever other scheme may be proposed.

(4) Chiastic

A. He appeared in a body,	Manifestation on earth
B. was vindicated by the Spirit,	Acceptance in spiritual realm
C. was seen by angels,	Comprehension by heavenly beings
C.' was preached among the nations,	Comprehension by human beings
B.' was believed on in the world,	Acceptance in earthly realm
A.' was taken up in glory.	Manifestation in heaven

Since chiasm (a literary structure that involves the repetition, in reverse order, of words, phrases, or, as here, ideas) was an acceptable structural scheme in ancient times to draw attention to the successive ideas and their relationships, it is legitimate to consider the possibility of one here. But one must be careful not to go beyond the intention of the author and force such a scheme on a text improperly.

THE HYMN IN **its context.** This hymn is a magnificent conclusion to chapters 2–3. But it is more than that—it is a climax and a crux. It is a *climax* in that it is a distinctive literary form, it comprises essential truths relevant to the preceding verses, and it brings the reader to a high point of praise. It is a *crux* in that it forms a pivotal doctrinal hinge between the preceding chapters, where Paul has been discussing "how people ought to conduct themselves in God's household" (3:15), and chapter 4, where Paul discusses how to confront the heresy he first mentioned in chapter 1.

Paul has made it clear that wise, godly ministry and leadership in the church are essential to the maintenance of doctrinal purity and that doctrine and behavior are closely related. As noted above, the qualifications for eldership in 1 Timothy do not include a doctrinal test. That omission is significant in that it purposefully puts the weight on personal morality and character. But this hymn shows that doctrine lies at the heart of it all. It is profoundly Christological. It draws attention, whichever literary scheme is closest to the original intention, to the various events that brought glory to our Lord. The dominant idea is that he who was one with the Father in the eternal past and unseen by human beings, was revealed at his incarnation. By the Holy Spirit, by the heavenly beings who welcomed him on his ascension, and by those human beings who heard and believed the preaching about him, he has been accepted and honored. The images of this hymn are representative, but not exhaustive. They provide both a means of praise (one can hardly simply *study* this passage!) and a model for further praise.[4]

Hymnology and Christology. There are some great hymns to Christ that celebrate the successive steps of his ministry, death, resurrection, present glory, and coming glory. Others range over aspects of his being and works. Among these are "Crown Him With Many Crowns" (Matthew Bridges and Godfrey Thring), "Thou Who Wast Rich Beyond All Splendour" (Frank Houghton), "At the Name of Jesus" (Caroline Maria Noel), "Jesus! The Name High Over All" (Charles Wesley), "The Head That Once Was Crowned With Thorns" (Thomas Kelly), "Join All the Glorious Names" (Isaac Watts), and "We Come, O Christ, to Thee" (E. Margaret Clarkson). The two most recent of these are those by Houghton and by Clarkson. We will comment on the contribution of contemporary praise songs under the Contemporary Significance section.

The truths that are so strikingly presented in the Christological hymn of verse 16 have endured through the centuries and within the multiple societies that have succeeded that of first-century Ephesus. The fact that Scripture includes such a condensed, structured hymn should validate the enterprise of reproducing the essential doctrines about Christ in ways that are acceptable vehicles of truth in each culture. Nations, tribes, and various groups have regularly conveyed truth for generations in many different ways, such as songs, narratives, anecdotes, actions, and interactive dialogue. There is a "story to tell to the nations," and it calls on the best of our God-given abilities to tell it well.

The church year and the lectionary can provide a framework and biblical context within which to stir remembrance of the major aspects of Jesus' life and ministry. But there are other ways as well. It is not necessary, as in the Middle Ages, to paint or enact the events in Jesus' life, but there are ways to make the story clear in each age. The "Jesus Film" has done this marvelously in our day.

The function of the hymn of verse 16 is apparently to remind the believers at Ephesus, through Timothy, about the foundation of the church that cannot be destroyed by false teachers. The doctrine of Christ (Christology) is the unchanging sine qua non of Christian theology. Since there will always be opponents of the gospel, this hymn is always necessary and foundational.

The inclusion of a hymn that omits the cross is not an oversight, since its main theme, the coming of Christ as an epiphany, with his vindication and acceptance in heaven and earth, is appropriate here. The epiphany theme is

---

4. Young (*Theology of the Pastoral Letters*, 59–68) summarizes this passage together with others on Christology in the Pastorals.

repeated at various points in the Pastoral Letters (1 Tim. 6:14; 2 Tim. 1:10; 4:1, 8; Titus 2:11, 13; 3:4). Sub- or anti-Christian teachings are often veiled in vague religious language. In contrast, this hymn on the manifestation of Christ is by its very nature open. These things, as Paul said, "[were] not done in a corner" (Acts 26:26).

PROCLAIMING THE TRUTH of Christ. The centrality of Christology needs constant emphasis. The years leading up to the writing of this commentary have witnessed a renewed interest in the Jesus of the Gospels, an interest that has unfortunately been marked by the skepticism of the "Jesus Seminar" and resulting publications. At the same time notable evangelical and Catholic leaders have declared their common allegiance to certain central doctrines, including the deity of Christ. Whatever other areas of agreement are necessary for cooperation in social, moral, or evangelistic enterprises, Christology must always be the essential foundation for any fellowship.

In 1998 the Southern Baptists held their annual convention in the Mormon territory of Salt Lake City. This occasioned considerable discussion on both sides as to whether the Mormons should be considered genuine Christians. One of the issues regarding Mormons continues to be the meaning attached to biblical terms concerning Christ and his sacrificial death, resurrection, and ascension. The present hymn contributes significantly to all Christological discussion.

Numerous studies of the religion of "Baby Boomers" and of "Generation X" have pointed out that contemporary hymnology is more an expression of personal intimacy with God than a static statement of objective truths about God. (It should also be noted, however, that some of the most passionate hymns about Christ came from monasteries in the Middle Ages.) Also for this generation the learning of truth must be accompanied by its application. Eternal truths must have immediacy. A distant God must also be immanent. That which is static must be transformed into what is active. Aimlessness and hopelessness must be addressed.

The message of the Christological hymn in 3:16 is appropriate to these concerns. Its very structure rests on verbs rather than nouns. It centers on the Christ who came to us and the response he has received and deserves to receive further from us. The proclamation of Christ evokes a response. There is a sense of purpose and hope as Christ moves, so to speak, from his incarnation to his ascension. Those who feel misunderstood can identify with the Christ who needed vindication. Those who feel alone as Christians can be encouraged by the reminder of how widespread faith in Christ really is in our world. Those who are self-centered can be reminded by this Christocentric hymn where the center of our attention and affection belong. Along with all this there must still be an objective Christological foundation.[5]

Traditional and contemporary church music. If any generation has needed to sing, it is ours, though in many ways we are passive in our music. As we go along with our portable CD players, it is hard to conceive of a past generation that did not have CDs, radios, TV, or multimedia computers. We may not sing ourselves as much as our ancestors did, but we do love to listen. However, apart from the productions of perhaps one classical music station per major city, what we hear on most stations appeals by its beat and emotion rather than by soaring melodic lines, much less by cerebral counterpoint.

Much traditional Christian hymnody, it is said, lacks the characteristics that move us today, such as a focus on single themes. Those who criticize contemporary "praise songs" sometimes maintain that they are not as biblical as the old hymns. While that has been true of many "choruses" and other songs of recent decades, it is not true of the best of contemporary praise songs. Many of them are quotations from Scripture, often from the Psalms. A strong defense of contemporary worship music by theologian John M. Frame appeared in 1997.[6]

Each period of church music has had its emphases and its omissions. In planning a series of worship services that will be uplifting and honoring to God, we should make sure that there is a rich and varied doctrinal content. If there is enthusiastic emphasis on joy and victory, we need to be sure that attention is also given to the cross, suffering, and discipleship. We want to be careful not only to celebrate Christ, but also God as Father and the person and work of the Holy Spirit. The exaltation and present intercession of Christ at the right hand of God the Father seems rarely mentioned if at all, and the present hymn with its focus on the heavenly reception of Christ could well be incorporated to help rectify that neglect.

One's private devotional times can also be immensely enriched by meditating on hymns from various periods of Christian history. It is the nature of hymn books to have the hymns topically listed, a means of making sure that the great doctrines of the faith are covered. One way to construct a list of possible hymns and songs for use in church worship is to start with such

---

5. It is a mistake to think that this has been absent from contemporary worship music. One thinks of one of the earlier of the contemporary songs, Melody Greene's "There Is a Redeemer," as a fine example.

6. See his *Contemporary Worship Music: A Biblical Defense* (Phillipsburg, N.J.: Presbyterian and Reformed, 1997).

a passage as 1 Timothy 3:16, examining its doctrinal content, its usefulness in offering praise, and its potential in instructing the Christians who sing it.

Other key passages can be also examined. The Psalms, of course, are obvious, but again they do not contain the whole range of biblical theology. Colossians 1 and Philippians 2 have yielded great hymns and praise songs. But important as they are, one's own private worship of God can also profit from such carefulness in spanning the various doctrinal themes in hymns and songs and weaving them into the time alone in God's presence.

Preachers bear the responsibility of conveying the "mystery of our religion" in many sermons over a lifetime. The heresies that threaten us will differ from those at Ephesus, but the essential Christological message is relevant and must be proclaimed over and over. The individual verbal affirmations in verse 16 ("appeared," "was vindicated," "was seen," "was preached," "was believed on," "was taken up") move from the presentation of Christ and his claims to his earthly and heavenly acceptance. This is the goal of Christian evangelism and missions: faithful preaching and teaching, effective witness and apologetics. To reaffirm this is the constant joyful task of believers.

1 Timothy 4:1–5

🔥

THE SPIRIT CLEARLY says that in later times some will abandon the faith and follow deceiving spirits and things taught by demons. ²Such teachings come through hypocritical liars, whose consciences have been seared as with a hot iron. ³They forbid people to marry and order them to abstain from certain foods, which God created to be received with thanksgiving by those who believe and who know the truth. ⁴For everything God created is good, and nothing is to be rejected if it is received with thanksgiving, ⁵because it is consecrated by the word of God and prayer.

"THE SPIRIT CLEARLY says" in 4:1 prompts the question, "Where?" When Paul addressed the elders of the Ephesian church—the same leaders who were now facing heresy—he warned of coming doctrinal defection (Acts 20:17–35). In the course of that talk he referred to the Holy Spirit both in connection with his own actions and with the elders' appointment. We know from this and other instances that Paul was conscious of the Spirit's direct activity in connection with that church. We also know that the Spirit inspired Paul in the writing of his letters, which included predictions about coming defections (e.g., 2 Thess. 2:1–11). In 1 Corinthians 7, when Paul did not have a direct command of the Lord Jesus on a matter, he wrote, not his own opinion, but what he understood the Spirit of God was teaching (cf. vv. 10–12, 40).

We know too that Jesus predicted the coming of deceitful false prophets (Matt. 24:11; Mark 13:22). Among the letters to the seven churches in Revelation 2–3 was one to Ephesus, which predicted the church's opposition to false apostles (Rev. 2:2). These letters were given to John by the glorified Lord, but also said to express "what the Spirit says to the churches" (2:7; see also 2:11, 17, 29; 3:6, 13, 22). Therefore we know that what Jesus said was also what the Spirit said: "The Lord is the Spirit" (2 Cor. 3:17). Paul therefore may have been referring to the Lord Jesus' teaching about coming heresy, to warnings the Spirit included in the inspired Scriptures, or to prophecies the Spirit gave to believers and communicated to the churches in the Lord's name (1 Cor. 14:26).

"Later times," an expression found only in this passage, picks up the concept of time as viewed in phases. Jewish thinkers spoke of the present age and the age to come. From the Christian perspective we are already participating in the blessing of the coming age, since the Messiah has come. While conscious of a wait until he returns, we are in the new age, in the kingdom, and already experiencing the "heavenly realms" (Eph. 2:6; cf. Col. 3:1-4). Hebrews sets up a contrast between "the past [when] God spoke to our forefathers through the prophets" and "these last days," when "he has spoken to us by" the one who is no less than his own Son (Heb. 1:1-2). These "last days" are characterized by the pouring out of God's Spirit on men and women, young and old, and the availability of salvation by calling on the name of the Lord (Joel 2:28-32; Acts 2:17-21), but also by "scoffers" who reject God's truth (2 Peter 3:3; Jude 18).

In 1 Timothy 4:1 Paul refers to those who "abandon the faith." The verb used here (*aphistemi*) occurs in a number of passages in classical Greek literature, in the LXX, as well as in the New Testament to describe an act of separation or withdrawal.[1] The implication in its use here is not simply that they carelessly fall away, but that they abandon or "renounce" (NRSV) the faith (i.e., the doctrine) that they formerly held.

This text gives us a behind-the-scenes glimpse and reveals that the real perpetrators of heresy are not only the heretics but the evil spiritual forces that deceived and taught them. This recalls Ephesians 6:12, which informs us that our spiritual battle is not against human beings but against unseen spiritual powers. The word "deceive" (*planao*) occurs several times in the Pastoral Letters. Paul refers pointedly to religious deception,[2] and such terminology marked disputes among preachers in paganism as well as in the sphere of Christianity.

The apostle's use of the active and passive forms of that verb, "deceiving and being deceived," occurs notably in 2 Timothy 3:13. Two further points of interest there bear on the present passage. (1) One is the reference to "evil men and impostors [*goetes*]." That latter word was a common term of abuse in the first century (a "sorcerer"), describing people perpetrating a scam of some sort, such as used to wander across the Roman empire, cheating or swindling

---

1. A few examples among many in the Old Testament are Gen. 14:4; Num. 14:9; 2 Chron. 21:8; 29:6 (where it means to be unfaithful in a context of turning away from the Lord and his temple); Ezek. 20:38 (where it means to rebel). It occurs several times in the New Testament in a neutral or good sense (e.g., "turn away" in 2 Tim. 2:19). The negative meaning appears in the interpretation of the parable of the soils in Luke 8:13, regarding those who "fall away" in the time of testing. In Heb. 3:12-14 those who "turn away from the living God" are contrasted with those who are not "hardened by sin's deceitfulness" but "hold firmly till the end." The related noun, *apostasia*, is the source of our English word "apostasy" and is used in 2 Thess. 2:3 for the coming rebellion, when the "man of lawlessness" is revealed.

2. See esp. 2 Thess. 2:3-5.

people. Not only Christian, but pagan wandering preachers accused each other of being a *goes* or a *magos* (in its meaning of a sinister magician). Those who went to hear such persons had to be on guard against the religious or philosophical scam artists departing from the truth and deceiving others.[3]

(2) A second point of comparison between this passage and 2 Timothy 3:13 is that both describe a worsening situation (the impostors "will go from bad to worse"), although the latter does not use the phrase "later times." In his Olivet eschatological discourse, Jesus predicted that impostors would "deceive even the elect—if that were possible" (Matt. 24:24).

Paul's emphasis in 1 Timothy 4, however, is not so much on the human deceivers as on the supernatural powers that cause people to be deceived. They are called "spirits" and "demons," and as such have superhuman influence. These evil spirit beings work through evil human beings, "hypocritical liars." Three things characterize them: They are not what they seem to be, what they teach is false, and their own consciences are burned to the point of insensibility.

The two false teachings cited in verse 3—"forbid[ding] people to marry" and "order[ing] them to abstain from certain foods"—are not easy to understand. A clue may be found in 2 Timothy 2:18, where the teaching that the resurrection is past receives stern disapproval. The idea that Christians have already entered the next age has, as we have seen, an aspect of truth, but not the way it was apparently being taught by these heretics. For them this is not a matter of the new life in the Spirit or of personal discipline in cases where marriage may, under certain circumstances, be considered unwise.[4] Nor does the second element seem to be fully explicable in terms of personal dietary convictions, Jewish food laws, or refraining from meat offered to idols.[5] Rather, the error seems to be a judgment against all marriage and against certain foods[6] as being wrong in themselves.

This conclusion is strongly countered by Paul's statement in verse 4 that "everything God created is good." If this false teaching has some affinity with the prohibitions Paul criticizes in Colossians 2:21 ("Do not handle! Do not taste! Do not touch!"), it may share with the Colossian heresy—and other teachings that eventually took the form we know as Gnosticism—the premise that the material world, or some aspects of it, were evil. The only

---

3. For a description of how wandering preachers frequently denigrated each other using such terminology, see Walter Liefeld, *The Wandering Preacher As a Social Figure in the Roman Empire* (Ann Arbor: University Microfilms, 1968), 272–99.

4. Paul deals with that in 1 Cor. 7, and in the course of his instructions he makes it clear that marriage in itself is not wrong or unspiritual.

5. Paul deals with such matters in, among other places, Rom. 14 and 1 Cor. 8.

6. The NIV inserts the word "certain" before foods. Since the word is general, and we may assume that these people did eat, they must have selected some and rejected other types of food.

clearly relevant information we have in 1 and 2 Timothy, however, is that some taught the resurrection was past. In some way the heretics were imagining an altered or heightened spiritual environment, in which marriage and certain foods were unnecessary, even wrong.[7]

Paul indicates that such ideas are false when he says that people who "believe and . . . know the truth" receive the food that God created with thanksgiving. We may assume by analogy that Paul would say the same about marriage, but as the passage goes on it deals only with food. Close observation of the semantic patterns is necessary here:

God created [food] . . .
> [which false teachers **forbid**]
>> to be **received**
>>> with **thanksgiving**
>>>> by those who believe and know **the truth**.

Everything God created is good
> and nothing is to be **rejected** [as false teachers do when they forbid food]
>> if it is **received**
>>> with **thanksgiving**
>>>> because it is consecrated by **the word of God** and prayer.

To reject food is to negate God's creative work. To receive it and be thankful are to acknowledge that work and our dependence on God. There is a vital cause-and-effect connection between the true God and the created world, something the Gnostics later denied because of their mistaken idea that the world was evil and could only have been created by an intermediary, not directly by God himself. The false teachers were clearly thankless, a sin that lay at the core of human rebellion against God (Rom. 1:21).

How much the confusion of these heretics may have been a distortion of Jewish food laws is not certain. Peter himself had to recognize that no food was "impure that God has made clean" (Acts 10:15). Jesus had earlier dealt with the misapplication of Old Testament dietary laws by stating that "nothing outside a man can make him 'unclean' by going into him" (Mark 7:15). The emphasis on receiving implies a conscious act of accepting food from the

---

7. Towner, offers a valuable observation: "But it is also possible that this behavior reflected the attempt to enact the life of resurrection paradise by following the model given in Genesis 1 and 2, before the fall into sin" (Towner, *1–2 Timothy & Titus*, 104–5). He refers to Jesus' teaching that in the resurrection there will be no marriage (Matt. 22:30) and suggests that "vegetarianism seems to have been the rule in Eden/paradise."

hand of the God who created it. From the basic dependence on God for our "daily bread" (Matt. 6:11) to the experiencing of the beautiful mystery of marriage (Eph. 5:32), also rejected by the false teachers, we are to receive God's gifts with thanksgiving.

Thanksgiving, prayer, and the Word of God render the food legitimate to eat. While this does not mean that a formal act of blessing is necessary every time food is taken, it does suggest that an acknowledgment of its source and of the fact that "everything God created is good" is appropriate and desirable. Each account of the Lord Jesus' feeding of the five thousand and the four thousand is careful to mention that he gave thanks (Matt.14:19; 15:36; Mark 6:41; 8:6; Luke 9:16; John 6:11), and, of course, Jesus gave thanks before breaking the bread and distributing the wine at the Last Supper (Matt. 26:26–27; Mark 14:22–23; Luke 22:17, 19). Also Jewish table benedictions have a long tradition.

We know that what is secular can be "sanctified," that is, given over to God and considered to belong to him. If an unbelieving spouse and the couple's children can be "sanctified" in the sense of 1 Corinthians 7:14, certainly God's gift of food can be consecrated and eaten, no matter what doctrinal reason the heretics may have to the contrary. This consecration is accomplished by "the word of God and prayer."

In spite of several suggestions as to what specific Scripture Paul has in mind in verse 5, the use within Paul's writings of the expression "word of God" has a broader referent than the Old Testament. More to the point, when the Pastorals refer to *specific* biblical texts, the phrase "word of God" is *not* used to introduce them (1 Tim. 5:18; 2 Tim. 2:19); and when the Pastorals employ the *single* word *logos* ("word"), it does not refer to a specific text (see comments on 4:6; 2 Tim. 2:15; 4:2; Titus 1:3). This does not mean that Scripture is ruled out, but most likely the author has in mind the truth of God (known, of course, mainly from Scripture) that is recalled in the prayer of thanksgiving.[8]

FALSE TEACHING IN the "later times." This section relates not only to the foregoing passages with regard to the ongoing concerns about false teachers but also, in a particular way, to the hymn of 3:16. There is a contrast between the open truths of the hymn and the

---

8. Kelly's proposal has merit, that the prayer is "the actual prayer of blessing" and the Word "the excerpts from Scripture which, according to Jewish custom, formed [the prayer's] content" (Kelly, *Pastoral Epistles*, 97)—if one allows that along with "excerpts from Scripture" one could include "truths from Scripture."

deceitful lies described in 4:1–3.[9] The insidious nature of the false teachings described in this chapter as well as the teachings themselves characterize the "later times."

What period of history does this refer to? It is not unusual to find in the oral or written traditions of a culture a tribal memory of an early golden age. Such an age was remembered as a time of great accomplishment and peace. Civilizations rise and fall. Biblical history itself chronicles cycles of degeneration. In fact, the dispensational analysis of history concluded that every "dispensation" ended in failure as regards the ability of people to please God. Beyond this dreary path of failure lies what both Old and New Testaments speak of as the "day of the Lord," a day on which God acts decisively. Those who complacently expect God to bring them special blessings when that time comes, while irresponsibly disobeying God, need to learn that the day of the Lord for them means not joy but judgment (Amos 5:18).

The expression used in verse 1, "later times," does not refer to that specific point in time, but it does contain the idea of a period preceding that day. It recalls the somewhat similar phrase "the last days." A form of that phrase is used in Hebrews 1 to refer to the time of Christ in contrast to the time of the Old Testament (Heb. 1:2). Peter, in Acts 2:17, uses the same phrase to interpret Joel 2:28. In other passages the phrase looks ahead to a significant time of God's decisive action (Isa. 2:2; Hos. 3:5; Mic. 4:1; John 6:39–40, 44, 54; 11:24; 12:48; James 5:3; 2 Peter 3:3). In both this passage (1 Tim. 4:1) and in 2 Timothy 3:1 (which refers to "terrible times"), a description of the last days seems to be intended to alert the readers of what has already begun to take place. While times of greater moral degeneration may yet come, there would seem to be little point in Paul's citing these times in the context of the Pastoral Letters if the conditions they describe were not taking place at the time of this correspondence.

The three forms of the expression just cited ("in these last days," Heb. 1:2; "later times," 1 Tim. 4:1; "last days," 2 Tim. 3:1) seem to allow that the conditions described could, in one form or another, take place in any period of intense moral decline or doctrinal deviation during the church age and prior to the "day of the Lord." It is useful to see what problems may be expected to recur during these last days. (1) One problem is departure from the faith (see also 2 Peter 2:1–22; Jude 8–16, which spell this out vividly). (2) Behind

---

9. There is no grammatical break between 3:16 and 4:1. The use of a conjunction (*de*) signals a connection. It is true that it is customary in Greek grammar to connect most sentences with a conjunction, usually omitting it only when a new section or topic is being introduced, but when present its function must be observed. In this case it is not a strong conjunction (indicated only loosely by "now" in NRSV and omitted in NIV), yet its presence does indicate a level of continuity.

this apostasy are evil spirits. Surely not all error comes directly from Satan or demons, but repudiation of the faith and of truth is often demonically inspired. The devil is "the father of lies" (John 8:44). (3) The demonic spirits have human associates through whom they do their work; thus it is not surprising that his teachings "come through hypocritical liars" (1 Tim. 4:2).

Principles for receiving God's gifts. The characteristics of the false doctrines that follow in the text may stem from a Gnostic-like, if not actually pre-Gnostic asceticism. The prohibitions may seem at first so particular and limited in scope that it is difficult to offer general principles dealing with them. Mere abstinence from specific foods is not unusual for a culture, but denying people the right to marry is uncommon except in some cults and religious orders.

Paul outlines several principles here that apply to any rules proposed in regard to these matters. (1) All things have been created by God and are, as stated repeatedly in Genesis 1, good. (2) God's created gifts are to be received and not rejected. (3) God's gifts are to be received with thanksgiving. (4) The consuming of God's gifts should take place with an understanding of the truth and with faith and is to be consecrated by the Word of God and prayer.

It is a paradox that many people who have sought to be religious have tried to do so by rejecting God's own created gifts. This is not the same as Christian fasting, which is a temporary exclusion of food or whatever else might distract us from full devotion to God. Normally, however, the Christian gladly accepts all of God's provisions for a healthy and contented life.[10] The problem with centering on what one does or does not consume as a rule for spirituality is that it directs attention away from God as creator and provider and from the true nature and practice of spirituality. "For the kingdom of God is not a matter of eating and drinking, but of righteousness, peace and joy in the Holy Spirit" (Rom. 14:17).

FACING THE "LAST days." Wherever we may be today within the total span of the church age and however far we may be into the "last days," most would agree that there seems to be intense activity now on the part of deceiving spirits. Beliefs and practices that were usually only confronted by overseas missionaries a few generations ago are now found throughout North America. This is not the same as demon possession (also a threat in our times), which is the control of an individual by one or more evil spirits. What is in view in the present passage is the evil activity of blinding people to truth and persuading them of error.

---

10. The sins of greed and excess are dealt with in ch. 6.

The risen Jesus told Paul to go to the Gentiles "to open their eyes and turn them from darkness to light, and from the power of Satan to God" (Acts 26:18). Even persons who do not exhibit evidence of demonic control can be under the "dominion of darkness" and need to be brought "into the kingdom of the Son [God] loves" (Col. 1:13). Satan also deceives nations (Rev. 20:3). When these are added to the "made in America" cults, the opposition to biblical truth is formidable. The spirit of pluralism and postmodernism makes it difficult to confront competing systems of belief without incurring the charge of intolerance. In the 1960s many Christian parents were dismayed and perplexed when their children, who had grown up under orthodox Christian teaching, turned to Eastern religions. Later decades saw the coming of "New Age" teachings.

The situation has grown increasingly complex since then. Scripture tells us that one of the gifts God gives his church is distinguishing between spirits (1 Cor. 12:10). This gift is urgently needed today. But one does not need special gifting to study God's Word and learn sound doctrine against which to test various claims. Churches that teach God's truth clearly, that emphasize major doctrines, that avoid a dogmatic attitude about things that matter less (the so-called *adiaphora*), and that stress love as the goal of God's commands are well able to deal with false teachings. They are in a good position to teach young people, who will be faithful to the truth and to Christian life.

Discerning between kinds of abstinence. Are there examples today of the kind of prohibitions issued by the false teachers in this passage? We can cite the Shakers, a sect that has forbidden marriage and has almost died out as a result. Many religions have had food laws of one sort or another. This passage has sometimes been used to critique the Catholic church, whose priests do not marry and who were expected (at least until several decades ago in the United States) to abstain from meat on Fridays. These practices, however, do *not* correspond to the intensely evil teachings of the reprobate false teachers, who are Timothy's enemies.

This passage, therefore, clearly should not be used in an arbitrary way to condemn people for one or another form of abstinence. Romans 14 deals with this matter fully. The important truth to apply today from the present passage is that we should beware of people who are deceitful, whose teachings are contrary to Scripture (possibly originating in demonic sources), and whose practices are a result of their evil origin. The specific error that must be addressed is the assumption that God's creation in part or in the whole is not good.

It would be trite, of course, to mention that some things, though part of creation, are harmful and ought not to be ingested. Poisons and certain drugs were never intended to be food. Tobacco has been at the center of much concern over the past decades, and tobacco executives have recently had to face charges of increasing sales by seeking to ensnare especially young people into dependence. Less clear is the use of alcohol. On the one hand, Scripture celebrates the joys of wine or its medicinal use (1 Tim. 5:23); on the other hand, it cautions moderation (3:3). But in the passage before us, it is not a matter of adverse chemical or social effects, but of denial of the inherent goodness of the material world.[11]

Asceticism and withdrawal from society can result from extreme self-discipline, from an under-evaluation of some parts of creation (assuming that they are good but dispensable), or from the belief, exemplified by the Gnostics, that the material world is inherently evil. It is the last of these that must be rejected. The others are matters of priority. God has created a wonderful world to be enjoyed—beauty, order, music, color, fragrance, and form, among many other delights.

---

11. While Buddhism, for example, has views on this world, desire, and the nature of the ultimate "state" (or non-state) of Nirvana, which are different for Christians, even that is not the same as Gnosticism. It is perhaps a simple devaluing of the material world that should be addressed in our own culture from this passage.

1 Timothy 4:6–10

IF YOU POINT these things out to the brothers, you will be a good minister of Christ Jesus, brought up in the truths of the faith and of the good teaching that you have followed. ⁷Have nothing to do with godless myths and old wives' tales; rather, train yourself to be godly. ⁸For physical training is of some value, but godliness has value for all things, holding promise for both the present life and the life to come.

⁹This is a trustworthy saying that deserves full acceptance ¹⁰(and for this we labor and strive), that we have put our hope in the living God, who is the Savior of all men, and especially of those who believe.

THE REFERENCES TO "the truth" (v. 3) and "the word of God (v. 5) lead Paul to remind Timothy of his training in the "truths of the faith and of the good teaching that you have followed" (v. 6), an important emphasis in the Pastoral Letters. The phrase "brought up" represents the Greek word for "nourished," a significant description of the life-supporting role of teaching in the growing Christian. Some, it is true, remain infants in regard to their spiritual development (1 Cor. 3:2). Not Timothy, however, for he has received nourishment in the faith. The New Testament lists three sources of his teaching: biblical knowledge from his mother and grandmother (2 Tim. 1:5; 3:14–15); experience in the church, inferred from Acts 16:2; and training-in-service under Paul. The present tense in the word "brought up" implies that this process of nourishment and growth is continuing.

The "teaching" Timothy has received, referred to here as "good," is usually described as "sound" in the Pastorals (1 Tim. 1:10; 2 Tim. 4:3; Titus 1:9; 2:1). In 1 Timothy 4:13 teaching appears as one element in Timothy's ministry to others (see comments on that verse). In the present section also, the things Timothy has learned are to be taught to others, specifically "to the "brothers" (v. 6). Paul uses the term *brothers* frequently enough with reference to both men and women (e.g., Rom. 12:1) to justify including "and sisters" in a contemporary translation. Without doubt, in other words, Paul intends women to learn these things too (cf. 1 Tim. 2:11). These people are probably not only the leaders, but the church as a whole, who need to know and respect Timothy's credentials. This letter will be in Timothy's possession, ready to be produced at any time that his delegated authority needs affirmation.

To "point these things out" (v. 6) is one way to express Timothy's assignment. "Command and teach" in verse 11 is a stronger way of putting it. By doing this he will be a "good minister of Christ Jesus." "Minister" (*diakonos*) is a word for anyone who serves God, as well as for the special group described in 3:8 (see comments). Paul uses this word in his letters for himself and for any who serve with him in the work of evangelism and mission (Rom. 16:1; 1 Cor. 3:5; 2 Cor. 3:6; 6:4; 11:23; Col. 1:7, 23, 25; 4:7).

The negative side of this commission is avoiding involvement in fruitless "godless myths and old wives' tales." Such teachings not only lack verifiable substance ("myths") or religious sanction ("godless," the word used here has an assortment of meanings stemming from the idea of territory outside the precincts of a sacred temple), but are no more dependable than "old wives' tales." This reference sounds sexist and discriminatory of the elderly to our modern ears, but was an idiomatic expression useful in describing vacuous tales such as elderly women told their grandchildren.[1] Whether intentional or not, this description of the godless, undependable teachings of the heretics forms a contrast to Timothy's rigorous training in godliness and to the "trustworthy saying" referred to in verse 9.

This training in godliness is so important that it far surpasses physical training (v. 8). Since Paul says that the latter has "some value," commentators and preachers have postulated, with varying degrees of emphasis, an exhortation to Timothy to keep himself physically fit. It is important to see the semantic pattern here. In the last clause of verse 7 two significant words appear: "train" (*gymnaze*) and "godliness" ([*pros*] *eusebeian*; the NIV translates the entire phrase by "to be godly"). Paul picks up the root *gymnaz-* in verse 8, expresses it in noun form ("training"; Gk. *gymnasia*), and makes the observation that this does have "some value." But his emphasis is not there. He picks up the word "godliness" (*eusebeia*) and makes a structurally parallel statement, substituting *eusebeia* for *somatike gymnasia*, "physical exercise" and *pros panta*, "for all things" for *pros oligon*, meaning, loosely, "for a few things":

somatike gymnasia	*pros oligon*	*estin ophelimos* ("is beneficial")
eusebeia	*pros panta*	*ophelimos estin* ("is beneficial")

The emphasis is clearly on the second clause, with the first one functioning as a basis for comparison, not as a command to Timothy to get a lit-

---

1. See Plato, *Republic* 1.350, as well as the information under γραῦς in LSJ, 359. By contrast, see the type of teaching children should receive from their mothers and grandmothers (2 Tim. 1:5).

tle exercise or as a demeaning of athletic training. The *pros panta* ("for all things") in the second clause is amplified by a further comment that this holds promise for "both the present life and the life to come." This implies that Paul's "some value" refers to the relative brevity of this life in comparison with what is to come. It is possible that this thought follows on Paul's rejection of the asceticism of the false teachers (vv. 1–5), but the text does not establish a direct connection.

The "trustworthy saying" (see comments on 1:15) referred to in verse 9 is probably the words found in verse 8 rather than in verse 10. A similar diagram to the one I constructed above to determine the flow of the text is used by Knight to show that verses 8 and 9 belong together and constitute a familiar saying.[2] A further and perhaps stronger reason to why verse 10 is likely not that "trustworthy saying" is that it is introduced by the conjunction *gar*, often translated "for," and seems to provide an explanation or reason for what precedes, rather than being a quotation brought into the text. It points to verse 8 as the grounds for Paul's instructions.

The next clause in verse 10 begins with the Greek word *hoti*, which can mean either "that" or "because." Understood as "that," it could introduce a quotation such as the "trustworthy saying." However, as already noted, this is likely not the case. If the word *hoti* therefore means "because," it offers the reason why Paul struggles, which, in turn provides the basis for his words to Timothy in verse 8, which constitute the "trustworthy saying." Expressed, then, in reverse sequence, verses 8–10 suggest: "We hope in God, the Savior, and thus we work hard; we do this because of the promise of life to come that rewards training in godliness." If this is the correct understanding of the clause relationships, the note of hope is dominant here, expressed in the "promise ... [of] the life to come" (v. 8) and in "hope in the living God."

The NIV interprets these verses differently, understanding verse 10b to be the "trustworthy saying." By starting a new paragraph at verse 9 it separates "This is a trustworthy saying" from the preceding material. Then it deals with the problem of the *gar* clause intervening between verse 9 and the second clause in verse 10 by making it parenthetical and translating *gar* "and" rather than "for." The result is: "This is a trustworthy saying ... (and for this we labor ...), that we have put our hope...." The NRSV, by contrast, keeps everything in the same paragraph and has the sequence: "... the life to come. The saying is sure and worthy of full acceptance. For to this end we toil ... because we have our hope set...."[3]

---

2. Knight, *Pastoral Epistles*, 199.

3. See also the NLT for a similar structure. The UBS Greek text has a period after verse 8 and a semicolon after verse 9, thereby linking the "trustworthy saying" with what follows. A footnote shows the punctuation interpretation of various translations. The reader of the

Two phrases in verse 10 require careful attention lest they be misunderstood: "Savior of all men" and "especially of those who believe." These words could be taken to mean that God ultimately saves everyone (an idea called universalism), though believers experience this in some special way. But this is not the case, for several reasons. (1) Paul, Jesus, and Scripture in general make it clear that not all are saved, for some deliberately refuse to accept God's saving grace.

(2) While the term *savior* can be taken in a nontheological sense—that is, that God cares for all, heals them, and rescues them from harm—this does not fit the usage of "Savior" in the Pastoral Letters.

(3) The word "all" in Scripture often refers to believers, the context making this clear.

(4) In the present context "all" may mean "all kinds of," a possibility supported by the use of *anthropos*, which refers to humanity (it should be indicated by the translation "people," not "men," as in NIV).

The second phrase, "especially of those who believe," is not the best translation of the Greek words used here; more likely it means "in particular" or "I mean" (as it does in Gal. 6:10; perhaps also Phil. 4:22; 1 Tim. 5:8, 17; 2 Tim. 4:13; Titus 1:10–11).[4]

CONFRONTING HERESY ON a personal level. The protection of the flock is a main (though not the only) responsibility of shepherds. Paul's speech to the Ephesians elders in Acts 20 emphasizes this. The predators would, he said, "distort the truth" (v. 30). Now Timothy must participate in caring for that same flock and confront the error that did intrude.

But in spite of the severity of the error, this passage does not instruct Timothy further as to the theological issues. Paul does, it is true, refer to Timothy's Christian heritage, citing the "truths of the faith" and the "good teaching" he has followed. But Paul's promise is not that if Timothy will "point these things out," he will conquer the deceiving spirits, defeat the false teachers, or save the flock from error, important as those effects would be. Instead, Paul concentrates on Timothy himself as a "good minister of Christ Jesus." He goes on in the next section (4:11–16) to exhort Timothy

---

NLT will note that unlike most other translations, it translates each occurrence of *pistis ho logos* differently, here using eight words. Unfortunately this does not alert the reader to the repetition of a formula and thus fails to communicate clearly the fact that Paul is citing a *series* of quotations he considers of great significance.

4. See T. C. Skeat, "'Especially the Parchment': A Note on 2 Timothy IV.13," *JTS* 30 (1979): 173–77.

about his personal life. As has often been said of missionaries and others who serve Christ, the person is more important than the work.

Paul follows this commendation with the instructions to avoid completely the "godless myths" he is encountering. But again Paul does not describe these myths or "old wives' tales" or show Timothy how to combat them. This, of course, adds to our frustration in trying to determine the exact nature of the heresies Paul wants Timothy to oppose. This very fact, however, is a strong indicator that the Pastoral Letters are not primarily a handbook either on church order or doctrine. As we have frequently noted, this letter is unique in its thoroughgoing blending of doctrine and life. The real message of the Pastoral Letters is not one or the other of these but the combination of both.

Therefore, in the current passage Paul refers to the false teaching, but instead of expanding on this he immediately speaks of the *way* Timothy is to live and to respond to that teaching. The antithesis to becoming involved with these myths and tales is not, in this context, to bring an arsenal of theology against them but to be godly. The rigorous but strange lifestyle of the heretics has to be met with an equally rigorous lifestyle of godliness. This has immense value "for both the present time and the life to come." Surely all this does not mean that we are never to combat error point by point with truth, just that such is not the main message of *this* book. The mixture of error and ungodliness is adversely compared to the blend of truth and godliness. That is the message for all cultures and all times from this passage.

Myths, tales, and hope. Without losing that main thrust of the passage, we must also consider the fact that every age has its own myths and tales. Those who have studied ancient Greco-Roman religions have realized that while the names of the gods are prominent, it was the folk religion that controlled the lives of the people. Fertility, protecting the boundary lines between properties, and personal health were what concerned the people and called for religious action. Myths and tales have been spread by word of mouth, by pagan priests, by printed page and telephone, and now by the Internet. There is no standard of truth and no screening of error on the Internet, and even Christian resources that contain blatant error are picked up and repeated literally around the world.

The conclusion of verse 8 directs our attention to the life to come. The minute we talk about that we are in the realm of hope. This is not as prominent in the Pastoral Letters as it is in Romans 5 and 8 or in the magnificent lines of 1 Peter 1:3–9. But it is here, and it serves as a reminder not to be preoccupied with our present situation, either with present evil or with present activity, to the exclusion of the "forward look." God is "living," transcending all of our present experiences, and he is Savior. As such he rescues us from all present circumstances as well as from our sins.

KEEPING FOCUSED IN the age of technology. We live in a time when Christian leaders are both better known and, therefore, a greater potential benefit or deterrent to the gospel than perhaps at any other time in recent memory. This, of course, is true in large measure because of the exposure to Christian leaders in television and other media. Also, the founders of new churches themselves tend to be the visible focus of those churches. The very qualities that enable them to be successful in church planting and growth—aggressiveness, practical skills, and the ability to speak God's Word to a contemporary audience—are qualities that bring them to prominence.

Television programs, Christian radio, and Christian publications naturally feature the successful preachers and church builders. This puts a heavy burden on these servants of Christ. Very early in his ministry, Billy Graham determined to keep all finances above board and never to be alone with a woman other than his wife.[5] Not all have followed that wisdom, however, and the fall of those who have not is far better known today than it would have been fifty years ago. That is not always because the preachers are more vulnerable, but because they are more visible.

This passage urges self-discipline. That is implied in the comparison of godliness with physical training. Godliness is not passive but active. As physical training develops the body and as aerobic exercises improve the function of the heart, so a godly walk has its beneficial effect on one's character. Attempts to minimize the importance of physical training are heard less these days than before research showed the effect of exercise and good diet on one's life span. It does have value, as Paul affirms in verse 8, but the importance of spiritual and moral health far exceeds that.

Spiritual formation. In recent decades the term *spiritual formation*, long used by Catholics, has been more common among Protestant evangelicals. There is a recognition that conscious attention should be given to such areas as spiritual growth, moral and ethical awareness, practical appropriation of Scripture, immersion in prayer and meditation, and involvement in the community of faith. Evangelical seminaries formerly tended to concentrate on academics. In general they assumed that since spiritual growth should be the responsibility of the church, the seminary did not need to include this in its curriculum. What attention was given to the spiritual aspect of ministry training was largely in chapel services and small groups.

---

5. Billy Graham, *Just As I Am* (New York: HarperCollins; Grand Rapids: Zondervan, 1997), 128.

Now, however, more deliberate spiritual direction and specific courses on spiritual development are appearing as part of the academic curriculum in Christian colleges and seminaries. One example is the cooperation of the Bannockburn Institute and Trinity International University to foster seminars to facilitate this process, not only in the educational but in the business community as well.[6]

What is still sometimes neglected in both church and school is the development of *character*. Prayer, Bible reading, meeting attendance, witnessing, worship, obedience to specific biblical texts, moments of spiritual insight, and even revival are all tremendously important. Isolated acts and events, however, do not necessarily develop character. Character is developed by bringing these spiritual disciplines to bear together on our lives, on our attitudes and decisions, and on our relationships and actions.

The tools of our trade in the various phases of Christian ministry today are extraordinary, and it is possible to become too involved with the amazing variety of technology available to us. The use of such tools as electronic equipment, the Internet, and CD-ROM resources has already (according to the confession of some) occupied too much attention and time. To the extent that this may distract us from time alone with God and from the worship of and dependence on God, it can move us away from the goal of 1 Timothy 4:6–10.

Not only is it easy to become too involved in technology, but we can also be preoccupied with our own battles with evil. First Timothy 4 opened with a reference to the teachings of demons, so Paul is consciously dealing with the unseen world in the matters at hand. But his instructions to Timothy do not concentrate on that. They rather deal with his development of character and with discipline. Nor does Paul focus only on what Timothy was involved in at the time. He looks ahead on the basis of the promise that godliness holds "for both the present life and the life to come."

This introduces the topic of "hope in the living God" and elevates the focus of the minister of Christ, who may tend to be mired in the mud of daily duties. When Paul was listing what he had suffered for Christ, he added in 2 Corinthians 11:28, "Besides everything else, I face daily the pressure of my concern for all the churches." Pastors, missionaries, and others who feel the burden not only of those who may be lured by false teachings (as those in Ephesus), but also of all believers in their daily struggles, can learn from verses 8–10 of our passage to look up and hope in the living God. He is the Savior of all, and he cares infinitely more for the people among whom we labor daily than even we do.

---

6. One of the Institute's enterprises is The Center for Personal and Relational Growth, which was established to promote spiritual development. The address of the Institute is 2065 Half Day Road, Bannockburn, IL 60015, USA.

1 Timothy 4:11–16

𝕚𝕮

COMMAND AND TEACH these things. ¹²Don't let anyone look down on you because you are young, but set an example for the believers in speech, in life, in love, in faith and in purity. ¹³Until I come, devote yourself to the public reading of Scripture, to preaching and to teaching. ¹⁴Do not neglect your gift, which was given you through a prophetic message when the body of elders laid their hands on you.

¹⁵Be diligent in these matters; give yourself wholly to them, so that everyone may see your progress. ¹⁶Watch your life and doctrine closely. Persevere in them, because if you do, you will save both yourself and your hearers.

VERSES 11–16 CONTAIN a series of important imperatives that summarize and enlarge on the preceding sections. Once again we are confronted by *parangello* (see comments on 1:3), whose classical meanings range from "give orders" to "exhort" to "cheer on." Here, with the impersonal object "these things," it means "to command." Just as Paul commanded Timothy and authorized him to give commands in 1:3 and 5, so again in 4:11 Paul tells Timothy, "Command and teach these things."

In 1:3 Timothy was to command certain individuals "not to teach false doctrines any longer." Having issued a negative imperative regarding teaching falsehood, Paul now gives a positive imperative to Timothy to teach the truth about which he has been reading in this letter. Paul does not define "these things" clearly. The possibilities are: (1) the doctrinal statement at the end of verse 10, "who is the Savior of all men, and especially of those who believe"; (2) the content of the trustworthy saying (v. 9, probably referring to v. 8); (3) everything since the previous occurrence of "these things" (v. 6); (4) all of the doctrinal statements in the letter; or (5) everything in the letter that is applicable to the church at Ephesus. In view of the fact that "these things" appears repeatedly,[1] it is most likely that here and elsewhere it refers to (5). At the same time, the word was triggered by the immediately preceding statement(s), and thus (1) and (2) are certainly not excluded.

---

1. See, e.g., 1 Tim. 3:14; 4:6, 11, 15; 5:7, 21; 6:2; 2 Tim. 2:2, 14; Titus 2:15; 3:8.

John Stott observes that verse 11 speaks of the responsibility for Timothy to pass on Paul's instructions to the churches while verse 12 expresses his youthfulness. These two verses stand in "dramatic contrast," in which Timothy is "called to Christian leadership beyond his years."[2] This contrast is not a passing phenomenon but expresses the heavy plot (if one can call it that in an letter) of gleaming truth opposing dark error with a relatively young warrior leading the charge, wielding a sword given him by the aging apostle.

The encouragement not to let people despise his youth (v. 12) raises the question of Timothy's age. In the story of the rich young ruler the same word (*neotes*) refers to an earlier period in his life, though probably not as young as the word "boy" in some translations could imply (Luke 18:21, NIV). In Matthew the man is called a *neaniskos*, which can describe a man from his mid-twenties to his thirties (Matt. 19:20, 22). After giving examples of the age range described by the word in ancient literature, Knight makes the useful point that in Acts 7:58 Luke used the same word to describe Paul.[3] If, as is probable, Timothy was in his thirties, words such as "young" and "youth" might give the contemporary reader the wrong impression, since we generally reserve these words for people in their teens and early twenties.

The pervading theme of the letters, which is the necessary blend of sound doctrine and godly living in the life of church leaders, reappears here. There is no single passage in the Pastorals where all of the requisite virtues (or doctrines, for that matter) occur together. In this passage the key word is "example" in five areas: speech, life, love, faith, and purity. These are specific enough but, taken together, they are also comprehensive enough to constitute an appropriate "example" (*typos*).

Lock understands *typos* to be "not so much 'a model for the faithful to follow,'" on the analogy of 1 Thessalonians 1:7, as "a model of what the faithful are" (supported by Titus 2:7).[4] Timothy's lifestyle "will make its appeal to all men ... and attract them to complete salvation." He thinks that 1 Peter 5:3, "being examples to the flock," is not a proper parallel to 1 Timothy 4:12, which he understands as being an example to outsiders. Knight takes the opposite position.[5] While an exegetical choice must be made between these two, the ultimate outcome is the same, as exhibited in Paul's desire for others to follow his example as he follows Christ (1 Cor. 11:1). Thus, if Timothy models Christian virtues to the Ephesian believers, they will become examples along with him to the unbelieving world. But at this stage, Timothy is to be

---

2. Stott, *Guard the Truth*, 119.

3. Knight, *Pastoral Epistles*, 205.

4. Lock, *Pastoral Epistles*, 52.

5. Knight, *Pastoral Epistles*, 205.

an example *to the believers*. The preaching and teaching referred to in verse 13 is one way in which he can set an example in "speech." Later Paul cautions Timothy against quarreling (6:3–5; 2 Tim. 2:14–16).

The word "life" (v. 12) translates *anastrophe*, which can describe one's conduct or behavior in a particular circumstance (Gal. 1:13) or a way of life (Eph. 4:22). Here it means the latter, in conjunction with the traits of character expressed in love, faith, and purity. This is a reprise of 1:4–5.

"Until I come" (v. 13) is a "real time" reference and therefore serves both to support genuine Pauline authorship of the letter and to place Timothy's commission in context. His duties are not those of a pastor as we conceive of that ministry today, since the word "until" introduces the idea of a limited or uncertain duration in Timothy's ministry, dependent on the time of Paul's return. In that connection the text does not give any indication that the reading, preaching, and teaching of Scripture is the whole, or even the main, duty of a pastor. It is, however, the main duty of Timothy as he represented Paul in the doctrinal conflict at Ephesus.

Nevertheless, given the fact that the elders at Ephesus were instructed to guard against heresy (Acts 20:28–30) and that the foremost ministry of elders is preaching and teaching (1 Tim. 5:17), the teaching of God's Word is clearly of utmost importance in the church, even if it is not the specific ministry of every shepherd or elder. Likewise it should be noted that this text does not imply that the reading, preaching, and teaching of Scripture is the main component of worship. Fee observes, "Although this certainly refers to what Timothy is to do in public worship, it is too narrow a view to see this as intending to provide a model."[6] He cites biblical references showing that "public worship included prayers (2:1–7; 1 Cor. 11:2–16), singing (Col. 3:16; 1 Cor. 14:26; cf. 1 Tim. 3:16), charismatic utterances (1 Thess. 5:19–22; 1 Cor. 11:2–16; 12–14), and the Lord's supper (1 Cor. 11:17–34)."

Timothy's reading of the biblical text with comments and homily reflects the use of Scripture in the early church as well as in the synagogue. In Luke 4:16–21 we have an example of the synagogue procedure, where Scripture was read and commented on. Exhortation was secondary to the Scripture itself. Acts 13:13–15 shows the difference even more clearly: "After the reading from the Law and the Prophets, the synagogue rulers sent word to [Paul and Barnabas], saying, 'Brothers, if you have a message of encouragement for the people, please speak.'" Knight notes that the word for "encouragement" (*paraklesis*) is the same as that for "preaching" here in 1 Timothy 4:13.[7]

---

6. Fee, *1 and 2 Timothy, Titus*, 107.
7. Knight, *Pastoral Epistles*, 207–8.

The word "Scripture" is not in the Greek of verse 13 but is implied, since the reading of Scripture was customary in worship services. The importance of the reading of sacred Scripture underlines the significance of Paul's asking that the church at Colosse have his letter to them read in the church at Laodicea and that the letter to Laodicea be read in the Colossian church. Stott says, "These are extraordinary instructions. They indicate that the apostles put their writings on a level with the Old Testament Scriptures."[8]

Verse 14 contains not only a urgent word to Timothy, but a message of affirmation to those in the Ephesian church who would also be hearing this letter, and a glimpse, for later readers like ourselves, of an important event in Timothy's life. Paul refers here to Timothy's "gift" (*charisma*, the same word as in 1 Cor. 12). We may assume that this gift, like those in that chapter, was an endowment by the Holy Spirit. We may also assume that it was a spiritual ability that one could fail to draw on, although going through the motions of ministry. To "neglect" it will hinder Timothy's spiritual effectiveness.

Two visible actions took place when Timothy received his gift: the utterance of a divine prophetic word and the laying on of hands by the body of elders. The Greek prepositions indicate that the laying on of hands accompanied (Gk. *meta*, "with") the bestowal of the spiritual gift, but that it was "through [*dia*] a prophetic message" that the gift was actually given. However, the fact that in 2 Timothy 1:6 Paul says that the gift was in Timothy "through [*dia*] the laying on of [his] hands" may mean that the distinction between prepositions does not exclude the laying on of hands along with the prophetic message as the channel through which the gift was given. What is most important to note is that the text does not say that the gift was the bestowal of some office.

It is common to call this action an ordination. Kelly even uses that term in his translation of the verse.[9] Apart from issues of ecclesiology (the significance of ordination) and of church history (ordination as we know it was not practiced until two centuries later), there are two basic interpretive issues: the biblical significance of the laying on of hands and the Jewish practice of ordaining rabbis.

(1) In the Old and New Testament laying on of hands was more than symbolic. A simple placing of hands on a person might accompany a blessing or healing. A "laying on" or "imposition" of hands (the verb *samak* implies leaning and not merely touching) accompanied the appointment of Joshua as Moses' successor (Num. 27:18, 23). According to Deuteronomy 34:9

---

8. Stott, *Guard the Truth*, 121.
9. Kelly, *Pastoral Epistles*, 107.

he received an additional gift of the spirit of wisdom. In contrast, the installation of elders in Numbers 11:16–17, 24–25 did not include the laying on of hands. When the Levites were set apart to a special service (Num. 8:14, 19) and when Paul and Barnabas were set apart for a special work (Acts 13:2), there was an imposition of hands (Num. 8:10; Acts 13:3). In these cases the laying on of hands was done by peers, not predecessors or superiors.

(2) There is no evidence that in the time of Paul rabbis were ordained by the laying on of hands. This was done to admit people to the Sanhedrin (*m. Sanh.* 4:4), but such a practice was not equivalent to rabbinical ordination. While it was formerly thought that rabbinic ordination provided the background for 1 Timothy 4:14, more recent studies have shown that not only is there little if any evidence that the ordination of Jewish rabbis in Paul's day employed the laying on of hands, there is actually some evidence to the contrary. Note also that the function to which rabbis were ordained was different from that of Timothy. What is most important in Timothy's case is that he received a spiritual gift, of which a prophetic word and the laying of hands were visible affirmations.[10]

Verses 15–16 follow naturally on what preceded. The sacred endowment he received and the sacred task that lies before him requires wholehearted commitment, but it also requires that there be no inconsistency in his life. Paul does not hesitate to repeat the instruction that Timothy combine "life and doctrine." He must watch these because others are looking on; they are to "see [his] progress." In fact, it is for this very purpose (*hina*, "so that") that he is to be so diligent.

The call to perseverance in verse 16 is in accordance with Paul's words to others (Rom. 11:22; Col. 1:22–23; cf. Acts 13:43). What is surprising is not that Timothy will be saved if he perseveres (this thought is already in 1 Cor. 15:2) but that he can "save both [himself] and [his] hearers." In the context of the Pastoral Letters, with their emphasis on the necessity of the Lord's servant leading a godly life under the scrutiny of others, this verse can best be interpreted by stating it negatively: "If you do not combine godliness

---

10. On the laying on of hands, see Marjorie Warkentin, *Ordination* (Grand Rapids: Eerdmans, 1982); Lawrence A. Hoffman, "Jewish Ordination on the Eve of Christianity," *Studia Liturgica* 13 (1979): 11–41; Edward J. Kilmartin, "Ministry and Ordination in Early Christianity Against a Jewish Background," *Studia Liturgica* 13 (1979): 42–69; Stephen Westerholm, *Jesus and Scribal Authority,* Coniectanea Biblica N.T. Series 10 (Lund: CWK Gleerup, 1978), 26–39; Everett Ferguson, "Laying on of Hands: Its Significance in Ordination," *JTS* 26 (1975): 1–12; and David Daube, *The New Testament and Rabbinic Judaism* (London: Athlone, 1956), 224–46.

with proper doctrine in your life, you will give the lie to your own claim to salvation and be a hindrance to others who seek to be saved."

ON DOCTRINE AND **life**. Ordination sermons and charges are often based on 2 Timothy 4:1–5, and they usually center on the *duties* of ministry, especially preaching. But this passage exhibits that blending of doctrine and *life* that is characteristic of the Pastoral Letters. The initial words in 1 Timothy 4:11 set forth the ministry of authoritative proclamation and teaching. While this is Timothy's charge, it is also indirectly a charge to the congregation to obey the command and to learn the teachings. What follows, however, is specifically for Timothy, where there is a blend: verse 12 emphasizes life, verse 13 emphasizes ministry and the Scripture, and verse 14 emphasizes Timothy's gift.

We are never told how old Timothy was at the time, but clearly he was young enough for some to have held back the respect he was due. As speech therapists can testify, preachers sometimes seek their help in an attempt to speak in a lower pitch than is normal for them so that they can achieve a sound of authority. Paul advocates nothing of that sort here. The attention and respect that Timothy should receive must come from the example of his life. The "speech" that is mentioned, far from being an artificial display of oratory in a stentorian voice, is to be gracious and worthy of a Christian. The word "life" has to do with general conduct, while the words "love . . . faith and . . . purity" represent specific areas of life.

Ministries of Christians will differ from situation to situation, and the qualities mentioned in verse 11 can be exercised in any ministry in any place at any time. The preaching ministry of verse 13, on the contrary, is specific and focused. Over the centuries in liturgical churches the Eucharist has been central, and in Calvinistic and other churches the preaching ministry has usually been the visible focal point. More recent emphasis on spiritual gifts in some churches and on seeker services in others has changed this perspective somewhat, but the proclamation of the word of truth will always have a prominent place. This is especially important wherever, as in Ephesus, there is error to be corrected with truth.

The "public reading" of Scripture may not seem as important with the wide availability of Bibles in the vernacular, but where the Scriptures are not available or where there is a high degree of illiteracy it is essential. This reading and the exposition of Scripture would have been new and fresh to the ears of many in Timothy's congregation. A challenge to all preachers is to be sure that the Word is accessible, effective, and understandable, both publicly and privately. No congregation ever gets beyond the need for the exposition of the Word of God.[11] If a church is doing its job in evangelism, it is a perpetual kindergarten. There will always be those who need the fundamentals. Paul's charge to Timothy about the Scriptures will never need modification in essentials, even if the method and language of the reading, preaching, and teaching may vary.

The gift of God. To accomplish his task Timothy must depend on the gift that God gave him at the laying on of hands. While the nature of that gift is not defined, it was without question a supernatural endowment. Timothy received something he did not otherwise possess. It may have been new courage, confidence, or boldness. It may have been some specific ability. Whatever it was, that occasion marked a definite work of the Holy Spirit.

Likewise, the "prophetic message" was a work of the Holy Spirit. In accordance with the teaching about prophecy in Scripture, this was not merely some wise saying on the human level. Rather, God was speaking. Together this gift and this prophecy were God's special way of enabling Timothy for his ministry and of showing those present that he was indeed a special minister of Christ Jesus. The primary function of the actual laying on of hands may have been to convey the spiritual gift, or it may have primarily expressed the confidence and commendation of the elders. If I may write personally, the recollection of having hands laid on me by respected elders and pastors has given me peace and assurance in times when I have had doubts about my calling and ministry.

 THE LAYING ON of hands. In applying verse 14 about the laying of hands on Timothy, we need to use care lest we read too much into it or not derive all we should. It is both less than and more than what is assumed in ordinations today, depending on the denominational theology of ministry. (1) In the sense that it is *less,* most ordination rites today are intended to convey an ecclesiastical status and privilege not given to Timothy. If what Timothy experienced was equivalent to ordination and a pattern for ordination today, we face several historical obstacles.

(a) There is no clear instance of ordination in the New Testament. Other instances of the laying on of hands were for different purposes. Paul and Barnabas had already been in Christian ministry when hands were laid on them in Acts 13, and the ministry for which they were set apart was not a life-

---

11. See W. Liefeld, *New Testament Exposition* (Grand Rapids: Zondervan, 1984) for methods of going from text to sermon.

time ministry but was "completed" with the conclusion of their first missionary journey (Acts 14:26).

(b) Moreover, while the laying of hands on Timothy has been compared to rabbinic ordination, there is no rabbinic evidence that the latter was performed with the laying on of hands (see above).

(c) Furthermore, the nature of rabbinic service and authority was different from that of Christian ministers. The early church saw a development of practice, with changing patterns regarding the use of hands in what we would now call confirmation and then in what we know as ordination. The rite of ordination did not become firm until the third century. If in ordination we bestow a rank liturgical or privilege that the ordinand did not previously have, we are going beyond Timothy's experience, at least as it is described in the Pastoral Letters.

(d) There is no evidence that Timothy—or anyone else in the early church as described in Acts and the New Testament letters—was given the exclusive right to preach, baptize, or preside at the Lord's Table, as though these were rights that "laypeople" did not have.

(2) There is a sense in which the imposition of hands on Timothy was *more* than is usually attributed to ordination in many Protestant churches today. By and large in these churches ordination centers on what the participants are doing rather than on what God is doing. Charismatic churches would be an exception here, but there is usually little sense that God is giving the ordinand a *spiritual gift* at the time of the ordination. Nor is there any audible *prophecy* being mediated from God to the ordinand. What is typical is that as the ordinand kneels and receives the laying on of hands, prayer is offered up on his or her behalf. That such prayer is important hardly needs to be said, but it is an action of human beings reaching up to God rather than an action of God reaching down to the ordinand.

This does not mean that ordination should be discontinued, but rather that it should be reexamined as to its significance. Timothy's experience may not be an exact model, but it does have valid elements and lessons, as does the setting apart of Paul and Barnabas in Acts 13. Those who serve God on special assignments and in special ministries ought to be so recognized, affirmed, and commissioned. Prayer is important, but hearts should be opened for God to respond in whatever way he chooses.

It should be recognized that this is not the elevation of a privileged cleric to a superior exclusive class (as was the Old Testament priesthood), but the acceptance of one whom God has given to his church to work not above, but among, the people of God. The commissioning of missionaries may perhaps be more closely compared to the laying of hands on Paul and Barnabas than on Timothy.

Timothy is told here not to neglect the gift he has thus received. God is honored and his work is forwarded not simply by the *memory* of our ordination but by allowing the spiritual gifts God has given to *operate* fully and powerfully through us. Whether this gift is the ability to preach and teach as Timothy was commanded to do here, or courage (as 2 Tim. 1:6–7 may imply), or if it is something else unexplained here and perhaps different for each of us, we are exhorted through this text to keep it in mind and in force.

1 Timothy 5:1–16

D O NOT REBUKE an older man harshly, but exhort him as if he were your father. Treat younger men as brothers, ²older women as mothers, and younger women as sisters, with absolute purity.

³Give proper recognition to those widows who are really in need. ⁴But if a widow has children or grandchildren, these should learn first of all to put their religion into practice by caring for their own family and so repaying their parents and grandparents, for this is pleasing to God. ⁵The widow who is really in need and left all alone puts her hope in God and continues night and day to pray and to ask God for help. ⁶But the widow who lives for pleasure is dead even while she lives. ⁷Give the people these instructions, too, so that no one may be open to blame. ⁸If anyone does not provide for his relatives, and especially for his immediate family, he has denied the faith and is worse than an unbeliever.

⁹No widow may be put on the list of widows unless she is over sixty, has been faithful to her husband, ¹⁰and is well known for her good deeds, such as bringing up children, showing hospitality, washing the feet of the saints, helping those in trouble and devoting herself to all kinds of good deeds.

¹¹As for younger widows, do not put them on such a list. For when their sensual desires overcome their dedication to Christ, they want to marry. ¹²Thus they bring judgment on themselves, because they have broken their first pledge. ¹³Besides, they get into the habit of being idle and going about from house to house. And not only do they become idlers, but also gossips and busybodies, saying things they ought not to. ¹⁴So I counsel younger widows to marry, to have children, to manage their homes and to give the enemy no opportunity for slander. ¹⁵Some have in fact already turned away to follow Satan.

¹⁶If any woman who is a believer has widows in her family, she should help them and not let the church be burdened with them, so that the church can help those widows who are really in need.

THE NEXT LARGE section of this letter (5:1–6:2) is about relationships. Given the repeated emphasis in the Pastoral Letters on the importance of blending sound doctrine and godly living, it is not surprising that Paul devotes so much attention to an area of life that offers so much potential for a public display of inner character.

Relationship in the Christian Family (5:1–2)

VERSES 1–2 PROVIDE a terse introduction to the topic. The instructions are comprehensive, covering all four possible relationships: older men, younger men, older women, and younger women. The instructions are not directed to these groups, as they would be in the usual household instructions, as to *their* responsibilities. Instead, they are directed to Timothy to guide him in *his* relationship to *them*.

The first of these is in the singular, "older man"; the others are plural. In this context it is clear that the Greek word *presbyteros* refers to age, not to a church elder. Although Timothy has been given considerable authority to deal with false teaching and false teachers, his attitude to the older men is not to be harsh even if they need correction. This is especially so because his relationships in the church are like those in the family household. Also, since the Lord's servant "must not quarrel ... [but] must be kind to everyone" (2 Tim. 2:24), Timothy certainly must not treat an older man "harshly." The verb used here for "rebuke" (*epiplesso*) means to strike out at someone (in a figurative usage here, to strike verbally).

This prohibition is followed by a contrasting imperative, which governs the three following instances. The positive verb "exhort" is *parakaleo* (translated as "urge" in 1:3; 2:1; 6:2). The word "urge" does not fit the present English sentence structure (e.g., the sentence does not say what Timothy is to urge younger men to do), and the translation "preach" (4:13 translates the related noun as "preaching") would be too strong. The other two relationships need little explanation, other than to stress the importance of the Lord's servant treating younger women "with absolute purity."[1]

Caring for Widows (5:3–16)

"SORTING OUT WIDOWS was not only a pastoral headache in the early church, it has also proved to be an exegetical one for modern commentators."[2] At first

---

1. For an important study on the household theme in the Pastoral Letters see David C. Verner, *The Household of God*, SBLDS 71 (Chico, Calif.: Scholars, 1983), 161–66.

2. B. W. Winter, "Providentia for the Widows of 1 Timothy 5:3–16," *TynB* 39 (1988): 83.

glance, it may seem obvious who is a widow, or even who is a widow in need. Why does Timothy and those with whom he serves need help in sorting them out? The basic topic seems to be providing financial help for needy widows, but there are several questions associated with this that need to be addressed. The text implies that the following questions were being asked in the church: (1) Which widows truly are in need? (2) What is the responsibility of family and other relatives? (3) How can the church determine which widows qualify for inclusion on their list? (4) How should the church deal with women who do not qualify for the list?

The main problems faced by the exegete are: (1) Why does this passage occur where it does in the Pastoral Letters ? (2) How should we understand the phrase "really widows" (NRSV; NIV has "who are really in need," v. 3)? (3) What is the "list"? Is it only for financial aid, including all "real" widows, or is it a special list of widows who have a role of honor or service in the church, perhaps similar to the order of widows in the postapostolic church? (4) Why is it assumed that a widow who does not qualify for the list is likely to fall into a dissolute lifestyle and follow Satan? (5) Does this passage contribute to the problem many commentators see in this letter of women being victimized, especially by false teachers?

In the ancient Roman empire, life was short. People were considered old in their forties. There were few widowers; the men died early.[3] Widows might be wealthy and thus their attractiveness to men could be more than physical beauty. Young wealthy widows would be especially desirable. This probably describes the social context of the church in which Timothy ministered at Ephesus. We may assume that there were more unmarried women than available men and that some of these might become financially destitute while others could fall into a dissolute lifestyle and eventually into the hands of Satan himself.

Care of widows was important in Jewish tradition. "The LORD . . . God of gods and Lord of lords, the great God" is the one who "defends the cause of the fatherless and the widow" (Deut. 10:17–18). God's people were to do the same. "Do not take advantage of a widow or an orphan" (Ex. 22:22). "Do not deprive the alien or the fatherless of justice, or take the cloak of the widow as a pledge" (Deut. 24:17). "Cursed is the man who withholds justice from the alien, the fatherless or the widow" (Deut. 27:19; cf. Isa. 1:17; Zech. 7:10).

The Jewish concern for widows appears also in the New Testament: "Religion that God our Father accepts as pure and faultless is this: to look after orphans and widows in their distress and to keep oneself from being polluted

---

3. L. P. Wilkinson, *The Roman Experience* (Washington, D.C.: Univ. Press of America, 1974), 26.

by the world" (James 1:27). Acts 6:1–6 reveals the concern the early Jerusalem church had for the widows, first those who were Hebrew-speaking and then those who spoke Greek. As for the Greco-Roman world outside of Judaism, a widow was to be cared for by her sons in her husband's home or, if that was not possible, she was to return to her parental home.[4]

One factor that may have been at work behind the scenes of 1 Timothy is the ancient concept of honor and shame. "Recognition" in verse 3 translates the Greek verb for "to honor" (*timao*). Does this word refer to financial help, which seems to be the case with a similar noun (*time*) in verse 17 (see comments below)? It should be observed by way of background that a married woman participated in her husband's honor, assuming that she had the appropriate sense of shame. This shame was not the same as being ashamed because of bad behavior, nor was it merely connected with modesty. Malina and Neyrey state that

> women not under the tutelage of a male (e.g., notably widows and divorced women) are viewed as stripped of female honor (i.e., "shameless"), hence more like males then females, therefore sexually predatory, aggressive, hence dangerous. Only remarriage would restore their true sexual roles, but often this is not socially possible. This points to the precarious position of the widow and divorcee.... Such cultural attitudes toward widows are articulated in 1 Tim 5:3–16.[5]

First Timothy 5:3–6:2 comments on three groups of people—two of them social groups (widows and slaves) and between them an ecclesiastical group (elders). This seems to account for the placement of the present passage, especially if the idea of "honor" is a connecting thread (5:3, 17; 6:2). Women also receive attention in chapter 2 and elders in chapter 3. The topic of money comes up again in chapter 6. As is typical in the Pastoral Letters, topics are scattered rather than grouped together.

Summary of Paul's argument. The topic now being widows, how should the church address their needs—social, personal, and religious? The first step was to determine financial need. Paul makes it clear that not all those whose husbands had died deserve this support. Some are being cared for and some are not living in a way that commends themselves support. So it is necessary to limit the definition of "widow" for the purpose of determining who gets support.

After instructing Timothy to honor those who are "really" widows (v. 3), Paul defines them first as those who are alone and have no family members

---

4. Winter, "Providentia for the Widows," 85.

5. Bruce J. Malina and Jerome H. Neyrey in *The Social World of Luke-Acts: Models for Interpretation*, Jerome H. Neyrey, ed. (Peabody, Mass.: Hendrickson, 1991), 44.

to care for them. Moreover, they must trust in God in contrast to living for pleasure (vv. 5–6). The three characteristics cited in verse 11 identify those who are to be put on "the list" (see below for comments on what this list is). To be placed on "the list" a widow must be over sixty (v. 9), must have been faithful to her husband (v. 9b), and must have had a reputation for "good deeds" (v. 10). The next verses (vv. 11–15) explain why younger widows should not be on this list. The section concludes with a reprise on a family's care for its own widows, now focused on female family members (v. 16).

Specific details. The meaning of the opening verb, "honor" (*timao* in v. 3; NIV, "give proper recognition") is clear. In addition to the background ideas about honor mentioned above, this verb has a noble history signifying the honoring, even the revering, of worthy persons. What is not certain is whether in this passage it has an extended meaning of honoring by providing a monetary gift or stipend. That meaning probably attaches to its related Greek noun *time* (v. 17), close enough to this passage to warrant consideration. That verse directs that the elders "who direct the affairs of the church well are worthy of double honor, especially those whose work is preaching and teaching." The meaning "honorarium" or "financial support" is made probable by verse 18 that follows: "For the Scripture says, 'Do not muzzle the ox while it is treading out the grain,' and 'The worker deserves his wages.'"

Yet shortly thereafter, slaves are told to "honor" (NRSV) or "respect" (NIV) their masters. In that circumstance it does not imply the giving of funds. In other words, *timao* can mean simply "honor" or "respect" in the present passage as well. It is true that financial support is the subject of this passage, but that fact does not require such a meaning in verse 3. Moreover, even if there was an official, remunerated order of widows, that is not directly dealt with until verses 9–10. The NIV "give proper recognition" is perhaps weak, but it does point to the purpose of the passage, which is to urge that the church identify those widows who deserve support.

The verb *timao* is in the imperative in verse 3, indicating that it is not optional whether one gives widows what they deserve. The honor and support of widows are responsibilities the community must seriously undertake. But the passage has both a positive and a negative purpose. Positively, those who are "really" widows must be located and helped; negatively, those who are not deserving should be excluded. It is as though those who do not qualify for help should not be considered widows at all.[6] That is not to ignore their grief; rather, it is to determine their financial need. In that sense, this section is not a "pastoral" passage as we think of the word.

---

6. The NIV "widows who are really in need" paraphrases the Greek "really widows," losing some of the attention-grabbing impact, but accurately expressing its meaning.

Verses 4–8 establish a connection between one's "religion" and one's concern for others. It may stem from the Ten Commandments, the fifth of which is, "Honor your father and your mother, so that you may live long in the land the LORD your God is giving you" (Ex. 20:12). The command here, "honor," may be the catchword between this passage and that. Even though there is no direct connection, there is an important truth in common: One who is truly religious will respect others, a truth found also in the so-called "second" great commandment about loving one's neighbor. Jesus' teaching in Mark 7:9–13 (on not using allegedly religious excuses to avoid duties, such as caring for parents) contains that commandment also. James 1:27, quoted above, lauds looking after orphans and widows.

Paul specifies in verse 8 that family members must care for their own or else they will be considered worse than unbelievers, and verse 4 makes it clear that those family members most responsible are the widow's children. The religious dimension is also underscored by the conclusion of verse 4, that "this is pleasing to God." One cannot be truly religious and please God when ignoring the needs of human beings, especially those in one's own family.

But if the widow's family is responsible to God for the way they treat her, she in turn is responsible to God for her attitude and life (v. 5). The description of a widow in need as one who is "really" a widow" is now repeated from verse 3. Her four defining attributes are: (1) She is left "all alone"; (2) she "puts her hope in God"; (3) she "pray[s] and . . . ask[s] God for help"; and (4) she does so "night and day." These may be in ascending order of importance in selecting worthy widows. It is not enough to be alone, for one can be alone and lonely but not look to God. One can indeed trust in God but not devote oneself to prayer.

Verse 5b contains two words, both meaning prayer, one being a more general term (proseuche, "pray"), the other (deesis, "ask," less frequent in the New Testament), suggesting a pleading for help. The latter implies petitions for the widow herself and for others, while the former suggests devotional expressions of worship. The phrase "night and day," along with the verb "continues," expresses total devotion. It reminds us of the aged Anna, "a widow . . . [who] never left the temple but worshiped night and day, fasting and praying" and who testified concerning the infant Jesus (Luke 2:37).

The spiritual qualifications for "real" widowhood receive emphasis by means of the contrast with the widow who lives a self-serving life (v. 6). The rare Greek word that describes her (spatalao) occurs in only two other biblical passages, the LXX of Ezekiel 16:48, which describes Sodom, and James 5:5, where it describes the rich who live in "self-indulgence." It is not simply that this widow enjoys life while the "real" widow lives in somber austerity, but that she grossly seeks her own pleasure to the neglect of others, while the worthy widow derives pleasure from the Lord. The self-seeking one is "dead even while she lives," an interesting phrase occurring within a passage about those who have suffered the death of another. This could refer to her relationship to God (as in Eph. 2:2).

It is important (v. 7) that Timothy relay this command about the worldly widow as well as the other commands so that the church will not be laid "open to blame." Such a concern for what others might think about Christianity occurs elsewhere in the Pastoral Letters (see the clauses expressing purpose in Titus 2:5, 8, 10). The implication in these verses is that unbelievers are looking for inconsistencies to criticize.

This section concludes (v. 8) with a warning about those who do not provide for their families. A strong word, used in James 3:14 ("deny the truth") and in Jude 4 ("deny Jesus Christ"), occurs here: The irresponsible person has "denied the faith." Paul does not clarify what is meant by "worse than an unbeliever," but 1 Corinthians 5:1 describes a person who commits a sin not even found among pagans. According to Romans 2:14 Gentiles can still do by nature what the Jewish law (which they do not have) teaches. The Greco-Roman literature mentioned above shows concern for widows. Christians, therefore, should not sink below the moral standards of the unbelievers around them.

In verses 9–10 Paul explains what is necessary for a widow to be "put on the list." The NIV calls it a "list of widows" for clarification, but some argue that this is a list of a specific kind of widows, that is, those who are in the "office" of widows, serving in special ways that other widows do not. We do know there was an order of widows in the postapostolic church, which apparently grew out of the instructions in this passage. Later there was an order of virgins as well, and eventually convents were established. Widows were called "the altar of God," showing the respect they had for their devotion to God.[7] Ignatius spoke of "virgins called widows"[8]—a reference to the choice of these women not to remarry but to live for God.

Hippolytus (A.D. 170–235) was cautious about which widows would qualify to belong to the order of widows:

> When a widow is appointed she is not ordained but she shall be chosen by name. But if she lost her husband a long time previously, let her be appointed. But if she lately lost her husband, let her not be trusted. Even if she is aged let her be tested for a time for often the passions grow with him who gives place for them in himself. Let the widow be

---

7. Polycarp, *Epistle to the Philippians* 4.3.
8. Ignatius, *To Smyrna* 13.1.

instituted by word only and let her be reckoned among the enrolled widows.[9]

At the end of the fourth century, the *Apostolic Constitutions* developed further instructions, including that a good widow should be modest and not greedy and be found "sitting at home."[10] This shows us a trajectory from 1 Timothy 5 through the fourth century that assumes an order or office of widows. Hippolytus insisted that widows not be ordained to clerical office, though some apparently did consider them appropriate candidates for some kind of ordination because they constituted such a distinct group of ministry within the church.

But does 1 Timothy teach that there should be an *official* order of widows in the church? One of the marks of an "office" from a sociological point of view is a specific selection marked by some kind of installation. Another is that there is usually some stipend.[11] It would be useful to know whether the widows' "enrollment" implied some kind of official installation and whether the financial help mentioned here constituted remuneration for service. But there is little hard evidence on this in Scripture or any other early Christian writings, and this may be a reading back of later circumstances.

Another consideration, of course, is whether the New Testament envisions any office other than for elder and deacon, if indeed the term *office* is even appropriate there. One problem is that no Greek word for "office" (e.g., *prostasia*, referring to leadership authority) is used in the New Testament. The KJV used the word "office" eight times in the New Testament, but in none of the texts is there a specific word for "office."[12] The widespread use of the KJV meant that to generations of readers "office" seemed a normal concept.[13]

---

9. *Apostolic Tradition* XI.1.4.5. He added, "But she shall not be ordained because she does not offer the oblation nor has she a liturgical ministry. But ordination is for the clergy, on account of their ministry. But the widow is appointed for prayer, and this is a function of all Christians."

10. *Apostolic Constitutions* 3.7.

11. B. Holmberg, *Paul and Power* (Philadelphia: Fortress, 1978).

12. In Rom. 11:13 the KJV has Paul saying, "I magnify mine office," but the word "office" here is simply *diakonia*, "service." In 12:4, "All members have not the same office," the Greek is *praxis*, "function." The word "office" in 1 Tim. 3:1, "If a man desire the office of a bishop," represents *episkope*, "oversight." In the phrases "let them use the office of a deacon" and "used the office of a deacon" (1 Tim. 3:10, 13) the Greek word translated "office" is simply a form of *diakoneo*, "serve." In three instances, the KJV inserts "office" into a phrase referring to the [Jewish] "priesthood" (Luke 1:8, 9; Heb. 7:5).

13. "Office" may be distinguished from function in that the former implies a position that always exists and requires an incumbent. If a senator dies, for example, someone else must be appointed to fill that office. On the other hand, an attorney general may appoint a special prosecutor to function for a time for a particular purpose.

There may be one clue as to the whether an order of widows for service existed this early. That is in 1 Timothy 3:11, where there are specific instructions for "women" (see comments). The question as to whether these constituted an order parallel to elders and deacons or whether they were the wives of deacons may be answered that the deacons' wives served in a ministry that *later* became organized separately from that of their husbands. If so, the ministry of widows may have had a similar history, from an informal group to a recognized order. It is anachronistic, however, to say that "1 Timothy speaks of widows who are to be enrolled as members of the clergy."[14]

We should also observe that the reference to giving widows honor (NIV "recognition") in verse 3 need not imply enrollment in any special list, but the verb *katalego* in verse 9 does.[15] However, without further evidence, that difference is not enough to postulate two distinct categories, general "honor" (meaning financial support) and acceptance into an order of widows for service. Conceivably the recognition itself constituted an official "installation" and the "honor" of verse 3 involved a remuneration for service, but the section introduced by verse 3 does not seem to describe an official order as much as do verses 9–10, where (significantly) no remuneration is mentioned.

We take the position, therefore, that the "list" is mentioned first in verse 9 because Paul is giving more specific details about qualification for support (such as specific age). There is no question that the verb which both NIV and NRSV translate as "be put on the list" means selection and enrollment. Thus, even if it does not mean enlistment in an order of service, it certainly means listing in a definite, openly recognized group qualified to receive financial assistance.

The age of sixty (v. 9) was considered old in the ancient world, but it was the time Plato determined best for entrance into priestly service in his ideal state.[16]

The meaning of the next qualification is debated. Literally it is "[the] woman [or wife] of one man," but that does not solve the problem. Does it mean "married only once" (NRSV) or "faithful to her husband" (NIV)? The same phrase (adapted to gender) describes deacons in 1 Timothy 3:2 (see comments). It is equivalent to the Latin word *univira* (the gender was normally feminine; it was customarily applied to women). The word was applied to the noble Roman matrons and has even been found in tribute on tombstones. However, as divorce increased in the Roman empire, these strong-minded matrons were no longer assumed to have been married only once, and other

---

14. Kroeger and Kroeger, *I Suffer Not a Woman*, 91.
15. One example given by BAGD is military enrollment (412).
16. See his *Laws* 757d.

honorific terms were used. Conversely, the term *univira* came to be used for women in *other* social classes who *had* been married only once.[17]

This made the expression available for the new and growing Christian church. Eventually the church used it in a more particular way, to designate those who did not marry after widowhood.[18] It would seem, therefore, from secular and pagan usage that the expression denotes someone married only once. But it has been argued that to assign this restrictive meaning to our passage results in an inner contradiction. That is, although Paul requires that widows who receive remuneration must not have married a second time (v. 9), his word to younger widows is that they *should* remarry (v. 14). But his advice to younger widows may have been intended to provide them with financial support through their second husbands as well as to keep them from immorality. We must keep in mind that the issue at hand is whether or not to give financial aid, not a judgment on remarriage. How the church should respond to the needs of young widows who later become widowed again after a second marriage is not stated.

Perhaps the best conclusion we can come to is that Paul here expresses an *ideal* of no remarriage. The phrase used here (and in 3:2) then corresponds to the marital status that earned respectability in the society in which the early church functioned. The terminology was in flux, and within the Christian community at that time it had a meaning more related to the moral life of the individual than to whether he or she had remarried. Therefore the translation "faithful to her husband" (NIV) probably best conveys the intent of the qualification.

The phrase in verse 10, "well known for her good works" has similarities to one of the qualifications for elders in 3:7: "He must also have a good reputation with outsiders." Both clauses have a word derived from the root *martyr*- (lit., "witness": "well known" and "reputation") and a form of *kalos* ("good"), though in a different grammatical relationship. As with elders, a widow's reputation is important for recognition in the church. Her good deeds should be of "all kinds." Paul states this generality after citing four distinct examples: "bringing up children, showing hospitality, washing the feet of the saints," and "helping those in trouble."

The contrast between younger and older widows in verses 11–15 is stronger than one might have expected. It is not merely that younger widows are likely to remarry and therefore not need financial help. They are to be refused rather than be enrolled, because their sensual desires may well

---

17. Majorie Lightman and William Zeisel, "*Univira*: An Example of Continuity and Change in Roman Society," *Church History* 46 (1977): 25–26.

18. Ibid., 30–32.

come between them and Christ. The verb (*katastreniao*) contains the idea of luxuriating or giving way to lustful impulses. In Revelation 18:9 the basic form of that verb, *streniao* ("live in luxury, live sensually"), describes the kings of the earth living in luxury with Babylon. The related noun (*strenos*) occurs in 18:3, where it means sensuality or luxury. The problem is not in young widows remarrying, since Paul counsels remarriage of young widows in verse 14. It is rather that they allow their impulses to alienate them from Christ, as is indicated by the relationship of the noun *Christos* to the verb.

Given that perspective, it is not surprising that these young widows will be judged (v. 12). They have "broken their first pledge." This may mean a pledge that they took when enrolled on the widows' list, but that could only have been the case before, or in spite of, Paul's restrictions on younger widows. It could refer to their initial promise to follow Christ, but that is not the usual way of describing conversion. It is difficult to determine with precision what the "first pledge" means, but it is clearly a commitment they have broken.

These are rather sweeping comments on how precarious the situation of young widows was (see below for some moderating considerations). But there is yet a further problem, the tendency of the younger widows to use their freedom to avoid responsibility (v. 13). This does not imply that women are more prone to idleness than men (see 2 Thess. 3:6–15, where it is probably men, not women, who are idle). Naturally the use of spare time to visit friends allows for the possibility of gossip, but is that a greater likelihood for remarried widows?

The preferred alternative (v. 14) is for the younger widows to remarry, not to satisfy their lusts but to assume responsibility for having children and managing their homes. It is worth noting that Paul advocates having children, but he gives no reason why. Perhaps this is to be interpreted on the basis of 2:15. A simple practical reason might be that having children to care for might reduce any tendency to go "about from house to house." But surely he would not counsel having children for the second reason unless he also believed that having children was desirable in a marriage, and would that be any more reason for a remarried widow than for any other wife?

Paul also counsels the young widows to "manage their homes." The word for "manage" is *oikodespoteo*, which, with its cognates, has an interesting history. The verb and related nouns were used in astrology for the ruling planet in a "house." In the noun form it could be used to describe the father of the family or the master of house, as in Matthew 10:25: "If the head of the house has been called Beelzebub, how much more the members of his household!" Given the commanding role astrology had in ancient times and given the domineering role of Beelzebub in pagan thought, *oikodespoteo* is a remarkable term to use for the responsibility of the remarried young widow over her household.[19] It indicates that this woman would have a strong management role in her new family.[20]

The concern lest there be "opportunity for slander" accords with verse 7 (see comments above). The "enemy" could take advantage of a bad situation, and Paul immediately identifies that enemy as "Satan" (v. 15). Since some of the young widows had already "turned away to follow Satan," we understand why there are such harsh words about judgment in verse 12. Satan can take advantage of human sins and weaknesses (1 Cor. 7:5; 2 Cor. 2:11; Eph. 4:26–27).

Once more, and in conclusion (v. 16), Paul counsels family members to care for widows to prevent additional burden on the church. The person who should help is a believing woman.[21] The end of the verse shows Paul's concern for truly needy widows. If, along the way, he changed the topic from widows in need to widows in an order of service, he has now clearly moved back to his initial concern.[22]

DEALING WITH PEOPLE. A Christian's relationship with other people is certainly not less important than other aspects of Christian life, nor is it simply one responsibility among many. Not only did Jesus make forgiveness of others a condition for our own forgiveness (Matt. 6:14–15), but he also said that if we only love those who love us and if greet only our brothers and sisters, we are doing no more than the despised tax collectors and the pagans do (5:46–47). If this is important for any Christian, it certainly crucial for Christians in positions of leadership.

Yet the same person whose smooth voice is heard on the radio or whose cheery words are read in a publication may, behind the scenes, be a demagogue. Sadly, sometimes the more important a Christian leader becomes the

---

19. See LSJ, 1204.

20. This text should be kept in mind when assessing the role of the wife in a family.

21. It is possible that Paul used a masculine word rather than a feminine, though the manuscript evidence is weighted toward the feminine as the original text. This would not be the first time that an ancient copyist changed the text to give preference to the male.

22. For further study, see also the following: M. Bassler, "The Widows' Tale: A Fresh Look at 1 Tim. 5:3–16," *JBL* 3 (1984): 23–41; R. A. Campbell, "*kai malista oikeion*: A New Look at 1 Timothy 5.8," *NTS* 41 (1995): 157–60; Verner, *The Household of God*, 161–66; Paul Veyne, ed., *A History of Private Life. 1. From Pagan Rome to Byzantium*, trans. Arthur Goldhammer (Cambridge, Mass.: Harvard Univ. Press, 1987), 75, 497–98, 535, 568, 598, 604; B. W. Winter, "Providentia for the Widow."

less important he thinks his associates are. It was not to be that way with Timothy even if someone needed correction; the young pastor was not to rebuke that person harshly but to exhort him as though he were his own father (v. 1).

That was Paul's instructions concerning men older than Timothy. But neither was he to be harsh with young men; they were to be treated as brothers. One wonders how many pastoral associates or interns have given up Christian ministry because of harsh criticisms from a mentor. There is, of course, no indication that the men and women mentioned in this passage were working closely with Timothy. And given the low view of women prevalent in those days, it was possible for even a sincere Christian man to slip into a feeling of superiority to his sisters in Christ. It is certainly possible for missionaries in any culture to lack the respect they should have for women, especially if they do not receive respect from the men in their own ethnic or social group. It is also easy for men, including or perhaps especially those in Christian ministry, to "use" younger women in the congregation in the pursuit of their own goals.

The needs of widows. The instructions in verses 1–2 prepare for Paul's giving attention to a needy group in the first century, the widows. It is instructive to see how he employs his blended treatment of doctrine and life with regard to this subject. In verse 4 the children and grandchildren of a widow "should learn first of all to put their religion into practice." I have had the experience of seeing very religious people virtually neglect their parents when they were older and in need. Sometimes children who have the means to give help shirk their duty and leave it up to a sibling, perhaps an unmarried woman, to care for the parents. Those who hear such a person preach, sing, or pray beautifully may have no idea that they have not put their "religion into practice." The words of verse 8 are amazingly strong in asserting that one who does not provide for his or her family has "denied the faith and is worse than an unbeliever." "The faith" here is the body of Christian doctrine. The individual has not only failed to put doctrine into practice but has denied it.

The exact social position, and economic position as well, of a widow will vary in different societies. Available resources will also vary. Customs regarding remarriage also differ from culture to culture. Christians must proceed thoughtfully to determine what is the best way to put doctrine into practice and to express love and respect in caring for widows in their society.

The needs of the elderly, and especially of widows, are universal, though they do not receive equal help in all societies. One hesitates to say that they are a problem, because, in addition to the attitude that word reveals, for an elderly person to think of herself or himself as a problem can add to a sense of uselessness, burden, and perhaps guilt. Although the need is universal, both widows and the elderly are viewed and treated in different ways. Some cultures traditionally have multigenerational homes, with each generation feeling loved and wanted and with those who are bereaved or aging staying on through their declining years. Other cultures devalue older people by ignoring them as they languish in sparse circumstances or by indifferently removing them from the family home and, in a cursory way, putting them in a "retirement" home. By contrast, when newly married couples establish a home that is monogenerational (until children arrive), they thereby effectively, if not deliberately, remove themselves from parents, grandparents, aunts, and uncles who may eventually need care.

Some families, wanting to do what is best for an older person, find a suitable retirement community or home, but then suffer immense guilt for not giving personal care in their own home. I recall my own mother saying, "This is the worst day of my life," as we were driving her to a fine retirement home, lovingly administered by a friend of ours. But within a few months, as we were driving her back there after Thanksgiving at our house, she surprised us by saying how glad she was to be going back to where her friends were! She lived there peacefully until she was ninety-four.

How then can we determine what is best for widows, based on 1 Timothy 5:3–16? What principles does Paul express? We must consider the needs of the widow, the responsibilities of her family, and the responsibilities of the widow herself.

(1) *Determining needs.* We should be sensitive to the actual needs of widows. Many widows today have considerable wealth through investments, retirement programs, and inherited funds. But there are needs of a different nature that are easily misread. Sometimes, when a woman is bereaved, it is assumed that she is unable to make the ordinary daily business decisions formerly made by her husband. The family may underestimate her latent ability, fail to take her sensitivity sufficiently into consideration, and make decisions for her. A common action is to insist that she leave her home and move into a different situation, leaving familiar surroundings and friends. This decision is often made too quickly and without adequate consultation with the individual. Again, we must be sensitive to her real needs.

(2) *Family responsibilities.* The care of a widow is primarily the responsibility of her family. Even when other sources of help are available (such as the church in Paul's day), the family ought to assume responsibility. It may seem trite to suggest that in our contemporary society, where a widow may be some distance from her family members, the frequent use of mail and phones is welcome; many widows feel neglected and forgotten. A phone call or visit is more important than money or a gift. I recall how much it meant to my own mother when she was in her nineties and struggling to hold on to her

memory, for me to bring a street map of the neighborhood she knew as a child and help her recall the delights of her childhood in that way.

Each circumstance provides opportunity for creative support of widows, especially the elderly. Often in my own pastoral ministries and in visiting friends of my mother, I have heard widows complain that they rarely hear from their families. The other side of the coin is that their families often do not know what to do or say. As with people dying from a wasting disease, it is often difficult to see them and to carry on a meaningful, encouraging conversation. If an elderly person—and we should enlarge this beyond widows—lives in or visits a home with younger people who, in turn, have children, the situation may have other difficulties. The younger generation will probably be engrossed in their own affairs and, at mealtimes, be involved in conversation about their activities and opinions. The older person is cut off without anything to contribute and perhaps will not even understand the vocabulary used. Decreased hearing or incipient dementia complicates the problem further.

The most obvious responsibility of families is financial, as Paul states in verse 4 of our passage. He offers the reminder that for us to take care of a parent or grandparent is really a repayment for the years of care he or she has given us. As the senior person gets older, we may find ourselves in a position of being a parent to our parents, especially as their mental acuity diminishes. Older people may not realize how much their family are paying for their support. Worse, they may become suspicious that their children or grandchildren are taking their money or possessions. Sadly, this is sometimes true. But even in good situations, elderly people may develop a fear of being "taken." They may squirrel away their own funds and then blame others for robbing them. Such circumstances give Christian families a difficult but wonderful opportunity to "honor your father and your mother" (Ex. 20:12).

The Bible also teaches that caring for widows is a religious duty (see, again, James 1:27). We cannot claim to be pleasing God while neglecting a widow, especially one in our own family. Verse 16 indicates that a believing woman should take care of any widows in her family. This may suggest a greater sensitivity on the part of women to widows, but it may also reflect a time when men were the wage earners and women were normally at home, where they could take care of needy family members. The point Paul makes, however, is that the women should try to assume the burden so the church does not have to. That is a matter of thoughtfulness for others.

(3) *The widow's responsibilities.* Reciprocally, the widow has a responsibility to seek God on her own, to trust him, and to pray for others continually. Verse 9 implies that she should continue to honor her husband. She should do good deeds, caring as much as possible for others, to the extent that she earns a

reputation for doing this. It may take a while after bereavement, but a widow must learn to trust God for her needs and future, looking to him "night and day (v. 5). Then she can turn her attention to the needs of others (v. 10).

As for younger widows, in many cultures they have already had a good education and can enter or reenter the marketplace. Many will remarry. Of course, all single people need to guard their sexual desires (as all people should) and refrain from improper relationships. It is appropriate for younger widows to remarry without reproach and start a new family. Also, since Paul counsels remarried widows to manage their households, we may assume that he has the same expectation of all married women. While Paul could be interpreted as thinking that the only management role women should have is in the home, the text does not say that. The striking thing is the strength of the word "manage." This should speak to men who, in their eagerness to be "head," attempt to micromanage their homes and intrude into all areas of home management. Verse 14 affirms women who devote their gifts to the management of their homes.

 **WIDOWS IN WESTERN society today.** The age at which women become widows has varied, of course, from generation to generation and country to country. Barring accidents and pernicious diseases, women today in Western societies are more likely to survive childbirth and various infectious diseases to live into their seventies, eighties, and nineties. Better economic preparation is being made for the care of women, and insurance policies for extended care are readily available. In other cultures extended families are, so to speak, self-insured by the existence of several generations and several workers in one household. Yet some regions of the world have no built-in care patterns, and the provisions of this passage are more relevant.

At the same time, however, medical costs and costs for care facilities have skyrocketed in the United States. We have a need today of planning for our own advanced years as well as helping our parents to prepare for theirs. Some people think that good investing and the purchase of good insurance policies evidence a lack of faith. Yet failure to provide means that someone else will have to provide—perhaps another relative, perhaps the government, perhaps the church.

It is relatively easy today to secure the necessary information from publications and institutions, and to solicit the advice of gerontologists and geriatric specialists who can help in understanding the circumstances of advanced age psychologically, medically, sociologically, and so on. Churches can provide counseling, programs, and financial help as well as spiritual care to those who are left alone. There are many widows—and widowers as well—grieving and struggling alone in single room occupancy hotels and institutions and on the streets. There is plenty of opportunity to blend our own faith and practice in these days to care for widows.

James 1:27 and 1 Timothy 5 refer to literal widows. There are literal orphans also who need help (James 1:27). There are, however, parallel situations in our contemporary world in which we can express the same blend of doctrine and life in helping those in need. Today there are many divorced people who are alone, hurting, feeling misunderstood, and perhaps having financial need. There are also children of divorces; recent studies have shown that divorce usually has an effect on children that continues even into their adult lives. They are not orphans, but they are children in need of love, which means understanding and care. There are also children who have been abused. They and abused women (with a few men as well) give opportunity for Christians to combine their faith with practice. In these matters James and the Pastoral Letters share the conviction that "religion" must be blended with deeds. Our churches should be centers of healing.

Among the books surrounding me in my study are *Beyond Widowhood*,[23] *Women as Widows*,[24] *Bereavement: Counseling the Grieving Throughout the Life Cycle*,[25] and *Our Aging Society*.[26] These books are a testimony to the attention that has been given in recent years to both aging and widowhood. These two topics are, of course, related, having to do in large measure with the increasingly large proportion of our society represented by the term *senior citizen*. Many communities have mutual support groups for the elderly and for the bereaved, the vast majority of whom are widows. Social Security has specific provisions for surviving spouses. Health care is available for the elderly, notably through Medicare. Private insurers even offer long-term care insurance, nursing home insurance, and other special packages.

Because of such programs, it could be said a few years ago that Christians in general no longer had the need that existed in earlier generations to provide for the elderly and widows. Government entitlement programs were doing what families used to do. In the 1990s, however, it became clear that the aging population was too large for these programs. Republicans seized on the question of whether Medicare would shortly be bankrupt. The skyrocketing costs of health care became a hot political topic, with business

---

23. By Robert C. DiGiulio (New York: Free Press, 1989).
24. By Helena Znaniecka Lopata (New York: Elsevier, 1979).
25. By David A. Crenshaw (New York: Continuum, 1990).
26. By Alan Pifer and Lydia Bronte, eds. (New York: W. W. Norton, 1986).

and government trying to affix responsibility on the others. The future burden on today's younger generation is a matter for deep anxiety (along with college costs!).

Work and preparing for retirement are subjects of not a few books, magazines, and newsletters. Age discrimination is a feared monster both among those who need to keep working in order to live and among employers, who need caution in discharging a worker of declining abilities, lest there be a lawsuit. And at the end of the road are the questions of "quality of life," euthanasia, doctor-assisted suicide, and living wills with instructions for termination of "heroic measures."

Suddenly the church has had to open its eyes to the fact that Christians will once again have to consider what they should do for the aging and for widows. An exemplary program for senior citizens launched some years ago by the LaSalle Street Church in Chicago continues to point the way for urban churches to care not only for their own but also for those in the surrounding community. The love of Christ is expressed in food, pastoral care, legal counsel, and low cost housing. When a fire took the lives and homes of senior citizens in a nearby single resident hotel, LaSalle Street Church held a memorial service for the whole community.

Specific ways to help. There are several specific ways in which Christians today can help meet the needs of those who are "really widows."

(1) They can have a church member qualified for hospice care, so that if a person is near death, that person will understand what the surviving spouse is experiencing and perhaps also participate in the final days of care, enlisting other Christians to help also.

(2) The church can assist in the stages of bereavement. There is plenty of help for people in the early stages. Not all go through the same sequence of grief, but understanding the forms grief takes helps those who desire to bring comfort and encouragement.

(3) It would also be good to have at least one of the church membership, perhaps a deacon, become acquainted with the government entitlement programs, such as Social Security, Medicare, and Medicaid, including enrollment procedures, timing, and computation of benefits. That person might also be able to find out certain financial information, such as retirement plans, plans that are tax deferred, and 401K programs, and how to roll over benefits paid after retirement in time to prevent taxation. Many of the elderly feel unable to manage their affairs wisely, especially older women without business experience.[27] This means not only being alert to help in practical matters, but also

---

27. Others may be well able to make wise financial decisions and would feel demeaned by too much help.

being aware of the deep apprehension over their future financial health. Pastors, friends, and lay counselors should be aware of this pervasive anxiety.

It is a sensitive matter to evaluate the actual financial needs of a widow. The ways in which a portfolio can be structured are varied, and many tend to be fearful and cautious in revealing their financial matters to others. Nevertheless, if 1 Timothy 5 is to be applied, some responsible persons need to be informed of the extent of need. Preferably more than one person will be involved, so there is no opportunity or suspicion of manipulation.

(4) Attention must be given also to the family. They may have different perspectives on an aging relative's financial security and on what decisions are best. Some may be unwilling or feel unable to provide assistance, so 1 Timothy 5:4 and 16 may have to be explained to them. It may even be that family members will seek personal benefit. Some may try to convince the widow to make large gifts to them. This could not only benefit them personally at her expense, but could be done under the guise of avoiding estate taxes, when actually they have in mind reducing the person's visible assets so she will be qualified for state aid, in effect causing the government to take over their responsibility.

(5) Pastoral visits to widows are also important. I once visited the widow of an elderly Christian. Both husband and wife had been deeply spiritual and had a son who was a missionary. When I entered I noticed that she was addressing envelopes. She told me that she was sending gospel "tracts" to everyone in the local phone book. Then she told me that she had a spiritual concern she wanted to talk over with me. She said that she was not sure she was saved. I felt like saying that this was ridiculous, given her love for God and her desire to see other people come to the Lord through her project. But I realized that this was a manifestation of her deep grief; perhaps it was a feeling that she had not been worthy, and so God took her husband. Whatever the case, she needed to be helped to assurance and into a continuing relationship with her Lord as taught in 1 Timothy 5:5 and 10.

Younger widows. So far, a good deal of the teaching of 1 Timothy can be applied with an intelligent and spiritual understanding of the individual circumstances and feelings of the older widow. The instructions for young widows, including the age at which one becomes qualified for support, are more difficult because of the differences in perceptions of aging in different cultures and in different periods of history. Younger women today have usually been able to establish careers or at least secure employment. They can keep in good health and have ways of maintaining their physical appearance.

It is still true, as implied in the text, that to many men younger women are more attractive sexually, but a woman's sexual desire continues longer than has often been thought. Some recent research seems to show that men decline more rapidly than women in the later years. But age seems to have little to do with being idle and going around visiting people (or, today, making phone calls). Using free time to go on-line and search the Internet to establish contacts, including the use of e-mail, is another matter, however. Younger women are more likely to be adept with computers. The Internet allows those who want to establish contact with men easily to do so. The moral problems of cyberspace are well known, and Satan is still able to lure women as well as men into dangerous situations. Thus, the warnings of 1 Timothy 5:11–15 are still applicable.

Women should be encouraged (if they are reluctant) to remarry, and age is not the dividing line it used to be. Likewise, women hardly need to be encouraged to manage their homes, especially given the access they have to women's literature on the home and to Christian materials about bringing up children and relating well to spouses. They will also probably have more general background and education to help them be good managers.

In all of this we must remember that in Paul's instructions to Timothy, it is the church that should accept responsibility for widows. Even though there are various resources available today that were unavailable and not even conceived of in Paul's day, the government is not able to do it all, nor should it. The church is still a "household," the family of God.

1 Timothy 5:17–6:2

THE ELDERS WHO direct the affairs of the church well are worthy of double honor, especially those whose work is preaching and teaching. [18]For the Scripture says, "Do not muzzle the ox while it is treading out the grain," and "The worker deserves his wages." [19]Do not entertain an accusation against an elder unless it is brought by two or three witnesses. [20]Those who sin are to be rebuked publicly, so that the others may take warning.

[21]I charge you, in the sight of God and Christ Jesus and the elect angels, to keep these instructions without partiality, and to do nothing out of favoritism.

[22]Do not be hasty in the laying on of hands, and do not share in the sins of others. Keep yourself pure.

[23]Stop drinking only water, and use a little wine because of your stomach and your frequent illnesses.

[24]The sins of some men are obvious, reaching the place of judgment ahead of them; the sins of others trail behind them. [25]In the same way, good deeds are obvious, and even those that are not cannot be hidden.

[6:1]All who are under the yoke of slavery should consider their masters worthy of full respect, so that God's name and our teaching may not be slandered. [2]Those who have believing masters are not to show less respect for them because they are brothers. Instead, they are to serve them even better, because those who benefit from their service are believers, and dear to them. These are the things you are to teach and urge on them.

THESE VERSES CONTINUE the section on personal relationships (see comments on 5:1–2). The first topic in this segment is how the church should relate to elders (5:17–25). Verses 17–18 deal with the respect and material help that elders deserve. Verses 19–20 deal with the possibility of elders being accused of sinning. Verse 21 is a general command that, in this context, applies to the way elders are treated. Verse 22 seems to arise from the potential problem of sinning elders. It is difficult to relate verse 23 to the context, but verses 24–25 continue the theme of private and public sin triggered by verse 20. In 6:1–2 Paul moves to the topic of slaves and how they should live as Christians.

Honoring Elders (5:17–20)

THE INSTRUCTIONS IN 3:1–7 concerning "overseers" certainly apply to elders, but since the usual Greek word for elder (*presbyteros*) does not occur there, this is the first unambiguous occurrence of substantial instructions concerning them. "Direct the affairs of the church well" (v. 17) is an enlargement on the Greek words for "rule well."[1] The verb used here is *proistemi*, the same one employed to refer to overseers and deacons managing their families (3:4, 12). The adverb "well" (*kalos*) also appears both in that context and this one.

While the reference to the "respect" (3:4) that an overseer should have from his children is different from the "double honor" referred to here, it is significant that evidence of an elder's dignity and recognition appears in both contexts. Commentators differ as to whether the phrase "double honor" means (a) respect, (b) remuneration, or (c) both; and whether, if it is (b), it means that they should receive literally twice as much remuneration as elders who do not rule well or who do not minister the Word. In support of (a), honor was far more important in that society than in ours and would have been a deeply valued "reward" to the worthy elders. In support of (b), Paul elsewhere argues strongly for proper financial support for the Lord's servants (cf. 1 Cor. 9:14, where he also uses the Deut. 25:4 quotation about not muzzling the ox).[2] Finally, since the provision of needs would have been a practical expression of honor, the two possible meanings need not be mutually exclusive, and thus (c) is possible.

While the word translated "especially" (*malista*) can have the sense of "that is" or "I mean" (see 4:10; 5:8; 2 Tim. 4:13; Titus 1:10, and comments on those passages), here it probably means "especially." We may infer that elders as a group had the responsibility of leadership, that all of them had to be doctrinally strong and to teach effectively, but that only some of them devoted enough time to preaching and teaching to make additional financial support necessary. This argues for the meaning "remuneration" or for *both* "honor and support."

---

1. The participial construction in the Greek here includes the adverb for "well" between the article and the participle. This, along with the use of the perfect tense, implies that the people in view here have established themselves as those *characterized* by good leadership.

2. See also Jesus' instructions to those he sent out in Matt. 10:10 and Luke 10:7. In each the word "worthy" is used, as here, with *trophos* ("nourishment," i.e., daily provision of one's needs).

With verse 19 the passage takes a sharp turn from *honoring* to *accusing* elders, though the elders are still honored by the exercise of caution in making an accusation. The instructions here are unambiguous. The Old Testament requirement of two or three witnesses (Deut. 19:15) is appropriately applied here. Its use is crucial here not because elders are more important than others but because the reputation of an elder is so important to the witness of the church and because Satan can use disgrace to his own ends (cf. 3:7).

The present tense of the word "sin" in verse 20 implies that the elder in question not only has been proved guilty of the sin charged, but persists in it. Since the reputation of God's people in the world is so important in the Pastoral Letters (see also Titus 2:5, 8, 10), if an elder's sin comes to light (with at least two or three witnesses testifying about it), it must be dealt with publicly. But John Stott observes:

> Such a public rebuke, though an effective deterrent, must be the last resort, however. It is a safe rule that private sins should be dealt with privately, and only public sins publicly. It is neither right nor necessary to make what is private public, until all of the possibilities have been exhausted.[3]

Further Instructions About Sin and Purity in the Church (5:21–25)

THE WARNING IN verse 21 to avoid "partiality" and "favoritism" seems a matter of common sense and courtesy. However, since Timothy is working closely with the elders, his natural tendency might be reluctance to act strongly against a leader who has sinned. Paul initiates these instructions with the heavy artillery of a solemn warning just short of an oath, calling on "God and Christ Jesus and the elect angels" as witnesses (cf. also 2 Tim. 2:14; 4:1 and comments). The reference to the "elect angels" here is perplexing, especially since the expression occurs nowhere else in Scripture. It is possible that "elect" simply emphasizes the importance of the angelic witnesses. Yet it may also emphasize God's sovereign right to choose angels, or perhaps it refers to the angels' ability, as God's servants and unlike human beings, to choose not to sin.

Timothy should not only exercise great care in the matter of accused elders and in avoiding impartiality, but he should "not be hasty in the laying on of hands" (v. 22). The argument has gone back and forth over the years as to whether this is the imposition of hands in the sense of 1 Timothy 4:14

---

3. John Stott, *Guard the Truth* (Downers Grove, Ill.: InterVarsity, 1996), 139.

or the accepting back, through that same sign, of a repentant person (presumably a former elder).

Some interpret the caution Paul encourages here in terms of early church practice, but this may be anachronistic when applied to the apostolic period. Nevertheless, Hanson acknowledges that the practice of reconciliation of the excommunicated by the laying on of hands by a bishop "is not attested till more than one hundred years after the author's time," but he feels that this is the more natural interpretation.[4] Among the earlier commentators of the twentieth century Lock has a detailed, though concise, discussion with historical references. He too chooses the reception of the penitent sinner.[5]

While this is possible, the only reference to laying on of hands so far in the Pastoral Letters is 4:14. Therefore other commentators think the "hasty" action is selecting a wrong person for eldership. But Paul's warning not to "share in the sins of others" and his exhortation to Timothy to keep himself "pure" imply the actuality or the possibility of sin in the original selection of the erring elder.[6] Clearly *neither* action—selecting or disciplining—should be done in such a "hasty" manner as to be undiscerning, careless, or slack as regards to sin. To be neglectful in these matters is to commit sin oneself. The injunction to Timothy to "keep yourself pure" (cf. also 4:12; 5:2) can be understood as referring particularly to a possibility of association with evil or as a general command.

The most natural explanation for Paul's comments in verse 23 about wine is that his mention of purity provides a bridge to the issue of abstinence. The dangers of excess drinking were well known in the ancient world. Those who took the Nazirite vow were to abstain from wine during the period of their separation (Num. 6:3–4). John the Baptist abstained from wine altogether (Luke 1:15; 7:33). However, according to the Pastorals elders were simply to avoid drunkenness or addiction (1 Tim. 3:3; Titus 1:7). It is natural that Timothy would question whether he should take wine at all. It is possible that, like the Corinthians who asked Paul several questions in a letter (see 1 Cor. 7:1), Timothy may have raised the question with Paul. The apostle not only allows Timothy to take "a little wine" for reasons of health, but he commands him to do so. Then, picking up the matter of sin, private and public once more, Paul makes the point in verses 24–25 that sooner or later both sins and good works will become public.

---

4. Hanson, *The Pastoral Epistles*, 103.

5. Lock, *The Pastoral Epistles*, 63–64.

6. Fee, *1 and 2 Timothy, Titus*, 131–32; Knight, *Pastoral Epistles*, 239; Oden, *First and Second Timothy and Titus*, 152; Stott, *Guard the Truth*, 139–40.

Slaves and Masters (6:1–2)

THE FINAL EXAMPLE of relationships in this section is that of slaves and masters. Reprising the idea of honor from 5:17, Paul counsels slaves to give their masters "full respect." The reason for this is similar to the reasons he gives in Titus 2:9–10 for proper behavior by slaves, women, and young men (cf. 2:5, 8)—the Christian's reputation in the community (cf. also 1 Tim. 3:7; 5:14). Disrespectful and disobedient Christian slaves could bring terrible disgrace on the gospel.

The large number of slaves in ancient society and in the church meant that they could not be left out of an extended treatment of human relationships. The Pastoral Letters do not conform to the usual pattern of social codes (*Haustafeln*, which deal with the various roles or stations in life; cf. Eph. 5:21–6:9).[7] Here the dominant theme is not some traditional pattern of mutual relationships (submission, love, etc., as in Ephesians), but godly behavior in the various relationships of life and the effect of this on Christian witness. In the case of slaves they are given instruction here with no corresponding message for masters.

Slaves are under a "yoke" (v. 1). While it was unnecessary to use that graphic word (since the term *slavery* itself conveys their miserable condition), "yoke" emphasizes that slaves have no rights of their own. Paul is not "rubbing this in" but rather setting the stage for his strong word that both in general (v. 1), and particularly when slaves have a Christian master (v. 2), they should give (positively) "respect" and (negatively) not disrespect. The Greek word translated "respect" in verse 1 is the same as the "honor" due elders in 5:17; the word rendered "to show less respect" is the same one used in 4:12 regarding those who may "look down" on Timothy.

Rather than taking advantage of Christian masters "because they are brothers," the slaves are to remember that their owners are also "believers" and beloved (NIV "dear to them"). The passage is straightforward except for the final phrase, "those who benefit from their service [*euergesis*]." Since *euergesis* refers in Greek literature to service done by a superior to an inferior, it makes the natural reading unusual. However, the alternatives also have their short comings, so the NIV is probably preferable.

The section concludes with a familiar exhortation to teach and encourage "these . . . things" (*tauta*, see comments on 4:11). While that word probably refers, as usual, to what has preceded, and therefore in the NIV stands as a conclusion of the paragraph, verse 3 flows naturally from it because that verse sets up the antithesis of false doctrine. The editors of the standard

---

7. On this whole topic see David C. Verner, *The Household of God*.

Greek text place this sentence at the beginning of a new paragraph, as does the NRSV.

SHAME, HONOR, AND **relationships**. Concepts of shame and honor are culture-sensitive. Studies of the significance of honor and shame in specific New Testament instances have been helpful in the understanding of relevant biblical passages.[8] Understanding why Scripture enjoins someone to respect a particular class of people, such as how slaves here are told to respect their masters or how Ephesians 5 tells husbands to love their wives, may be difficult. In the latter case American ideas about love and marriage need to be scrutinized in comparison with ancient Jewish or Roman assumptions regarding the relationship between husband and wife.

Many societies have fostered honor and respect for the elderly, although this has been changing in modern times. While in 1 Timothy 5:17 it is not clear whether the word *time* ("honor") means simply honor or honorarium (see comments above), honor is certainly involved, and the principle cited here is found in the Old Testament (see v. 18; cf. also 2 Tim. 2:6). Hard work should be compensated in the church as well as in society.

A deep respect for elders carries over to the problem of alleged sin among elders. Charges brought by individuals are not to be acted on precipitously. The Old Testament principle of multiple witnesses is important in such cases. The principle here seems to be that when the word is out that an elder has been living sinfully, the correction must also be public.

In all of this we should keep in mind the human situation. The social context is a relatively small group of individuals who have been meeting in one or more homes, who have developed an intense relationship with one another, and who are also related to one another. The number of people in a house church related to each other would have been proportionally much larger than in a church of, say, two hundred people. In addition, other associations existed, such as slaves and masters and perhaps clients and benefactors. In such circumstances favoritism could easily overshadow fairness.

Once we have the proper prospective and sense of proportion with regard to the scene of the New Testament church, we can proceed to make the proper application in our own circumstances. Fairness must always be observed. It is not unknown in churches that a leading figure has been caught

---

8. One useful study of this topic in Luke's writings is Jerome H. Neyrey, ed. (*The Social World of Luke-Acts: Models for Interpretation* (Peabody, Mass.: Hendrickson, 1991).

in terrible sin, but is let off easily because of strong personal attachments in the congregation.

Such defections cannot be completely foreseen and prevented, but care in the selection of elders is an important proactive measure, as verse 22 points out. The shallow way in which many churches have election for church office can increase the possibility of problems later. These instructions were first of all given to Timothy himself, and as such they are a warning to all those who through missionary and evangelistic activity establish churches or who are looked up to as founding leaders. Such people must keep apart from sin themselves and keep above charges and countercharges. Church leaders and others can, through precipitous action, lose their own objectivity and purity.

Alcohol in the Christian's life. Verse 23 seems to stand in isolation from what proceeds and follows it, while verses 24–25 seem to belong to verses 17–22. Having noted that, we can briefly comment on verses 23–25 in sequence. Christians who travel internationally for the first time are often struck by the fact that perspectives vary widely among Christians regarding such matters as the use of alcohol. It is not always easy to extract principles from Scripture that apply to such practices universally, but this one seems quite clear. The principles are: (1) Total abstinence from alcohol is not required; (2) wine is advisable, at least under certain health conditions; (3) the use of wine is to be done in moderation ("little wine").

This passage does not deal with larger issues of social drinking, alcoholism, or attitudes toward alcohol that are indigenous to different countries or regions. Elsewhere Scripture issues strong warnings about alcohol (Prov. 20:1; 32:31; Eph. 5:18; 1 Peter 4:3). At the same time 1 Timothy 4:4–5 reminds us that "everything God created is good, and nothing is to be rejected if it is received with thanksgiving, because it is consecrated by the word of God and prayer."

Verses 24–25 pick up the matter of the seriousness of a sinful life. The point here, of course, is that in regard to what we have done, both evil and good will one day be revealed. Although written in a different context, this reflects the truth of 2 Corinthians 5:10. The difference is that there it is before the judgment seat of Christ that we give account, whereas here neither sins nor good deeds can be successfully hidden permanently.

SUPPORTING THE LORD'S **servants.** In his autobiography, *Just As I Am*, Billy Graham describes the circumstances under which he decided that it would be better to receive a salary from his organization rather than a love gift from the audience at the end of each crusade.

There had been newspaper reports about the amount of money Graham was receiving through those love gifts. To prevent rumors and embarrassment he was advised to receive a salary that would "compare favorably with that of a typical minister in any average large-city church."[9] Although the salaries of athletes today are unconscionably high, the public is more critical of public officials and preachers who take in too much money.

Perhaps it is time to revisit the world of the first century and reflect on what the New Testament has to say on the subject (see comments in the Contemporary Significance sections of 6:3–10, 11–21). It is difficult for churches to find a yardstick by which to measure the appropriateness of salaries for the pastoral staff. Billy Graham was advised to accept a salary commensurate with that of an urban pastor, but is this the best way to determine a pastor's salary? One proposal that has merit is to ascertain the salary of an educational administrator (high school) in the community; there is enough of a similarity between education and at least some of the ministries of a typical pastor to warrant such a comparison. This is preferable to matching salaries with those of successful business people in the church or community, even though the church may think that pastors deserve equal compensation with community business leaders.

All of this raises the question as to whether a pastor should even have a salary. In one church I served, I wanted to live "by faith," but the church, which had a good number of fine, successful people, were afraid that anything like a "love gift" would be too much. We eventually settled on an arrangement whereby my income varied according to giving, but was carefully monitored by the treasurer. One danger is that the pastor becomes a professional who is paid like those in the secular world, expecting larger and larger amounts year by year and perhaps ultimately going to a church that will pay him even more. Another danger is that a so-called senior pastor will receive an amount inappropriately more than that received by others on the church staff. One further consideration is that the reputation of the church and, therefore the reputation of the Lord himself (concerns that are prominent in the Pastoral Letters) must not be harmed by an obvious failure to provide a decent living for the pastoral staff.

Problems of defection among leaders. It is not appropriate in this section to enlarge in detail on contemporary problems of moral defection among church leaders. Rather, I offer the following observations. (1) The circumstances of moral defection are often complicated by the existence of heavy demands in contemporary ministry, of increasing tensions within the home, and of the high number of people entering ministry who come out of broken and abusive homes.

---

9. Graham, *Just As I Am* (Grand Rapids: Zondervan, 1997), 185–86.

(2) When a pastor has not had stable, loving support and moral encouragement in early life, when he or she is tired, often occupied in counseling people with sexual problems, and when he or she is busy with frequent evening meetings that interfere with time at home with family and especially with spouse, temptations, especially of a sexual nature, can be strong.

(3) Added to this are the burdens of spiritual warfare—the fact that a pastor is a likely target of the enemy of souls and of the realities of temptation described in James 1:13–15 that we all face. Understanding and counseling are needed in such situations.

(4) Finally, such understanding and counseling do not preclude definitive action on the part of the church, such as that which is described in this section of 1 Timothy.

Applying master-slave relationships. First Timothy 6:1–2 concludes the theme of chapter 5, which contains "Advice About Widows, Elders and Slaves" (as the NIV entitles it). Paul's instructions here pertain only to slaves, not (as in Eph. 6:5–9; Col. 3:22–4:1) to both slaves and masters. He makes two points: Masters deserve full respect (vv. 1–2a), and slaves should give Christian masters even better service (v. 2b). This section provides yet one more example of the blending of doctrine and life.

The reason for giving the masters full respect is so that God's name and the apostolic teaching not be slandered. This respect is to show itself in good service. This is a work ethic that embodies the two "great commandments" (although they are not mentioned here). For slaves to love God fully and to love their neighbor (in this case, their masters) as themselves will mean that they must serve their masters well, thus bringing honor to God (cf. Titus 2:2–10). The mention of slaves does not imply Paul's approval of slavery. Unfortunately, it has been so applied. All this accords with the teaching of the Pastorals, which exhibits the concern of these letters that Christians bring honor to God in all their relationships.

1 Timothy 6:3–10

IF ANYONE TEACHES false doctrines and does not agree to
the sound instruction of our Lord Jesus Christ and to
godly teaching, ⁴he is conceited and understands nothing.
He has an unhealthy interest in controversies and quarrels
about words that result in envy, strife, malicious talk, evil suspicions ⁵and constant friction between men of corrupt mind,
who have been robbed of the truth and who think that godliness is a means to financial gain.

⁶But godliness with contentment is great gain. ⁷For we
brought nothing into the world, and we can take nothing out
of it. ⁸But if we have food and clothing, we will be content
with that. ⁹People who want to get rich fall into temptation
and a trap and into many foolish and harmful desires that
plunge men into ruin and destruction. ¹⁰For the love of money
is a root of all kinds of evil. Some people, eager for money,
have wandered from the faith and pierced themselves with
many griefs.

Original Meaning

DURING THE COURSE of this letter, Paul has
returned again and again to the need for both
sound doctrine and godly living. This theme is
not developed in a connected logical way as
though he were writing a treatise. It is presented instead as we might expect
for a veteran missionary writing a letter of an urgent nature. He deals with a
subject, follows through some implications of it or enlarges on certain aspects,
and then later comes back to it again, dealing with it in a slightly different way.

Description of the False Teacher (6:3–5)

PAUL'S LAST DESCRIPTION of the false teachers was in 4:1–5, which he followed by a contrasting word to Timothy as to how he should act as a good
servant of the Lord. In the present passage, verses 3–5 describe the false
teachers and verse 6 establishes a contrast triggered by the repetition of the
word "godliness."

Another major section like this occurs in 2 Timothy 3:1–9, though the contrast there is not with Timothy but with Paul's own life (vv. 10–11). It is significant that in both 1 Timothy 6 and 2 Timothy 3 one of Paul's criticisms of the

false teachers has to do with greed. Here it occurs at the crucial middle of the section; in 2 Timothy 3:1–9 it occurs at the beginning (v. 2). In both passages, however, greed is contrasted with true godliness. Financial greed is also mentioned in yet another section about false teachers (Titus 1:10–16, esp. v. 11).

The fact that Paul does not hesitate to attribute financial motives to the opponents of his gospel not only triggers his insistence on combining godliness with sound teaching, but also reflects a convention in the Greco-Roman world, that of using such charges as a means of discrediting one's opponents.[1] It must be stressed, however, that this is no mere convention here; polluting the gospel message by financial gain was, and is, a serious matter.

Verse 3 opens with a conditional clause, "if anyone teaches false doctrines." Paul has already made it clear that there are indeed people who do this, and the conditional clause is a normal way of expressing an assumption. It might be better to translate it "anyone who" or "whoever" (NRSV). The verb for teaching false doctrines (*heterodidaskaleo*) appeared in 1:3 (see comments). This is still his concern.

The false doctrine runs counter to "sound instruction" and "godly teaching." Both expressions are thematic in the Pastorals. The word "sound" represents the participle of the verb *hygiaino*, conveying the idea of being in good health (see comments on 1:10).[2] The NIV "instruction" represents the plural of *logos*, which has a broader meaning than just "words." Thus, it need not refer to the specific words of Christ, though it is sometimes taken to do so (as in NRSV). The Pastorals do not cite specific quotations of Christ that the heretics contradict. Rather, their teaching is against the basic doctrines that he taught his followers. The word "godly," which modifies "teaching," is a significant word in the Pastoral Letters, where it refers both to the character of individuals and to doctrine.[3]

---

1. The first-century Jewish historian Josephus called the revolutionary Theudas a *goes,* a sorcerer, the same word he used to describe an Egyptian false prophet and a band of outlaws (*War* 2.13.5, 6 [261, 264]; *Ant.* 20.5.1 [97]). Any missionary of a new religion might be accused of being a *magus* (i.e., a charlatan magician). Elsewhere Paul referred to contrasting opinions concerning himself with the words "genuine, yet regarded as impostors [*planoi*]" (2 Cor. 6:8). He asserted in 1 Thess. 2:3 that his "appeal" did not "spring from error or impure motives." The impure motives in question often involved greed, so Paul defends himself further by saying that he did not use a "mask to cover up greed" (v. 5) and that far from being a (financial) "burden" to them he worked "night and day" (v. 9). For other examples see W. Liefeld, *The Wandering Preacher As a Social Figure in the Roman Empire* (Ann Arbor: University Microfilms, 1968), 272–87. See also comments on 4:2.

2. See also 2 Tim. 1:13; 4:3; Titus 1:9, 13; 2:1.

3. In 1 Timothy it occurs in 2:2; 3:16; 4:7, 8, as well as in the present passage in vv. 3, 5, 6, 11; it also occurs in 2 Tim. 3:5; Titus 1:1. The cognate verb occurs in 1 Tim. 5:4 and the adverb in 2 Tim. 3:12; Titus 2:12.

The person who "does not agree" to the truth "is conceited and understands nothing" (v. 4; "a pompous ignoramus," REB; cf. 1:7; 3:6). A somewhat similar description appears in Romans 1:21–22, 25, 28. The person who rejects "healthy" doctrine has an "unhealthy" or morbid obsession with "controversies and quarrels about words." Lock calls them "hair-splitting—fights in which words are the weapons and perhaps also the object; there is no reality behind them."[4]

The five results listed for these quarrels all have to do with disruptions in interpersonal relationships: "envy," "strife" (a contentious disruption of relationships, which often arises from envy), "malicious talk" (*blasphemiai*, in this case slandering one another, not God), "evil suspicions," and "constant friction." Not only the friction but all of these dysfunctional attitudes occur among people who have three characteristics: a "corrupt mind," "robbed of the truth," and driven by a perverted concept of "godliness." The false concept is that godliness (here perhaps in a more ordinary sense of "religion") is a way to make money.

Contentment and True Godliness (6:6–10)

IN VERSE 6 Paul picks up the word "gain" from verse 5 and contradicts the utilitarian view of godliness criticized there. There *is* great gain in godliness, but only if it is combined "with contentment," the opposite of greed. The word "contentment" is *autarkes*, a word used by the Stoics for the virtue of self-sufficiency. Paul used this word in a Christian sense also in Philippians 4:11, "I am not saying this because I am in need, for I have learned to be content whatever the circumstances."

It is interesting that Paul does not speak here of Christ being our contentment. No doubt that was still true for him, but the point he makes in verse 7 is expressed in an aphorism much like our "you can't take it with you." Verse 8 specifies the essentials necessary for contentment, "food and clothing." This embodies Jesus' strong teaching against greed and regarding trust in God for material needs in Luke 12:13–34 (see also the prayer, "Give us today our daily bread," and other teachings in the Sermon on the Mount in Matt. 6:9–13, 19–34).[5]

The point of verses 9–10 is not that wealth is wrong but that desire for it is. Three phrases make that clear: (1) "people who *want* to get rich," (2) "the *love* of money is a root of all kinds of evil," (3) and "some people, *eager* for money" (italics added). The NIV properly avoids the definite article before the

---

4. Lock, *Pastoral Epistles*, 68.

5. See also Young, *Theology of the Pastoral Letters*, 19, 33–34, commenting on Reggie M. Kidd, *Wealth and Beneficence in the Pastoral Epistles*.

word "root" because Paul is not saying that the love of money is *the* root, and the NIV inserts "kinds of" to show the implication of the word "all" before "evil."

The closing words of verse 10 show the interconnection between covetousness and departure from "the faith." Once again we see the contrast between the combination of true godliness and faith on the one hand and evil motivation and unbelief on the other. The familiar verse 7 is not only a truism; it is a powerful fact that should motivate our living. In fact, the whole section of verses 6–10 is familiar to our ears.

THE BACKGROUND FOR **Paul's concern.** As noted earlier Paul apparently became increasingly concerned with the murky mixture containing the dregs of false doctrine and sinful character of the false teachers. This is different from the nasty accusations that ancient preachers, both philosophic and religious, used to hurl at each other. Paul is not merely trying to demean the opposition. He is trying to show the connection between evil people and the evil teachings they are foisting on the Christians at Ephesus.

Timothy is facing an intellectual perversion here, shown in the persistent pursuit of details that do not edify but stir up controversy. These false teachers apparently have two wretched goals in their religious instruction: financial gain and sexual conquest (see also 2 Tim. 3:6). This, of course, is the picture novelists have portrayed of evangelists—in some cases, with justification. Religion provides a marvelous cover for evil. In a later century but still in the context of the Roman empire, the satirist Lucian described religious and philosophical preachers, many of them itinerants, who used their profession to gain money and sex. One example was Alexander the false prophet, who sold prophecies for a price and settled in an area where people were superstitious and gullible. He also found a rich patroness.[6] A more famous figure was Peregrinus. This man was always seeking attention, finally demonstrated when he immolated himself on a pyre at a Greek festival with everyone looking on. During the course of his checkered career, Peregrinus discovered that itinerant Christian preachers were royally hosted and supported by sincere Christians. He converted from Cynicism to Christianity for a time.[7]

To follow a religious profession for the sake of personal gain was already well known in Paul's day. He told the Thessalonians that he did not want to

---

6. Lucian, *Alexander.* See also W. Liefeld, *The Wandering Preacher As a Social Figure,* 85–88.
7. Lucian, *Peregrinus.* See also Liefeld, *The Wandering Preacher As a Social Figure,* 53–59.

be a burden or indebted to any of them and, therefore, as he preached the gospel he worked at a trade "night and day" (1 Thess. 2:3–9). He preached full time only when Silas and Timothy arrived from Macedonia, possibly because they brought supplies from believers there (Acts 18:5; cf. Phil. 4:10–19).[8] In contrast to all those "who think that godliness is a means to financial gain" (v. 5), Paul's assertion that "godliness with contentment is great gain" (v. 6) is a strong personal testimony. Here is a marvelous example of blending religion and practice, godliness and contentment.

The "love of money." After urging his readers to have this contentment with basics of food and clothing, Paul establishes an aphorism that is often misquoted and almost always quoted apart from its context: "Love of money is a root of all kinds of evil" (v. 10). It is often rightly pointed out that Paul does say that money is the root of all evil, it is *the love of* money that nourishes evil. Furthermore, it is not *the* root of all evil, but *a* (NIV, NRSV) root or "at the root" (NLT) of *all kinds* of evil, as implied by the Greek text.

In another master stroke of blending doctrine and life, Paul states that "some people, eager for money, have wandered from the faith" (v. 10). We have seen that in the Pastoral Letters the word "the" before "faith" implies that it is not one's personal trust in Christ but the body of Christian doctrine that he has in mind. Greedy motives lead away from the truth. Paul will pick this theme up in the next section when he tells Timothy to "fight the good fight of the faith" (v. 12).

All of this demonstrates the importance of having proper motivation in ministry. Our hearts are deceitful indeed; the love of money (even though we may profess a simple lifestyle) and degenerate lust (even though we may preach sermons against it) have moved to make shipwreck of the ministries of far too many people. How much more dangerous it is when these drives run wild in the hearts of those who are not even believers.

KEEPING OUR CHECKBOOK "in balance." We human beings seem to find it hard to keep our balance. With regard to the current section, we tend to avoid offending anyone and consequently mute the implications of the truth. Paul makes it clear that evil motives at least sometimes lie behind evil doctrines. Yet to accuse those who do not agree with orthodox doctrine of sins of greed or other unworthy motives can easily overstep on the other side. We should never forget that Paul was inspired

---

8. The use of a begging bag by wandering Cynic preachers may be one reason Jesus told his disciples not to take such a bag (Luke 9:3; 10:4).

by the Holy Spirit as he wrote, and what he wrote was truth because it was indeed the Word of God. We, by contrast, do not have that unerring judgment regarding people's motives. Not only can we turn people away today if our lives do not support what we are claiming, but we can turn people away because we accuse others of the same. This takes much discernment from God and a delicate blend of love and boldness.

In the past, fundamentalist Christians heavily criticized the Catholic Church for its material possessions. In the August 4, 1997 issue of *Time* magazine, the Mormons were put under the same searchlight. But there are plenty of lavishly built churches and lavish homes owned by Protestant preachers with expensive cars to guard our thoughts and speech in this matter. There may be fewer Christians than we think who are truly content with food and clothing. Unfortunately, we may regard the "simple lifestyle" only as a noble gesture ensuing from the 1960s.

It would not hurt preachers—or any of us, for that matter—to draw up a series of pages with two columns, one labeled "need" and the other "want," and to list in the appropriate columns our homes with their market value, our cars, perhaps the number of clothes and shoes we have, and other items that need that kind of assessment, and then to set these lists before God in a time of prayer, determined to take the proper action as a result of our evaluation. One friend who had earned enough to live comfortably sincerely offered to God to downsize significantly and recalls the fear he then experienced as to what this might mean!

1 Timothy 6:11–21

❦

BUT YOU, MAN of God, flee from all this, and pursue righteousness, godliness, faith, love, endurance and gentleness. ¹²Fight the good fight of the faith. Take hold of the eternal life to which you were called when you made your good confession in the presence of many witnesses. ¹³In the sight of God, who gives life to everything, and of Christ Jesus, who while testifying before Pontius Pilate made the good confession, I charge you ¹⁴to keep this command without spot or blame until the appearing of our Lord Jesus Christ, ¹⁵ which God will bring about in his own time—God, the blessed and only Ruler, the King of kings and Lord of lords, ¹⁶who alone is immortal and who lives in unapproachable light, whom no one has seen or can see. To him be honor and might forever. Amen.

¹⁷Command those who are rich in this present world not to be arrogant nor to put their hope in wealth, which is so uncertain, but to put their hope in God, who richly provides us with everything for our enjoyment. ¹⁸Command them to do good, to be rich in good deeds, and to be generous and willing to share. ¹⁹In this way they will lay up treasure for themselves as a firm foundation for the coming age, so that they may take hold of the life that is truly life.

²⁰Timothy, guard what has been entrusted to your care. Turn away from godless chatter and the opposing ideas of what is falsely called knowledge, ²¹which some have professed and in so doing have wandered from the faith.

Grace be with you.

Original Meaning

THE APOSTLE IS ready to draw his letter to a close. This entire section is directed to Timothy, who is to distance himself from the false teachers and continue to live a life dedicated to the Christian faith. Paul also includes some parting instructions that the young pastor must offer to those who are rich in the world.

Honoring God by Fulfilling His Calling (6:11–16)

THIS SECTION OPENS with a strong contrast, "But you," by which Timothy is commanded to distance himself from the people described in verses 3–10. Paul addresses him as a "man of God," a phrase used only here and in 2 Timothy 3:17 in the New Testament. It appears a number of times in the Old Testament, including references to Moses (Deut. 33:1; Josh. 14:6; Ezra 3:2; title to Ps. 90), Samuel (1 Sam. 9:6), David (2 Chron. 8:14; Neh. 12:24, 36), Elijah (1 Kings 17:18), and Elisha (2 Kings 4:7). At first glance it seems to refer to strong leaders. But while it may have been used in this way for King David, the two references given for him use it in connection with his instructions concerning the role of the Levites in worship. It should be noted that the expression in the New Testament uses the generic *anthropos* ("human being," not "man" in the sense of male).

Several imperatives follow in short order. "Flee [*pheugo*] from all this" refers to the evils mentioned in verses 3–10. While in the moralistic literature of the period *pheugo* could have the sense of shunning or avoiding, the fact that it is immediately followed by "pursue" presents a vivid picture of a person escaping from evil and running after good. Timothy is to pursue a series of virtues that will help him to maintain the character that Paul has been mandating throughout the letter.

- "Righteousness" here is not the forensic righteousness of Romans but the integrity of life described by the word "upright," which was ascribed to Zechariah and Elizabeth in Luke 1:6.
- "Godliness" is the familiar word *eusebeia*, prominent in 6:3–6.
- "Faith" is one of the first virtues mentioned in the Pastoral Letters: God's work is "by faith" (1:4). At times the term *faith* refers to doctrine (esp. with the definite article), at other times it is a virtue or a quality of one's relationship with Jesus.
- Among the virtues in the Pastorals frequently linked with faith is "love" (see 1:5, 14; 2:15; 4:12; 2 Tim. 1:13; 2:22; 3:10; Titus 2:2).
- After faith and love come "endurance and gentleness" (see also Titus 2:2 for endurance in the Pastoral Letters). The word for "gentleness" is unique in the New Testament; it may seem a strange word here, given that the next imperative is "fight."

The verb "fight," however, refers to an athletic contest, not military combat, and we also know that Timothy was to be kind and gentle as he was instructing unbelievers (2 Tim. 2:24–25). Actually the context of 6:12 is not a conflict against other people; it is the "good fight of the faith," which is Timothy's own "athletic contest" for personal mastery.

In this connection Timothy is to "take hold" of eternal life. He has received this from God and is to appropriate it now. The aorist tense used in this imperative does not mean that it is a one-time event. For Timothy to "take hold" of eternal life means to appropriate what God has given him, since he has already been "called" to it. (Of the various aspects of calling in Scripture see 2 Thess. 2:13–14.) A more specific meaning of "taking hold" of life is seen in 1 Timothy 6:19, where rich people are to take hold of life in the sense of using their wealth for good, thereby laying a foundation for their future in the "coming age."

The significance and time of Timothy's "good confession" (v. 12) is debated.[1] The problem may be more a matter of English than of Greek, because the literal rendering, "Take hold of the eternal life to which you were called and you confessed the good confession," is somewhat jarring. In Romans 10:10 Paul says (lit.) "with the mouth confession is made for [*eis*] salvation." Note, however, if that passage were considered a parallel to the construction in the present passage, it would make eternal life contingent on one's personal confession.

There are two aspects of the NIV in verse 12b that affect interpretation. (1) One is that the *time* of the confession is the same as the time of Timothy's calling and laying hold of eternal life. Given that, we face a problem, for it distorts somewhat the comparison with the confession of Christ Jesus before Pontius Pilate (v. 13). That confession had nothing to do with conversion on the part of Jesus, nor was it a confession in front of a friendly crowd, such as would be the case if it is analogous to Timothy's baptism or the laying on of hands (cf. 4:14). But that latter problem exists anyway, unless we postulate some experience of opposition that Timothy had in which he made a good confession.[2] Since the calling mentioned here has to do with Timothy's

---

1. The NIV ("when you made your good confession") links the confession with the calling in a temporal way. The NRSV ("for which you made the good confession") likewise introduces a link, assuming that the prepositional phrase *eis hēn* that introduced the verb of calling (where it is translated "to which") also introduces the verb of confessing (where it is translated "for which"). The NLT for some reason omits the calling completely. Like the NRSV they construe the clause about the confession as a relative clause, introduced by the relative pronoun "which," with "eternal life" as the antecedent. The idea that both verbs continue the metaphor of fighting was rejected by Ellicott (*Commentary on the Epistles of St. Paul*, 108) and others in the mid–nineteenth century and does not seem to have appeal to commentators in the twentieth century.

2. Almost all commentators see the situation as a "friendly" one. Lock (*Pastoral Epistles*, 71), Fee (*1 and 2 Timothy, Titus*, 150), Kelly (*Pastoral Epistles*, 141), Stott (*Guard the Truth*, 57) and Scott (*Pastoral Epistles*, 77) hold that this was a baptismal confession. Ellicott (*Commentary on the Epistles of St. Paul*, 108), Knight (*Pastoral Epistles*, 264–65), and Towner (*1–2 Timothy & Titus*, 143) think it was at commissioning or ordination ceremony. Both options are

receiving of eternal life and since it took place long before the incident of 4:14, this probably refers either to his baptism (which, it must be acknowledged, is a conjecture) or to some other experience early on in his Christian life. (2) The concluding phrase, "in the presence of many witnesses," almost certainly refers to more than just a few elders laying hands on him.

Verse 13 contains another solemn charge by Paul, introduced by the word *parangello,* "I charge" (see also 1:3; 4:11; 5:7; 6:17). It is made "in the sight [lit. presence] of God," with the additional description "who gives life to everything." This, along with the following reference to Christ as the other witness to the charge, gives this command great solemnity and force. The reference to God as life-giver is a reminder that Timothy and all beings are dependent on him for daily existence. The reference to Christ as a good confessor is a reminder of the brave and noble example Timothy has to follow.

The first question that faces us in verse 14 is that of identifying "this command." Paul uses three different nouns for "command" in the Pastoral Letters: *epitage* (1 Tim. 1:1; Titus 1:3; 2:15), *parangelia* (1 Tim. 1:5, 18), and *entole* (present passage and Titus 1:14; see comments on 1 Tim. 1:1, 5). Fee conveniently summarizes the various understandings of the referent for "command": (1) the exhortations in 1 Timothy 6:11–12, collectively understood; (2) an alleged baptismal charge to which allusion is made in verse 12; (3) an ordination charge; (4) the whole Christian faith thought of as a kind of new law; or (5) a commandment to Timothy to persevere in his own faith and ministry, as in 4:16, so as to save himself and others.

Referring to 6:20 and 2 Timothy 4:7, Fee chooses the last option as one that "really summarizes the basic thrust of the letter, that Timothy will best stem the tide of the false teachers as he himself is steadfast in his faith and calling." While it is frustrating exegetically to be unable to identify a single specific command in either chapter 1 or here, this very ambiguity points to the fact that God is calling and directing Timothy repeatedly through various means. His call to eternal life is the beginning of a process of calling and directing in which the apostle Paul plays a significant part.[3]

Paul's command has moral overtones. It was not only a *charge* to *do* something, but a *mandate* to *be* something: "without spot or blame." Grammatically the words "without spot or blame" are adjectives modifying "command." The implication, however, is not that the command itself could be soiled, but that Timothy's response to it could be muddied, thereby bringing both his mission and commission into disrepute.

---

presented equally in Dibelius/Conzelmann (*Pastoral Epistles*). Hanson (*Pastoral Epistles*, 110–11) thinks it refers to his baptism with a reminder given at his ordination. Calvin (*Commentaries*, 163) considers it a reference to the whole ministry of Timothy.

3. See the Bridging Contexts section for further observations on this topic.

The word translated "without spot" (*aspilos*) elsewhere describes the perfection of Christ as the sacrificial lamb (1 Peter 1:19) and the character expected of Christians (James 1:27; 2 Peter 3:14). "Without … blame" (*anepilemptos*) only occurs in the Pastorals (see also 1 Tim. 3:2; 5:7). It picks up the theme in the Pastorals of not giving others any opportunity to lay blame on the behavior of Christians. In the first instance it is applied to elders; in the second, to the conduct of affairs for widows. Here it applies specifically to Timothy.

The "appearing" (*epiphaneia*) of Christ refers to his second coming (see also 2 Tim. 1:10; 4:1, 8; Titus 2:13). The related verbal (*epiphaino*, see Titus 2:11; 3:4) refers to the appearing of God's grace at the first advent of Christ (see comments on Titus 2:11, 13). Timothy's specific teaching mission at Ephesus was to be carried on until Paul came (1 Tim. 4:13), but his whole Christian ministry was to be carried on for a lifetime or until the appearing of Christ. Similarly, the missionary journey for which Paul and Barnabas were commissioned by the laying on of hands in Acts 13:2–3 was completed by the time of 14:26, but Paul continued his service for the Lord until he had "finished the race" (2 Tim. 4:6–8). This latter passage, like the present one, refers to the appearing of Christ. It perhaps carries the idea of an accompanying public approval of one's ministry.[4] The fact that Paul expects both Timothy and himself to continue in ministry until the appearing of Christ is one of the reasons to reject the idea that the Pastoral Letters were written at a time when Paul, or perhaps a later writer, had given up the hope of his being alive at the return of Christ.

The doxology in verses 15–16 employs rich, lofty vocabulary to exalt God. It is introduced by a statement that includes the previous reference to the appearing of Christ. This statement emphasizes the sovereignty of God, who will bring about that appearing "in his own time" (or "at the right time," NRSV).[5] God is " blessed" (*makarios*; see Eph. 1:3 for another word of blessing or praise, *eulogetos*). He is the "only Ruler"; in the doxology of 1 Timothy 1:17 he is the "only God." *Dynastes* (trans. "Ruler" here) is used elsewhere in the New Testament only in Luke 1:52 and Acts 8:27. The word was used in secular Greek for important officials and for the chief Greek god, Zeus. Since the expressions "King of kings" and "Lord of lords" were also used outside of Scripture during this period, Paul was apparently deliberately employing terminology familiar to his readers in order to express the supremacy of the true God.[6]

---

4. In 2 Thess. 2:8 Paul refers to the judgment of the "lawless one," who will be destroyed by the "splendor" (*epiphaneia*) of Christ's coming (the familiar *parousia*).

5. See 2:6, where the phrase is translated "proper time"; Titus 1:3, where it is translated "appointed season."

6. See Deut. 10:17; Ps. 136:2–3 for "God of gods" and "Lord of lords." In the New Testament the combined phrase "King of kings and Lord of lords" does not occur until Rev. 19:16, although the reverse, "Lord of lords and King of kings," occurs in Rev. 17:14.

Another unique characteristic of God celebrated in this doxology is his immortality. The adjective *monos* here emphasizes that only God is not subject to death. Some hold that it is theologically inappropriate to refer to the "immortal soul" of anyone who has not received God's eternal life. They believe that human beings only have immortality if God bestows this on them (1 Cor. 15:53–54).[7]

This is the God who lives in light that cannot be approached.[8] The light of God exposes all that is evil (Eph. 5:11–14). He is surrounded by light (Dan. 2:22; cf. Ex. 3:5) and dressed in a robe of light (Ps. 104:2). Moreover, God would not let Moses look directly at his face, "for no one may see me and live" (Ex. 33:20). That fact is reinforced by Paul here. Just as human beings do not have immortality by nature but are granted this by grace, so those who have been unable to see because of sin will one day be like him when he appears, "for we shall [then] see him as he is" (1 John 3:2). These truths are exclusively true of God, and therefore he deserves "honor and might forever."

Words to the Wealthy (6:17–19)

VERSE 17 CONTAINS one final occurrence of the verb *parangello*, "command" (see comments on v. 13; also 1:3.) It may seem strange that Paul returns to subject of wealth in this paragraph, having already dealt with it in verses 5–10. We know, however, that the early Christian churches did not lack members of the upper, wealthier class. In whatever way they may have gained their wealth, possibly before they became believers, they now had it and needed instructions as to how to use it. (1) Such people are to recognize that wealth is temporary, "in this present world," and will last only until the appearing of Christ just alluded to. (2) They should not be arrogant. (3) They are not to "put their hope in wealth," because that is "so uncertain."

This warning is followed by a strong adversative *alla* ("but") and the positive instruction that responds to the negatives point by point in a kind of chiasm: their hope is to be in God, he is the one who "richly provides us with everything for our enjoyment," and instead of being arrogant they are to "do good" and "to be generous and willing to share" (v. 18). All of this is set within

---

7. The Greek word for immortality (*athanasia*) and its cognates were used in Greek literature for the gods and, in an honorific way, of some human beings (LSJ, 30–31). On the immortality of God see comments on 1 Tim. 1:17; on the immortality that God bestows on believers see comments on 2 Tim. 1:10. For a thorough evaluation (and rejection) of "conditional immortality" see Millard J. Erickson, *How Shall They Be Saved?* (Grand Rapids: Baker, 1996), 217–32.

8. For references to occurrences of the word "unapproachable" (*aprositos*) in other Greek literature (its only New Testament use is in the present passage), see LSJ, 230.

the anticipation of "the coming age" (v. 19), marked by the appearing of Christ in God's own time (vv. 14–15). The word for "age" (NIV) is implied but not expressed in the Greek text. The "firm [lit., good or beautiful] foundation" for what is to come replaces the uncertainty of wealth (v. 17). Just as Timothy is to take hold of eternal life (v. 12), so the wealthy are to "take hold of the life that is truly life."

Conclusion (6:20–21)

VERSE 20 BEGINS a final personal word to Timothy. It is difficult to know what was "entrusted" to him (see comments on 2 Tim. 1:12, where something is entrusted to God; 1:14, where something is entrusted to Timothy). In the present context it may refer to the endowment Timothy was given when hands were laid on him (1 Tim. 4:14).

But immediately after telling Timothy to "guard" this, Paul writes about turning away from "what is falsely called knowledge." This command seems to be a summary of all the exhortations in this letter to follow truth and oppose heresy. If so, probably what was "entrusted" and to be guarded carefully was the "sound teaching." This certainly seems to be the case in 2 Timothy 1:14, which is preceded with a reference to keeping this "pattern of sound teaching" (v. 13). It is especially important for Timothy to do this because some have embraced falsehood and "wandered from the faith" (1 Tim. 6:21); note that Timothy was charged in 1:3–7 to correct those who have "wandered" in this way.

Bridging Contexts

SOME CHRISTIANS MAKE a practice of reading over on a regular basis a book or portion of Scripture that they find especially significant. This may be the Psalms or Proverbs or perhaps the Sermon on the Mount. First Timothy 6:11–21 could be a candidate for such repeated attention.

The expression "man of God" is frequent in the Old Testament, normally referring to a prophet. The only other occurrence of the term in the New Testament is also in the Pastorals (2 Tim. 3:17), where the Scripture equips "the man of God . . . for every good work." Since these New Testament passages do not seem to be directed to prophets, we may conclude that they apply to all men and women who serve the Lord. If this is true, it is easy to bring this truth into the modern age.

Concern for God's glory. This section begins with our inner life and character (v. 11). Paul allows for the fact that every Christian faces struggles (v. 12). He reminds the reader of the eternal life that all God's people have, though the circumstances of any special calling we may have will vary among us. Whatever those circumstances may have been in Timothy's life, they involved making a "good confession" before others. All of us can look back to the example of Christ before Pilate, and all of us can look forward to the future appearing of Christ. Both should motivate us to fulfill God's call and command to us.

God is on the throne and is worthy of not only our obedience but our worship as well. The concerns Paul has shown in this letter about maintaining sound doctrine and maintaining Christian character appropriate to that doctrine are ultimately concerns for the reputation, the glory, of God. The several doxologies in the Pastoral Letters are, therefore, pertinent to and apt expressions of that blend of doctrine and life.

The Christian's battle of faith. If the command to "fight the good fight of the faith" refers to Timothy's ministry, it must be taken in accord with the instructions in the Pastorals not to be quarrelsome and antagonistic. If, on the other hand, this is an inner battle, as seems reasonable given the context, it describes what Christians typically experience. Gaining victory as we engage in our struggles may be one aspect of "tak[ing] hold of ... eternal life." As noted above, wealthy people take hold of the true life by using their wealth for the good of others and with a view to the future. On that analogy Timothy and Christians in various life situations can prepare for the future by using what God has given them in this life.

In the Original Meaning section we discussed the possible connection between Timothy's calling, his confession, and his laying hold of that life. We may be confident that God's calling to eternal life has itself an eternal dimension. God's decision did not just happen when Timothy was in the presence of the witnesses (v. 12). That confession, affirming God's call, was made at a particular time—possibly, as we have seen, at Timothy's baptism. The example of Christ before Pilate (v. 13), however, was not at some spiritual event such as baptism, but a moment of opposition; this suggests that we may be called on at any time to give our confession. Paul then looks ahead to the time of consummation, when Christ will appear, and concludes with a doxology to the God who is immortal and who will receive "honor and might forever."

The realization that Christ will be appearing in glory is a great motivator for obeying him "without spot or blame." According to 2 Corinthians 5:10, we will all appear before the judgment seat of Christ. This in itself should motivate us to good behavior, but the appearing of Christ on earth should also move believers to holy living and holy serving. So should the reminder in this passage of the holy God, who "lives in unapproachable light."

Confession. Our common use of the word "confession" can cause a misunderstanding of verses 12–13. A search through dictionaries and examples of usage reveals that most people understand this word to mean acknowledgment of sin. It usually has to do with the admission of a fault or a crime and is often used with reference to admitting our guilt to God or to a court. There is, however, a traditional use to indicate the firm acknowledgment of a doctrinal truth (as in the great "confessions" of the church's faith). It is also firmly in the Christian's vocabulary as a verbal acknowledgment of our faith in Christ (Rom. 10:9–10).[9] The words "confess" and "confession" can, therefore, be retained and its meaning explained. Every generation of believers will have opportunity, perhaps under duress, to confess their Lord before unbelievers.

Christians and their wealth. Paul knew that many false teachers, both professing Christian and outright pagan, had mercenary motives. In Thessalonians 2:1–9 he makes it clear that this was not true of him. But he also has advice for those whose wealth is not necessarily gained by guile or kept in greed. Wealth can cause arrogance and lead people to put their whole dependence on it (v. 17), but believers should use their wealth generously in doing good to others. We do not know what kind of "treasure" awaits such people, but we know that good use of their resources in some way lays a foundation for their future in the "coming age." This is their way of taking hold of "the life that is truly life" (v. 19).

SPIRITUALITY. CHRISTIANS HOLD different views of what constitutes spirituality and how it is "attained." Some are activist, engaging in spiritual "exercises," procedures, and programs. For others passivity is the ideal, with an emphasis on abiding in Christ. Even when we minimize our human role, however, there are legitimate struggles. It takes decision and deliberate action to arise early enough in the morning for Bible reading and prayer; skipping a late night TV show helps. Likewise, it takes concentration to overcome distractions as we are interceding in prayer for others.

It also takes insight and objectivity to deal with our own personality. What we may think is a spiritual humility and despondency over sin on our part may actually be human personality factors that need to be dealt with. And what we interpret as spirituality or the lack of it in others may also simply be a matter of personality. In other words, we all too easily rule out the human element when we are evaluating spirituality.

---

9. In Matt. 10:32–33 and its parallel, Luke 12:8–9, the NIV and some other modern versions translate the Greek "whoever acknowledges me" rather than "whoever confesses me."

For Paul, however, spirituality involves things *to do*. "Flee," "pursue," and "fight" are active verbs. "Take hold" also requires positive decision and action. The development of Christian character, so important in these letters, involves wise decisions and swift obedience. (1) The Christian needs to know what to flee. In 2 Timothy 2:22 it is "the evil desires of youth." First Corinthians 6:18 tells us to flee sexual immorality; 10:14 warns us to flee idolatry.

(2) We also need to pursue peace (1 Peter 3:11–12, quoting Ps. 34:12) as well as "righteousness, faith, love and [again] peace" (2 Tim. 2:22). The list here in 1 Timothy 6:11 is longer, including some of the previous group: "righteousness, godliness, faith, love, endurance and gentleness." Without being wooden or legalistic, we would do well to select one of these goals along with a contrasting action to flee several days to check and improve our behavior.

(3) The "fight" may well begin with our decision to do this. It is possible that the larger, more encompassing spiritual battle will ensue, since Satan is always seeking ways to "devour" us (1 Peter 5:8). My personal observation, however, is that some Christians are too ready to blame personal failures on Satan instead of on their own "evil desire" (James 1:13–15).

Confessing Christ. This passage also teaches us to give a good confession. At any point a believer may be called on to confess Christ. For some it has been a circumstance of persecution, with the threat of torture for those who make that confession instead of a denial. While that circumstance does not exhaust the meaning of this passage and may not touch many who read this commentary (or its author), it is a possibility for many around the world at this very moment.

There will always be those who try to compel Christians to curse Jesus, but we must, and can, by the Spirit say "Jesus is Lord" (1 Cor. 12:3). The words of Peter are to be kept in mind, "But in your hearts set apart Christ as Lord. Always be prepared to give an answer to everyone who asks you to give the reason for the hope that you have" (1 Peter 3:15). The closing words of that verse, "but do this with gentleness and respect," are similar to the emphasis in the Pastoral Letters (e.g., 2 Tim. 2:24–26).

Doxology and worship. The doxologies in the Pastorals are uplifting, directing our hearts to the God who is worthy of all worship and honor. We can miss a great opportunity, however, if we simply read these words in the course of our study or wait until the worship leader incorporates them into a Sunday morning service. They are there for our use at any time!

It is often said that our personal times of prayer should include worship. Such worship can be expressed, of course, in our own words—words inspired by the Spirit in the depths of our minds and hearts. It can also come through the words of hymns and devotional writings. This is not only a helpful way to expand our worshipful thoughts and vocabulary, but also a means of joining in the voices of people from other Christian traditions as part of the great worshiping church worldwide. This has exciting possibilities. Personally, for example, I find it wonderfully stretching to offer an evening hymn when it is evening somewhere *else* in God's world, joining in with, and praying for, the believers in that time zone.

Best of all, however, is to worship God in his own words—through the Psalms, the songs of praise in Revelation, and other passages. This doxology, celebrating, along with 1 Timothy 1:17, the immortal God, is a wonderful instrument of worship. It also can be a means of recalling the universal church and all those—believers on earth and in heaven, angels, and other beings—who for an eternity will worship God together.

Responsibilities for the wealthy. It may seem abrupt to go directly from such an exalted passage to one about material wealth, but it is not abrupt in God's world. All we are and have is his. Those with wealth have a special opportunity to put their hope in the God, who "richly provides us with everything for our enjoyment." They also have the freedom to share their wealth.

The context of Paul's aphorism about the love of money in verse 10 is (1) the importance of godliness with contentment, (2) the fact that we cannot take any of our possessions into the afterlife, and (3) the desire for wealth, which can bring temptation and destruction. Now, in an upbeat mood, Paul adds the privilege of sharing and the opportunity of "tak[ing] hold of . . . eternal life" by using the material blessings of earthly life to do good.

I often recall my friendship with a couple who had a large home, beautiful swimming pool and cabana, two expensive cars, and a plane. I knew them both well enough to realize that at the end of the summer they were exhausted from having many church groups in to use their pool, after whom they had the job of cleaning up. I knew also that the husband used his plane for the Lord's work, in particular flying an evangelist to his meetings, and that the wife, among other "good works," gave untold hours in charity work. Close friends of theirs were likewise involved in charities and ministries that many people were unaware of. It is not money, but *love of* money that is the potential hazard, and these people understood that fact and longed not for money but "for [the Lord's] appearing" (2 Tim. 4:8).

In contrast, as I write, people are streaming over the border to an adjoining state where they can buy lottery tickets for a jackpot worth a quarter of a billion dollars. The drawing is tonight, and the news is full of pictures and sound bites (one man said if he won, he would have "women everywhere").

Dealing with false teachers. We, like Timothy (and Titus), have a trust (v. 20). In the process of discharging that trust, we, like they, are sometimes assigned to deal with not only error but with the sins of the false teachers. It is easy to become entangled with some of the problems we seek to solve. In the process of extricating other people from error we must be careful not to engage in the kinds of dissension and argumentation they employ. If what they teach is "falsely called knowledge," our temptation may be to argue the points beyond what is useful in order to display their error.

By contrast, we may abstain from any direct encounter and choose instead to see it all as a work of Satan to be dealt with only by prayer. It is significant that Satan is not mentioned here and, in fact, those in error are said to have "wandered" from the faith. While that may be a deliberate choice, there certainly are many who wander inadvertently. They need prayer, for Satan does blind people's eyes, but they also need loving and careful instruction. All the while, in keeping our trust, we must be sure that we ourselves turn from the "godless chatter" and "opposing ideas." In so doing, we need the grace Paul mentions at the close of the letter (v. 21b).

2 Timothy 1:1–7

P AUL, AN APOSTLE of Christ Jesus by the will of God,
according to the promise of life that is in Christ Jesus,

²To Timothy, my dear son:

Grace, mercy and peace from God the Father and Christ
Jesus our Lord.

³I thank God, whom I serve, as my forefathers did, with a
clear conscience, as night and day I constantly remember you
in my prayers. ⁴Recalling your tears, I long to see you, so that
I may be filled with joy. ⁵I have been reminded of your sincere
faith, which first lived in your grandmother Lois and in your
mother Eunice and, I am persuaded, now lives in you also.
⁶For this reason I remind you to fan into flame the gift of
God, which is in you through the laying on of my hands. ⁷For
God did not give us a spirit of timidity, but a spirit of power,
of love and of self-discipline.

Original Meaning

THE FACT THAT we have three Pastoral Letters
permits some useful comparisons. In 1 Timothy,
which sounds an alarm against false teaching, Paul
not only describes the heretical teachers in strong
terms, but he also employs strong words of command as he writes his delegate in Ephesus. Paul "commands" Timothy; Timothy is then to "command"
the congregation. Paul's opening description of himself as an apostle (1 Tim.
1:1) includes the noun "command." In contrast, while the letter to Titus was
also written because of false teachers, the tone is more positive. Paul's opening words in this letter about his apostleship speak of "the faith of God's
elect and the knowledge of the truth that leads to godliness."

Paul's Greeting (1:1–2)

HERE IN 2 TIMOTHY, Paul connects his apostleship with the "will of God,
according to the promise of life that is in Christ Jesus." As in Titus, the salutation includes the idea of life, and, like both other Pastoral Letters, it provides a realistic picture of the author, the recipient, and the problems in the
congregation. However, there is a marked poignancy in this letter that is
absent from the others. Paul refers to his imprisonment and suffering (1:8),

reflects on his grief that many have deserted him (v. 15), and later returns to that theme after he expresses what seems to be an anticipation of imminent death (4:6–18). Although in the canon the two letters to Timothy are placed together, followed by Titus, the tone of this letter leads many to place it chronologically after Titus as Paul's final written words.

On Paul's apostleship (v. 1), see comments on 1 Timothy 1:1. His reference to the "will of God" stands alone in the Pastoral Letters, though it is not unique among the Pauline letters (see 1 Cor. 1:1; 2 Cor. 1:1; Eph. 1:1; Col. 1:1).

But why does Paul add the words "according to the promise of life that is in Christ Jesus" in 1:1? He referred to eternal life in Titus 1:2, but that has to do with faith and knowledge of the truth, not, as here, directly to Paul's apostleship. The idea of promise appears elsewhere in Paul's writings—especially in Galatians, where his argumentation includes reference to the fact that the "promises" were given to Abraham long before the law was introduced (Gal. 3:15–22). The reason for a reference to "the promise of life" here in 2 Timothy is that "Paul's mission is to make known that this promise receives fulfillment through fellowship with Christ."[1] The phrase also reminds us of 1 Timothy 4:8, where the "promise" relates both to the "present life" and "the life to come."

The words "according to" in the NIV translate the preposition *kata* ("for the sake of," NRSV). Opinions differ as to the significance of the preposition and its phrase. Ellicott says *kata* denotes "the *object* and *intention* of the appointment . . . 'to further, to make known the promise of eternal life.'"[2] Kelly translates it "in reference to."[3] For Lock the phrase "gives the standard by which God chose [Paul] and to which his Apostleship must be true"[4] (See my comments on Titus 1:1–4, where *kata* appears four times. Its first use in Titus, where it may convey the idea of appropriateness, seems close to this passage, and I have suggested that John 2:6 provides another example.) The word *kata* probably indicates that Paul's apostleship is not so much to *promote* the promise (Ellicott) as it is to be in *accordance* with it (NIV).

The reference to "Christ" in verse 1 is one of thirty-two in the Pastoral Letters, almost always along with "Jesus." In that combination, 2 Timothy almost always places "Christ" before "Jesus," and it is usually thought that at this time "Christ" was being used primarily as a title. That order, however, is not uniform (see 1 Tim. 6:3, 14; Titus 1:1; 2:13; 3:6). This does not, of course, require a late date for the Pastoral Letters. The word "Christ" is first of all a

---

1. Kelly, *Pastoral Epistles*, 153.
2. Ellicott, *Commentary on the Epistles of Saint Paul*, 121.
3. Kelly, *Pastoral Epistles*, 153.
4. Lock, *Pastoral Epistles*, 82; Knight adopts Ellicott's view (*Pastoral Epistles*, 364).

title ("Messiah" or "Anointed One"). In Philippians 1 (to take an example of an acknowledged Pauline writing) "Christ" occurs eighteen times, and it appears both alone and with the name Jesus in both orders. The prepositional phrase "in Christ Jesus" may be one of many uses by Paul where it conveys the idea of close relationship or union.

In verse 2 Paul identifies Timothy as his "dear son," a more natural and personal expression than "my true son in the faith" (1 Tim. 1:2; see also Titus 1:4). Paul repeats "my son" at the beginning of the exhortation in 2 Timothy 2:1. The rest of 1:2 in the salutation is similar to that in 1 Timothy 1:2 and Titus 1:4 (see comments on 1 Tim. 1:2), except that the latter omits the word "mercy."

Remembering Timothy's Faith and Spiritual Giftedness (1:3–7)

UNLIKE 1 TIMOTHY 1:3–7 and Titus 1:5–9, the references in this passage to the recipient of the letter do not take the form of a commission. They are more reflective, beginning with thanksgiving to God for reminiscences about Timothy. The content of this section is closer to typical elements in Greco-Roman letters than is the case in 1 Timothy or Titus. It was customary to offer kind, sometimes flattering, comments about the recipient. Paul is tender and sincere in his thoughts. But he also slips in some remarks about his own service to God before he continues with his comments about Timothy.

The word "serve" translates *latreuo*, which often refers to worship, especially with regard to the offering of worship in a cultic context. In the LXX this, of course, was the divine worship offered to God in his temple. To translate it "serve" loses the sense of the worship context, but to translate it "worship" would fall short of indicating that the form it took in Paul's ministry was active service. The reference to his "forefathers"[5] recalls his Jewish heritage (Phil. 3:4–5) in a positive way. Paul's "clear conscience" recalls his insistence on this qualification for deacons in 1 Timothy 3:9 (see also 1:5, 19). Although in Philippians 3 Paul rejected any works-oriented righteousness as a means of salvation, here he has a clear conscience about the sincere service he has offered God in company with faithful Jewish ancestors.

What follows is a pattern of words about remembrance. (1) Paul remembers Timothy in his prayers. Two expressions describe his perseverance in prayer for Timothy. (a) He does so "constantly." Paul uses words in this word group elsewhere also to describe that which is incessant (prayers in Rom. 1:9; 1 Thess. 1:2; 2:13; 5:17; anguish over his unbelieving "brothers" in Rom. 9:2–3). (b) He prays "night and day." It does not mean that Timothy is never

---

5. The Greek word does not exclude women, although in Greek literature *gyne* could be added to specify a female ancestor.

out of his thoughts, but that during his frequent prayers around the clock he never fails to mention the young pastor. Paul's constant prayers for the Thessalonian believers, along with his reference to working "night and day" so that he would not burden them, are worth consulting (1 Thess. 1:2, 3; 2:9, 13; 3:10; 5:17; cf. also 1 Tim. 5:5, about the widow who "continues night and day to pray").

(2) Next, Paul remembers Timothy's tears (v. 4). We do not know the occasion referred to. It may have been when Paul left Ephesus (1 Tim. 1:3), since we do not know of any further meeting between the two. The important thing is what it says about their relationship. Clearly Timothy is not the only one who is sad, for Paul longs to see Timothy so that he himself may be "filled with joy."

(3) Paul then recalls Timothy's "sincere faith" (v. 5). Comparing this passage with Acts 16:1–3, we gather that the opinions of his acquaintances differed as to the kind of home in which Timothy grew up. It is clear that his mother was Jewish, which meant that Timothy was Jewish also. But her marriage to a Gentile meant a break in her relationship to her religion. Thus, on the one hand Timothy was "technically an apostate Jew because he was uncircumcised," and on the other hand was viewed by Gentiles as virtually Jewish.[6] In order to clarify his status and to protect his own acceptance in the synagogue, Paul had Timothy circumcised. Yet it was already clear to Paul when he met him that Timothy had an authentic Jewish faith, thanks to the piety of his mother Eunice and his grandmother Lois.

(4) The fourth remembrance is actually a reminder Paul gives Timothy to fan God's gift into flame (v. 6). This may presuppose a lessening of Timothy's effectiveness. We do not know the length of time between the two letters to Timothy, nor do we know the effect that the confrontation with the false teachers at Ephesus may have had on him. Paul's words do not necessarily mean that Timothy's passion had abated, though the verb translated "fan into flame" can have the sense of rekindling a dying fire. The basis of Paul's exhortation ("for this reason") is Timothy's faith (v. 5), so we know that there is no lapse there.

In understanding verse 7 it is common to do "mirror reading," that is, to assume that the mention "of power, of love and of self-discipline" implies that Timothy lacks these and that, because "timidity" is mentioned, this is his problem. It seems reasonable to assume that the inner abilities that God gave Timothy for ministry—power, love, and self-discipline—were being weakened as a natural timidity began to take over. On this reading, in order to

---

6. F. F. Bruce, *The Acts of the Apostles: Greek Text With Introduction and Commentary*, 3d rev. (Grand Rapids: Eerdmans, 1990), 352.

overcome a natural reticence to speak and act with confidence, Timothy needs to allow the spiritual gift to resume its dominance and restore a higher level of effectiveness in his ministry. This reconstruction takes into account all of the elements of verses 6–7.[7]

It remains to observe the wording with respect to the bestowal of that "gift [*charisma*] of God," which was "through [*dia*] the laying on of [Paul's] hands." This may imply that Paul was one of the elders who laid hands on him (1 Tim. 4:14). There is a difference between this wording and that of 1 Timothy 4:14, where the bestowal of the gift was "through [*dia*]" prophecy, "with [*meta*]" the laying on of hands by the group of elders. It may be that Paul now wants to emphasize that his (and the elders') role was not only to accompany the bestowal of the gift but to be involved in it as well.

The use of the word *anazopyreo*, "fan into flame," raises a theological issue: Can an inward spiritual gift of God die down like a fire and be rekindled by an act of the will? Does one have control over that which is the sovereign work of the Holy Spirit of God? A true understanding of this verse must be consistent with the proper answer to those questions. The fact that in 1 Corinthians 14:22–40 Paul teaches the regulation of spiritual gifts shows that Christians have responsibility for their use. The very word translated "self-discipline" means taking responsibility to be moderate or to act reasonably. It implies that the individual exercises control. For the Christian, the motivation and power to do this comes from the Holy Spirit, but we must respond by making the right decisions and taking the right actions.

The "spirit" mentioned in verse 7 is probably the Holy Spirit himself, not the human spirit. It is something God gave and was probably part of the gift mentioned in verse 6. The gift seems to have been a measure or kind of power, love, and ability to control oneself that is beyond our normal capacities, which comes only from the Holy Spirit. He is not the kind of Spirit who brings fear.

---

7. Most commentators have understood this reference to timidity (or "cowardice," *deilia*) to describe Timothy. They may support this by referring to 1 Cor. 16:10, where Paul tells the Corinthians, "See to it that he has nothing to fear while he is with you." C. R. Hutson contests this rendering ("Was Timothy Timid? On the Rhetoric of Fearlessness [1 Corinthians 16:10–11] and Cowardice [2 Timothy 1:7]" in *Journal of the Chicago Society of Biblical Research* 42 [1997]: 58–73). He proposes for the Corinthian passage: "If Timothy comes, recognize that he is fearless toward you." He holds the reference to timidity in the present passage to be comparable to the rhetoric of philosophers to their students, intended to appeal to their sense of shame so that they would *not* be timid. There is nothing in Acts or in any of Paul's other letters to suggest that Timothy was timid. On the contrary, he was a strong associate of Paul's, who should not be disdained for any reason but accepted as his envoy. It was not a "quavering tenderfoot" that Paul sent "to deal with the fractious Corinthians" (ibid., 62). That may be true, but Timothy still may have had a natural timidity that surfaced in the more hostile environment in Ephesus.

Bridging Contexts

THE SENSE OF urgency under the duress of a command and against the forces of evil that characterizes 1 Timothy is past. So is the sense of conflict against lying, deceitful enemies that marks the opening of Titus. In contrast, 2 Timothy opens with the reminder of the "promise of life" in Christ. That does not mean that all opposition is gone. Already in 1:15 Paul reflects on his own unhappy circumstances and feelings of abandonment. The presence of evil and heresy at Ephesus is clearly indicated in the rest of the letter.

Nevertheless, one has the sense in reading this letter of two friends talking. They are on the alert for trouble, but are reflecting mainly on their own lives and on how they are fairing in the conflict. Paul appears more as a mentor than as a commander. In 1 Timothy 1 he marveled at the grace of God in saving him and calling him to ministry. In 2 Timothy we see an additional element: Paul is suffering (1:11–12; 2:8–10; 3:10–13), but is trusting God for the future. Most scholars understand 4:6–8 as expressing his sense of impending execution. Picture Timothy reading this letter privately with deep emotion, possibly sharing some of it with the church (perhaps less of it than of the first letter, though eventually he gave it out for "publication"). We can only imagine his feelings when he read this again after Paul's death.

The promise of life in Christ. It is not surprising, then, given Paul's anticipation of his death, that he opens this letter with a reference to "the promise of life that is in Christ Jesus." This does not mean that we have a different Paul (or a different person). He is still concerned with the importance of keeping "a clear conscience" as he was in 1 Timothy 1:5, 19, but immediately he turns attention to Timothy and *his* feelings. Within a few lines he has again combined faith with conscience. This time, however, it is the faith of Timothy's mother and grandmother. To the names Lois and Eunice can be added those of Monica (the mother of St. Augustine), Susanna Wesley (the mother of John and Charles), and generations of Christians who have effectively instructed and prayed for children and grandchildren. The emphasis we sometimes place on 2 Timothy 2:2 about discipling others can be equally placed on this passage on the importance of the Christian nurture of one's family.

Whatever the statistics may be concerning earlier generations, it seems that now all too often, although many young people from non-Christian families are turning to Christ, many children from Christian families are turning away from him. We are the beneficiaries of much literature on parenting, and yet seem to have great difficulty in passing on our Christian values and faith to our children. To observe this is not to lower guilt on anyone, but to observe the importance of Christian character and instruction in the home. Even at the early stage of Christianity represented in 1 Timothy 1 there were those for whom the way of salvation was paved by the faith of parents and grandparents.

A home where there were at least some earnest Jewish believers was a wonderful place of preparation for personal faith in the Messiah. Someone once coined the expression, "God has no grandchildren." To the extent that this means that each generation must come to God freshly and that we are not saved by the faith of our parents if they are God's children, it is true. However, Christian history has shown, and those of us who have been in the Lord's work over a long lifetime have observed that when people come to Christ, there are often parents, grandparents, or others in their background who have long and earnestly prayed for their salvation.

Those "others" may well be Sunday school teachers. Not long ago a funeral service was held for a man who had many friends and had been a vibrant witness for Christ, but who had never held a major leadership position in the church. The dominant image portrayed of him, however, was of a faithful Sunday school teacher. Many of his former students were there and gave testimony of his faithfulness and total devotion to them—a devotion that extended far beyond Sundays. His model, influence, and prayers will affect their lives for decades.

Timothy's gift. The reference in verse 6 to fanning God's gift into flame adds to our understanding of the laying on of hands first mentioned in 1 Timothy 4:14. It is perhaps strange that throughout church history so much emphasis has been put on the laying on of hands as a ritual by which one is installed in an *office*, when the biblical emphasis is so clearly on the impartation of a spiritual *gift*. Apart from issues of biblical interpretation and of ecclesiastical practice, it must be said that it is probably easier to subscribe to an act of ordination that declares a change in status than to believe that, when people lay their hands on an individual, God himself is actually, through them, giving that person a new gift or power from the Holy Spirit. Yet that is precisely what both texts teach, and what Paul goes on to discuss in 2 Timothy 1:7.

This is not to deny that God's gifts may also come to believers at conversion or in subsequent circumstances. Nor does it deny that all believers have spiritual gifts from God. In fact, verse 7 implies that they do, by speaking of the gift that God gave to "us" (unless Paul was restricting that to just Timothy and himself). Nevertheless, in this case Timothy clearly received, through the imposition of Paul's hands, a gift from God that he either did not have before or did not have in the same manner or to the same extent. In some way the Holy Spirit brought to Timothy's human spirit new "power . . . love and . . . self-discipline" (v. 7). Christians are often in a dilemma over whether to "let go and let God," that is, to yield to God and passively wait for him to transform them spiritually or to be actively shaping their own Christian character.

The issues are deep and complex—too much for detailed treatment here. But they should not be overlooked, and they are raised at this point by the reference to the endowment given to Timothy at the laying on of hands. Was this a gift of the Holy Spirit himself, who brings with him the power, love, and self-discipline we need, or did the gift consist of qualities and abilities? If the gift is the Spirit, did Timothy not have the Spirit prior to this occasion? Was the gift a fresh anointing of the Spirit; and, if so, is there some Scripture that clearly describes and explains this supplementary endowment of the Spirit? And in either case, was the gift something that Timothy would not otherwise have possessed?

That may have been the case with "power," but was it the case with "love"? The power to exorcise demons is probably not in view; rather, it is probably the power to bring people from darkness to light (Acts 26:17–18). This is not something we can do. But is not love something for which we are responsible ourselves—both as an act of obedience to the two great commandments and as an expression of mature Christian character? And what about "self-discipline"? Is that something we wait to receive from God or is it our responsibility to achieve? The fact that Timothy was to stir this gift into flame implies that he himself bore responsibility for its nurturing.

The answer to such questions must at least include several considerations. Power, love, and self-discipline are not commodities; they are attitudes and actions. As such they are not static gifts wrapped in a package that we can possess. They must be exercised by the individual. But to the extent that the motivation and the will to exercise them are weak or lacking, these must come from God.

Ever since the famous incident in which it was realized that an increase in the effectiveness of work by factory employees was caused not by a quantitative change in the level of lighting but by the realization of the workers that someone was concerned enough for them to experiment with the lighting, motivational studies have been carried on intensively. Our performance in any activity depends largely on what motivates us. This, of course, involves not only external prompting, but our inner disposition and sense of values. Fear can be a powerful motivator both positively and negatively. As noted above, Timothy's problem may not have been fear, timidity, or cowardice, but all three can affect us deeply. In certain situations fear can either cause us to depress the brake or kick the accelerator. Cowardice only operates the brake. The trio of power, love, and self-discipline forms an impressive and effective counterforce to timidity.

TODAY'S TIMOTHYS. MISSION leaders today are meeting a different kind of volunteer than they were accustomed to a couple of generations ago. The same is true of admissions counselors at seminaries and often of pastoral search committees in churches. An extraordinary number of applicants grew up in non-Christian families and many (whether the families were Christian or not) suffered through the divorce of parents and/or were abused. The "old days" when a pastoral candidate had grown up with a knowledge of Christian doctrine, had studied Greek, Latin, and perhaps ancient history in college to prepare for seminary, and then took a seminary course in the classical tradition have long since disappeared. Today's mission boards and executives need to be sensitive to individual life histories and the emotional health of their candidates and missionaries on the field. It is a tribute to the grace of God and the self-discipline of such candidates that they have been able to overcome the effect of years of drugs and free love in America to enter the service of God.

The skills and professional knowledge needed for service to God today can be gained in many ways. What is less attainable are character and wisdom. These are qualities that are sometimes lacking in professional religious figures. The seminary, church, mission, or other parachurch organization can help candidates for service by concentrating as much as possible on their personal and spiritual well-being. Psychological testing and appropriate counseling should not be viewed negatively but with appreciation. Today's Lois and Eunice may be an InterVarsity staff member and a seminary teacher, and today's Paul may be a mission executive.

It is never too late to foster the development of character or wisdom in the Lord's servant, but we do not want to forfeit the opportunities of early nurturing. It is still the sober task of parents and grandparents to monitor their own lives and parental care so as to give their children a healthy upbringing. Grandparents, who used to pray for their grandchildren with happy optimism, now need to be proactive in their prayers, anticipating the weaknesses of even the finest Christian homes as well as the forces against their grandchildren's spiritual development in the neighborhood, school, and workplace.

Also gone, for the most part, are the days when a young person who is faithful in Sunday school and who perhaps assists in various ministries will be noticed in the church, taken under the care of the pastor or others, and shepherded into Christian ministry. Today pastors, elders, Sunday school teachers, youth leaders, and others need to be praying for young men and women to respond to God's call to Christian life and service. Here also we need to be proactive, prayerfully searching for those who may be suitable for special ministries and encouraging them personally. A large number of those who go on to such ministries and missionary work have left home for education or other purposes, many being converted while at college and university, and are now asking churches that barely know them to support them financially in ministry.

What young Timothys today need especially is personal mentoring, but not merely mentoring in the sense of giving information and offering guidance. Too often that becomes a means of control and the reproduction of ourselves in the other, accompanied by all our agendas and opinions. We may think we have discipled or mentored a person when they adopt our outlook on things, pray as we do, witness as we do and, if it is a pastoral relationship, preach as we do. The word "clone" comes to mind.

In the ancient *Life of Apollonius of Tyana*, a pagan figure apparently shaped in the literature to make him seem like a superior competitor to the Christians' Jesus, there is a curious scene about him climbing into a boat. His disciples artificially imitate his every move as they follow him into it. That is not what Christian discipling and mentoring are about. To mentor a Timothy means to be available, to spend time with him or her, to understand the differences, and to seek to facilitate rather than to control the use of that person's distinctive gifts. An athlete runs the race alone but does so after months or perhaps years of training and encouragement. And that may not be done just by a coach, but by others who are close to the athlete. In Paul Timothy had a person who was close to him, who listened and understood him, who recognized his individual giftedness, and who had confidence in him.

The role of the church. A picture is developing in these letters of a servant of God who functions independently of, but in close fellowship with, the church. Timothy was nurtured by a believing mother and grandmother. He was well thought of in the church (Acts 16:2). He assisted Paul in carrying out the decisions of the church at Jerusalem (16:4). He received the laying on of hands by the church elders (1 Tim. 4:14). Today, when many people are coming to Christ apart from the church, it seems in accordance with this picture for them to be encouraged into church fellowship and to function in cooperation with the church leadership. While on occasion great missionaries and others have had to act independently because church leaders have lacked vision, the healthy church will encourage and facilitate the ministry of those who seek to serve the Lord.

This picture includes Timothy's assumption—and our assumption—of responsibility for *character development*. God's gifts are not a substitute for personal character; they assist in its development. While it is true that a missionary acts in love to help a repulsive victim of a wasting disease because God has given the gift of love by his Spirit, it is also true that the missionary makes a conscious decision to respond to that love, to grow in it personally, and to put it into action where it is deeply needed. Just as Timothy could resist a paralyzing sense of shame when he witnessed (as well as avoiding an embarrassing sense of shame over the imprisonment of his "supervisor" Paul) because of the gifts God had given him (see comments on 1:8), so we also can experience the effect of these gifts in our lives.

There is, in short, a mutuality in which God's supernatural gifts and our response in obedience and character development work together. The gifts alone may result in visible accomplishments, but unless those gifts are allowed to work inwardly as well as outwardly, the spiritual and character development they should produce will not take place. They will be like faith without works and like the gifts of 1 Corinthians 12 without the love of 1 Corinthians 13. In short, churches, like parents and grandparents, must be much more alert to find and encourage Timothys and provide them with the prayer, spiritual resources, and support they need to serve God.

Even if we do all this, however, it is still the Spirit of God who gives the necessary endowment for Christian ministry. It was that way in generations past when sometimes rough, ill-educated individuals, who were looked on with dismay rather than expectation by church leaders, went out in the power of God alone, and saw him work in wonderful ways. It is true now, when many of those in significant movements of our time, like YWAM and Promise Keepers, have little formal training in theology. It is perhaps ironic, but also significant, that while many pastors who have labored through biblical studies and theology in seminary deliver simplified sermons to attract and win seekers, laypeople with little, if any, biblical or theological education are teaching Sunday school classes, small home groups, and community-wide Bible studies to people hungry for deeper teaching. These teachers and learners are some of today's Timothys, motivated by the Spirit of God and needing all the encouragement and training they can get.

Another way to encourage Timothys in our times is to give support and personal encouragement to minority students and those from emerging countries. Seminaries need scholarship funds. Also there are organizations, like the Christian International Scholarship Foundation, who help support promising Christian workers from emerging countries. They select those who are already proven leaders but who need advanced studies to serve the Lord even more effectively in their home countries. Likewise, Bible schools and seminaries overseas need help from their North American brothers and sisters.

The necessity of prayer. The most important factor of all in the life of Timothy may be discerned in these few words in verse 3: "Night and day I constantly remember you in my prayers." Timothy needed the ongoing specific faithful prayers of his mentor. The writer of this commentary, like many other Christians in our day, not only has benefited from the prayers of others but has the privilege and responsibility of receiving prayer requests almost daily from missionaries and others in the Lord's work. E-mail makes it possible to know and bring needs immediately before God.

But it is not necessary to know the immediate circumstances of the Lord's servants in order to pray faithfully for them "night and day." The prayers of Paul, the faith of Timothy's mother and grandmother, the confidence of those who laid hands on him, and the gift of God given to him all lead to the conclusion that begins the next section, "So do not be ashamed to testify about our Lord, or ashamed of me his prisoner" (1:8).

2 Timothy 1:8–18

S O DO NOT be ashamed to testify about our Lord, or ashamed of me his prisoner. But join with me in suffering for the gospel, by the power of God, ⁹who has saved us and called us to a holy life—not because of anything we have done but because of his own purpose and grace. This grace was given us in Christ Jesus before the beginning of time, ¹⁰but it has now been revealed through the appearing of our Savior, Christ Jesus, who has destroyed death and has brought life and immortality to light through the gospel. ¹¹And of this gospel I was appointed a herald and an apostle and a teacher. ¹²That is why I am suffering as I am. Yet I am not ashamed, because I know whom I have believed, and am convinced that he is able to guard what I have entrusted to him for that day.

¹³What you heard from me, keep as the pattern of sound teaching, with faith and love in Christ Jesus. ¹⁴Guard the good deposit that was entrusted to you—guard it with the help of the Holy Spirit who lives in us.

¹⁵You know that everyone in the province of Asia has deserted me, including Phygelus and Hermogenes.

¹⁶May the Lord show mercy to the household of Onesiphorus, because he often refreshed me and was not ashamed of my chains. ¹⁷On the contrary, when he was in Rome, he searched hard for me until he found me. ¹⁸May the Lord grant that he will find mercy from the Lord on that day! You know very well in how many ways he helped me in Ephesus.

JUST AS THERE was a verbal pattern of terms relating to remembrance in 1:3–7, so there is another pattern of words having to do with shame and suffering in verses 8–12. This, along with a reference to Paul's imprisonment (v. 8), is picked up in verse 16 in regards to Onesiphorus, who "was not ashamed of my chains." The theme of suffering in verse 8 (*synkakopatheo*, lit., "suffer together") occurs again in verse 12 (the simple verb *pascho*, "suffer"), and it reappears in 2:3, once more in the compound form *synkakopatheo* ("endure hardship"; NRSV, "share in suffering").

Verses 13–14 make no reference to shame, suffering, or imprisonment, but they do mention for the first time in 2 Timothy the theme of "sound teaching" that is characteristic of the Pastoral Letters.

No Cause for Shame (1:8–12)

VERSES 8–12 FORM one long sentence in Greek. It is introduced by the word "so" (or "therefore"), indicating that Timothy's ability to resist being ashamed lies in the gifts of power, love, and self-discipline (v. 7). The word translated "be ashamed" (*epaischynomai*) is a compound verb with a more intense meaning than the simple form from which it is derived (*aischynomai*). In this context being ashamed stands in contrast to joining with Paul in suffering. Elsewhere in the New Testament this verb is also used in a construction of contrast, specifically with confessing Christ. That is consistent with this passage, "do not be ashamed to testify of about our Lord." "Ἐπαισχύνομαι plays a special role in the confessional language of primitive Christianity. It can designate the renunciation of Jesus Christ by a human being or the renunciation of a human being by the son of man."[1]

In this way Timothy can join Paul in "suffering for the gospel." This very suffering is "by the power of God" (cf. the word "power" in v. 7). Verse 9 shows two ways in which God has expressed that power. One is by saving us; the other, by calling us. In the Pastoral Letters the verb "save" appears several times (1 Tim. 1:15; 2:4, 15; 4:16; 2 Tim. 1:9; 4:18; Titus 3:5). The verb "call," however, only appears in these letters in 1 Timothy 6:12 (see comments). There the calling is to eternal life; here the implication is that it is "to a holy life." The NIV infers this from the dative phrase meaning (lit.) "with a holy calling."

First Corinthians 1:2 says we are "called to be saints [or to be holy]." According to 1 Thessalonians 4:7, "God did not call us to be impure, but to live a holy life [lit., in holiness]." In those two passages and the present one, the NIV assumes that since the action of calling has both a subject and an object, and since we know that God is holy, the holiness referred to extends to the life of the people called. The emphasis in this verse is on the sovereign nature of God's call, which is not dependent on what works we may do.

The importance of the phrase "because of his own purpose and grace" (v. 9) can be realized more fully by noting Ephesians 1:3–14, where Paul

---

1. A. Horstman, "αἰσχύνομαι," *EDNT*, 1:42–43. See Mark 8:38 and parallels; also Rom. 1:16, where the negative expression "I am not ashamed of the gospel" stands for the positive idea of being willing to take a stand and confess the truth of the gospel. In this context that process includes a willingness to be identified with those who represent Christ, even when they are humiliated.

makes it clear that God's grace is founded on his eternal purposes. That passage employs a remarkable series of words, phrases, and grammatical constructions that express the idea of God's purpose, wisdom, good pleasure, and plan, through which we are brought to salvation. The same concept is fortified in 2 Timothy 1:9 by the time reference, indicating that grace was actually given us "in Christ Jesus *before* the beginning of time," but that "it has [only] *now* been revealed" (emphasis added).

Three words in verse 10 are of special importance in the Pastoral Letters. (1) The word translated "revealed" (*phaneroo*) occurs in the important creedal statement in 1 Timothy 3:16, "he appeared in a body," and in Titus 1:3, "and at his appointed season he brought his word to light." Connected with this idea of manifestation is the related word *epiphaneia*, denoting the appearance of Christ (1 Tim. 6:14; 2 Tim. 4:1, 8; Titus 2:13; see comments on Titus 2:13, along with 2:11; 3:4, which contain the verb "appear"; Paul uses the same terminology to refer to both the first and second coming of Christ).

(2) The word "Savior" is also significant in the Pastoral Letters since, apart from 2 Peter, this noun is relatively infrequent in the New Testament (see also 1 Tim. 1:1; 2:3; 4:10; Titus 1:3, 4; 2:10, 13; 3:4, 6). One of the distinctives of the Pastoral Letters is in the attribution of salvation directly to God. In the rest of the New Testament, salvation, which in the Old Testament is God's work, is now the work of Christ. (For the identification of God as Savior in the Pastorals see comments on 1 Tim. 1:1; see also the linking of God and Christ as Savior in Titus 2:13.)

(3) The long Greek sentence that began in verse 8 continues with a participle ("having destroyed"), which is used adjectivally to describe the activity of Christ at his appearing. The clause is a *men* ... *de* construction, a means of balancing two members of alternative statements. This section can be literally translated, "who *on the one hand* had destroyed death and *on the other hand* has brought life and immortality to light through the gospel." The first action, which Christ did on the cross, needed to be accomplished before the second. Christ, we might say, put death out of commission. True, it is still a final enemy to be destroyed (1 Cor. 15:26), but even now it is not a threat to the believer. Moreover, we know that Christ made it possible for us to *have* eternal life through his resurrection, but the emphasis here is on that which "brought life and immortality *to light*" (emphasis added). What accomplished that was the gospel.

This gospel was already being proclaimed by Christ during his lifetime; he predicted his resurrection as well as his suffering and death (Matt. 16:21 and elsewhere), and the content of what Paul identified as "the gospel" and as primary in his preaching included "that he was raised on the third day according to the Scriptures" (1 Cor. 15:1–4). These truths are so important that it is almost surprising that Paul has not incorporated "a faithful saying" here that summarizes them. It may be that he is actually quoting parts of some early Christian affirmation.

As he did in 1 Timothy 1:12–16 and briefly in 2 Timothy 1:3, Paul now speaks of his own ministry (v. 11) on behalf of the gospel. The three ministries he mentions in this verse—preaching, apostleship, and teaching—are all related to that gospel. For Paul to function in these three capacities required God's specific action. It was not something Paul chose for himself, although he was grateful for that appointment.

The three words "herald," "apostle," and "teacher" are not intended to be mutually exclusive in this context, but rather to express three distinctive ways in which Paul serves the gospel.[2] The fact that "herald" appears first (rather than "apostle") suggests that Paul is not drawing attention to his status or authority but rather to the ways in which he forwards the cause of the gospel. The herald naturally comes first as the person who makes the announcement, who first brings the good news. The "teacher" explains God's truth with a view to edifying the church. The word "apostle" describes Paul's special commission, in the fulfillment of which he did both proclaim and teach, but which had other dimensions (such as representing the sender, the Lord Jesus Christ, and fulfilling his will wherever he went). Knight observes that Timothy was not an apostle, but Paul can encourage him by being a model of the herald and of the teacher, both being ministries that Timothy himself can carry on by following Paul's example.[3]

As Paul nears the end of his sentence, he gathers up in verse 12 what he has said about testifying to the gospel and declares that it is for this reason that he is "also suffering these things" (NIV: "I am suffering as I am"), probably meaning that suffering is also part of his commission, as it is Timothy's (cf. 3:12). Having alluded back to verse 8 regarding suffering he adds that, as he has counseled Timothy, he himself is not ashamed. This statement is followed by a strong affirmation in the middle of verse 12, introduced by the conjunction *gar* ("because"), providing the grounds on which he is able to state that he is not ashamed. This is accompanied by the affirmation "I know," followed immediately by the familiar "whom I have believed" clause, including God's guarding "what I have entrusted [lit., my deposit] to him for that day."

But what has been entrusted, and to whom? In 1 Timothy 6:20 Timothy is responsible to guard a deposit entrusted to him. In 2 Timothy 1:14 Timothy again is charged with keeping "the good deposit," in this case, "with the help of [lit., through] the Holy Spirit who lives in us." Since Timothy is

---

2. Note that the same three words appear in 1 Tim. 2:7, and in the same order.

3. Knight, *Pastoral Epistles*, 377–78.

instructed in verse 13 to "keep ... the pattern of sound teaching" he heard from Paul, it seems clear that the deposit entrusted to Timothy in verse 14 is the teaching. But God is the one who will guard the deposit in verse 12. "My deposit" in this verse seems to be a reference to Paul's ministry. Thus, the sequence of thought in verses 12–14 is as follows: Paul is doing his part in suffering for the sake of the gospel, committing his life and ministry to God as a deposit for the future day of reckoning. Timothy, for his part, must guard the teachings God has entrusted to him, and God has given him the Holy Spirit to help him do this.

Keeping the Pattern of Sound Teaching (1:13–14)

OUR UNDERSTANDING OF verses 13–14 must take into account the foregoing discussion on verse 12 and the use of the term *sound teaching* through the Pastorals (1 Tim. 1:10; 6:3; 2 Tim. 4:3; Titus 1:9, 13; 2:1–2; see esp. the discussion on 1 Tim. 1:10, which is important for the understanding of the meaning of "sound teaching" here). The Greek word translated "pattern" in verse 13 can have any one of three meanings: a sketch or outline, a model or pattern, or "a rhetorical figure by which a matter was vividly sketched in words."[4] Here it probably refers to a detailed model to be followed scrupulously. This accords with all the language, especially in 1 Timothy, pertaining to authoritative commands that Paul gives Timothy.

The emphasis given to "pattern" (being the first word in the Greek sentence), considered along with the key phrase "sound teaching" and with the instruction about guarding the deposit in verse 14, makes it unmistakably clear that Timothy is not at liberty to deviate from the apostolic teaching. The words "with faith and love in Christ Jesus" echo the dimension of personal piety that characterizes the Pastoral Letters, beginning with 1 Timothy 1:4 (faith), 1:5 (love and faith), and 1:19 (faith).

The Kindness of Onesiphorus (1:15–18)

VERSES 15–18 REVEAL some of Paul's personal feelings. This section picks up the theme of suffering and shame that begins and ends verses 8–12. It also provides a basis for Paul's exhortation to Timothy in 2:1. What could have been "a cause of depression to the affectionate and faithful Timothy" becomes "an inspiriting and quickening call to fresh efforts in the cause of the gospel."[5]

The nature of the desertion of "everyone in the province of Asia" (v. 15) has been a matter of debate. Possibly prior to this writing some from Asia had

---

4. LSJ, 1,900.
5. Ellicott, *Commentary on the Epistles of Saint Paul,* 130.

been in Rome during Paul's imprisonment there and had not supported him. It is also possible that some doctrinal defection is in view, given the fact that the verb translated "deserted" here (*apostrepho*) refers to doctrinal defection in 4:4 and Titus 1:14. However, the context in the present passage contains nothing to suggest that the desertion was anything other than personal (cf. the use of this word in Matt. 5:42; 26:52; Luke 23:14; Acts 3:26; Rom. 11:26; Heb. 12:25, which is not associated with doctrine). The word translated "everyone" is often used in a general sense and must not be taken here to mean a total defection. Various suggestions have been made as to what significant group Paul has in mind but, as Knight says, "Timothy knows about the event, but unfortunately we do not."[6] Phygelus and Hermogenes are not called heretics, as Hymenaeus and Philetus are (2:17), but probably are two stalwart associates whose defection hurt Paul the most.

Onesiphorus stands in beautiful contrast to the others. Taking up the theme of Paul's imprisonment and the natural tendency of associates to be ashamed of him, Paul specifically says that Onesiphorus "was not ashamed of my chains." He "refreshed" Paul and in the populous city of Rome acted quickly and busily. Paul feels so warmly toward Onesiphorus that he repeats the word "mercy" in verse 18. "That day" is the same day mentioned in verse 12, when the present age is concluded and God brings appropriate judgment or reward. Paul concludes with a reference to the help Onesiphorus gave him in Ephesus also, something about which Timothy knows "very well."

Several specific points require attention. (1) In verse 16 Paul offers an indirect prayer[7] that the Lord will show mercy to the household of Onesiphorus.

(2) Using the same indirect prayer mode in verse 18, Paul asks that Onesiphorus may "*find* mercy ... on that day" (italics added), a change in wording. Some think that is a clue that Onesiphorus has died. This change, however, is probably simply a stylistic move on Paul's part, picking up the word "find" from the end of verse 17, thereby asking that the one who *found* Paul will also *find* mercy. Moreover, while a reference to "that day" may imply that Onesiphorus has died and is awaiting the resurrection, Knight points out that Paul refers to "that day" in connection with himself in 1:12, and he is still alive.[8]

(3) The repetition of a prayer for mercy in verses 16 and 18 is not in itself troubling, since it can be explained from Paul's deep feelings. The problem is rather that in the first instance it is not Onesiphorus himself but his "household" that is the object of the prayer. Some scholars have also suggested on

---

6. Knight, *Pastoral Epistles,* 384.

7. Wiles called such indirect prayers "wish-prayers" (G. T. Wiles, *Paul's Intercessory Prayers,* SNTSMS 24 [Cambridge: Cambridge Univ. Press, 1974]), 45–155.

8. Knight, *Pastoral Epistles,* 386.

the basis of *this* aspect of the text that Onesiphorus has died. But Knight points out in 1 Corinthians 1:16 that Paul speaks "about a man's household while that person is still alive" (though Stephanus's household is not mentioned separately from him, as is the case here). It does not, therefore, seem possible to determine whether Onesiphorus has died or not, and it does not matter for the application of the text.[9]

GRACE AND **God's purposes.** Immense and powerful truths are compressed in verses 8–10, ready to explode into the minds of the readers. Paul has already uncoiled some of these in his letter to the Ephesians, and the gist of Ephesians 2:1–7 finds expression in Titus 3:3–7. If Ephesians 2 teaches salvation by God's *grace*, Ephesians 1:3–14 teaches the fact of God's eternal *purposes*. Those verses contain an amazing combination of Greek words and grammatical constructions that express wisdom, forethought, and purpose. A number of these are concentrated in verse 11: "chosen," "predestined," "plan," "purpose," and "will." Therefore, when Paul here in 2 Timothy 1:9 writes of God's "purpose and grace," he may well be summarizing the teachings of Ephesians 1–2. Also when he says that God has saved us and "called us to a holy life" and that we have received this grace "before the beginning of time" (2 Tim. 1:9), he is expressing the truth of Ephesians 1:4: "For he chose us in him before the creation of the world to be holy and blameless in his sight."

To point all this out is not simply to review the exegesis. It helps us see the importance of God's purpose and God's grace in Paul's own theology. The fact that this "has now been revealed through the appearing of our Savior, Christ Jesus" (v. 10) carries on the strong emphasis in the Pastoral Letters (seen in 1 Tim. 3:16; 6:14; 2 Tim. 4:1, 8; Titus 2:11, 13; 3:4). The fact of the *epiphaneia*, the appearance, of Christ, with all the Christological and apologetic force of that teaching, would certainly help remove timidity and shame from Timothy's heart (2 Tim. 1:7).

The sequence of revelation and redemption is also important. God gave his grace in Christ "before the beginning of time" (v. 9), but it is only "now" that it has been revealed through the appearance of Christ. Similarly again in Ephesians (2:11–18), as God is expressing the contrast between the for-

---

9. If it could be proved that Onesiphorus has died, then Paul would be offering a prayer for the dead. But since the matter is unresolved and there is no justification elsewhere for such prayers, this passage cannot be used to support this practice. Knight argues that v. 16 is not a direct prayer to God but an expression of Paul's hopes.

mer state of Gentiles who are apart from Christ and their present situation in Christ, Paul uses the contrasts of distance ("far" and "near") and of time ("then" and "now"). He goes on to explain how another aspect of revelation, the "mystery" regarding the union of believing Jews with believing Gentiles into one body, had not been made known previously "as it has now been revealed by the Spirit to God's holy apostles and prophets" (Eph. 3:2–6).

The destruction of death. Perhaps the most powerful antidote to Timothy's timidity and tendency to shame is to realize that Christ "destroyed death" and "brought life and immortality to light through the gospel" (v. 10). Paul elsewhere brands death as "the last enemy to be destroyed" (1 Cor. 15:26). Death is an enemy, not a friend. Nevertheless for the believer it is our "entrance into glory."[10] In Hebrews 2:14–15 we learn that Jesus shared in our humanity "so that by his death he might destroy him who holds the power of death—that is, the devil—and free those who all their lives were held in slavery by their fear of death." For Christians all apprehension about what lies beyond death is gone; we have been brought into life and given immortality (which "mortal" human beings do not have by nature), and this has removed fear and, in Timothy's case, timidity and shame.

The active destruction of death and the devil, who holds its power, is not heard as often as other aspects of the saving death and resurrection of Christ. But it deserves to be proclaimed. No wonder Paul was convinced that the Lord could guard that "deposit" until the future day.

Shame in Middle Eastern culture. Shame is a powerful deterrent to righteous action. There was a social aspect to honor and shame in the ancient Near East and in the Mediterranean world of Paul, and it still exists in some cultures today (though it is not common in North America). It can be a powerful motivator or a hindrance to action. The shame in view here may derive from a deviation from expected behavior, but it may well be more of a personal sense of embarrassment. Either can be a hindrance. To give testimony is a public act; shame and embarrassment are also public. To identify, in the presence of others, with something they disapprove of is always difficult. It would be natural for Timothy to be ashamed of the Lord, given the facts that "the message of the cross is foolishness to those who are perishing," and that "we preach Christ crucified: a stumbling block to Jews and foolishness to Gentiles" (1 Cor. 1:18, 23).

The figure of Paul in prison must also have been an embarrassment to Timothy. It is significant that words about shame occur four times in 2 Timothy, a large number in proportion to the size of the book. In addition to

---

10. From the hymn "Jesus Lives," original text by Christian Fuerchtegott Gellert (1715–1769).

Paul's calling on Timothy not to be ashamed (1:8), he affirms that he himself is not ashamed (1:12) and that Onesiphorus was not ashamed of Paul's "chains" (1:16). Furthermore, Timothy is to be an approved worker who does not need to be ashamed (2:15). The very fact that Paul brings this issue up several times shows a natural tendency for Christians to be ashamed of Paul the prisoner. It is no wonder that in verse 7 Paul has assured Timothy that God has not given him a spirit of timidity. The spirit of power mentioned there enables one to participate in suffering for the gospel (v. 8).

There are two main reasons why Paul and Timothy are not to be ashamed. (1) The gospel reveals God's initiative, "his own purpose and grace," that existed before time began. (2) Along with that, the appearance of Christ meant that death has been "destroyed." His appearance, therefore, "brought life and immortality to light through the gospel." This is a powerful message. (3) A further reason, on Paul's own part, for not being ashamed is his confidence in the Lord and his ability to guard the trust for the important coming day.

EMBARRASSMENT AS CHRISTIANS **today.** Reasons for humiliation or shame today in the Western world are very different from those in Paul's day. While it is true that there are people around the world who are in terrible suffering and in prison, for the most part this is not so among those who are reading this commentary. Also we have become used to people *voluntarily* submitting themselves to imprisonment for causes they consider just. One thinks of the civil disobedience of the 1960s and 1970s and more recently of those who have been imprisoned during abortion protests. While there certainly are mixed feelings about these, the situation is different from that of the apostle Paul, a lone figure in the non-Christian world, forcibly imprisoned for the sake of the gospel. Our embarrassment over the way some preach the gospel is more likely to be over their personal attitudes and methods.

There is another fact to be considered on this issue. Because claims for the exclusiveness of the gospel run counter to today's doctrine of tolerance for all views, Christians do stand out for their witness to truth. But it is not only tolerance that is the problem, it is the common idea that *no* system, even one's own, can claim absolute truth. Most agree it is appropriate for a "born-again Christian" to give a "testimony," but to go beyond that to make strong *truth* claims is frowned on. To make matters worse, many Christians today are poorly prepared to explain the biblical and theological foundations of and reasons for their faith. Few are able to set forth clearly the implications and effect of the death of Christ beyond the initial fact of our salvation from the penalty of sin.

Nevertheless, though we may still need maturing in our understanding of Christian theology, we can testify for the Lord and even, if necessary, suffer for it. In North America at least, bigots can with impunity ridicule Southern Baptists, Catholics, antiabortionists, and other religious people, whereas the same slanders against other minorities would rightly elicit public rebuke. To many of us, and perhaps especially to children and young people, the disapproval and mockery of peers is a fate worse than imprisonment. So we can experience a kind of humiliation and shame. For those with children who feel that way, perhaps an explanation of the basic elements of this passage will help. But an understanding of the way our children feel and our assurance to them that we do understand will be an important part of our encouragement to them.

Persecution throughout the world. As for those enduring literal imprisonment, whether justly or unjustly, we need to be aware of the massive number of people—Christians, but others also—who are imprisoned and otherwise persecuted around the world. Some have been held hostage by guerrillas in Columbia. Some languish in Chinese and African prisons, victims of totalitarian regimes. Atrocities are committed by Muslim fundamentalists and other radical religious groups. People still die in the Middle East and Northern Ireland. The influence of Nazis, Communists, the Ku Klux Klan, and other oppressive groups has not been erased from society. North American Christians must not ignore the victims of hatred around the world. The "household of Onesiphorus" needs to be expanded to offer help to those unjustly suffering today.[11]

Those who are imprisoned for just reasons are not to be neglected either. The ministries of Prison Fellowship and others on behalf of prisoners have both biblical and humanitarian grounds for their work and its support by Christians. Those who cherish freedom ought to be the first to care for those whose freedom is gone—whatever the reason and whatever the length of the sentence—and who live in confinement, often with regret, remorse, and repentance, sometimes with a feeling of hopelessness and futility and always

---

11. Recent articles in *Christianity Today* 42 (1998) on persecution include Alford Deanne, "Imprisoned Evangelicals Dispute Accusations of Terrorism" (Feb. 9, 1998), 94; (unsigned) "Assemblies of God Church Attacked" (Feb. 9, 1998), 87; Beverly Nickles, "Restrictions on Religion Get Uneven Enforcement" (April 6, 1998), 20; David L. Miller, "Columbia's Bleeding Church" (May 19, 1998), 40–43; and on into *Christianity Today* 43 (1999): (unsigned) "Christians Killed, Churches Burn" (Jan. 11, 1999), 24; Michael Fisher, "The Fiery Rise of Hindu Fundamentalism" (March 1, 1999), 46–48; Frederica Mathewes-Green, "Can We Survive Persecution" (March 1, 1999), 68–69.

with consequences. How many Christians eager to a call from God to some kind of service are eager for this one?

Holding a pattern of sound teaching. This is the first example in 2 Timothy of the characteristic theme of the Pastorals: the blend of sound teaching with godly living. Here the "pattern of sound teaching" is to be blended with "faith and love in Christ Jesus." In this case, "faith" does not have an article and so may have to do with the application of faith in daily life rather than to the body of Christian doctrine (as it so often signifies in the Pastoral Letters). We are used to the words "sound teaching" in these letters, but the idea of a "pattern" has an added significance. A pattern or standard does not allow for deviation. There are objective ways of discerning when someone has deviated from a standard. Whether adding to, subtracting from, or changing the nature of a predetermined standard, no change is to be tolerated.

The most recent example in North America on a large scale of Christians vigorously holding to the standard "pattern of sound teaching" is the fundamentalist-modernist controversy of the early 1900s.[12] The rise of "higher critical" studies of the Scriptures, combined with other factors, resulted in large-scale defections from historic teachings of the Christian church. Many major seminaries and denominations have witnessed a marked departure from clear biblical teachings, especially concerning the person and work of Christ.

The publication of a small series of books on the essentials of the faith, called *The Fundamentals*, gave rise to the term *fundamentalists* for those who held to theologically orthodox doctrines. Some pastors were defrocked and removed from their pastoral ministries, while others attempted to work from within the major denominations and were called compromisers by those who took the path of separation. This situation was complicated by the rise of neoorthodoxy, but eventually the fundamentalist movement gained strength. A growing number have preferred to be called *evangelicals*.

The whole movement of those who held to the "pattern of sound teaching" became strong and recognized. The teachings they held in common included the doctrine of Scripture, and one's view of Scripture became increasingly important. Today the term *fundamentalism* has become widespread and has come to describe the more conservative elements in various religions around the world. The early Christian fundamentalists have for the most part passed off the scene. Major issues now confronting the church that need to be tested against the pattern of sound teaching are pluralism and postmodernism.[13] It is crucial that Christians today reach an understanding

---

12. George M. Marsden, *Fundamentalism and American Culture: The Shaping of Twentieth-Century Evangelicalism 1870-1925* (Oxford: Oxford Univ. Press, 1980).

13. See Bridging Contexts section of 1 Tim. 2:1-7.

as to what is included in the standard or pattern to which we must adhere and what are legitimate, flexible areas of difference.

Our well-intentioned desires to determine the issue of the day and always be contemporary may cause some of us to intrude what may be subsidiary issues (possibly our own agendas) into our witness, teaching, and preaching. Conversations, Sunday school classes, and the pulpit can become a means of making our own commentary on social, political—even religious—issues, to the detriment of the gospel and the whole counsel of God. We can even do this in the name of sound teaching. Paul's reference to God's "purpose and grace" should call us back to his primary intentions for his church. We have been given a trust, whether we feel we are "only" laypeople (not a biblical concept) or leaders. The gospel must shine brighter than our own agendas, however relevant and important they may be.

Paul knew that as a herald he had an important message to proclaim. As an apostle he was to represent the One who sent him and *his* agenda, and as a teacher he had been given the "pattern of sound teaching" from which neither he nor Timothy, or any successive generations, should depart. This passage calls on *all* contemporary Christians to reassess how well we are communicating the revealed gospel and the doctrinal context.

The instruction in verse 13 was in terms of keeping or holding the standard; verse 14 speaks of guarding a deposit. This is not by one's own ability but "with the help of the Holy Spirit who lives in us." Both the keeping of the pattern and the guarding of the deposit have been difficult at various stages of church history. Calls to compromise, outright persecution, exclusion from fellowship, and burning of books are some of the ways in which the Lord's servants have been treated when they have affirmed God's truth over against error.

Personal element in Paul. It is not clear whether doctrinal differences are the reason why people in the province of Asia deserted Paul (v. 15). Neither is it clear why he mentions two names in particular. Because of the vagueness of his language here and the lack of reference to any particular doctrinal issue, it is probable that this was a personal loss of friendship and support among some of those in the western part of Asia Minor from whom he expected such help. The example of Onesiphorus stands in wonderful contrast. It is interesting that Timothy already knew of both the desertion and of Onesiphorus's help. It shows something of the warm relationship between Paul and Timothy that he would have shared something so personal with him.

At various places in the Pastoral Letters—as well as sprinkled throughout the Pauline corpus—we see the human side of Paul in his remarks about other people. Romans 16 is a wonderful example of his appreciation for fellow workers. It does not take much imagination to picture this missionary, who has forfeited a stable personal life, the joys and warmth of a family, and the hope of a second and third generation of physical descendants to carry on his name and perpetuate his values, as having especially keen feelings about both the affirmations and the criticisms of associates. For Paul, therefore, to lose the confidence of another Christian was probably more traumatic than a modern pastor's loss of a member of the pastoral staff.

If even we tend to "take things personally," how much more this single, dedicated, and exhausted missionary! Yet we can to a degree identify with him, and so can all those who have served God in sensitive relationships with other Christians—whether in isolated mission outposts, among the clergy in a medieval cathedral, in a contemporary Christian radio station, in a convent of mercy, or among the staff of Caesar's household. Christians need one another, and those who criticize or depart in anger have a responsibility to be open and loving toward those who may be hurt by their actions. We could well use a "theology of dissent" in our Christian relationships.

2 Timothy 2:1-13

Y OU THEN, MY son, be strong in the grace that is in Christ Jesus. ²And the things you have heard me say in the presence of many witnesses entrust to reliable men who will also be qualified to teach others. ³Endure hardship with us like a good soldier of Christ Jesus. ⁴No one serving as a soldier gets involved in civilian affairs—he wants to please his commanding officer. ⁵Similarly, if anyone competes as an athlete, he does not receive the victor's crown unless he competes according to the rules. ⁶The hardworking farmer should be the first to receive a share of the crops. ⁷Reflect on what I am saying, for the Lord will give you insight into all this.

⁸Remember Jesus Christ, raised from the dead, descended from David. This is my gospel, ⁹for which I am suffering even to the point of being chained like a criminal. But God's word is not chained. ¹⁰Therefore I endure everything for the sake of the elect, that they too may obtain the salvation that is in Christ Jesus, with eternal glory.

¹¹Here is a trustworthy saying:

> If we died with him,
>   we will also live with him;
> ¹²if we endure,
>   we will also reign with him.
> If we disown him,
>   he will also disown us;
> ¹³if we are faithless,
>   he will remain faithful,
>   for he cannot disown himself.

THIS SECTION, BEGINNING with the emphatic pronoun "you" and accompanied by personal words that address Timothy as "my son," presents an exhortation to Christian service. It is free from the references to heresy and conflict that characterize much of the Pastoral Letters.

The opening verses picture three qualities that should characterize Timothy: strength (v. 1), foresight (v. 2), and endurance (v. 3). Verses 4–6 contain three images: a military image, an athletic one, and an agricultural one. Verses 8–10 encompass two foci: the remembrance of Jesus Christ, and endurance for the sake of the elect. To put it another way, Timothy, like Paul, should focus on the gospel and on the salvation it brings. All this is followed by another of the "faithful sayings" in the Pastoral Letters, this time dealing with conditions and results.

Forceful Words About Hardship (2:1–7)

FOLLOWING THE EMPHATIC "you," verse 1 continues with the word "then." This causes the reader to reflect on the exhortations and events referred to in chapter 1 and leads to the exhortation to "be strong." The words "in the grace" may refer to the sphere of Timothy's ministry, which indeed is "in Christ Jesus." But it can also be an instrumental construction, in which case the grace of Christ enables Timothy to be strong. In either case, it recalls Titus 2:11–14 (written earlier than 2 Timothy), where Paul informs what the grace of God "teaches us."

Verse 2 may seem an unexpected intrusion into the flow of thought. But the need for what Paul teaches and commands to be passed on by Timothy (and Titus) pervades the Pastoral Letters. In this case Paul does not refer to a direct command or written instruction but to his teaching as heard by Timothy and other "witnesses." The NIV phrase "in the presence of many witnesses" can also be translated "through many witnesses" (cf. NRSV). The problem with this rendering, however, is the implication that Timothy did not hear the teachings himself.

Perhaps the idea expressed here is confirmation by witnesses. Fee suggests that it was "attested to" by a number of people, "a needed emphasis in light of the many defections at Ephesus."[1] The word "entrust" is from the same root as the word translated "what I have entrusted" in 1:12 and "deposit" in 1:14. The teachings of Paul are something valuable that require "reliable" people to care for it and pass it on. The NIV "men" is unwarranted in the context, since the Greek word used (*anthropos*) is a generic term.[2]

The people to whom Timothy is to entrust Paul's teachings must also be "competent" (*hikanos*). "Compentent" is probably a better translation than the NIV's "qualified," since, although *hikanos* can have that meaning, it raises

---

1. Fee, *1 and 2 Timothy, Titus*, 241.

2. Knight (*Pastoral Epistles*, 39) assumes from 1 Tim. 2:12 that only men could teach: "Their task was 'to teach' an audience that included the entire church, a task forbidden to women because of the men in the audience (1 Tim. 2:12; cf. 1 Cor. 14:34ff.)." He assumes three things: that the audience was the whole church, that women could not do this, and that the recipients of the teaching here in verse 2 were "presbyters/overseers."

questions of qualifications that cannot be answered from this passage, unless it simply refers back to the quality of faithfulness. Perhaps the thought is similar to that of *didaktos*, which describes the ability to teach required of elders (1 Tim. 3:2; see comments). That need not imply that these people are elders, as Knight has assumed.[3]

It is understandable why these instructions appear in a passage about being strong and enduring hardship. It would be natural for Timothy to use his strength and gifts to continue confronting heretics and wrestling with problems, but it is sometimes more difficult to train and motivate others to carry on one's work. With Paul's impending execution, however, the instruction of others might weigh heavily on his mind. His reference to entrusting a deposit in 1:12, 14 immediately prior to this point in his letter may have triggered the thought in Paul's mind of instructing others to carry on after Timothy, which he expressed as soon as he had an appropriate context.[4]

The three images in verses 3–6 appear elsewhere in Paul, but with different emphases. The military image here has to do not with warfare but with disciplined obedience; the athletic image deals less with success and more with conformity to the rules; the agricultural image stresses hard work.

The military image is introduced by the instruction to "endure hardship with us." The verb used here also occurs in 1:8 ("join with me in suffering"; see comments) and the basic verb "to suffer" appears in 1:12. But the verb *kakopatheo*, as used here, has to do with being in distress. A related noun conveys the idea of misery or suffering, while another related noun describes "laborious toil, perseverance."[5] The NIV is justified, therefore, in translating the verb in the context of 2:3 as "endure hardship" rather than "suffer" (as in NRSV and NLT).

Verse 4 is clear in its insistence on devotion to duty and to one's commanding officer over against succumbing to diversions that may interfere with military duty. By Paul's time the Roman empire had long since secured its dominance, but to maintain the borders was a continuing task. The military forces were everywhere, and rapid troop movements were made possible by the famous Roman road system. Soldiers were especially concentrated

---

3. Ibid.

4. Hanson (*Pastoral Epistles*, 128–29) observes, "We certainly have here a doctrine of succession, but it is succession in teaching rather than succession in authorized office." He then quotes 1 Clement on apostolic succession (chs. 42, 44) and, holding that Clement wrote "perhaps 15 or 20 years" after an unnamed author wrote the Pastoral Letters, seeks to show that the short period of time between the two writings saw a development in thought toward apostolic succession. (Hanson thinks that the Pastorals were written around 100–105.)

5. See LSJ, 862. Verse 4 is clear in its reference to devotion to duty and one's commanding officer over against succumbing to diversions that could interfere with military duty.

at the far-flung borders, where insurrections were especially likely. This meant extensive training. There could be no weakening of resolve, skill, or strength. Daily discipline was enforced; diversions could not be tolerated. Because of the extensive distribution of the troops, Paul's image of the soldier's devotion was immediately recognizable and impressive.

Paul writes elsewhere about athletic competition, especially in 1 Corinthians 9:24–27. In that passage the emphasis is on personal training and discipline; here it is more on keeping the rules. Both are with a view to winning. Athletic contests were popular and highly valued in the Greco-Roman tradition. Cities were proud of their arenas, and winners were highly honored. We may be used to deliberate fouls and displays of personal flaunting in sports today, but keeping to the rules was expected in Paul's day.

Likewise, Paul refers elsewhere to the right of the Lord's servants to receive financial gain from their work (cf. 1 Tim. 5:17–18; see also 1 Cor. 9:7–14). But the message of this passage is that when the (eschatological) rewards are bestowed, priority should be given to those who have worked the hardest. The word "first" is part of the imagery and should "not be pressed in regard to Timothy's situation."[6] This image of the farmer, like the other two, is well chosen. Unlike countries today with their urban sprawl, everyone in Paul's day knew the image of the hardworking farmer. No farm machinery lessened their arduous work. All three analogies, like Jesus' parables and parabolic sayings, require reflection, so Paul tells Timothy in verse 7 that the Lord will give him insight.

Reasons for Enduring Hardship (2:8–13)

VERSE 8 MOVES from analogy to history. Whatever encouragement Timothy may receive from verses 1–7, it is the resurrection of Christ, the promised messianic descendent of David, that provides the strongest motivation. Picking up the references to suffering and imprisonment in 1:8 and the reference to chains in 1:16, Paul refers in 2:9 to his own suffering in chains "like a criminal," but adds that "God's word is not chained." This recalls the ending of Acts, where in spite of his imprisonment Paul preached "without hindrance" (Acts 28:31).

Paul turns in verse 10 to his own willingness to endure anything necessary "for the sake of [*dia*] the elect" (see 1 Tim. 5:21 on the "elect angels"; Titus 1:1 on "the faith of God's elect"). The words that follow, "that they too may obtain the salvation that is in Christ Jesus, with eternal glory," have elicited discussion. The whole concept of election stands to the side of the present

---

6. See Knight, *Pastoral Epistles*, 395.

passage, because Paul's emphasis here is not on the matter of election, predestination, and the sovereignty of God, but on the need to *facilitate the salvation* of the elect. However one may address the matter of election, the conversion of a person involves the faithful ministry of the saving gospel.

Paul's question in Roman 10:14—"How, then, can they call on the one they have not believed in. . . . And how can they hear without someone preaching to them?"—is relevant here. The words "with eternal glory" are unusual in that they combine a word ("eternal") that refers to God only once in the Pastoral Letters (1 Tim. 1:17) and five times to the believer's eternal life (see 1 Tim. 1:16; 6:12; 2 Tim. 2:10; Titus 1:2; 3:7) and another word ("glory") that, apart from this passage, only refers to glory of God (1 Tim. 1:17; 3:16; 2 Tim. 4:18). The present verse leads into the "trustworthy saying" of verses 11–13 since living and reigning with Christ involves participation in his eschatological glory.

The "trustworthy saying" (v. 11) is one of five in the Pastoral Letters (see comments on 1 Tim. 1:15; see also 3:1; 4:9; Titus 3:8). The present saying is the only one that can be called poetic. The structural features are obvious, particularly the "we" . . . "him" pattern and the protasis ("if") and apodosis (consequence) alternation. The repeated "with" (representing the verbal prefix *syn*) occurs in three of the first four verbs. The use of the word "endure" in verse 10 is apparently the trigger that causes Paul to include verse 12a (with no *syn*). The other verbs allude to biblical teachings about dying and raising with Christ (esp. Rom. 6:3–11) and participation with Christ in his coming reign (Matt. 19:28; Rev. 5:10; 20:6; 22:5).

While verse 11 can have overtones of martyrdom, the fact that in the Romans passage just cited Paul has already written strongly about spiritual identification with Christ in his death, the spiritual allusion is the most natural reference.[7] Given the fact that this saying is clearly intended as an encouragement to endure in view of all that has preceded it in 1:8–2:10, the words about dying and living also have a hortatory force. That is to say, Paul is not merely stating a spiritual or theological fact; he is calling on the reader to experience what it means to die with Christ.

Paul is not simply thinking of something historical, though it is based on the historical death of Christ, and certainly not of something physical, for we have not actually been put to death. Rather, there is a personal identification with Christ in his death, portrayed in baptism, that is supposed to mark the end of the *sinful kind of life* we previously lived. But this calls for a conscious "dying" with Christ: "In the same way, count [or consider] yourselves dead to sin but alive to God in Christ Jesus" (Rom. 6:11). If 2 Timothy 2:11 deals

---

7. For a discussion and rejection of the martyrdom interpretation see ibid., 403.

with the kind of death and life referred to in Romans 6, the future tense "we will also live" refers to our present life in Christ (cf. Rom. 6:8).

In verse 12 the endurance is, by its very nature, lifelong. The reigning is not something of a spiritual nature in this life, but is eschatological. The word "disown" is a possible translation of the Greek *arneomai*, but since we tend to use it with regard to a parent disowning a son or daughter, it could give the wrong impression. The Greek word also means "to deny, refuse" or simply "to say no"; "repudiate" may be a proper translation here. Most of the occurrences of this word are in the Gospels, where we can find help for understanding its meaning here. In Mark 8:34, for example, Jesus teaches that we should deny ourselves, and verse 38 speaks of being ashamed of Christ and of his words.

This background is useful in understanding the transition from Paul's words about being ashamed in 2 Timothy 1:8, 12, which, in turn, provides background for 2:12. First John 2:20–23 pointedly connects lying and rejecting the truth about Christ with denial. We know from 1 Timothy 5:8 and Titus 1:16 that denial can be expressed in actions even when it is not articulated. Either speech or action is possible here in verse 12. It is therefore striking that while Christ will repudiate the person who repudiates him, verse 13 tells us that if we are faithless, he remains faithful, for he cannot repudiate himself.[8] More important, we can conclude from verse 13 that not only will our Lord not deny us in words, but also he will not disown us in deeds. This fact forms the basis (*gar*) for his continuing faithfulness toward us even if we are faithless.

Since the verb *apisteo* (v. 13) can mean to disbelieve or to be unfaithful or disloyal, opinions differ as to its meaning here. But its meaning must be in contrast to what God is. He is *pistos*, which cannot mean believing (God does not "believe") but "faithful." Thus the NIV translation ("if we are faithless") is correct. In summary, verse 13 affirms God's consistency and integrity. Although human beings may not keep faith with God, he will not break faith with us because he cannot be inconsistent with himself. It is difficult to know with certainty what Paul has in mind when he speaks of God's faithfulness. Is it being faithful to his people, to his own righteousness, or to his judgments? Since all three are true and supported throughout Scripture, we do not lose any truth by leaving this question open here. What is most striking is that the saying of verses 11–13 concludes with a magnificent statement about God's character: He cannot repudiate himself!

---

8. Other occurrences of this verb in the Pastoral Letters are in 1 Tim. 5:8; 2 Tim. 3:5; Titus 1:16; 2:12. For further material and references to other literature on *arneomai* see *TDNT*, 1.469–71; *EDNT*, 1.153–55; *NIDNTT*, 1.454–56.

WITH GOOD REASON this section is frequently
quoted and preached on. It is straightforward,
positive, and graphic. It includes illustrations from
common life, doctrine, and a memorable "trust-
worthy saying." There is a series of imperatives that summarize Timothy's
responsibilities: "Be strong" (v. 1), "entrust" (v. 2), "endure hardship with us"
(v. 3), "reflect" (v. 7, referring back to the illustrations of vv. 3–6), and finally
"remember" (v. 8). Because Christian ministry and witness will always require
the elements of strength and endurance mentioned in this passage, it calls for
the attention of Christians in every age and place.

Principles. Embedded in this passage are at least two important principles.
(1) The sound teaching Timothy has learned from Paul is to be passed on to
those capable of transmitting it to other generations. This is the lifeline of
Christianity. It has been said that Christianity is only one generation away
from extinction. While that is improbable, it is theoretically true in that
unless the life, faith, and teachings of vital Christianity are actively committed to the next generation, Christianity could become a footnote of history (cf. Jesus' question in Luke 18:8).

(2) Serving Christ is hard work, requiring total commitment. That is the
message of the military, athletic, and agricultural images. However great the
power of the Holy Spirit, unless Christians are wholly dedicated to the Lord
and personally committed to his work, the channels through which the Holy
Spirit wants to work will be clogged and atrophied. The fact that Paul urges
Timothy in verse 7 to "reflect on what I am saying" and that he needs God-given
"insight" into it show that these teachings require more than superficial assent.

Paul's gospel. As elsewhere, Paul follows his personal exhortations about
commitment with a reference to doctrine, in particular the doctrine of the
resurrection of Christ, the descendent of David the King. He goes so far as
to call this "my gospel," because he is committed to it, serves it, and to a
large extent has fashioned its contours. Because of his passion for this gospel
and the Savior for whom he suffered and was imprisoned, he once again
refers to his own experience and to the importance of endurance.

The closing "trustworthy saying" is sobering, because we could infer from
it that if we do not fulfill the conditions (e.g., dying with Christ), we will not
live with him. In fact, we can look to verse 10 and ask whether there are
those who would not receive salvation if Paul or others had *not* "endure[d]
everything for the sake of the elect." But this passage is not so much intended
to raise such questions as it is to spur Christians on to faithfulness.

The importance of faithfulness. In the centuries before the advent of
media resources that keep us informed of the activities of preachers and
other Christian leaders around the world, most Christians knew only of the

ministry of their pastor and other local servants of God, such as Sunday school teachers and parish nuns. Occasionally, perhaps, the ministry of some missionary, bishop, or itinerant preacher came to their attention. People revered those local men and women of God, whose saintly lives one would expect to be rewarded by God, though also in such small circles, any "warts" were also evident.

Today, by contrast, the average Christian hears much about of many talented figures across the continent and overseas who have reputations for extraordinary gifts and ministries. But we have little personal knowledge of these giants. Whether a person is a parish priest, the head of an international organization, or the feisty host of a Christian talk show, each one stands before the God who alone can look on the heart. We have little ability to judge who is truly obeying him from the heart, discarding worldly enticements. We do not know who is truly faithful, who is playing according to God's rules privately as well as publicly, and who actually works hard in all conditions, under sun and rain, cultivating the soil of the church and fostering the growth of Christians. It is possible to preach, lead, and give out information and opinion without necessarily being inwardly spiritual or effectively bringing others along in their faith.

God's servants are judged for their faithfulness, not for their accomplishments. Who of the preachers among us has not uncomfortably heard compliments about our sermons, while being conscious of our flaws and "feet of clay," or heard others lauded for their sermons when we are aware that they also share our sinful humanity? The sharper our swords or the more finely tuned the amazing computers of our brains, the more real is the temptation to think in terms of our accomplishments rather than of personal spiritual diligence and faithfulness.

This passage deals with the seriousness of our commitment to Christ. Note that eternal life is not dependent on our faithfulness in Christian service; the Lord remains faithful (v. 13). However, the place a Christian will have in the future reign of Christ is dependent on one's endurance for him. Jesus himself said, "Whoever acknowledges me before men, I will also acknowledge him before my Father in heaven. But whoever disowns me before men, I will disown him before my Father in heaven" (Matt. 10:32–33). The word rendered "disown" (or "deny") in that passage is the same as the one translated "disown" here in 2 Timothy 2:12. However distant the possibility may be that any given Christian may disown the Lord or become unfaithful to him, that possibility is left open here. Assurance comes in the last lines. Even if we prove unfaithful, the Lord will be faithful to his own promise, his covenant sealed with his own blood. Thank God for the commitment of Christ to us (v. 13) that undergirds this whole passage!

"Christian Unbelief" was the title of a talk I once heard on the subject of the tendency of Christians to assent mentally to certain doctrines but not believe them to the extent that they change their lives. It can also describe the attitude of those who have read verses 11–13, but have assumed that even if they do not follow Christ as diligently as others do, they will have an equally blessed future reigning with Christ. If Scripture means anything, it means that there *will* be a difference. This series of conditions and consequences teaches that there *are* consequences.

It is regrettable that, for a good part of the twentieth century, liberals, who did not believe in the authority of the Bible, nevertheless emphasized Christian ethics; whereas evangelicals, who were stronger in their faith in the biblical text, tended to neglect its teachings on ethics.[9] A comparable statement may be made regarding Christians' responses to this passage. Even though it has a poetic flavor and employs images, it contains teachings that accord with other biblical statements—as, for example, Jesus' words concerning losing our lives for his sake and being rewarded for what we have done, when the Son of Man comes in glory (Matt. 24–25).

DISCIPLING AND MENTORING **contemporary believers.** The contemporary Christian has advantages over those of prior generations in that helps for the Christian life are available on all sides. Christian bookstores are stocked with devotional and motivational works. Christian magazines, websites, and small groups are among the resources available to help us in our daily lives. Whereas Timothy had little to read besides Paul's personal letters, possibly an early form of the Gospels, and whatever Old Testament Scriptures were available to him, we have armloads of books and CDs.

The vivid imagery of verses 1–7 has been taken up and expanded in contemporary writings. The same is true for doctrinal works and books on apologetics and Christian evidences to support faith. In contrast, first-century citizens of Ephesus would have had little to help affirm and support their faith. The affirmation of verse 8, "Remember Jesus Christ, raised from the dead, descended from David," would have been especially valuable to them. Today Christians can help one another immensely by recommending and sharing books and other materials on the basics of the faith. Christians need to gather

---

9. Carl F. H. Henry's work, *The Uneasy Conscience of Modern Fundamentalism* (Grand Rapids: Eerdmans, 1947), was an exception to this generalization.

consciously resources about their faith and proactively declare the truths about Christ and the gospel.

What young Timothys today need especially is personal mentoring, but not merely mentoring in the sense of giving information and offering guidance. Too often that becomes a means of control and the reproduction of ourselves in the other, accompanied by all our agendas and opinions. We may think that we have discipled or mentored a person when they adopt our outlook on things, pray like we do, witness like we do, and, if it is a pastoral relationship, preach like we do. (The word "clone" comes to mind.)

That is not what Christian discipling and mentoring are about. To mentor a Timothy means to be available, to spend time with him or her, and to seek to facilitate rather than to control the use of that person's distinctive gifts. An athlete runs the race alone, but does so after months and perhaps years of training and encouragement. And not only the coach, but other friends and family may have a part in that encouragement along the way. In Paul Timothy had a person who was close to him, who listened and understood him, who recognized his individual giftedness, and who had confidence in him.

Faithful evangelism. It is awesome in the true sense to think that around the world today are Christians in all strata of society and in diverse ethnic groups who are faithful to the Lord. Some are people with little education and only a basic knowledge of the gospel but who put many of us to shame by their faithfulness to the Lord in incredibly difficult circumstances.

At the same time, many Christian organizations are working to facilitate the transmission of the truth from one generation to another. The work of the Navigators is well known, a ministry that from its inception sought to implement verse 2 in an organized way. It is a verse that can be applied not only to "one-on-one" transmission of biblical truth, but also to the larger, more complex ministry of churches, missions, and educational institutions like seminaries. Strong seminaries do not guarantee vital churches, but they do educate men and women who, if they are spiritual and faithful to the Lord, can lead churches in the proper direction. Sloppy theology and professional expertise that lack heart and wisdom, however, are not going to accomplish the task.

Whether, then, we do it personally, corporately, or institutionally, Christians need to be consistently obedient to these verses in order to provide for successive generations of disciples of the Lord Jesus Christ. The most successful evangelistic outreach will last only a generation if we do not diligently teach others "to obey everything" Jesus commanded (Matt. 28:20).

Monitoring results in a mobile society. At the same time as information is so widely available about our faith, our relationships with those with whom we share it are often more superficial than used to be the case. People move with greater frequency. Employment situations rapidly change. Younger generations move out rather than live in extended families (in spite of the number of young adults who are tending to stay at home until marriage). Our occasional contacts with people are fleeting, such as with fellow passengers on an airline flight. Therefore, those who are hardworking farmers in the imagery of verse 6 may never know on this earth whether seeds they have planted have taken root and grown. If we endure hardship for the sake of the elect (v. 10), we may not know whether our efforts have been rewarded in changed lives.

There is, therefore, a strong eschatological dimension to this passage. Faithful Christians may not see the results or reap its rewards until heaven. We must depend all the more heavily on the promises of this passage as well as respond in faith to its commands. Perhaps the reader of this commentary, like the author, has had the joy from time to time of learning how a word of witness, a conversation, a sermon, or perhaps something written in years previous had a significant effect on someone's life.

I received a phone call at supper time some time ago that began with the words, "I won't take time away from your dinner, but I want to thank you for the articles you wrote in *Decision* magazine." The caller was a neighbor who had previously showed little interest in spiritual things. A remarkable story followed about a desire that had surfaced several times over her lifetime to get to know God. One episode involved eagerly receiving *Decision* magazine, only to store it away for a more convenient time. Eventually, in her retirement, she took out the magazines and unexpectedly came across my articles. She had no idea that my wife and I had been praying for her. A few years after that, we—and then they—moved away. Had these moves taken place before she found the articles, we may not have known this side of heaven what God had done in her life.

2 Timothy 2:14–26

K EEP REMINDING THEM of these things. Warn them
before God against quarreling about words; it is of no
value, and only ruins those who listen. ¹⁵Do your best
to present yourself to God as one approved, a workman who
does not need to be ashamed and who correctly handles the
word of truth. ¹⁶Avoid godless chatter, because those who
indulge in it will become more and more ungodly. ¹⁷Their
teaching will spread like gangrene. Among them are
Hymenaeus and Philetus, ¹⁸who have wandered away from the
truth. They say that the resurrection has already taken place,
and they destroy the faith of some. ¹⁹Nevertheless, God's solid
foundation stands firm, sealed with this inscription: "The Lord
knows those who are his," and, "Everyone who confesses the
name of the Lord must turn away from wickedness."

²⁰In a large house there are articles not only of gold and sil-
ver, but also of wood and clay; some are for noble purposes
and some for ignoble. ²¹If a man cleanses himself from the latter, he will be an instrument for noble purposes, made holy,
useful to the Master and prepared to do any good work.

²²Flee the evil desires of youth, and pursue righteousness,
faith, love and peace, along with those who call on the Lord
out of a pure heart. ²³Don't have anything to do with foolish
and stupid arguments, because you know they produce quarrels. ²⁴And the Lord's servant must not quarrel; instead, he
must be kind to everyone, able to teach, not resentful.
²⁵Those who oppose him he must gently instruct, in the hope
that God will grant them repentance leading them to a knowledge of the truth, ²⁶and that they will come to their senses and
escape from the trap of the devil, who has taken them captive
to do his will.

Original Meaning

FROM THE WARM words of encouragement in 2:1–
10 and the lofty saying of 2:11–13 we suddenly
find ourselves back in the world of the Ephesian
church with its heretical teachers. This does not
mean discontinuity, for verse 14 refers back to what has just been said with

the exhortation to "keep reminding them of these things." But Timothy's act of reminding must be accompanied by an act of warning, an act so sobering that it is said to be "before God."

How to Deal With Destructive Teaching (2:14–19)

THE NIV "KEEP reminding" (v. 14) brings out the present tense of the verb. "Warn" is a participle, also in the present tense. This tense indicates that the task is not complete but requires constant attention. The relationship between indicative and participle suggests that the two are concurrent, with a positive action, reminding, and a negative one, warning. What Timothy has taught them is a point of reference for the warning.

The contemporary reader of the completed New Testament is well aware that words are important and that precise wording is necessary for precise theology. But here Paul is warning "against quarreling about words [*logomacheo*]."[1] Paul does not enlarge here on what the controversy is about, but rather offers two clear reasons against allowing it: It is without value and does no good, and it ruins the listeners and therefore does evil.

This is the setting against which Paul writes the well-known words of verse 15. The words "do your best" represents the Greek verb *spoudazo* in the Pastorals (cf. the related adverb in 1:17 [trans. "hard" in NIV] and Titus 3:13 [trans. "do everything you can"]. The idea is doing something with diligence and perhaps with haste and urgency. It communicates the idea of zeal. Timothy is to be concerned with God's approval and so must deliberately present himself to that end. "Approved" (*dokimos*) appears only here in the Pastoral Letters, though its antonym *adokimos* ("disapproved") occurs in 3:8 (NIV "rejected") and in Titus 1:16 (NIV "unfit"). Timothy is not simply to court God's approval but to be the kind of worker who is approved so that he can present himself to God. The word for "workman" was often used for agricultural workers.

The instructions to remind and warn begin, in the Greek sentence order, with the word *tauta*, "these things." Although an ordinary and seemingly unimportant expression, it is repeated several times in the Pastoral Letters and has considerable significance (see also esp. 1 Tim. 4:6, 11; 6:2; 2 Tim. 2:2; Titus 2:15; 3:8) to refer to the range of doctrines Paul has instructed Timothy and Titus to pass on. The two uses in this present chapter either refer to specific teachings (v. 2) or follow a saying that is obviously at least one element in the teachings (v. 14). This is another way in which the present passage picks up a pattern of careful provision for the promulgation of apostolic teachings.

---

1. The noun form related to this verb occurs in 1 Tim. 6:4, where the context is also about controversy, specifically that which is carried on in a malicious way.

It may be asked why anyone would think that a workman might be ashamed (cf. Rom. 1:16). Although the idea of shame is significant in 1:8–16, this is a different context, for there is no suggestion that this workman might be ashamed of his product, that is, the gospel. Rather, the following clause indicates that it is the *way* the work is performed that might or might not give reason for shame. This work is described in the word "correctly handles" (*orthotomeo;* lit., "cut straight"). Recent reference works and commentaries tend to agree that the cutting imagery is less important than the idea of correctness.[2] The only other biblical use of this verb is in the LXX (Prov. 3:6; 11:5), where it refers to making a straight path.

Verse 16 deals once again with the activities of the false teachers. Verse 14 had warned against useless, destructive quarreling, verse 15 urged a correct handling of the truth, and verse 16 counsels against "godless chatter" (see comments on 1 Tim. 6:20). This empty talk is devoid of religious value and consequently leads "into more and more impiety" (NRSV). Such talk is to be avoided, and there will be a progression downward toward ungodliness (a sarcastic statement). In contrast, 1 Timothy 4:15 describes true progress in godliness (using a similar word).

The sentence continues in verse 17 with a second reason for avoiding the godless chatter. "Their" refers to the false teachers. "Teaching" is *logos*, with the use of that word standing in strong contrast to "the word [*logos*] of truth" in verse 15. "Will spread like gangrene" is a mixed metaphor. "Spread" denotes the opportunity to expand; the word "gangrene," while accurate, expresses the idea not of the growth of foreign cells (such as with "cancer," NLT) but the progress of tissue decay.

Of the two false teachers named in verse 17, Hymenaeus was mentioned in 1 Timothy 1:20 (see comments), while Philetus is mentioned only here. The word translated "wandered away" (*astocheo*) occurs in 1 Timothy 1:6; 6:21, but a different word is so translated in 6:10. The imagery of the word used here is not that of a person inadvertently wandering off a path, but of deviating from what is good or true. Their error is in saying "that the resurrection has already taken place."[3] This refers to the future resurrection, which is like that of Jesus and not just a spiritual transformation (1 Cor. 15:35–49).

---

2. See, for example, H. Köster, τέμνω, *TDNT*, 8.111–12; R. Klöber, *NIDNTT*, 3.352; Fee, *1 and 2 Timothy, Titus*, 255; Knight, *Pastoral Epistles*, 411–12; Towner, *1–2 Timothy & Titus*, 182. How much the emphasis is on straightforward handling of the "word of truth" and how much is on proper interpretation of it is debatable, but the neutral "correctly handles" of the NIV is to be preferred over the "rightly explaining" of NRSV and "correctly explains" of the NLT.

3. Several important textual witnesses lack the definite article before "resurrection," and the UBS text inclusion of the article receives only a C rating. Nevertheless it is preferred.

This issue may seem unimportant, on which, like some other eschato-logical issues, room can be left open for debate. Yet this is an error that has negative implications regarding the bodily resurrection of Christ. It seems to value Hellenistic ideas opposed to the biblical celebration of body and soul together, and it may draw on negative pre-Gnostic ideas about the material world, including the human body. The seriousness of this error was, there-fore, probably not only in the surface teaching but in the underlying assump-tions and their view of what we would call biblical theology. Because of the implications of their teachings, they not only led some people astray, but actu-ally destroyed their faith (v. 18).

Verse 19 responds to this upsetting situation with the affirmation that "God's solid foundation stands firm." This verse could lose some of its force if we attempt to analyze the metaphors too closely. For example: Does *theme-lios* mean specifically a foundation or, more generally, the beginning stages of construction? Does the fact that solidity is important mean that Paul had the biblical stone imagery in mind (Isa. 28:16; Matt. 21:42; 1 Peter 2:6–8)? Did his occupation with household codes cause him to move from thoughts about members of the household to the "house" itself? Is he thinking of the foun-dation of the apostles and prophets as in Ephesians 2:20 and the structure that "grows into a holy temple in the Lord" (2:21–22, NRSV)? Or is 1 Corinthi-ans 3:10–17 his point of reference, where Christ himself is the foundation?

And what are we to do with the word "seal," a strange word to use in con-nection with a foundation, since it usually refers to the soft wax that was applied to scrolls and other documents and impressed with a signet ring? Apparently Paul is referring to an inscription and using the term *seal* as an overlapping metaphor because it conveys the idea of ownership. The next verse refers to "a large house," another building metaphor probably connected with, and therefore perhaps affecting the interpretation of, the foundation in verse 19.

Scripture verses and extrabiblical citations can be introduced in support of each of the foregoing options. Once we have collected the evidence, however, it is probably best to see that Paul is not singling out one descrip-tion to the exclusion of others, but rather merging several images to convey the idea of that which (1) is absolutely firm, (2) is owned by God, and (3) stands in spite of the presence of destructive persons like Hymenaeus and Philetus. God does, after all, own the building. The concepts of God's household, the church, the pillar, and the foundation have already been blended together in 1 Timothy 3:15.

The seal or inscription on God's solid foundation expresses two comple-mentary truths. The confusion introduced by the heretical teachers and defec-tions among the people are countered by the fact that "the Lord knows those who are his." Yet although God knows, we do not. Therefore, "everyone who confesses the name of the Lord must turn away from wickedness." Each of these affirmations has roots in other Scriptures. The first quotation is from Numbers 16:5, about Korah and others who were rebelling against Moses. It was necessary that God indicate who truly belonged to him and, as it turned out, that process judged the pretenders. The second quotation contains elements of Leviticus 24:16; Joshua 23:7; Job 36:10; Isaiah 26:13; 52:11 (cf. Luke 13:27; Acts 2:21; Rom. 10:13). It may be that Numbers 16:26–27, which described separation from the tents of Korah and his associates, whose judgment was imminent, is also in mind.

The Imagery of Household Utensils (2:20–21)

THE IMAGERY OF verses 20–21 continues the theme of false teachers and teachings in verses 14–19, which concluded with the necessity of turning away from wickedness. Paul then introduces a new imagery, that of utensils in a house, which is encompassed in the larger imagery of the house and household. The "large house" does not imply anything about the size of the church at Ephesus, but is in reference to the narrative world of the parabolic saying.

A large house, owned by a wealthy person, would have a variety of utensils. This is not simply a matter of better versus everyday tableware (as is implied in the word "ordinary" in NRSV). It is rather that some utensils are used for purposes that have an overtone of "dishonor," "disgrace," or "shame."[4] Such a purpose might be for removing excrement. This would be better understood by readers in cultures where, for example, the left hand is reserved for the dirty functions of living. It is this strong description that gives sense to verse 21 and its requirement to "cleanse" oneself from the latter group of utensils. This accomplishes the shift from the impersonal utensils of the image to the personal world of Timothy, who is to be "an instrument for noble purposes," "holy [and] useful to the Master."

Although it is customary for commentators to refer to Jesus' parable of the weeds (Matt. 13:24–30, 36–43) and to Romans 9:19–21, the imagery stands on its own. The lesson concerning personal holiness is clear, and the idea of being "prepared to do any good work" for the Master looks ahead to 3:17.[5]

Personal Advice About Handling Controversy (2:22–26)

THE WORDS IN verse 21 about cleansing oneself are now explained in plain language. Verse 22 presents two contrasting objectives: "the evil desires of

---

4. BAGD, 120.
5. Regarding "good works" and the importance of ethics in the Pastorals see Young, *Theology of the Pastoral Letters,* 28–46.

youth," from which one should flee, and the pursuit of "righteousness, faith, love and peace." The idea of fleeing and pursuing is similar to 1 Timothy 6:11, were the desired objects are "righteousness, godliness, faith, love, endurance and gentleness." Paul will also mention righteousness later in 2 Timothy in 3:16 and 4:8 (see also Titus 3:5).

The word "faith" (*pistis*) occurs thirty-three times in the Pastoral Letters; it can mean "faith" or "faithfulness," depending on the context. For "love" see also 1 Timothy 1:5, 14; 2:15; 4:12; 6:11; 2 Timothy 1:7, 13; 3:10; Titus 2:2. The word "peace" (*eirene*) does not appear elsewhere in the Pastoral Letters apart from the salutations. The word "pure" has the same root as "cleanse" in verse 21. The "heart" is, as throughout Scripture, the inner person, which is dedicated either to good or to evil.

Verse 23 warns against arguments that produce quarrels, which must not characterize the Lord's servant (v. 24). Verse 14 identified this quarreling as a kind of verbal warfare used by the opponents of truth. Thus, it must not characterize Timothy. There is a progression here from arguments that are "foolish and stupid" to outright controversy. The word *mache* ("quarrels") here refers to "battles fought without actual weapons."[6] The root of that Greek word is also evident in the verb translated "quarreling" in verse 14 and "quarrel" in verse 24.

The positive attitudes in verse 24 are significant. The word for "kind" (found only here in the New Testament) carries the idea of gentleness and stands in contrast to a controversial spirit. Timothy must have this attitude "to everyone." The next word, *didaktikos* ("able to teach"), is one of the qualifications for overseership in 1 Timothy 3:2. Paul is not teaching passivity; there is truth to be taught, and taught in a strong, capable way. The word translated "not resentful" appears only here in the New Testament and describes the way one handles evil opposition or pain. The NRSV's "patient" is not strong enough, while "patient with difficult people" (NLT) comes closer. The picture in the context is of meeting the opposition of aggressive, controversial people, absorbing the pain without losing one's temper and lashing back at them.

Verse 25 describes the required active response: instruction with a view to the "repentance" of the opponents. This instruction must be done "gently," which continues the attitude described in the previous verse. Timothy's arguments could not produce repentance; only God can do that. The noun "repentance" occurs only here within the Pastoral Letters, but it appears twenty-one times in the rest of the New Testament. The verb form is not found in the Pastorals but is used thirty-four times elsewhere. In the present

---

6. BAGD, 496.

context "repentance" is not used in connection with sin in general, but specifically with respect to opposition to the truth.

The spiritual need of repentance will lead to an acknowledging of the truth. Paul hopes that these opponents will "come to their senses," a phrase that translates a verb that can mean also "to become sober again." The key to the error and belligerent attitude of these heretics is their entrapment by the devil. Two passages show with special clarity the fact that unbelievers are held under the devil's power: Acts 26:18 and Colossians 1:13. The former contains Paul's commission to turn the Gentiles from "the power of Satan to God," which involves opening their eyes and bringing them out of darkness to light (2 Cor. 4:4). Some have held that "his will" in 2 Timothy 2:26 refers to the will of God, picking up the latter part of verse 25. More likely, however, it refers to the effect of the entrapment and captivity of Satan to do his will.[7]

Bridging
Contexts

A CHANGE IN the symphony. The powerful exhortations to Timothy about diligence and faithfulness (2:1–13) take an unexpected turn in this passage. Like a movement in a symphony that suddenly leads the hearer from a pleasing, coherent theme to a related yet new aural sensation, perhaps in the jarring notes of the brass section, Paul grammatically joins two different, yet related, themes in verse 14. He combines a reference to what has preceded ("keep reminding them of these things") with the surprising command, "Warn them before God against quarreling about words."

What seems even more surprising is that the command appears at first to be less important than the previous instructions. What, after all, is so important about quarrels concerning mere words compared with the powerful images of soldier, athlete, and farmer (2:1–7), the ringing doctrinal affirmation about Christ in 2:8, and the trustworthy saying about faithfulness to the Lord (2:10–13)? Moreover, the following verse (v. 15) contains the frequently quoted saying about proper handling of the word of truth. What, then, is the significance of and justification for the intrusion of this trumpet blast of what seems to be a minor theme in the symphony of chapter 2?

This question relates to the fact that Paul is obviously more concerned in these letters with how to handle doctrinal controversy than in explaining the

---

7. See Hanson, *Pastoral Epistles*, 142–43, for an excellent discussion of the issues here, leading to the conclusion just expressed.

intricacies of the doctrinal deviations themselves. Not that the content of heresy is unimportant; if that had been the case, these letters need not have been written. It is rather that Timothy, aware of the doctrinal issues, needs a reminder of their seriousness and how to deal with them and with their advocates rather than detailed treatment of their content.

On handling controversy. Paul does provide enough comment on the specific errors for Timothy to explain them to the Ephesians (and Titus to the Cretans), who are, as it were, looking over his shoulder at the correspondence. What Timothy, Titus, the elders, and the household churches need to know is how to keep these doctrinal controversies and their promulgators from tearing apart the churches. This concern over how to handle damaging controversies fits in with Paul's insistence on the Lord's servants maintaining a purity of life consistent with their purity of doctrine. In turn all this combines to hallow God's name and uphold his reputation.

This situation may be compared with the problem of how to dispose of napalm left over after the Vietnam war. There was no question about the content and danger of this substance. The question was how and where it could be safely transported and safely disposed of without exploding and the consequent spreading of this extremely hazardous material. That in itself resulted in a heated and "explosive" controversy.

If Timothy allows himself to be drawn into heated debates over minutia, he will be distracted from major concerns, be at risk of taking the low road of merely human argumentation, and be exposed to possible loss of respect from others. Such discussions are fruitless anyway and, worse, will "ruin those who listen" (v. 14). Paul also speaks of the "godless chatter" of the false teachers, and although their teaching will spread, the implication is that Timothy is unable to contain it by engaging in controversy on their level and, in fact, may actually contribute to its dispersion. The advice Paul gives recalls some of the wisdom in the book of Proverbs:

Whoever corrects a mocker invites insult. . . . Instruct a wise man and he will be wiser still. (Prov. 9:7, 9)

A man of knowledge uses words with restraint, a man of understanding is even-tempered. (17:27)

Do not speak to a fool, for he will scorn the wisdom of your words. (23:9)

Do not answer a fool according to his folly. (26:4)

There is an alternation in verses 14–19 that helps the reader get the full force of Paul's positive instructions:

(1) Some get into quarrels about words. Avoid that.
    It ruins others.
    (2) On your part be a good workman,
        with no cause for shame,
        handling the word of truth correctly.
(3) Some become involved in godless chatter. Avoid that also.
    The false teaching destroys others.
    (4) On God's part his foundation stands firm.
        He knows who are his.
        His people should turn away from wickedness.

This structure enables us to see divisive argumentation and false teaching from God's point of view. We can see its effect and how to counter it. Wrong doctrine wrongly taught needs to be countered by true doctrine correctly taught—and lived. God's foundation is firm and in no danger of toppling. God's knowledge is certain; we cannot deceive him. We should make sure that our outward behavior corresponds to our true relationship with God.

Living in God's household. The passage goes on in verses 20–21 to use the illustration of a household—an appropriate one considering that the Pastoral Letters address God's people as a household. In this case the household is not identified as the church, but Paul simply builds on the available image. Nevertheless, those from whom Christians should "cleanse [themselves]" are probably in the professing church. This is a crucial issue, for various groups and cults have used these verses to justify their separation from other believers to form independent churches, organizations, or movements. There is no call here for Christians to separate from each other, but rather it is a call for those who hold to the truth and live it to dissociate themselves from those who are evil in teaching and living. The result should be greater usefulness to the Lord.

The vocabulary describing the persons who do this is significant. They are useful for "noble purposes," in contrast to the articles in the illustration that are for filth and excrement. The word "noble" has to do with doing what is honorable. The person who cleanses himself or herself is "made holy." Christians are saints, God's holy ones. Such a person also becomes "useful to the Master," which recalls the right God has, like a potter, to mold us as he chooses in order for us to serve him in the most appropriate way. We are thus prepared to do "good works" (see also 3:17; 2 Cor. 9:8; Eph. 2:10; Phil. 1:6; Col. 1:10). The separation from the dishonorable articles is thus not the conclusive act; it must be followed by the changes in being and function.

Verses 22–26 begin with a restatement of the kind of person God wants us to be, but now without the imagery of the household articles and their functions. In verse 22 Paul speaks forthrightly in unmistakable terms about the moral characteristics God expects in Timothy and all believers. Significantly, this leads directly into an amplification of the instructions in verses 14 and 16 and deals with "foolish and stupid arguments" and "quarrels." Here it becomes clear that in addition to the previously given reasons for appropriate attitudes in the face of arguments, there is a practical goal. The servant of the Lord who does not quarrel but instead is kind will be able to teach others and perhaps see them repent, come to a "knowledge of the truth," "come to their senses," and "escape from the trap of the devil." It is sobering to realize that if the attitude of the Lord's servant makes these results possible, the opposite is also true: A wrong attitude on our part may, in spite of correct teaching, hinder others from coming to Christ.

ON DEALING WITH those who are not Christians. Fred Heeren, author of *Show Me God*, has engaged in stimulating dialogues with scientists with a secular viewpoint. He recently said, "If I've found any one thing to be key in getting through to skeptics today, this is it ... *Have an attitude of gentleness and respect toward unbelievers and their views.* Put negatively, the greatest single turn-off for skeptics is the Christian who sets up an us-versus-them argument between Christianity and science."[8] While the setting is different from that of the early church with its conflicts, this is good advice that accords with what Paul has been telling Timothy about his attitudes to those with whom he disagrees.

Another writer observes:

> When people on the streets are asked, What is a Christian? What do they stand for?, on nearly every occasion words come back such as anti-abortion, anti-gay, anti-feminist, anti-welfare, anti-this, anti-that. And words like harsh, self-righteous, intolerant, or mean-spirited. Yet another poll of people, asked what they think Jesus was like, almost universally returns with words like compassionate, nonviolent peacemaker, and reconciler. How do we explain the contradictions here? Either the popular conception of Jesus is mistaken, or we in the church have been following the wrong agenda.[9]

Second Timothy 2:14–26, like the rest of the Pastoral Letters, leaves no doubt that Paul was anti-heresy and anti-godlessness, but the point of this

---

8. Quoted with permission from the Summer 1998 "Partners in Outreach" update of Day Star Productions, Wheeling, Illinois.

9. Quoted with permission from a brochure distributed by *Sojourners* Magazine.

passage is that Timothy should not be argumentative and quarrelsome in his attitude, as the false teachers were. In this life we will always need to take some stands that are "anti," but the issue is whether we can do this in a way that will not involve us in sub-Christian quarreling, producing a sub-Christian reputation.

Some years ago a church attempted to apply this passage from 2 Timothy to their own situation. A small group had been started in an area that could benefit from a warm, gospel-preaching, Bible-teaching church. The pieces, so to speak, were all in place. The participants were well-taught Christians. They loved the Lord, devoted themselves to worship in a spirit and to a depth not usually seen in evangelical churches in those days, and had a desire to reach others for Christ. There was a good diversity in ages, and they fit well socially into the neighborhood.

Unfortunately, they were so intense in trying to follow what they thought was the teaching of this passage that they lacked the positive attitude toward others that it also taught, which could have produced the effects envisioned in verses 25–26. They were unable to achieve such goals because of a preoccupation with being separate from all those who did not agree with their doctrine at every point, including spiritually minded, Bible-believing Christians. Other nearby churches held most of their doctrines and had similar views of church polity, ministry, and worship. But for this group, cleansing themselves from the unclean articles in the household meant separation even from those sister churches. Only God knows what might have been accomplished and what people might have been won to the Lord by a winsome, open, and kindly attitude toward others.

Two personal illustrations. For another application, I might offer a personal illustration. Years ago I had the opportunity to take some doctoral courses in a major liberal seminary. This took place at a crucial time in American fundamentalism. Some of the more strident voices in fundamentalism were making it difficult for others, equally fundamental in their beliefs, to hold meaningful conversations with those of a different persuasion. Some of their attitudes and argumentation were close to what this passage warns against. In this climate I, for one, found it hard to explain my beliefs to others at the seminary. I had no disagreement with the essential doctrines of fundamentalism, but the personal attacks by others of my theological position on some of the very people I was then meeting and appreciating at the seminary made it difficult to represent conservative theology to them.

However, at one point I had the privilege of facilitating an invitation to New Testament scholar F. F. Bruce, who was visiting in the area, to speak in the seminary chapel. He began with words close to these: "It does not matter what we think the apostle Paul might have said, or what we wish he had said. What matters is what, in fact, he did say." Bruce then proceeded in a clear, gentle way to present a biblical message on the heart of Pauline theology.

Perhaps a second illustration will be useful. From time to time openings present themselves to have public debate, personal dialogue, or correspondence with prominent opponents of the Christian faith. (I still keep a letter from atheist Madeline Murray O'Hare in response to something I once wrote her.) One Christian apologist had opportunities to debate her and others of similar persuasions. After one such appearance, some were troubled by his combative, demeaning attitude to the antagonist. His response was, "I did not go there to save souls but to destroy a heretic." I believe the apostle Paul would have hoped rather to destroy heresy and save a soul.

Fruitful dialogue. Contemporary application of this emphasis in our passage should not be difficult if we share Paul's goals. It will always be more difficult to separate from those whose life and teachings are destructive if we know them personally than if they are merely names to us. Yet it should make us more concerned for them personally, and we can hope for an eventual turnaround if we do know them. In the house church setting Timothy must have had firsthand contact, perhaps weekly for a period of time, with the very people Paul warns him about.

In what circumstances, then, can we best engage in fruitful dialogue? There are forums that provide an open hearing for differing theological and biblical viewpoints, some involving participants from non-Christian religious and various philosophical perspectives. One thinks of the American Academy of Religion and the Society of Biblical Literature, but there are major societies in other disciplines also that relate to religion. Disagreement is expected and, if it is courteous and reasoned, it is respected. Such dialogue allows for dissemination of one's viewpoints as they may legitimately arise from the presentations and discussions, though one must not misuse the scholarly forms for confrontational evangelism.

On the local church scene, pastors and others may be involved in ministerial gatherings with ministers, priests, and perhaps rabbis, where, in a friendly setting, there can be an "appreciative inquiry" (to borrow a happy phrase) of other faiths. Without attacking others or questioning their integrity (which I have unfortunately heard done), a clear testimony is appropriate.

When, however, we are confronted with outright heresy by "wolves" seeking to destroy the flock and to tear a church away from its theological moorings, the rules change, and the Lord's servant should not get sucked into banter or debate. When the lines are drawn and the life of the flock is at stake, truth must confront error as openly and as forcefully as necessary.

2 Timothy 3:1–9

🔥

BUT MARK THIS: There will be terrible times in the last days. ²People will be lovers of themselves, lovers of money, boastful, proud, abusive, disobedient to their parents, ungrateful, unholy, ³without love, unforgiving, slanderous, without self-control, brutal, not lovers of the good, ⁴treacherous, rash, conceited, lovers of pleasure rather than lovers of God—⁵having a form of godliness but denying its power. Have nothing to do with them.

⁶They are the kind who worm their way into homes and gain control over weak-willed women, who are loaded down with sins and are swayed by all kinds of evil desires, ⁷always learning but never able to acknowledge the truth. ⁸Just as Jannes and Jambres opposed Moses, so also these men oppose the truth— men of depraved minds, who, as far as the faith is concerned, are rejected. ⁹But they will not get very far because, as in the case of those men, their folly will be clear to everyone.

CHAPTER 2 ENDED optimistically: The Lord's servant is to instruct opponents patiently, with the hope that God will graciously rescue them from Satan's grasp. But chapter 3 presents another, less optimistic reality, introduced with the mild adversative *de* ("but") and the command "mark this."

Terrible Times (3:1–5)

THE VERB "MARK" is the simple word "know," but in this context it serves as a jolting reminder to Timothy of a reality with which he must come to grips: "Terrible times" are coming. The adjective translated "terrible" can, in various contexts, mean violent (Matt. 8:28), fierce, or hard to deal with. "There will be" would normally describe a coming state of affairs, but it becomes clear in verse 5 that the future is now. Some have argued that a later pseudonymous author attributed this to Paul, using the future tense to make it appear as if Paul had correctly predicted what would take place.[1] However, Paul could

---

1. This is a variety of the old *vaticinium ex eventur* ("prophecy after the event") explanation of biblical predictions.

certainly draw on writings and sayings that spoke of future dangers and cast this in futuristic language, although he knew—and will soon make clear—that these things are already taking place.

The expression "last days" originated in the Old Testament (see Isa. 2:2). Note how Peter, quoting Joel 2:28 in his speech at Pentecost (or Luke, quoting Peter in Acts 2:17), recasts the prophet's "and afterward" as "in the last days." The section that follows (Joel 2:28–32; Acts 2:19–20) describes events both at the beginning of the church age and those that must take place "before the coming of the great and glorious day of the Lord" (Acts 2:20).[2] Isaiah too follows his reference in Isaiah 2:2 to the "last days" with a description of a "day" that the Lord Almighty has "in store" (2:12).[3] Such terminology occurs also in the Minor Prophets (e.g., Zeph. 1:14–18), in Jesus' teachings (Matt. 24:29), and in 2 Peter 3:10. The battle of Armageddon will take place on "the great day of God Almighty" (Rev. 16:14, 16).

While some chronological prophetic detailing is possible, the *day/days* terminology in Scripture seems flexible, directing attention to major events that characterize different phases of history. Unlike the present passage, 1 Timothy 4:1–3 (which describes "later times") has to do with doctrinal defection rather than with the moral depravity described here in 2 Timothy 3. All teaching about the last days is consistent with the idea of the present age as evil (Gal. 1:4) and with Paul's exhortation to make "the most of every opportunity, because the days are evil" (Eph. 5:16).

The reasons why the last days are so terrible are cited in verses 2–9, introduced by the word *gar* ("for," omitted in NIV). The list in verses 2–5 calls to mind the vice catalogues found in Greco-Roman literature.[4] Sometimes, as in the present passage, the perpetrators are listed rather than the evil deeds. Hanson vividly refers to those in this chapter as "vicious characters."[5] The descriptions in verses 2–4 have sometimes been grouped according to their verbal similarities in Greek. For example, the two words translated "lovers of themselves" and "lovers of money" begin with the Greek prefix *phil* (related

---

2. See also the use of this and similar terms in John 6:39, 40, 44, 54; 11:24; 12:48; Heb. 1:2; James 5:3; 1 Peter 1:5, 20; 2 Peter 3:3; 1 John 2:18; Jude 18.

3. See also such passages as Isa. 10:20, 27; 13:6, 9, 13; 14:3.

4. Romans 1:29–31 contains such a list: "They have become filled with every kind of wickedness, evil, greed and depravity. They are full of envy, murder, strife, deceit and malice. They are gossips, slanderers, God-haters, insolent, arrogant and boastful; they invent ways of doing evil; they disobey their parents; they are senseless, faithless, heartless, ruthless" (see also 1 Cor. 6:9–10; Gal. 5:19–22; 1 Tim. 1:9–10; 6:3–10).

5. Hanson, *Pastoral Epistles*, 144. For references to some Greco-Roman and secondary literature on such lists see Dibelius/Conzelmann, *Pastoral Epistles*, 115–16.

to love). The last three Greek words in verse 2 and all those in verse 3 (except "slanderous") begin with the so-called *alpha privative* (the use of an initial Greek alpha, which transforms a positive into a negative [similar to the English "un"]). The first two words in verse 4 begin with *pro;* more significantly, the two nouns in the last phrase of verse 4 have the same *phil* prefix as in verse 2 ("lovers of pleasure rather than lovers of God"), which, it might be said, summarize the whole section.

This drawing together of the first and last pairs of words by means of identical prefixes also brings "lovers of money" into contrast with "lovers of God," calling to mind Colossians 3:5, "greed . . . is idolatry" (cf. also 1 Tim. 6:10). "Boastful, proud" (2 Tim. 3:2) are two words that overlap semantically and can be translated "arrogant pride" (cf. Rom. 1:30). The word translated "abusive" ("blasphemers" in KJV and NKJV) is usually understood now as having a broad sense. It certainly can include "scoffing at God" (NLT) but its inclusion with other vices (as in Mark 7:22; Eph. 4:31; Col. 3:8) demonstrates that it can refer to the defamation of other human beings also.[6] A bad attitude to parents (2 Tim. 3:2) is seen in the extreme in 1 Timothy 1:9 and is disallowed among the children of elders in Titus 1:6 (see also Rom. 1:30).

"Ungrateful" and "unholy" (v. 2) may not seem to belong together until we realize that prior to the vice list in Romans 1:29–31 (referred to above), Paul had written, "for although they knew God, they neither glorified him as God nor gave thanks to him" (v. 21). To withhold thanks from God is a refusal to acknowledge that he exists or, at the least, to refuse to acknowledge that our life and all we have come from him. The NIV "without love" fails to bring out the specific kind of love that is missing: that which normally exists between family members (such as between parents and children). The NRSV's "inhuman" may be too strong. This missing element of love is expressed in Ellicott's use of a quaint but accurate definition, "destitute of love towards those for whom nature herself claims it."[7]

The meaning of the word "unforgiving" (v. 3) is helped by reference to its etymology. It conveys the attitude of a person who does not respond to a proposal for a truce; such a person refuses to be reconciled or placated. The Greek word for "slanderous" is translated by the NIV as "malicious talkers" in 1 Timothy 3:11. "Without self-control," when used in a vice list like this, refers not to relatively harmless matters such as diet, but to matters of moral failure. "Brutal" is a good translation for the next word, which means also "untamed" or "savage." "Not lovers of the good" (occurring only here in Greek literature) can, in a vice list, be interpreted more forcibly as "haters of good"

---

6. BAGD, 143.
7. Ellicott, *Commentary on the Epistles of St. Paul,* 152.

(NRSV). "Treacherous" conveys the idea of betrayal. "Rash" describes the attitude of a crowd out of control (cf. Acts 19:36). On "conceited" see 1 Timothy 3:6 and comments.

The amazing thing is that these people, consumed by their own vices, have "a form of godliness." This does not necessarily mean that they are in the church, but the fact that Paul counsels Timothy to "have nothing to do with them" may indicate that they are. Note how Paul makes it clear in 1 Corinthians 5:9–11 that believers are not to dissociate themselves from immoral people in the world, but from those in the church. The word for godliness (*eusebeia*) was commonly used to mean piety or religion. It appears frequently in the Pastoral Letters as a word for Christian piety (see 1 Tim. 2:2; 3:16; 4:7–8; 6:3, 5–6, 11; Titus 1:1). Whatever their "form of godliness" is, these people deny its power and thus reject the true God.

Victimization of Women and Others (3:6–9)

VERSES 6–9 CONTINUE the warning against the evil people so graphically described in verses 2–4. Since these evil hypocrites have a "form of godliness," they are able to seduce some people into believing their heresies. Those described in verse 6 are women, specifically described as *gynaikaria*—a diminutive, demeaning form of the word for woman. Since "little" may fail to convey the disparaging pathos of the word, translators have tended to expand its connotation with words such as "weak-willed" (NIV), "silly" (NRSV), "gullible" (NKJV), and "vulnerable" (NLT).[8]

It is important exegetically to understand this word as a particular class of women and not as a description of women in general, any more than the words in verses 2–4 describe men in general. These women may have been recent converts, possibly from lives of religious perversion or prostitution. Kelly forsakes objectivity when he says "it remains a fact that women, with their more intuitive and receptive approach, are in all ages particularly susceptible to proselytism, bad as well as good."[9] Lock's comment is more appropriate here: "They have become *caricatures* of true womanhood."[10] The fact that some women are being deceived by evil, hypocritical false teachers may help to explain why Paul earlier restricted women as he did (1 Tim. 2:11–15). It is reasonable to suppose that this was also taking place in churches beyond Ephesus, requiring a blanket restriction on his part.

---

8. Peterson's *The Message* paraphrases it "unstable and needy women."

9. This is similar to the misuse of 1 Tim. 2:14 about Eve's deception to support the allegation that cults are typically started by women. This is true of some cults, but ignores the heresies from the time of the early church to the present that have been started by men.

10. Lock, *Pastoral Epistles*, 107.

Paul's main point in verses 6–7 is not to malign women but to show the treachery of the false teachers. One of the ways in which these people carried on their skullduggery is underhandedly to "worm their way into homes" and victimize women. What these men do when they get into the homes is to "gain control over" the kind of women who will respond to them. This verb means literally "to take captive," but is, of course, not used in a literal sense here. If the word "captivate" (NRSV) were a little stronger—it usually conveys the idea of charming someone—it would be a clever choice.

The women who are taken advantage of in this way are "loaded down with sins." The same verb occurs in 4:3 about accumulating teachers and, with the prefix *epi*, appears in the postapostolic Epistle of Barnabas 4:6, in the phrase "compounding your sins." As Knight points out, this verb is in the perfect tense, indicating a condition they are in as a result of past sins, while the next verb ("are swayed"; lit., "are led") is a *present* participle.[11] While the word for "desires" is not in itself negative, it generally has a negative sense in the New Testament. These women are sadly "always learning but never able to acknowledge the truth" (v. 7). The point is that they are susceptible to further encounters of this nature and, ironically, cannot even gain the awareness of truth that Timothy's opponents might have through repentance.[12]

Verse 8 contains another description of the false teachers, this time by reference to "Jannes and Jambres," two figures known from extrabiblical literature. These are the names Jewish tradition gave to the Egyptian magicians who tried to imitate the signs performed before Pharaoh by Moses and Aaron (Ex. 7:11; 9:11).[13] What they had in common with the false teachers at Ephesus was that they also stood against the truth, had "depraved minds," and were rejected "as far as the faith is concerned" (cf. also Titus 1:16, where "unfit" is the same word translated "rejected" in the NIV here). Lock calls the reference to Jannes and Jambres an "*ad hominem* illustration," remarking that the false teachers are "fond of their Jewish myths and genealogies: well, the nearest analogy to themselves to be found there is that of magicians whose folly was exposed."[14] The "just as ... so also" construction makes the comparison clear.

This section with its dismal pictures concludes with some encouragement to Timothy. These heretics "will not get very far" (v. 9). Paul is being

---

11. "That their consciences are burdened by past sins and their lives controlled by such desires puts them in a weakened condition and makes them vulnerable to false teachers who 'capture' them as followers" (Knight, *Pastoral Epistles*, 434).

12. See 2:25, where the Greek expression translated "knowledge of the truth" is identical to that used in a verbal phrase here in verse 7.

13. Their names are found in Jewish rabbinical writings and some other literature in the early Christian centuries; see Carl E. Armerding, "Jannes and Jambres," *ISBE*, 2:966.

14. Lock, *Pastoral Epistles*, 107.

somewhat sarcastic here, as the heretics' only advance is toward ungodliness. Once more the comparison is made clear by the words "as in the case of those men." In a situation where the very nature of false teaching was that it fooled some people, such as the "weak-willed women," it would have been a great encouragement to Timothy to know that "their folly will be clear to everyone."

A DEGENERATING SOCIETY. An article containing a sobering description of contemporary youth made the rounds several years ago. It portrayed the disobedience of young people toward their parents, their failure to observe traditional norms of politeness, and so on. It was a bleak picture, and the reader was compelled to join in this lament over the direction of today's youth culture. It was only at the end of the article that one learned the author was an ancient Greek philosopher. Probably many generations have felt that it was their particular fate to live during a period when society (and not only the youth culture!) was rapidly degenerating. Verses 1–5 can compete for one of the most pessimistic descriptions in print. No doubt the files of many preachers contain clippings illustrative of the various categories of degeneracy in this paragraph.

It is easy in a Bible commentary, which is read mainly by people with high spiritual aspirations, to moralize piously about the evil world "out there." But while trying to avoid banal moralization, some comment is necessary. We cannot bridge contexts without identifying trends. It is not only the first-century heretics or our contemporary narcissistic culture that have lovingly stared at their own reflection. "Lovers of themselves" have strutted through many cultures and many levels of society. "Bad as I wanna be" and "having it my way" are now acceptable as public declarations, but they are not new. Even though we may evaluate self-esteem as a valid and healthy Christian attitude, we can easily find perversions in any religion or philosophy.

Greed and arrogance. Nor do we need to look far to find "lovers of money." Having ministered in wealthy communities in both eastern and central United States, I know that rich people can be either generous or greedy. The possession of wealth itself does not determine this. The same can be said for people below the poverty line. One of the most wealthy families I knew was not only generous but *sacrificially* generous. But the literature of any age or country has its stock figures of sheer greed.

Arrogance—whether fed by wealth or poverty or neither—takes many forms. In this passage "boastful," "proud," "abusive," "ungrateful," "unforgiving," "brutal," and "conceited" are some of its faces. Anyone who goes to the altar for worship without proper reconciliation with others, or who acts out the equivalence of a Corinthian Christian using the Lord's Supper as a means of partying with friends, shows that he or she is an arrogant lover of self rather than a lover of God and one's neighbor. We would probably not find partying at the Lord's Supper in most cultures, but there are other ways to disregard the rights of disadvantaged people. No doubt from first-century slaves to medieval serfs and to contemporary minorities there have been many ways in which this has been done, both subtle and openly outrageous.

It may come as a surprise that occasionally missionaries have in effect enslaved defenseless people, but it is, sadly, no longer a surprise that some ministers abuse women in their churches. The people in this passage have "depraved minds" and are not true lovers of God; they are opponents of the faith and people of "folly." Whenever such attitudes erupt in the church there should be discernment and discipline. The church must purify itself. Verses 10–17 will provide a contrast in the pure life of the Lord's servants, such as Paul and Timothy.

The experience of the women described in verses 6–7 was not unique in Ephesus. During the first centuries of our era the Roman empire was criss-crossed by itinerant merchants, entertainers, philosophers, cult leaders, and others seeking to propagate or to peddle their wares and ideas. Some of the methods of the wandering preachers were aboveboard. However, others had motives that were mercenary or worse. The actions of greedy itinerant preachers, from whom Paul sought to disassociate himself, provide a useful background to the actions of the false teachers described in this chapter. The vulnerability of some women in the Ephesian church may have a bearing on Paul's restriction of women's ministry in 1 Timothy 2:12.

A form of godliness. The amazing thing about 3:1–9 is not that people are boastful, proud, and conceited or that they are unforgiving or without self-control, but that these words can describe people who have "a form of godliness but [are] denying its power." Paul is not describing pagans engaged in crime or biological warfare but false teachers penetrating the Christian church. Non-Christians often level the charge that the church is full of hypocrites. Actually that charge is mild compared to the insidious character of these protean false teachers. They could adopt a "form of godliness," but in their "depraved minds" they were preying on vulnerable women. Unlike Paul (1 Thess. 2:5) they used a mask of piety to cover up greed.

There seemed to be two ways of looking at such people. They are clearly hypocritical with their "form of godliness," so to some degree they may for a while be undetectable. At the same time their rebellion is often overt, as has been the case as far back as Jannes and Jambres. Paul says that "their folly will be clear to everyone." It will therefore take some discernment on the part of believers to detect these opponents of the gospel even before their cover is blown.

SOCIAL DEGENERATION. WE have already cited some contemporary examples of social degeneration. If it were not that Paul has tied all this with the "last days," we could easily assume that he is referring to terrible people who were a threat to the church at Ephesus and leave it there. However, assuming that the downward spiral will not reverse itself, the final "last" days will become increasingly intense in their horror, right on to the end of history.

It was probably the story of the death of Kitty Genovese in New York City several decades ago that woke people up to the extent that self-love and disregard for others had come to characterize modern urban dwellers. The story, disseminated widely, is that one night this woman was attacked in the street right in front of an apartment building. Residents in the surrounding buildings heard her screams for help, could see the savagery from their windows, but did nothing to come to her aid. She died a horrible death.

Our quest for the contemporary significance of this passage in 2 Timothy is not difficult, once we recognize that every murderer and every disinterested, dispassionate observer like those in that New York scene contribute to the "last days." Supporting evidence from the media is hardly necessary to prove the point that contemporary society is in bad shape. It could be asked, of course, whether Western culture at the turn of the millennium is demonstrably worse than, say, the calculated frightfulness of Tiglath-Pileser III in Old Testament times or than the times of the worst Roman emperors. We could proceed through history, pausing to look at such horrors as medieval torture chambers, the gulags of Siberia, and ethnic cleansing in Bosnia Herzogovena. Along the way we could take note of the days of Al Capone, Bugs Moran, Lucky Luciano, and other gangsters with their disregard for innocent life. But then would have to acknowledge as well the sad victims of abuse in its various forms in our own day: the terrors of street gangs, drive-by shootings, and the tragic results of road rage on the highways. And according to the Bible's descriptions of "the last days," the darkest hours of social degeneration may be yet ahead.

Terrible as such things are (and "brutal" in verse 3 serves as a good contemporary description of them), the common thread through all of this is selfishness. "People will be lovers of themselves," and the expressions of that— pride, ungratefulness, lack of love for others, ingratitude, and sensuous pleasure—are descriptive of contemporary moral malaise.

Victims of abuse. The abuse of women is another example of our social malaise and of the relevance of our passage. It is true that there have been societies in many ages of history where women were abused in one way or another. One would hope that with an increased sensitivity to the position and self-respect of women in our day, there would be less abuse. While the specifics of the first century (e.g., temple prostitutes) are a thing of the past, male aggressiveness and sinful passions drive some men to abuse their wives and daughters (sometimes under the guise of "male headship").[15] Further, as is now widely realized, access to the Internet can yield vivid and sordid sexual information. The so-called "vice catalogs" in the New Testament can perform a salutary service as checklists for Christians to avoid today.

It is possible for pastors, day-care employees, youth leaders, and others in contemporary churches to play on the weaknesses of people who depend on them for religious guidance, even if not to the horrific extent of the objects of Paul's condemnation in this passage. We do not have the same circumstance of wandering preachers (although evangelists do travel, as do entertainers, sports figures, and business people, and such people have been known to prey on women). Yet in today's society privacy is easily gained, and the very people who come to a minister for help may develop an attraction for, and dependence on, the helpful pastor. Reciprocally, pastors can feel attraction to and sympathy for a seeker; such situations can lead to problems.

More than that, unscrupulous clergy can exploit people both sexually and in other less obvious ways rather than care for the very persons whose needs lead them to the church for help. If such individuals then leave the church, they may well tell others how the "church" or "Christians" prostituted them, and the reputation of God, which the Pastoral Letters are seeking to uphold, is sullied.

The evils described in this passage are relatively easy to identify. It is possible, however, for Christians to become so occupied with such evils outside the church that they are oblivious to the vulnerability of people to sinful "operators" within the church. Those who do home schooling or send their children to Christian schools and Sunday schools and who encourage their young people to attend church youth groups may have a false sense of security. Sex maniacs can invade youth groups, just as financial predators can have neat haircuts and run for church office. The greed of a naive Christian can give opportunity to such a crook, and a natural hunger for sex can make young people vulnerable to a leader they trust.

---

15. At this point I am drawing on personal knowledge that is confidential.

2 Timothy 3:10-17

YOU, HOWEVER, KNOW all about my teaching, my way of
life, my purpose, faith, patience, love, endurance,
¹¹persecutions, sufferings—what kinds of things happened to me in Antioch, Iconium and Lystra, the persecutions
I endured. Yet the Lord rescued me from all of them. ¹²In fact,
everyone who wants to live a godly life in Christ Jesus will be
persecuted, ¹³while evil men and impostors will go from bad
to worse, deceiving and being deceived. ¹⁴But as for you, continue in what you have learned and have become convinced
of, because you know those from whom you learned it, ¹⁵and
how from infancy you have known the holy Scriptures, which
are able to make you wise for salvation through faith in Christ
Jesus. ¹⁶All Scripture is God-breathed and is useful for teaching, rebuking, correcting and training in righteousness, ¹⁷so
that the man of God may be thoroughly equipped for every
good work.

IN VERSES 10-11 Paul both encourages Timothy
and counters the negative characteristics
described in verses 2-9 by adducing the example
of his own life. He has not hesitated to do this
elsewhere in the Pastorals (1 Tim. 1:12-16; 2 Tim. 1:8, 12-13; 2:8-10; 4:6-
8). Paul then moves to Timothy's life and what influences have shaped him
(2 Tim. 3:14-15). In doing so, Paul refers to what the Scriptures are and
what role they play in a person's life (vv. 16-17).

Paul's Sufferings (3:10-13)

PAUL'S AUTOBIOGRAPHICAL NOTES in the Pastorals serve several purposes. They
demonstrate the sovereign grace of God in his life, acknowledge that faithful service does bring suffering, and provide a model for Timothy. The present passage accomplishes the second and third of those purposes. It opens
with the emphatic "You, however," which calls Timothy as a witness to the
difference between the false teachers just described and Paul's teaching and
way of life. Paul chooses a verb (NIV "know all about") that means "to follow."
As Knight observes, this word has a double sense, both of being with Paul
to observe some of these things and "primarily, and more profoundly . . . of

the 'following' that takes place 'with the mind' and that 'understands' and 'makes one's own' that which one follows, as in 1 Timothy 4:6."[1]

The word "teaching" stands first in a list of characteristics that are positive contrasts to the characteristics of the false teachers in verses 2–5. This word for teaching (*didaskalia*) is prominent in the Pastoral Letters, occurring fourteen other times (1 Tim. 1:10; 4:1, 6, 13, 16; 5:17; 6:1, 3; 2 Tim. 3:16; 4:3; Titus 1:9; 2:1, 7, 10).[2] Not only is the occurrence of *didaskalia* at the beginning of this list important; it is repeated as the first important use of Scripture mentioned in verse 16.

As Paul's list progresses in verse 10, he is not flattering himself but rather showing where his values are, values that are not optional or relative but of absolute importance in the life of the Lord's servant. Not only Paul's teaching, but also his character distinguishes him from false teachers and the itinerant philosophers mentioned above. The word translated "way of life" occurs only here in the New Testament, but was common in classical literature. While "purpose" is not an unusual word (it occurs twelve times in the New Testament), its use here calls for attention because in 1:9 Paul has written of God's "purpose and grace" (see comments there). We must understand God's purpose as revealed in Scripture and order our lives to follow that plan.

In place of the familiar "faith, hope, and love" Paul replaces "hope" with "patience" and after "love" writes "endurance." These four words convey the idea of waiting a situation out with steadfastness, an appropriate action for a person who has hope. Paul has already alluded to his sufferings in the Pastoral Letters, but these refer to events in specific cities that took place prior to Paul's meeting with Timothy in Lystra (Acts 13:14–52 [esp. vv. 45, 50]; 14:1–5, 8–20 [esp. v. 19]; 16:1–2).

Although Paul mentions that the Lord rescued him from these persecutions (v. 11), he makes the point in verse 12 that "everyone who wants to live a godly life in Christ Jesus will be persecuted." This verse reinforces 1:8–12; 2:3, 9–10. It is striking that Paul cites the noun "persecutions" twice in verse 11 and a related verb once in verse 12. He moves from his own experience to that of Christians in general. The word *pantes* ("everyone") in verse 12 does not, in this context, mean everyone without exception, but rather everyone in general as opposed to just Paul himself. Persecution is not exceptional for those who want to live a life that is "godly" (the adverb *eusebos* has the same root as the word for religion or piety that is prominent in the Pastorals, see 1 Tim. 2:2; 3:16; 4:7–8; 6:3, 5, 6, 11; 2 Tim. 3:5; Titus 1:1).

---

1. Knight, *Pastoral Epistles*, 438.

2. The word "teacher" (*didaskalos*) occurs in 1 Tim. 2:7; 2 Tim. 1:11; 4:3. The verb "teach" (*didasko*) occurs in 1 Tim. 2:12; 4:11; 6:2; 2 Tim. 2:2; Titus 1:11. Another word for teaching (*didache*) occurs in 2 Tim. 4:2; Titus 1:9.

Having moved from the sole figure of Paul to all those who want to live a godly life in Christ Jesus, we now face the contrasting figures of "evil men and impostors" (v. 13). The NIV "while" (v. 13) translates the Greek *de*, which is usually translated "but." There is really a double contrast in this section: (1) between the godly in verse 12 and the evil people in verse 13, and (2) between those evil people in verse 13 and Timothy in verse 14. In addition to "evil" Paul describes these people as "impostors" (*goes*, a sorcerer or someone out to swindle the public) and describes them with two participles, "deceiving" and "being deceived." In this context *goes* clearly refers to people who make a practice of trying to mask their evil intentions to cheat others (see the contrasting attitude of Paul in 1 Thess. 2:3–5).

The tragedy of these impostors is compounded by the fact that they not only deceive but are themselves "being deceived." In a master stroke, Paul once again calls on the verb *prokopto* (lit., "make progress") to describe them ("will go from bad to worse"; see the related noun in 1 Tim. 4:15, used in a positive sense, and the verb *prokopto* in 2 Tim. 2:16, used sarcastically, as well as "not get very far" in 3:9).

The Importance of Scripture (3:14–17)

VERSE 14 BEGINS with the strong "but . . . you" and contains a call to Timothy to consistency in doctrine and conviction. Not only had Timothy "learned" the truth from Paul and others, he had become "convinced" of it. The reason for this lies largely with the integrity of the people from whom he learned it, such as his grandmother Lois and his mother Eunice (1:5). Surely Paul has himself in mind also.

The "holy Scriptures" refer to what we know as the Old Testament and what the Jewish people call the *Tanach*. Jesus, during the forty days between his resurrection and ascension, taught how the Scriptures pertained to him (Luke 24:32, 44–47). Salvation does not come automatically from reading the Scriptures, but they "are able to make you wise for salvation through faith in Christ Jesus."

Verses 16–17 are the strongest statement in the Bible about itself. We understand that the word "Scripture" (*graphe*) includes the New Testament, since 2 Peter 3:16 cites the writings of Paul among the "Scriptures" (also *graphe*). The word translated "God-breathed" (*theopneustos*) in the NIV is more commonly translated "inspired," which is less awkward but also less accurate. The term *inspired* is much too broad in its common usage today to convey the force of the Greek *theopneustos*, which is formed from *theo* (the root form of the word "God") and *pneustos* (from a Greek root having to do with breathing).

The main exegetical issue is where to place the unexpressed verb "is" and how to interpret the Greek word *kai* (which can mean either "and" or "even, also"). The first option is to understand the unexpressed "is" as coming after "all Scripture," so that the description "God-breathed" is true of all Scripture. In this case "God-breathed" and "useful" are *predicate adjectives,* joined by "and" (*kai*). The NIV adds a second understood "is" and thus renders this, "All Scripture is God-breathed and is useful. . . ." This is the understanding also in NRSV, NKJV, NLT, NASB, JB, and others. The alternative is to understand the verb "is" as coming after "God-breathed," and to understand the word *kai* to mean not "and" but "also." In this case, "God-breathed" is understood as an *attributive* adjective—that is, it is part of the noun phrase and thus defines (and *limits*) the subject. In this case it means, "All God-breathed Scripture is also useful . . ." (cf. REB, "All inspired Scripture has as its use . . ."). This leaves open the possibility that there is other Scripture that is not inspired and therefore not useful.[3]

It can be argued that the most natural reading is the first. (1) If "God-breathed" were attributive, it would more normally have been placed before the noun "Scripture." (2) "God-breathed and . . . useful" is a balanced phrase in itself. Many other arguments have been made, however, and many statistics are offered on each side of the issue. The tendency over the past decades seems to be toward the first option, and modern translations offer that as the preferred rendering of the text.[4] It has been argued that the main point of verse 16 is the usefulness of Scripture, not its inspiration. This is the logical direction of the text, but it is important to note that the inspiration of Scripture is foundational to its usefulness.

The first use of Scripture Paul lists is doctrinal ("teaching"; see v. 10 and comments). Its use for "rebuking" and "correcting" may not seem primary to the modern reader. However, given the major function of the Pastoral Letters to address the problem of false teaching in Ephesus and Crete, these functions have obvious significance. The appearance of these two words here is probably due to their strength and appropriateness in the overall context of correction. There may be a sequence intended here: first, refuting the false teaching that Timothy was confronting, and second, straightening everything out. The final item in the sequence is providing an ongoing "training in righteousness" (see the verbal form of the word "training" in Titus 2:11–14 and comments there). Structurally, "teaching" stands at the head of this series and the purpose of it all is expressed in verse 17, "for every good work."

The importance of good works in the Pastoral Letters cannot be overemphasized. These are the marks of the genuine servants and people of God

---

3. The NRSV (among others) provides this alternative as a footnote: "Every Scripture inspired by God is also [useful]. . . ."

4. The literature on this issue is extensive. Perhaps the finest contemporary discussion in a commentary is in Knight, *Pastoral Epistles,* 444–48.

in contrast to the false teachers. This emphasis is consistent with the repeated theme of the blending of sound doctrine and godly living, which starts with the reference to purity, faith, and a good conscience in 1 Timothy 1:5–19, then is evident in the qualifications for elders and deacons (ch. 3), is important in the life of Timothy as an example in the church (4:6–16), is seen in the requirements for widows who are supported (5:3–10), and is stressed in many other passages.

Verses such as 1 Timothy 2:10; 5:10, 25; 6:18; 2 Timothy 2:21; Titus 2:7, 14; 3:1, 8, 14 refer to good works. Other passages teach us that we are not saved by good works (2 Tim. 1:9; Titus 3:5). Two ministries in particular are called (lit.) a "good work"—that of overseers (1 Tim. 3:1) and that of an evangelist (2 Tim. 4:5). To affirm the inspiration of Scripture and the importance of strong doctrinal teaching, therefore, has strong implications both for the correction of error and the pursuit of good works.

THE BOOK. THIS passage offers four separate pictures, which stand in contrast to each other. (1) The apostle Paul and those like him are being persecuted for his faith and life. (2) The persecutors are portrayed as "evil" and "impostors." (3) Timothy and others like him are seeking to learn by reading this letter. (4) The fourth is not a portrait but a "still life" painting of a book—not just a book but *the* Book, which for two millennia now has encouraged those in the first picture, rebuked those in the second, and trained those in the third. The expression *still life*, while appropriate in artistic terms, is certainly inappropriate for the living Scriptures, which have brought life to untold millions of believers.

Verses 16 affirms that "all Scripture is God-breathed"; before and after that verse stand examples of what it can accomplish. It makes a person "wise for salvation through faith in Christ Jesus," and it has a series of functions— "teaching, rebuking, correcting and training in righteousness"—that thoroughly prepares one "for every good work." This encompasses the purpose expressed in Ephesians 2:8–10: *salvation* by grace through faith for *good works*.

The affirmation of inspiration at the center must not be isolated from this context of purpose. At the same time, one's belief about the meaning of inspiration must not be camouflaged by exclusive emphasis on those purposes. We have concluded that the "Scripture" referred to here includes both Old and New Testaments because of the reference in 2 Peter 3:16 to Paul's writings as "Scriptures." No distinction is drawn in the New Testament between Paul's letters and the other books as regards their divine origin and authority, so it is reasonable to apply 2 Timothy 3:16 to the entire Bible.

Defining an orthodox of Scripture. The period of reaction against "higher criticism" of the Bible saw successive attempts to define an orthodox doctrine of Scripture. (1) At first it seemed that a simple affirmation of Scripture as "inspired" would suffice.

(2) But the potential for vagueness in the meaning of that word made it insufficient, so the phrase "plenary (full) inspiration" came into use. That expression had the advantage of including the entire Bible in its affirmation, but still left some room for vagueness.

(3) "Verbal inspiration" clarified the extent and focus of inspiration beyond that of general ideas. This, however, introduced another misunderstanding, for "verbal" was sometimes misunderstood to mean "dictated." This conjured up a caricature of the biblical writers as sitting with their minds in neutral, mechanically writing down words and syllables they heard from heaven. Such a process would have excluded such factors as individual style, feeling, and insight. It also encouraged the wrong use of the word "literal," as in the question, "Do you believe that the Bible is literally true?" The intention of the question, of course, was to ask if one believes that every word is true, but if the question is taken "literally," it really inquires whether a person thinks that all the literature in the Bible is literal as opposed to *figurative.*

(4) Much care is therefore needed in choosing terminology that explains the meaning of inspiration accurately over against inadequate definitions and concepts. One definition that has gained wide acceptance is "inerrancy." Yet even this term raises questions. Does it mean that whatever appears in Scripture is true, whether regarding history, science, or theology, or does it apply to theological truths but allows, for example, for inadequate scientific knowledge on the part of ancient writers? Few would have a problem with such an expression as "as the sun set," for we accept that as an accommodation to a commonly observed phenomenon. But this introduces detailed discussions, such as whether the mustard seed is actually the "smallest of all seeds" (Matt. 13:32, NLT) universally, or only in Palestine, or only in the span of Jesus' knowledge. Such issues are not ignored by those who use the term *inerrancy,* but at the same time they prefer to focus on what Scripture specifically affirms, especially about itself, taking literary form and genre as well as purpose into consideration.[5]

In the process of dealing with such literary implications of various views of inspiration is the theological implication of the Greek word *theopneustos*

---

5. There are, of course, other issues, such as textual differences. At one level it can be said that small differences between manuscripts are secondary, no more of a problem than different transcriptions or translations, say, of a speech in Russian. The issue is not whether the copies are correct but whether the original was true. This all calls, however, for scholarly discussion that would take us far beyond the purposes of this commentary.

("God-breathed"). Can what is God-breathed contain error? The term *inerrant*, clumsy though it is, specifically addresses that question. Such discussions have occupied theologians and biblical scholars for decades, and rightly so. Meanwhile, the Scriptures are doing their work of leading people to salvation through faith in Christ and on to training for every good work.[6]

THE UNIQUENESS OF the Bible. In the days when street preachers were a common sight in New York City a man named Charlie King could sometimes be seen running around his hat, which was placed on a street corner near Times Square, shouting, "It's alive! It's alive!" When a crowd gathered he would pick up his hat, under which was a Bible and from which he would proceed to preach the gospel. At about the same time, a Christian organization in New York City that evangelized high school students was encouraging Christian students, however embarrassing it might seem, to carry a Bible with a red cover on top of their school books. In other quarters, evangelical churches, educational institutions, and other organizations were building statements into their creeds on the inspiration and authority of Scriptures, often incorporating the word "inerrant."

Any one of these attempts to feature the Holy Scriptures could have drawn criticism or ridicule, but each was a deliberate attempt to proclaim the unique importance of the Bible. There are many ways we can do this today; but unless the Word of God is obeyed, preached, and taught as it should be, we are neither giving it due honor nor letting it do its job.[7] Bible societies like the International Bible Society (which distributes the NIV), Bible publishers like Zondervan (which publishes the NIV), Wycliffe Bible translators and other missionaries who translate the Scriptures, Sunday school teachers who explain it, preachers who proclaim it—and everyone who studies it, lives it, teaches it, raises a family based on its teachings, witnesses from it, and prays to God and praises him from its message—all have a significant part in the application of Scripture.

---

6. On the topic of inspiration, in addition to such classic works as J. Orr's *Revelation and Inspiration* (1910) and B. B. Warfield's *Inspiration and Authority of the Bible* (1927), the articles "Inspiration" in *ISBE*, 2:839–49; "Inspiration, History of the Doctrine of" in *ISBE*, 2:849–54; and "Bible, Inspiration of" in *EDT*, 145–49 provide excellent summaries. The article "Bible, Inerrancy and Infallibility of" in *EDT*, 141–45 is also useful. Two volumes edited by D. A. Carson and John D. Woodbridge contain pertinent articles: *Hermeneutics, Authority, and Canon* (Grand Rapids: Zondervan, 1986) and *Scripture and Truth* (Grand Rapids: Baker, 1992; orig. publ. by Zondervan in 1983).

7. For a step-by-step explanation of how to build an expository sermon from the New Testament text see Walter Liefeld, *New Testament Exposition* (Grand Rapids: Zondervan, 1984).

Biblical preaching and teaching. Whether or not preachers choose a straight expository style, every sermon should bring the Bible to bear on whatever topics are discussed. We may say that good sermons come both from above and from below. They come from above (from the Lord) in that they have their source and their authority in the written Word of God; they come from below (i.e., where we live) in that the themes they deal with come in part from the experiences and needs of the congregation. A sermon that is not applied to contemporary life or that lacks contemporary significance may be a fine exposition of Scripture, but it is not an expository *sermon*, which, by definition, takes the circumstances of the hearer into consideration. A book that deals with computer circuitry or computer language may have technical excellence, but it is of little benefit to the user if it does not explain how to put the computer to use.

The other side of the coin is that exhortations have no substance, basis, or authority if they lack specific biblical foundation. Further, while a sermon on a single text can have great force, if we expect the listener to go home and derive further direction from Scripture, preachers must show how the text arises from the immediate and larger context and how to both understand and apply it. Whether or not a Sunday school student will love and study the Scriptures over a lifetime may in large measure be determined by how well the teacher both motivates and enables students to study on their own (yes, even children, if they are of an appropriate age level).

Teaching child and adult classes is not a privilege for the doctrinally elite. Bible classes can be unutterably boring if the teacher lacks the skills and motivation to make them interesting and relevant. (Someone once said that it is a sin to make the gospel boring!) The most mature and knowledgeable Christian is not necessarily the most competent teacher. It is not only a brave but a responsible pastor who is willing to disappoint a would-be teacher who is not competent or prepared, in order to foster the teaching ministry of someone who may be less mature but more inspiring and willing to prepare well. If we are going to have teachers who have known Scripture from their infancy (v. 15), we certainly have the means to motivate and equip them, provided that we are willing to devote ourselves to that significant task. Much as the church may trumpet the doctrine of biblical inspiration, unless we all live it and unless it is taught enthusiastically and skillfully, we may produce a result opposite to what we desire.

We may have expected that the final effect of a proper use of the Scriptures would be doctrinal maturity or knowledgeable ministry. Instead, Paul once more encourages good works (v. 17), showing that God is mainly interested in the life and actions of the believer, not simply or even primarily in professional church ministry. It is no accident that this passage on Scripture occurs in conjunction with the pictures of the persecuted Christian, the persecuting opponent, and the person who serves God. The Bible contains many pages of narratives concerning ordinary people who live, work, and walk in God's presence. It is these examples, along with specific doctrinal teachings, that equip us "for every good work."

2 Timothy 4:1–8

IN THE PRESENCE of God and of Christ Jesus, who will judge
the living and the dead, and in view of his appearing and
his kingdom, I give you this charge: ²Preach the Word; be
prepared in season and out of season; correct, rebuke and
encourage—with great patience and careful instruction. ³For
the time will come when men will not put up with sound doctrine. Instead, to suit their own desires, they will gather
around them a great number of teachers to say what their
itching ears want to hear. ⁴They will turn their ears away from
the truth and turn aside to myths. ⁵But you, keep your head in
all situations, endure hardship, do the work of an evangelist,
discharge all the duties of your ministry.

⁶For I am already being poured out like a drink offering,
and the time has come for my departure. ⁷I have fought the
good fight, I have finished the race, I have kept the faith.
⁸Now there is in store for me the crown of righteousness,
which the Lord, the righteous Judge, will award to me on that
day—and not only to me, but also to all who have longed for
his appearing.

Original Meaning

THE APOSTLE PAUL is ready to close his second
letter to Timothy. The present chapter constitutes his last recorded words. Verses 1–8 include
a charge to Timothy and a further reflection on
Paul's own life of service to the Lord. In verses 6–8, it becomes plain that the
apostle does not expect to live much longer but will be put to death as a
Christian.

The Charge to Timothy (4:1–5)

VERSE 1 BEGINS Paul's final exhortation and appeal to Timothy. The opening
is in the form of a charge rendered somber by evoking the presence of God
and Christ and by two additional words (in an oath format), the "appearing
[of Christ] and his kingdom" (see also 1 Tim. 5:21; 6:13). The seriousness of
this charge is heightened by a reference to the fact that Christ "will judge the
living and the dead." The Holy Spirit is not mentioned in this verse; judg-

ment is under the authority of God the Father, who has "entrusted all judgment to the Son, that all may honor the Son just as they honor the Father" (John 5:22–23; see also Acts 17:31; note also Paul's reference to "the Lord, the righteous Judge" in 2 Tim. 4:8).

We gather from the various biblical texts about future judgment that this will be a complex event. Not only will there be a comprehensive judgment before the great white throne, resulting in eternal life or death (see Rev. 20:11–15), but our lives as servants of the Lord will be evaluated before the judgment seat of Christ (2 Cor. 5:9–10). In 1 Corinthians 3:12–15, another text dealing with the future evaluation of our work, Paul specifically focuses on how each one has contributed to the growth of the church. Our lives should, therefore, be lived with a constant eye to the future, primarily to the "appearing" of Christ.[1] While that future appearing is to be desired (v. 8), it also will mean judgment and therefore is linked with the "kingdom," which expresses the reign of Christ (see also 2 Tim. 4:18). All of this adds weight to Paul's charge.

The contents of the charge are contained in verses 2–5. It opens with five commands. The first ("preach the Word") echoes the repeated instructions to Timothy and Titus regarding the teaching and preaching of God's truth. As in 2:9, 15 this truth is referred to as "the Word." Next, "be prepared" contains the idea of standing by, taking a position of readiness (Jer. 46:14); such preparedness should be a permanent part of Timothy's life. The third, fourth, and fifth imperatives ("correct, rebuke and encourage") reflect the necessity of a strong ministry in view of false teaching at Ephesus (cf. 3:16). The modifying phrase "with great patience and careful instruction" combines two dissimilar words, one denoting an attitude and the other content. Yet the two belong together because they are integral to Paul's message in the Pastoral Letters that both attitude and teaching are important. The word "instruction" can convey both the activity of teaching and the content of teaching. Here it is probably the former.[2]

Verse 3 explains the reason for the charge in verses 1–2. The Word must be preached because sound doctrine is going to be rejected. The future tense, like that in 3:1 (see also 1 Tim. 4:1), describes a situation that is already coming into being. The word "time" (*kairos*) has the same root as the words translated "season" in verse 2; it will reappear in verse 6 with reference to the time of Paul's impending death. Once again we encounter the expression "sound doctrine," which is both unique to and typical of the Pastoral Letters (see 1 Tim. 1:10 and comments; 6:3; 2 Tim. 1:13; Titus 1:9, 13; 2:8). The verb "to

---

1. Paul refers to this appearing (*epiphaneia*) in each of the Pastorals Letters (cf. 1 Tim. 6:14; Titus 2:13); in 2 Tim. 1:10; Titus 2:11; 3:4, this word refers to the first appearance of Christ.

2. For the importance of the content of the teaching see 3:10 and comments.

put up with" occurs fifteen times in the New Testament (note esp. 2 Cor. 11:1[2x], 4, 19, 20).

"Instead" represents the strong adversative conjunction *alla*. People will "gather [teachers] around them," the verb conveying the idea of heaping up an assortment of things (NRSV "accumulate"). These teachers are not teachers of truth but those who suit the "desires" of the people. This, then, becomes not only a matter of doctrine but also of moral character. People will listen eagerly because of "their itching ears," that is, ears that want to be soothed with agreeable pleasantries. Clement of Alexandria wrote sarcastically about a Sophist who spoke on various subjects, "scratching and tickling, not in a manly way, in my opinion, the ears of those who wish to be tickled."[3]

Verse 4 picks up the reference to ears, going from a metaphorical use to a literal meaning, as the people "will turn their ears away from the truth and turn aside to myths." The use of the definite article before "myths" suggests that Timothy is aware of such myths (see 1 Tim. 1:4 and comments; 4:7; Titus 1:14).

Verse 5 begins (like 3:10) with "but you." In spite of this movement away from the truth, Timothy is to (lit.) "be sober in all things." Of course, this does not suggest that Timothy will otherwise be fuzzy-minded because of alcohol, since he has needed encouragement to take even a little wine (1 Tim. 5:23). Yet perhaps a near literal understanding of the verb is appropriate. It is not enough to keep from losing his head; he must think clearly, fully aware of all that is going on. This means that he has to "endure hardship," an exhortation that recalls Paul's words about suffering in 2 Timothy 1:8, 12; 2:3.

"Do the work of an evangelist" (cf. Acts 21:8; Eph. 4:11) is a straightforward command, implying that Timothy might be so consumed with other needs and tasks that he is in danger of not pursuing the work he probably originally did with Paul on their travels together. To "discharge all the duties of your ministry" might seem counterproductive to the instruction to do the "work of an evangelist." Is Timothy to focus or not? The solution may be to keep just the singular "ministry" rather than, as in NIV, add the words "all the duties of." A more literal translation reads: "Fulfill your ministry." In these final words of Paul to Timothy, the young pastor should accomplish the task for which Paul left him at Ephesus (cf. also Col. 4:17, "Tell Archippus: 'See to it that you complete the work you have received in the Lord'").

Paul's Reflections on His Life of Service (4:6–8)

PAUL NOW OFFERS comments about himself. "Being poured out like a drink offering" alludes to the various libations common to many religions, but especially to the sacrifice of drink offerings in the Old Testament (Ex. 29:40–

---

3. See his *Stromata* 1.3.

41; Lev. 23:13; Num. 15:4–10; 28:7). Paul uses the same imagery in similar circumstances, such as the possibility of his execution in Philippians 2:17. There is, however, one striking difference. In that passage he says, "But even if I am being poured out like a drink offering," while here he writes, "I am already being poured out like a drink offering." When writing Philippians he hoped for further years of service. Now he realizes the end of his earthly ministry is near. The word "departure" was used for the departure of troops or of a naval ship for battle, though it is not limited to that imagery.

What Paul does next (vv. 7–8) has sometimes been used as an argument against the Pauline authorship of the Pastoral Letters. It seems out of character for him to speak of himself as he does, including the reference to the "crown of righteousness" that he expects the Lord to give him. Perhaps it takes someone who has completed years of active service to understand the frame of mind in which a Christian may feel free to express gratitude for being permitted to leave some accomplishments as a heritage. There may also be a sense in which the apostle had to experience a release by putting these things into words.

Paul makes three statements in verse 7, using a verb in the perfect tense to express each accomplishment: "I have fought," I have finished," " I have kept." "The good fight" probably has behind it an athletic rather than military picture (see 1 Tim. 6:12). Paul has used the adjective *kalos* (as here) for "good" in the Pastoral Letters more frequently than *agathos*. *Kalos* expresses the idea of what is beautiful or noble. It is a noble contest that he has been in.

The second athletic metaphor, "I have finished the race," recalls Philippians 2:16 (which is followed by the image of being "poured out," used above in verse 6). Paul also used stadium imagery effectively in 1 Corinthians 9:24, 26.[4]

Does "the faith" that Paul has kept mean the body of doctrine, as elsewhere (2 Tim. 1:12, 14; see also Eph. 4:5), or does it refer to Paul's personal faith? Either is possible. It is interesting to note that "to keep the faith" was a fixed expression in extrabiblical literature for those who remained faithful to God.[5] It is not inconceivable that Paul used a common expression but with the added meaning that is so important in the Pastorals.

The word "now" in verse 8 suggests "that which is left." "In store for me" recalls inscriptions regarding keeping a reward or favor, and even a punishment, in reserve for someone.[6] The idea of a "crown [or garland] of

---

4. Such data has been used to argue that a later author selected these graphic words from Paul's authentic writings to use in the Pastoral Letters under his name. It is reasonable, however, to assume that Paul himself recalled images that were meaningful to him in an earlier similar experience.

5. Dibelius/Conzelmann provide examples of this usage (*Pastoral Epistles*, 121 [note 18]).

6. Dibelius/Conzelmann, *Pastoral Epistles*, 121 (note 20).

righteousness" is unique here. Elsewhere we read of a "crown of life" (James 1:12; Rev. 2:10). In those two passages the Greek genitive "of life" may indicate apposition (i.e., what constitutes the crown is eternal life). The same may be true here; that is, the future crown *is* righteousness. Kelly says, however, that this "is open to the objections (*a*) that Paul's normal teaching is that the believer is already justified, and (*b*) that it is not easy to see how righteousness can be already prepared in heaven."[7] In the mid-nineteenth century Ellicott suggested that it did not have a "dogmatical," but a "practical" reference— that is, that a person who has lived righteously deserves his crown.[8] Knight sees it as "the permanent and perfect 'state of righteousness' . . . into which the Christian is brought by God."[9]

The sense, therefore, may be that Paul knows he has already received righteousness and that this righteousness has been stored up for him in heaven. Such a search for meaning is necessary because Paul himself would insist that, on the one hand, heaven is not gained by our righteousness and, on the other hand, that the righteousness God bestows is already ours. Whatever choice we make regarding the details, we must keep the fact of the "award" in mind.

The Lord who awards this crown is "the righteous Judge." That fact both offers the assurance that God is right in bestowing that crown and gives a sobering context in view of the fact that God "will judge the living and the dead" (v. 1). This is a wonderful thought for those who (lit.) "have loved [perfect tense of *agapao*] his appearing." Given the fact that the appearing has not yet taken place, "longed for" is probably a better rendering of *agapao* here than "loved." The word "appearing" is the significant *epiphaneia*, that future epiphany of our Lord Jesus Christ that provides motivation in the Pastoral Letters (see v. 1 and comments).

Bridging Contexts

THE PREACHING OF **the Word.** Among all of the verses in the sixty-six books of Scripture, 2 Timothy 4:2 is probably the most frequently heard in ordination services of ministers. It is selected, of course, because of the imperative "preach the Word," its comprehensive time reference ("in season and out of season"), its specific instructions about correcting, rebuking, and encouraging (which cover a good deal of the pastor's typical ministry), its reference to method ("great patience and careful instruc-

---

7. Kelly, *Pastoral Epistles*, 209.

8. Ellicott, *Commentary on the Epistles of St. Paul*, 172.

9. Knight, *Pastoral Epistles*, 461, referring to G. Schrenk, "δικαιοσύνη," *TDNT*, 2.210.

tion"), the solemn context of verse 1 (referring to God as judge and to the coming kingdom), and the word "charge" in verse 1 of the NIV and several other versions (an ordination usually includes a charge).

There is both a great benefit and a significant flaw in the use of this passage as an ordination charge. The benefit is the importance of the Word of God in ministry. But the flaw is that contextually Paul's charge to Timothy was intended for, and applied to, a particular situation. Neither that situation nor the "charge" in this passage match the job description of typical pastors today. We tend to read back into the Pastoral Letters the modern idea of a senior pastor, whereas in fact Timothy's work had to do mainly with confronting heretics and repudiating their teaching. There is no indication that he was to devote a large share of his time to the kind of pastoral ministry normally needed today in Christian churches. Of course, one can move in one direction or another in this matter (see the Contemporary Significance section). At this point what must be emphasized is the significant place of the ministry of the Word of God in *any* ministry.

Paul insisted on the preaching of the Word in view of the time that would come (and most readers of this passage today would probably say the time had already come) when people would not put up with sound doctrine (v. 3). It is human nature to hear only what we want to hear and to close our ears to anything that counters our distorted ideas of truth and pleasure. This calls attention again to the *context* of the charge to preach the Word here, similar to the context of the exhortation to "correctly handle the word of truth" in 2:15 (i.e., the context of heresy).

The personal in Paul's letters. Moving to verse 6, it is unfortunate—totally apart from the theological aspects of the authorship issue—that Paul has been read out of his own scenario. This is an author who "pops" in and out of his own letters—now reflecting on God's grace to him, now on his commission, now on his peaceful conscience, or, as here, now on his apprehension of the future. There are curious little touches (something like characteristic strokes and colors of a painter or like the little self-images that Rembrandt put in some of his paintings) that make the Pastoral Letters not only authentic but intriguing. Although, as just noted, in verse 3 Paul says that the time when people prefer heresy *will* come, in verse 6 he declares that the time for his own departure *has* already come.

One might have thought, given everything he has said about the existence of heresy at Ephesus, that the time *had* already come when people would reject sound doctrine, but that the prospect of his death was *less* sure. Apparently, however, Paul has no doubt that his personal fate has already been sealed, and that he is "already being poured out like a drink offering." The fact that he is so sure that his own time has come gives him another opportunity for a small self-portrait. This is no grandiose *"après moi la deluge"* ("after me the flood") statement. He is not placing himself on the stage of history as the one whose "season" of death allows the "season" of uninhibited defection from the faith. He is rather the servant of God who, although he has only done his duty (Luke. 17:10), knows that he will hear his Master's "well done" (Luke 19:17). Whether Paul knew it or not, his words, "I have fought the good fight, I have finished the race, I have kept the faith" were destined to spur on generations of the Lord's servants to do the same against all obstacles.

PREACHING AND OTHER **ministries today.** "Preach the Word" is a command that not only stirs the hearts of pastors but also excites all who love Scripture. It is one command that we are eager to obey. However extensive other ministries of pastoral staff and congregation may be, it is the Sunday sermon that gains the most visibility. Important as witnessing, counseling, discipling, comforting, planning, administrating, and intercessory prayer are, it is preaching that most seminary students look forward to. Few recognize the names or faces of those who spend endless hours in pastoral counseling, but mention Jonathan Edwards, Charles H. Spurgeon, or one of our great contemporary preachers such as Bill Hybels or Charles Swindoll, and there is immediate recognition.

This means several things: (1) Preaching is important and should be given an immense amount of prayer and preparation. (2) Preachers should make sure that they are doing what God intends for them, serving where God wants them and living as God commands them, for their influence for good or ill is enormous. (3) Congregations should give more of their own time to share in the church's ministries (and perhaps also enlarge the church staff), providing freedom from other time-consuming pastoral tasks that may not be areas of the preacher's giftedness or calling. (4) Balancing the above, Christians should recognize the importance of other ministries and not inflate the preacher's ego. It is already too easy for the preacher to neglect prayer and people in order to preach a polished sermon.

We have already noted that Timothy's role as an apostolic delegate to the church at Ephesus, where he was to concentrate on refuting heresy and heretics, is more focused than, and different from, the tasks occupying a typical pastor's time in the contemporary church. That, of course, does not mean that pastors are never called by God to be mainly involved in preaching and doctrinal teaching. Many senior pastors do little pastoring. While in some cases that may be mainly a concession to personal preference, such specialization accords with the fact that there is no biblical support for solo ministry in a church. That fact has received increasing attention in recent years and has led to a healthy emphasis on the ministries of all God's people and on the benefits of a multiple staff.[10]

It is both biblical and functionally useful to have a team of staff and elders who divide the responsibilities of preaching, pastoral counseling, administration, teaching, evangelism, missions, and other ministries. It is also wise to have some sharing of the pulpit; no one person has all the gifts of biblical knowledge, theological discernment, homiletics, pastoral sensitivity, and street smarts! It is unfortunate, given the biblical teaching on the diversity and significance of the various gifts in the body of Christ, for the one who has the preaching gift always to be known as "senior pastor," while another on the pastoral staff who spends countless hours in counseling is only an "associate pastor" with a lesser salary. It would be a great object lesson for the congregation to see a greater sharing of honor than is customary.

How, then, should the command to "preach the Word" be applied? Those who are so gifted and called should do it! They should preach with the authority of that Word.[11] And since the Pastoral Letters demonstrate throughout the need for shepherding, even though there is a focus on teaching truth against error, the preaching ministry of a church should be accompanied by broad, capably handled pastoral ministries.

As suggested earlier, sermons must be motivated both from below (i.e., the existence of human needs) and from above (i.e., the truths of the Bible). A good sermon will probably begin with an introduction describing a human circumstance that calls for divine help, but it will quickly move to the exposition of relevant Scriptures. Further, while the preaching of the Word (with the accompanying ministries of correction, rebuke, encouragement, and

---

10. Some of the many recent works worth consulting on pastoral leadership of staff and people are Jackson W. Carroll, *As One With Authority: Reflective Leadership in Ministry* (Louisville: Westminster/John Knox, 1991); James R. Hawkinson and Robert K. Johnston, eds., *Servant Leadership: Authority and Governance in the Evangelical Covenant Church*, vol. 1 (Chicago: Covenant Publications, 1993); James R. Hawkinson and Robert K. Johnston, eds., *Servant Leadership: Contemporary Models and the Emerging Challenge*, vol. 2 (Chicago: Covenant Publications, 1993); Calvin Miller, *The Empowered Leader: 10 Keys to Servant Leadership* (Nashville: Broadman & Holman, 1995); William R. Nelson, *Ministry Formation for Effective Leadership* (Nashville: Abingdon, 1988); Henri J. M. Nouwen, *In the Name of Jesus: Reflections on Christian Leadership* (New York: Crossroad, 1989); Eugene H. Peterson, *Working the Angles: The Shape of Pastoral Integrity* (Grand Rapids: Eerdmans, 1987); Norman Shawchuck and Roger Heuser, *Leading the Congregation: Caring for Yourself While Serving the People* (Nashville: Abingdon, 1993); Rick Warren, *The Purpose-Driven Church: Growth Without Compromising Your Message and Mission* (Grand Rapids: Zondervan, 1995).

11. See James I. Packer, "Authority in Preaching," in *The Gospel in the Modern World*, Martyn Eden and David F. Wells, eds. (Downers Grove, Ill.: InterVarsity, 1991). This volume is a tribute to that great expository preacher and evangelical leader, John R. W. Stott.

---

careful patient instruction) is especially important in a period of doctrinal crisis such as existed at Ephesus, it is also important in the ongoing proactive ministry of elders as they guard the flock. Biblical truth should be the main nutrient in the flock's diet. It is important in the overall direction of a church and is necessary for the spiritual development of a congregation.

The fact that the charge is given in the presence of the Judge and King (v. 1) increases its weight on us. Moreover, Paul's consciousness of the impending fate that will form the last page of the story of his earthly life (v. 6), to be followed only by the epilogue of his commendation in heaven (v. 8), is a compelling motive for anyone serving God in our day.

The duties of ministry. In between these great sentences is another one that is occasionally used almost as an add-on in ordination charges: "Keep your head in all situations, endure hardship, do the work of an evangelist, discharge all the duties of your ministry" (v. 5). These duties constitute the "et cetera" of our ministries as God's servants. They remind us of Paul's words after describing the sufferings he endured for Christ: "Besides everything else, I face daily the pressure of my concern for all the churches" (2 Cor. 11:28). The message for us today is not one more burden, but just as Timothy was not to limit the effectiveness of his ministry, consumed by the main item in his job description, so we today are encouraged to look around us at the marvelous variety of opportunities existing in our own communities.

These are not to be burdens or distractions, for we should, like Timothy, "keep [our] head in all situations" (v. 5). We must not be like the infamous young man who got on his horse and rode off in all directions at once. Neither should we fill our time with the easy things, but rather be ready to "endure hardship." And specifically, we must not so narrowly define our gifts as to exclude the basic task of evangelism. Granted that not everyone has this particular gift (Eph. 4:11 makes that clear), we should certainly all be witnesses, forwarding the work of evangelism. No doubt Paul saw in Timothy the gift of an evangelist.

We are to "discharge all the duties of [our] ministry," but that does not mean undertaking all the duties that others unload on us. Many pastors and missionaries see so many needs that they find it difficult to establish boundaries, while others find it difficult to have vision and see opportunities. It is possible also to choose ministries that are more comfortable, perhaps more in accordance with our own natural gifts and inclinations (such as counseling those in the church or doing routine administration and thus avoiding ministries that entail a high risk of conflict, tension, or danger). Urban ministries, pioneering work overseas, and contact with disease come to mind.

Here is another reason for pastors to keep their heads. Today those in Christian ministry have a resource that, for the most part, their predecessors did not have (or perhaps want). That resource is the "ministry of the laity"—the contemporary movement to see all God's people as ministers. Because of this awareness, a church pastor today is better able to encourage others in the church to share in various ministries without being accused of trying to avoid doing the work himself. The wise pastor will not simply give "jobs" to laypeople, but will stimulate them to cultivate their own visions of what ministries are needed and possible and of how they themselves (with the pastor's encouragement) can fulfill these ministries. We have a wonderful opportunity today to find new opportunities at home and abroad, to create new ways of reaching people for Christ, and to enable his church to grow.[12] Because of these contemporary circumstances perhaps verse 5 can be fulfilled in ways undreamed of in earlier centuries.

Passing the baton. Behind all these exhortations is the figure of the great apostle, ready now to commit the immense tasks he has been passing on to a younger man. This must have required a great deal of trust on his part. My wife, on reading this text and my comments on it, added this note: "How do you feel as a retired teacher? Can you turn it all over to the young?" That gave me reason to reflect, both as a retired seminary professor and as a retired pastor! Then, just before completing this section I had two phone calls. One was about a former student and his excellent teaching ministry overseas. The other was about another former student who is being sought as a pastor by several churches. How do I feel? I have cherished every God-given opportunity for personal ministry. Yet I cherish more the fact that his kind of ministry does not end with my retirement but continues in the hands of many competent Timothys.

---

12. The following books are helpful on empowering lay ministries. David Foy Crabtree, *The Empowered Church* (New York: Alban Institute, 1989); Robert J. Banks, *Paul's Ideas of Community: The Early House Churches in Their Historical Setting* (Grand Rapids: Eerdmans, 1980); Melvin J. Steinbron, *The Lay-Driven Church: How to Empower the People in Your Church to Share the Tasks of Ministry* (Ventura, Calif.: Regal, 1997); R. Paul Stevens, *Liberating the Laity: Equipping All the Saints for Ministry* (Downers Grove, Ill.: InterVarsity, 1985); R. Paul Stevens, *The Equipper's Guide to Every-Member Ministry: Eight Ways Ordinary People Can Do the Work of the Church* (Downers Grove, Ill.: InterVarsity, 1992). Some of the works mentioned elsewhere in this book on other topics also include discussions on lay ministries.

2 Timothy 4:9–22

❧

DO YOUR BEST to come to me quickly, ¹⁰for Demas, because he loved this world, has deserted me and has gone to Thessalonica. Crescens has gone to Galatia, and Titus to Dalmatia. ¹¹Only Luke is with me. Get Mark and bring him with you, because he is helpful to me in my ministry. ¹²I sent Tychicus to Ephesus. ¹³When you come, bring the cloak that I left with Carpus at Troas, and my scrolls, especially the parchments.

¹⁴Alexander the metalworker did me a great deal of harm. The Lord will repay him for what he has done. ¹⁵You too should be on your guard against him, because he strongly opposed our message.

¹⁶At my first defense, no one came to my support, but everyone deserted me. May it not be held against them. ¹⁷But the Lord stood at my side and gave me strength, so that through me the message might be fully proclaimed and all the Gentiles might hear it. And I was delivered from the lion's mouth. ¹⁸The Lord will rescue me from every evil attack and will bring me safely to his heavenly kingdom. To him be glory for ever and ever. Amen.

¹⁹Greet Priscilla and Aquila and the household of Onesiphorus. ²⁰Erastus stayed in Corinth, and I left Trophimus sick in Miletus. ²¹Do your best to get here before winter. Eubulus greets you, and so do Pudens, Linus, Claudia and all the brothers.

²²The Lord be with your spirit. Grace be with you.

Original Meaning

"DO YOUR BEST" (v. 9) translates the word *spoudazo* (cf. occurrences of this verb or its related adverbial form in 1:17; 2:15; 4:21; see also Titus 3:12). It conveys a sense of urgency that is here increased by the word "quickly." This may express Paul's desire to have Timothy with him as quickly as possible for some specific reason, or it may simply be practical advice to start out before the shipping lanes are closed for the winter (v. 21). Ancient travel had enough hazards; overland was especially difficult in winter, and sea travel was impossible. If Timothy was to follow the usual route going from western Asia Minor, the Aegean Sea, across Macedonia, and then finally crossing the Adriatic Sea (assuming Paul was in Rome), he could meet delays at a number of points on the journey.

The reason given here for Timothy's coming, however, is that Paul's companions have been leaving him. His distress will be compounded if Timothy is delayed by a long stopover because of the onset of winter. Demas has deserted Paul because he "loved this world" (the aorist participle simply expresses the cause of his defection, an interesting contrast to the perfect participle of the same verb *agapao* in verse 8, describing those who "have longed for" the appearing of Christ). Demas made a choice for the present world, an act that may be compared to that of Esau, who sold his birthright for an immediate meal of red stew (Gen. 25:29—34). Thessalonica, where he went, was perhaps his home, but this is uncertain. Demas is mentioned in Colossians 4:14, where he and Luke seemed to be in good fellowship together, and in Philemon 24, where he is mentioned with Luke, Mark, and also Aristarchus (who was from Thessalonica, cf. Acts 20:4). Titus has gone to Dalmatia, probably on a mission for Paul (see comment on Titus 3:12, locating Nicopolis in Dalmatia).

The statement in verse 11, "Only Luke is with me," conveys some pathos. Some think it also offers a clue concerning the authorship of the Pastoral Letters. Luke's presence would make it possible for him to function as a secretary writing the Pastoral Letters, possibly being given a good amount of freedom by Paul. This freedom, it is suggested, allowed him to articulate Paul's thoughts using some of his own writing style and vocabulary in doing so (see the Introduction). The mention of Luke as Paul's sole companion at this time is not contradicted by verse 21, where others are mentioned who send greetings to Timothy. In verses 9—12 Paul is apparently speaking only of those on his "team," his coworkers in the work of the gospel, though others are around.

"Get Mark" (v. 11b) implies that he is not at Ephesus and that Timothy should pick him up on his way to join Paul. The reason Paul wants Mark is that "he is helpful to me in my ministry." The present tense implies that Mark is already associated again with Paul. At some point after Paul's refusal to have Mark continue with him on his missionary journeys (Acts 15:37—40), a change took place in Mark or in Paul, or perhaps in both, that made it possible for Paul to trust Mark again as an associate in his ministry. The nature of Mark's ministry is not explained, but the word *diakonia* used here refers (in addition to the specialized ministry of deacons and its general use to describe servanthood for Christ) to the evangelistic work of Paul and his associates (1 Cor. 3:5; Eph. 3:7; 6:21; Col. 1:7, 23, 25; 4:7).

Tychicus (v. 12) appears at several points as an important associate of Paul (Acts 20:4; Eph. 6:21—22; Col. 4:7—9). Paul has "sent [him] to Ephesus," the aorist tense either indicating a simple past action, in which case Tychicus is already on his way there, or as an epistolary aorist (cf. Eph. 6:22; Col. 4:8) written from the perspective of Timothy, who will receive the letter after Tychicus has arrived in Ephesus (note that Timothy is probably in Ephesus; cf. 1 Tim. 1:3). In this latter case, Paul may be sending this letter to Timothy by the hand of Tychicus. Another possibility is that Paul has already sent Tychicus on a mission that will end in Ephesus after this letter arrives (carried by someone else). Paul may want Tychicus there to begin preparations to carry on the ministry after Timothy leaves to visit Paul.

The instructions in verse 13 as to what Timothy should bring on that trip have been carefully scrutinized by scholars. Clothing varied in those days, as now, according to climate and season, but also according to status. The robes used by senators and by philosophers were distinctive. Wandering Cynic preachers deliberately abraded their clothing to effect an appearance of poverty.[1] The cloak Paul had left at Troas was a common heavy outer garment. We need not assume that Paul has forgotten it; winter is approaching (v. 21) and, even in a relatively warm climate like Rome (if that is where Paul is), prisons could be damp and cold.

We do not know who Carpus is. The word "scrolls" may refer to writings made from papyrus, but the word was also used for writings in a general way. Commentators usually suggest (correctly) that Paul's scrolls included at least some of the Old Testament writings.[2] Given the frequent use that Paul makes of the Old Testament and given his rabbinical training, it would not be surprising if he possessed some of the Old Testament books. "Parchment" was a more expensive material, usually made from sheep or goat skin. It was more durable than papyrus and surpassed it in appearance; it could also be erased.[3] We do not know the contents of the parchments that Paul requested.

It is often overlooked that there is no "and" between the word "scrolls" and the word "especially" (malista), so the scrolls and parchments may not refer to different things. Rather, Paul may be saying that the scrolls are the parchments. A highly significant and much-quoted article by T. C. Skeat[4] has convincingly demonstrated that in some cases, including this passage, the word

---

1. Dibelius/Conzelmann discuss some of the technicalities about the word "cloak," providing source materials and quotations (Dibelius/Conzelmann, Pastoral Epistles, 123).

2. Knight (Pastoral Epistles, 467) points out the use of the term to refer to specific Old Testament passages, as in Luke 4:17; Gal. 3:10; Heb. 9:19; 10:7.

3. The availability of the ancient Sinaiticus and Vaticanus manuscripts today is due to the parchment codex form in which they were written (see I. A. Sparks, "Parchment," ISBE, 3:663).

4. T. C. Skeat, "'Especially the Parchments': A Note on 2 Timothy IV.13," JTS 30 (1979): 173–77.

following *malista*, usually translated "especially," does not refer to separate items but to the items themselves. We may translate *malista* either "I mean" or "that is."[5] A sound exegetical decision must be made in each case, because the context must determine whether *malista* is used in this equative sense or not.

It is impossible to tell whether "Alexander the metalworker" is the same person named in 1 Timothy 1:20. Paul does not offer any clear comment to distinguish the two from each other, although the word "metalworker" here could be understood as that kind of distinguishing comment. The further description in verse 14 (where the "great deal of harm" may have been part of the "persecutions" in 3:11) corresponds to the 1 Timothy reference. However, the warning to Timothy to "be on your guard against him" (v. 15) implies that this man is a current threat, whereas 1 Timothy 1:20 implies his excommunication ("handed over to Satan"). It is therefore less likely that this first named Alexander would continue to be a threat. Conceivably he could do a great deal of damage from the outside, especially if he was under some measure of control by Satan. Yet given the unknown space of time between 1 and 2 Timothy, it is possible that he was restored but, sadly, still "strongly opposed [Paul's] message."[6]

What does Paul mean by "my first defense" in verse 16? If Paul was tried and acquitted after the end of Acts and is now for the second time imprisoned and awaiting the disposition of his case, this verse could naturally refer to that previous circumstance. We can easily understand verse 17 that way, with the Lord giving Paul strength so that "the message might be fully proclaimed and all the Gentiles might hear"—that is, through Paul's further missionary travels. The "lion's mouth" could refer to the Roman emperor. On the other hand, "first defense" may refer to what was called in Roman law the *actio prima*, the first phase of his present trial.[7] In this case we would have to understand verse 17 about the future proclamation of the gospel in another sense than Paul's going personally to further countries and Gentile audiences.

Clearly the fulfillment of message is in some way through Paul himself and includes the hearing of the gospel by a significant audience of Gentiles. This

---

5. The issue is not particularly important here, but it is important in 1 Tim. 4:10 ("the Savior of all men, and especially of those who believe"); 5:8 ("if anyone does not provide for his relatives, and especially for his immediate family"); 5:17 ("the elders . . . are worthy of double honor, especially those whose work is preaching and teaching"); Titus 1:10 ("rebellious people . . . especially those of the circumcision group"); see comments on those passages. Another sensitive text is Gal. 6:10: "Therefore, as we have opportunity, let us do good to all people, especially [*malista*] to those who belong to the family of believers."

6. There is one more possibility: The future tense in "the Lord will repay him" may refer to a sentence that has not yet been carried out. That, however, seems less likely.

7. Ellicott, *Commentary*, 178; Kelly, *Pastoral Epistles*, 218.

could conceivably have happened in a preliminary hearing if an assortment of Gentile people were present, but it must be said that it is easier to fit this time of witness into the period between the trial at the conclusion of Acts and the present one. There are various ways to interpret the image of the "lion's mouth," so that does not restrict the reference to any particular defense. Whatever the reference, it is hard to understand that no one came to Paul's support at either trial. Yet he makes a strong point of this—note the emphatic "no one" and the use of the word "deserted" (used earlier of Demas in v. 10). Paul's "wish-prayer" that "it not be held against them" is a reminder of the words of forgiveness on the lips of Jesus at his crucifixion (Luke 23:34) and of Stephen's prayer for those who were stoning him as he was dying (Acts 7:60).[8]

It seems strange that Paul is telling Timothy all this, for especially if this is a reference to his first trial, Timothy would have already known the details. However, in ancient narrative it was not uncommon to have events repeated. This is a mini-narrative that leads up to verse 18, "The Lord will rescue me." This is the third reference in this section to "the Lord" and may specifically refer to Christ. The Lord's Prayer contains the petitions "lead us not into temptation, but deliver us from [the] evil [one]" (Matt. 6:13). The similarities to 2 Timothy 4:18a, which uses the same verb for "deliver" (*rhyomai*) and for "evil" (*poneros*), are obvious. The emphasis on "rescue" is aided by the use of *rhyomai* in verse 17 (NIV "was delivered"; cf. also 2 Cor. 1:10).

The phrase "every evil attack" (lit., "every evil work") picks up the reference to what Alexander the metalworker did (see comments on v. 14). It is questionable whether the future *sosei* should be translated "will bring me safely." This familiar verb appears seven times in the Pastoral Letters, usually in a reference to one's salvation, where God rather than Christ is usually the subject. If "the Lord" in this verse is God the Father (as in the Lord's Prayer), this would be one more instance of attributing salvation to God. The salvation Paul is referring to is "to [or for, NRSV] [God's] heavenly kingdom." The word "kingdom" reminds us again of the Lord's Prayer, "your kingdom come" (Matt. 6:10); the word "heavenly" recalls Ephesians 1:3, 20; 2:6; 3:10; 6:12. It is only the second use of "kingdom" in the Pastoral Letters (see 2 Tim. 4:1 and comments). Paul cannot refrain from a brief doxology at this point. The phrase "for ever and ever" is appropriate to his thoughts about the "heavenly kingdom."

Paul's final greetings and personal references in verses 19–21 are, in the best sense of the word, sentimental. "Priscilla and Aquila" have meant a great deal to Paul. The order of their names is significant. In 1 Corinthians 16:19 Aquila is mentioned first, as would be expected. However, Luke does not refer

---

8. Knight (*Pastoral Epistles*, 468–72) has a detailed discussion of the issues in vv. 16–17.

to the church as meeting at *his* house but at *their* house. In Romans 16:3 Paul mentions Priscilla's name first. The couple is also mentioned in Acts 18:2, 18, 19, 26. Verse 2 mentions Aquila's name first. Then Luke says (v. 18) that after Paul had been in Corinth "for some time," he traveled to Syria, "accompanied by Priscilla and Aquila." It is as though by that time Priscilla had gained more significant attention than her husband.

It was unusual in those times for a woman to be mentioned before her husband. A rare exception was a reverse order on an occasional gravestone. Knight suggests several reasons for this, including the possibility that Priscilla may have had a higher rank than Aquila or that this was "an expression of Christian courtesy extended to her because she is a woman."[9] However, if the reason was anything like these suggestions, one would expect the order of names to be the same in every text. The best explanation seems to be that she gained more prominence as their ministry continued. For example, in Acts 18:26 Priscilla and Aquila (mentioned in that order) invited Apollos to their home and "explained to him the way of God more adequately." Any application of 1 Timothy 2:12 should take the Acts passage into account.

The reference to the "household of Onesiphorus" (v. 19b) is a beautiful echo of 1:16–18. This may be a wonderful testimony to the entire household or, poignantly, a sympathetic word to his bereaved family if he had died. The possibility of his death is suggested by the unusual fact that his household is mentioned rather than Onesiphorus himself.

"Erastus" (v. 20) may be the same person mentioned in the same breath as Timothy in Acts 19:22. Romans 16:23 also mentions an Erastus, "who is the city's director of public works" (the city there, presumably, is Corinth, from where Paul wrote Romans). In that case he would have had considerable stature and, indeed, may be the Erastus mentioned on an inscription at Corinth.[10] Paul's mention of Erastus here in 2 Timothy 4:20 without further description implies that Timothy knows him. The mention of Corinth here does establish a possible link with that city's director of public works. The problem of this identification, however, is the absence of a link between the Acts passage (where Erastus is in Ephesus) and Romans 16:23. Moreover, the name Erastus was a common one. The identification must, therefore, remain at best a possibility.

"Trophimus" is also mentioned in Acts 20:4 in company with Timothy. He is "from the province of Asia." In Acts 21:29 he is called "Trophimus the

---

9. Knight, *Pastoral Epistles*, 475.

10. The inscription reads: "Erastus in consideration of his aedileship laid this pavement at his own expense"; see J. H. Kent, *Corinth* VIII\3. *The Inscriptions* 1926–1950 (Princeton, 1996), 99, quoted in Bruce, *The Acts of the Apostles: Greek Text with Introduction and Commentary*, 3d ed. (Grand Rapids: Eerdmans, 1990), 414.

Ephesian." It may be significant in connection with Paul's involvement in miraculous acts, including healing (Acts 14:8–10; 28:7–9), that Trophimus was left "sick in Miletus."

In verse 21 the verb *spoudazo* occurs (see v. 9 and comments), giving a note of urgency to Timothy's projected trip to see Paul "before winter" and the closure of the sea lanes. Paul then cites several otherwise unknown people: Eubulus, Pudens, Linus, and Claudia. Linus has sometimes been linked by speculation with one of the early bishops of Rome,[11] but the name is too common to allow any positive identification. It may also be questioned whether there was such a thing as the rule of a single bishop in the first century. The word translated "brothers" may include sisters. Given the fact that many passages in Paul's writings referring to "brothers" clearly in their context include sisters, to add "sisters" in translation is legitimate.

"The Lord" is mentioned one final time at the end of this letter. Whether this word refers to God or to Christ, it is in the person of the Holy Spirit that the Lord is present with our spirit (John 14:15–27). The closing greetings are typical of ancient letters, but "grace be with you," like "grace, mercy and peace" in 1:2, has a distinctly Christian and Pauline meaning.

PEOPLE, PEOPLE, PEOPLE. Only God knows the number of people who have read the names of Demas, Crescens, Titus, Luke, Mark, Tychicus, Alexander, Priscilla, Aquila, Onesiphorus, Erastus, Trophimus, Eubulus, Pudens, Linus, and Claudia and have seen in them the faces of those who have affected their own lives for good or ill. This may have taken place, as with Paul, in times of extremity. The pathetic words "no one came to my support, but everyone deserted me" have probably been true of many forgotten saints. But so have the words "but the Lord stood at my side and gave me strength."

This section, along with closing greetings, is often read hastily at the end of a series of Bible studies on 2 Timothy. Since there is no danger of giving away the "end of the story," it might not be a bad idea for this section to be read at the *beginning* of a series of messages on this letter. If indeed all four chapters were written in the circumstances described in the final section, Paul's thinking (whether it is obvious to us or not) was affected by what was happening to him through the influence of these people. It is not a condescension but realism to let Paul the apostle be Paul the man. The picture of these associates of Paul can be meaningful, therefore, to help us

---

11. Irenaeus, *Against Heresies* 3.3.3.

understand both Paul's circumstances and those of Christians throughout church history.

In Paul's case, we learn that his immense efforts to "present everyone perfect in Christ" (Col. 1:28) were not always successful. While 2 Timothy describes things at the end of Paul's ministry (when a corresponding change of circumstances and attitudes can be expected among one's companions), we can assume that departures, defections, and sickness were common events in his long service to the Lord. After all, Paul had earlier written of the daily "pressure of [his] concern for all the churches" (2 Cor. 11:28).

Healing. The reference to Trophimus being left "sick in Miletus" raises the issue of healing. If healing can be claimed either as being "in the atonement" or as the assured result of believing prayer, why did Paul not have the theological understanding or mature faith to effect Trophimus's recovery? While a lengthy treatment of this perennial issue is not possible here, it can be noted that for whatever reasons, Trophimus (and Paul) had to deal with an illness that apparently interfered to some degree with Christian ministry. It is perhaps significant that discussions on the matter are usually subsumed under the topic of healing rather than of sickness. While health is the normal and desired state, Christians often need to grapple with its absence.[12]

Edwin Hui mentions some of the personal effects of sickness, such as "a sense of physical failure, mortality or despair due to a loss of control over one's destiny." There can also be a sense of isolation and "diminished self-esteem."[13] Surely Paul would have sought to alleviate his friend's sufferings, but perhaps he would also have gently reminded him that God can bring good out of sickness, especially if one seeks the Lord during the distress. The literature and hymnody of Christianity has been wonderfully enriched by those who wrote out of such experiences. Sickness is not to be sought or misused out of a perverted martyr complex, but it can be an opportunity for a closer walk with God that may in God's goodness benefit others as well.[14]

Patterns throughout church history. It is difficult to know to what extent we are to draw principles from Paul's comments on the various people he mentions in this section. As always, we must remember that he wrote under inspiration, and therefore his public citation of faults does not necessarily

---

12. A significant exception is the excellent and practical reference work *The Complete Book of Everyday Christianity*, Robert Banks and R. Paul Stevens, eds. (Downers Grove, Ill.: InterVarsity, 1997), which has articles on "Healing," "Health," and "Sickness."

13. Edwin Hui, "Sickness," *Everyday Christianity*, 895.

14. A powerful classic book that records many personal testimonies in this regard is the popular *Streams in the Desert*, by Mrs. Charles E. Cowman, originally published in 1925 and recently rereleased by Zondervan (1997).

give us the liberty of commenting negatively on people. Yet there is benefit in recognizing that certain characteristics and behavioral patterns do reappear in the global church in spite of cultural differences. There will always be those who choose the present world to the detriment of personal fidelity, those who are always "on the road" in Christian ministry and leave others to struggle with loss of companionship and help, those who "desert" the Lord's servants for unexpressed reasons, those who cause great harm to the Lord's servants and oppose their message, those who offer warm and perhaps sacrificial hospitality to missionaries, those who become sick or are otherwise unable to be active in ministry, and, thank the Lord, those who faithfully stand by Christians in need even if it means being the only ones who do so. We all have our own lists.

While the church—and church historians especially—has focused on public figures, such as pastors, teachers, great leaders, and prominent spokespersons, there are multitudes of others whose stories are likewise important to God and to the progress of Christianity. I think of people who influenced and helped my early ministry: Mrs. Zinke and Mrs. Chan, who prayed for me; the chairman of the deacons and his wife, who always had a word of encouragement (and whose lives were cut short by a drunk driver); my parents, aunts, and uncles; and Dr. J. Oliver Buswell Jr., whose clear Bible exposition made me want to do the same. Every servant of God who reads these words can recall similar people in his or her life. And the name of every leader mentioned in our church history books can be joined by the names of many to whose spiritual encouragement they are indebted.

In the days before pipe organ bellows were powered by electricity, a famous organist once gave a recital. He announced each piece in advance with, "I shall now play...." After the intermission he announced his next number, but when he began to play there was no sound. At that point a face appeared from around the corner of the pipe chamber and a young voice said, "Make that, 'We shall now play....'" The boy resumed his pumping of the bellows and the concert went on.

In earlier years I used to hear many missionary reports that left the impression that the missionary labored mainly alone. Rarely did he or she refer to other missionaries or organizations working in the area. Even less frequently did a missionary portray the Christian "natives" who did hard evangelistic work, served the church, or helped the missionary. That picture has changed considerably in recent years. Perhaps the best application of the vignettes Paul draws of his associates is to learn how to share the spotlight with others and how to be a helper to the Lord's servants. In this way we can evaluate our own behavior and role in ministry.

PRAISE AND BLAME. From the ideals mentioned in the previous section we can move to the specifics of contemporary life. Paul wrote 2 Timothy in the conscious environment of Death Row. If the faces of those named were vivid to him as he wrote Timothy, so also are those of our companions whose successes and failures, fidelity and defection either encourage or plague us to the end of our days. Those who minister for the Lord today do so in the real environment of persons whose comings and goings have permanently affected our life and ministry.

It may not be an executioner but an ex-companion who causes the most pain, and the time may come when a Christian leader must speak frankly about sin and defection among colleagues. Such a step is to be avoided if possible. Restraint is important, and we do not have the same inspiration as Paul did and must be careful about judging motives. Nevertheless, at times others need to know, if only to prevent further harm.

In my own years of ministry since my first charge as interim pastor at Northport Baptist Church in Long Island, New York, while doing graduate study (exactly fifty years ago as I write), I have seen many people overlooked at times when recognition has been given. In contrast there are others who have been wonderfully celebrated—such as a Sunday school teacher whose ministry exceeded fifty years and another whose life was devoted to successive generations of classes. The organ dedication of a Presbyterian church was recently enhanced by a fascinating, detailed recognition of *every* person who had given time, help, ideas, energy, and wisdom as well as money to the project. Later someone commented on the legendary thoughtfulness of that church in recognizing those who serve behind the scenes.

At the same time, recognition is sometimes given where it is not deserved. Prominent people may be singled out for approbation because of their position. Paul makes no such mistake, but is bluntly honest. Sometimes election to church office is little more than a payback to an influential figure. The same names may appear in church office year after year while spiritual workers behind the scenes go unrecognized with their larger gifts untapped for the church.

Jesus said, "From everyone who has been given much, much will be demanded" (Luke 12:48). Christians who have been given prominent positions of leadership, seminary positions, and journalistic and other media opportunities have sometimes used their platforms to criticize, severely and publicly, sincere Christians with whom they disagree. Rarely has any such critic been called to account as Paul would have done. In contrast, in a major city several pastors felt the obligation to speak out regarding the elders of a large nearby church who failed to discipline an errant prominent pastor. Contemporary Christians need to be more concerned about the reputation of God than about the reputation of fallible leaders. The response must not be carnal, or damage will be done in reverse, but it must be carried out in the spirit of Galatians 6:1–10.

Facing death. With the graying of America and with increasing openness about death, there is a greater awareness of what it means to face its closeness. Retirees may keep busy, but realize that their productive years are diminished or gone. Grandparents may enjoy their grandchildren and know that they are loved and appreciated by them, but they may also be conscious that they are no longer in the mainstream of action or conversation. Successive wedding anniversaries are celebrated with the unspoken apprehension that this may be the last one together. Genetic and pharmaceutical progress in extending life only prolongs the "final stages."

In some parts of the world persecution threatens to shorten life. Terrorists, rebels, and oppressive governments all bring Paul's uncertainty of living forcibly into the lives of many. Those who are near death for whatever reason—even believers, who know the glory that awaits them—are sometimes reluctant to yield to the inevitable. Perhaps it is the sadness that accompanies a feeling of spiritual work unfinished (in contrast to Paul's "I have finished the race"). Perhaps it is the grief of becoming the bereaver, so to speak, leaving loved ones alone to grieve their departure. Perhaps it is a sense of being overtaken in the prime of life. As one whose academic life has been accompanied by pastoral ministry I know what it is to tell a dying person that it is "all right" to let go. I had to tell that to my own ninety-four-year-old mother.

To say farewell is also a good and thoughtful act on the part of the one facing death. Too many people have been unwilling to deal realistically with the prospect of death. They then lose the opportunity to say that last word of forgiveness or to ask for it. Maybe feelings or secrets that seemed important to hide during life should be revealed *if* (with emphasis on that word) it would be beneficial to do so. Paul made his feelings clear. He gave Timothy closure on their relationship. He expressed his feelings regarding some people, feelings that for one reason or another were beneficial to acknowledge. At the same time, Paul was not courting death. He had already decided on an earlier occasion that as wonderful as being present with the Lord was, it was more needful for him to remain alive to serve the church (Phil. 1:21–26). The point is that he was *ready* to die, and that readiness speaks to us.

It is a blessed person who has the love of a warm household like that of Onesiphorus, of a dear friend like Trophimus, the burden of whose illness we share, or of someone we desperately hope will come to us "before winter" (if we may extend the implications of that phrase beyond its immediate reference). We are not alone, especially since, unlike Paul's day, people are as near as the phone or e-mail. As the winter of our lives approaches, we need these friends to "come," even if only electronically. I have become aware that friends of long ago, especially some older ones, are getting back in touch with me after years without contact. I am moved by this and am doing my own part in this reunion. Our winter may arrive at a different stage of life than for others, but it is appropriate to seek the presence of friends and to offer them the same blessing.

Titus 1:1–16

PAUL, A SERVANT of God and an apostle of Jesus Christ for the faith of God's elect and the knowledge of the truth that leads to godliness—²a faith and knowledge resting on the hope of eternal life, which God, who does not lie, promised before the beginning of time, ³and at his appointed season he brought his word to light through the preaching entrusted to me by the command of God our Savior,

⁴To Titus, my true son in our common faith:

Grace and peace from God the Father and Christ Jesus our Savior.

⁵The reason I left you in Crete was that you might straighten out what was left unfinished and appoint elders in every town, as I directed you. ⁶An elder must be blameless, the husband of but one wife, a man whose children believe and are not open to the charge of being wild and disobedient. ⁷Since an overseer is entrusted with God's work, he must be blameless—not overbearing, not quick-tempered, not given to drunkenness, not violent, not pursuing dishonest gain. ⁸Rather he must be hospitable, one who loves what is good, who is self-controlled, upright, holy and disciplined. ⁹He must hold firmly to the trustworthy message as it has been taught, so that he can encourage others by sound doctrine and refute those who oppose it.

¹⁰For there are many rebellious people, mere talkers and deceivers, especially those of the circumcision group. ¹¹They must be silenced, because they are ruining whole households by teaching things they ought not to teach—and that for the sake of dishonest gain. ¹²Even one of their own prophets has said, "Cretans are always liars, evil brutes, lazy gluttons."

¹³This testimony is true. Therefore, rebuke them sharply, so that they will be sound in the faith ¹⁴and will pay no attention to Jewish myths or to the commands of those who reject the truth. ¹⁵To the pure, all things are pure, but to those who are corrupted and do not believe, nothing is pure. In fact, both their minds and consciences are corrupted. ¹⁶They claim to know God, but by their actions they deny him. They are detestable, disobedient and unfit for doing anything good.

Original Meaning

IN THE ORDER of writing, Paul's letter to Titus almost certainly came close on the heels of 1 Timothy and well before 2 Timothy (see the Introduction). Like Timothy in Ephesus, Titus was left by Paul on the island of Crete to organize the church and deal with a crisis situation of false teachers who had infiltrated the church.

An Expanded Introduction (1:1–4)

IT IS NATURAL to compare the opening lines of this letter with those of 1 and 2 Timothy. Doing so may indicate differences between the two letters not only as regards Paul's relationship to the recipients but also as regards the distinctive missions of these two apostolic delegates. In any given instance, however, a difference between the two letters may only be a matter of style or of emphasis rather than of substance.

One difference appears at the very beginning. Paul identifies himself both as "a servant" (*doulos*, "slave") of God and as "an apostle" (v. 1).[1] The word *doulos* appears in Philippians 1:1, a letter he coauthored with Timothy. In all the other Pauline letters, except 1 and 2 Thessalonians (which were authored by Paul, Silas, and Timothy), Paul identifies himself simply as an apostle. Paul does not use *doulos* in a self-deprecating way. A slave was owned by another person to whom obedience was required. If slavery meant obligation, apostleship meant authority, but both meant responsibility.

The following words appear in the opening lines of both Titus and 1 Timothy: "command," "hope," "true son" (2 Timothy has "dear son"), "faith," and a prepositional phrase with *kata*. There are also the customary references to God and Christ as well as to grace and peace (Titus lacks "mercy"). In Titus 1:3 Paul refers to the proclamation entrusted to him by the "command of God our Savior"; in 1 Timothy 1:1 he is an apostle "by the command of God our Savior and of Christ Jesus our hope"; in 2 Timothy 1:1 he is an apostle "by the will of God."

Four prepositional phrases beginning with *kata* (lit., "according to") in verse 1 of the salutations of the Pastoral Letters call for attention. In 1 Timothy 1:1, "by the command [*kat' epitagen*] of God" expresses the basis of Paul's apostolic calling. In 2 Timothy 1:1 the idea of God's command is replaced by the phrase "by [*dia*] the will of God," but this is followed by *kat' epangelian*

---

1. The Old Testament refers to Moses as the "servant of the LORD" in Deut. 34:5; Josh. 1:1, 13, 15 and frequently elsewhere in that book. The same expression is used of Joshua in Josh. 24:29; Judg. 2:8, and of David in the heading of Ps. 18 and 36. This recalls also the "servant passages" in Isaiah and the ministry of Christ as the Servant of the Lord.

("according to the promise"). This phrase expresses not so much a basis for Paul's call to apostleship as it does a correspondence with God's promises. Two occur in Titus 1:1. Commentators stumble in trying to interpret the first of these: "for [*kata*] the faith of God's elect and the knowledge of the truth." The preposition *kata* does not seem to have the usual idea of basis or correspondence here.

The issues involved can be seen in Kelly, who questions whether, as some think, it means that "Paul preaches in accordance with the orthodox faith"—in other words, that "his message [is] in some way regulated by other people's faith." He understands it instead as meaning "in relation to" or "concerning," pointing to "the sphere in which Paul exercises his apostleship and the ends he hopes to achieve by it."[2] The probable meaning is not that Paul's message conforms to "other people's faith," but that his *mission* is in accordance with the faith of God's very elect (i.e., a true faith) and with the truth that needs to be reaffirmed at Crete. The use of *kata* in the New Testament closest to its meaning here is John 2:6, referring to the stone water jars such as the Jews used "for [*kata*] ceremonial washing." They were *appropriate for* and *in accordance with* that purpose.

This discussion should not overshadow but rather emphasize the double object ("faith" and "knowledge") of that preposition. The faith that Paul wants strengthened in the church at Crete is not some vague pliant subjective feeling but the faith of God's "elect," who stand in the tradition of the Old Testament people of God. The word "elect" is not intended here to emphasize predestination but rather to identify these people as God's own (Ps. 105:42–45, esp. v. 43; Isa. 65:9; cf. Rom. 8:33). "Knowledge of the truth" is important in Titus, just as it is in 1 and 2 Timothy (cf. 1 Tim. 2:4, 7; 3:15; 4:3; 6:5; 2 Tim. 2:15, 18, 25; 3:7–8; 4:4; see also v. 14 in the present chapter). The false teachings at Ephesus and Crete can only be corrected when truth is understood, but the same emphasis that characterizes 1 Timothy—namely, the blending of sound doctrine with godly living—is important here in Titus and is expressed already in Titus 1:1.

The correspondence between "truth" and "godliness" is expressed by yet another use of *kata*, this time before the word "godliness." This expression probably means "truth that is appropriate to godliness" rather than "that leads to godliness" (NIV) or "truth that shows them how to live godly lives" (NLT). Genuine godliness requires a genuine foundation of truth. The false teachers lack both.

The same "hope" that enlivens Paul's correspondence with Timothy (1 Tim. 1:1; 3:14; 4:10; 5:5; 6:17; 2 Tim. 2:25) appears here. It may seem

---

2. Kelly, *Pastoral Epistles*, 226.

strange that "faith and knowledge" rest on hope. However, this hope does not arise from the human heart, but has been "promised before the beginning of time" by "God, who does not lie." This in effect propels the Scriptures to the foreground.[3] This hope of eternal life that depends on the Word of the God "who does not lie" is also certain because it follows on our having been "justified by his grace" (3:7).

There is a chronological contrast between verses 2 and 3, "before the beginning of time" and "at his appointed season" (see 1 Tim. 2:6; 6:15). The testimony of the saving work of Christ and the future appearing of Christ are both said to be at its "proper [own] time" (1 Tim. 2:5–6; 6:14–15). However the word "appearing" (*epiphaneia*) used in 1 Timothy 6:14 and in Titus 2:13 (regarding the "blessed hope") is not used in the present passage, but rather *phaneroo*, "to reveal, bring to light, manifest." These concepts are related. Note how in 2 Timothy 1:10 God's grace has been revealed (*phaneroo*; NIV, "brought ... to light"), and it is coupled with "the appearing [*epiphaneia*] of ... Christ." "Word" in Titus 1:3 is not the Scriptures but God's message, the gospel. The means by which this message came to light was the "proclamation" (NRSV, probably a better translation of *kerygma* than the NIV "preaching").

The responsibilities of being faithful to a trust ("entrusted") and obedient to "the command of God" are combined in this passage (cf. 1 Tim. 1:11 on being entrusted with the gospel; also 1:1, 3, 5; 4:11; 6:14, 17–18). Paul uses the emphatic "I" (*ego*) both here in Titus 1:3 and in 1 Timothy 1:11. His responsibility is emphasized not only by the ideas of a trust and a command, but by the preposition *kata* placed before the word "command," now with the sense of "in conformity to" or "in accordance with." This phraseology gives Paul not only responsibility, but also authority. He did not ask for this trust, it was given him by God's command.

God is "our Savior" and as such has the right to decide how his saving message is to be announced. The address to Titus and the rest of the salutation are straightforward and brief. On the phrase "true son" and the other words of greeting see comments on 1 Timothy 1:2.

The Need for Elders (1:5–9)

"I LEFT YOU" in verse 5 does not mean that Paul simply dropped Titus off on the island of Crete but implies that Paul himself was there and then left Titus behind. Paul had been there briefly one previous time on his way as a prisoner

---

3. Cf. 2 Peter 1:16–21, which, after presenting the transfiguration as an assurance of the truth about Christ, says, "And we have the word of the prophets made more certain ... for prophecy never had its origin in the will of man, but men spoke from God as they were carried along by the Holy Spirit."

to Rome (Acts 27:7–15). Crete had been the scene of the great Minoan civilization but had languished in relative obscurity for more than a millennium. It was incorporated into the Roman empire in 67 B.C. Judaism was active there during the time of the New Testament, and some Cretans were in Jerusalem when the Holy Spirit was poured out on Pentecost (Acts 2:11). The existence of a Christian community after that was probably what drew Paul there for a visit after his release from Roman imprisonment. This group of believers were apparently not well organized. If Paul made only a brief stop there, it is understandable why he left Titus to rectify the situation.

There is some ambiguity in the words "straighten out what was left unfinished," because "straighten out" implies the existence of something that needs correction, while "what was left unfinished" implies something not yet complete. Put together, the words imply that there was some residual disorganization after Paul left, which could be remedied by what had not been done before: appointing responsible leadership. The island, approximately 156 miles long and ranging from 8 to 35 miles wide, had a number of towns scattered throughout it. In each of these towns Titus is to appoint elders. The requirements for elders that follow are probably more for the Cretans to learn than for Titus.

The Greek word in verse 5 for "appoint" is *kathistemi*. Of the ten words translated "ordained" in the KJV this is the only one that has a clearly "official" meaning (besides its use regarding the high priest in Heb. 5:1; 8:3).[4] The word for "elders" (*presbyteroi*) in Titus is apparently the same as the *episkopoi* in 1 Timothy 3 (see comments there and in Introduction).

The first requirement for an overseer in 1 Timothy 3:2 is to be "above reproach" (lit., "cannot be criticized"). Here in Titus 1:6 the word "blameless" is a different word (lit., "cannot be accused"). The dominant idea in both lists is that an elder must have an untarnished reputation. On the translation "husband of but one wife" and related issues, see comments on 1 Timothy 3:2; it is probably better to translate this "faithful to his wife."

There is a significant difference between the latter part of verse 6 and 1 Timothy 3:4. In 1 Timothy the elder is to manage his family well and "see that his children obey him with proper respect." Here the elder's children are to "believe," as well as not be open to the charge of being "wild and disobedient." This seems to make the parent responsible for a child's salvation, and,

---

4. The other words translated "ordain" are ordinary words, such as *tithemi* ("to place, do, arrange, set in place"; see 1 Tim. 2:7, where the KJV has "ordained" and NIV "appointed"). They are not hierarchical terms, and none of them refers to the pastor of a church. This language pattern of the KJV has undoubtedly affected views of ordination over several centuries, by making it appear that the New Testament church had a technical term for ordination. The NIV improves on this by putting "ordain" in the footnotes as an alternative to "appoint."

by extension, would make church leadership dependent on the elders' children. But the Greek word translated "believe" is an adjective (*pistos*), which can also mean "faithful" or "trustworthy" (see 2 Tim. 2:2, where it is translated "reliable" in the NIV and "faithful" in the NRSV). Thus, the meaning here may be broader than it seems at first. The fact that the emphasis in both 1 Timothy 3 and here is that elder be a person of good reputation, coupled with the fact that he receives his children's "respect," makes it probable that this is the emphasis here.

The NIV inserts an unwarranted "and" between "believing" and "are not open to the charge of being wild and disobedient," as though the latter were an additional requirement. Instead, the second phrase enlarges on the meaning of that previous word. Elders must be open to any inquiry about their children's behavior, which again is a matter of reputation. Good and wise parents can influence their children's actions and encourage them to be trustworthy, but they cannot control their spiritual response to God. The children should not incur any accusation of being "wild" (the word used here is translated "debauchery" in Eph. 5:18 and "dissipation" in 1 Peter 4:4) or "disobedient" (cf. Titus 1:10, where this word is translated "rebellious"). Thus, the phrase in verse 6 describes outrageous behavioral activity that would bring public disrepute on the eldership and the church.

In verse 7, *episkopos* ("overseer") is used, suggesting that overseers and elders are identical. An alternate view is that the word means "bishop," or at least an individual with a broader span of responsibility than (other?) elders. If so, the qualifications that follow are specific to bishops rather than merely to elders. However, with no break in the flow of characteristics but being an integrated whole (as in 1 Tim. 3:1–7), this is unlikely. Rather, the opening *gar* (NIV "since") implies that this is not an additional series of requirements but an explanation or foundation for what has preceded.

The overseer/elder is to be "blameless" (the same word as in v. 6) for a specific reason: He acts as God's steward (*oikonomos*; NIV, "entrusted with God's work"). The series of qualifications that follows specifies behavioral patterns that cannot characterize an elder if he is to be considered blameless. No elder should be "overbearing"—a word used to describe the terrible false teachers of the last days in 2 Peter 2:10 (NIV, "arrogant"); it can also be translated "self-willed" or "stubborn." "Quick-tempered" is a weak translation of an adjective that denotes not merely a matter of losing one's temper, but of being inclined to anger, irascible. The next three characteristics to be avoided—drunkenness, violence, and pursuit of "dishonest gain"—have counterparts in 1 Timothy 3:3, 8 (see comments there).

The desirable characteristics cited in verse 8 include two that appear in 1 Timothy 3:2: hospitality and self-control (on the latter, the same idea with related words occurs in 1 Tim. 2:9, 15; 2 Tim. 1:7; Titus 2:2, 4–6, 12). "Righteous" describes God in 2 Timothy 4:8; in 1 Timothy 1:9–10 the word is used for "the righteous," who stand in contrast to the lawbreakers. The word for "holy" can also mean pure or devout (cf. 1 Tim. 2:8). The last word, "disciplined," does not appear elsewhere in the New Testament but its cognates do, including the aspect of the fruit of the Spirit translated "self-control" (Gal. 5:23).

Note that these characteristics are not intended to be unique to elders, for in one form or another they describe the ideal character of all Christian men and women. Their function here is to portray a morally well-rounded person, who will not disgrace the Lord and his church.

It may seem strange that more is said in Titus (1:9) about the need for an elder to be doctrinally sound and able to refute heretics than was the case in 1 Timothy 3:1–7, since the former letter deals more strongly and repeatedly with false teachers and teaching. While the present passage does go on to talk about the need to refute error (Titus 1:10–16), the content here is less strong than in 1 Timothy and is pursued further only in 3:9–11. The difference may be that in Ephesus elders already existed (Acts 20:17–35), the need for doctrinal instruction by elders was already apparent, and the great need was to realize that sound doctrine needed to be blended with godly living in contrast to the lives of the heretics. In Titus, on the other hand, although the Cretan soil was ready to nourish erroneous ideas, the need for teaching elders may not have been pointed out to them previously. Kelly says that the "twofold task of building up the faithful and eliminating error" in the latter part of Titus 1:9 is the elders' or overseers' "chief challenge."[5]

The Circumstances of the Church on the Island of Crete (1:10–16)

THIS SECTION INTRODUCES the people whose teachings must be opposed by doctrinally capable elders. Although the spectrum of false teachers at Crete seems to be more narrow than those in Ephesus addressed in 1 Timothy, with the focus in Titus being on the "circumcision group," there are enough of them to be called "many" and to constitute a major problem. The first descriptive word is "rebellious," the same word translated "disobedient" in verse 6. Clearly if an elder's children acted the same way as the opponents did, he would have little credibility.

---

5. Kelly, *Pastoral Epistles*, 32. Young (*Theology of the Pastoral Letters*, 74–84) has a section on sound teaching in the Pastorals, followed by useful treatments of "teaching and learning in the ancient world" and on the popular philosophers. The concluding brief section in that chapter questions whether doctrine in the Pastoral Letters is to be equated with later orthodoxy. Like the rest of her stimulating book, this section calls for interaction.

"Mere talkers and deceivers" does not, as the NIV may imply, mean that they are not much of a threat because all they do is talk. Rather, the word translated "mere talkers" means talking idly or at random; we might say "shooting from the hip." And the word with which it is joined ("deceivers") means that they deceive the heart or mind.[6]

Paul has the "circumcision group" particularly in mind (on the meaning of "especially" [*malista*], see comment on 1 Tim. 4:10; 2 Tim. 4:13). The meaning here is not that people in the circumcision group cause more problems than others do, but that the rebellious people *are* the "circumcision group." There is an urgency about this. Whereas some of the false teachers in Ephesus targeted certain women (2 Tim. 3:6), the false teachers at Crete are turning *whole families* upside down. Perhaps the "things they ought not to teach" include the kind of legalistic practices that, when followed by some members of a family, disrupt relationships. Further, these teachers on the island of Crete are not operating out of sincerity but "for the sake of dishonest gain," just like the false teachers at Ephesus, who were seeking personal profit (1 Tim. 6:5). It is not surprising, given the presence of greedy false teachers, that Paul has insisted that elders specifically avoid such a reputation (v. 7; cf. also his comment about deacons in 1 Tim. 3:8).

The quotation in verse 12 that begins "Cretans are always liars" has caused much discussion.[7] (On the use of what we would today consider an ethnic slur see Bridging Contexts below.) An academic issue concerns the origin of the quotation.[8] Paul himself does not consider the author of this saying to be a prophet, but appeals to common understanding in the ancient world that he was. This gives the quotation more validity. The function of the quotation is to provide a reason for distrusting the false teachers and to point out that people in a society that promotes laziness and the satisfying of base desires easily foster the desire for "dishonest gain" in their false teachers. It

---

6. For an understanding of these two words and their cognates see LSJ, 1084 and 1954.

7. Dibelius/Conzelmann, *Pastoral Epistles*, 135, quoting Polybius, *Histories* 6.46, on this topic: "So much in fact do sordid love of gain and lust for wealth prevail among them, that the Cretans are the only people in the world in whose eyes no gain is disgraceful." In that quotation "sordid love of gain" translates the Greek *aischrokerdeia*, a cognate of *aischrokerdes*, a trait Paul says should not characterize elders (see v. 7 and comments above).

8. On this matter see especially Lock, *Pastoral Epistles*, 132–35; Dibelius/Conzelmann, *Pastoral Epistles*, 136–37. There is evidence that Epimenides, to whom the quote is attributed, was considered a prophet in ancient times. Other Greek writers also criticized the Cretans, with lying being only one of the charges. The reason for that being singled out may be that the Cretans made a preposterous claim that Zeus was buried on their island. This, of course, was not only highly offensive to Callimachus, whose scores the Cretans on that point in his *Hymn to Zeus*, but to others as well. Any people who brazenly claim to have the actual grave of the chief of the immortal gods and not be ashamed of that claim can certainly not be trusted.

could be argued that the church members and leaders were subject to the same characteristics as members of that Cretan society. However, if the core of the church was Jewish (Acts 2:11 indicates that the converted Cretans were at the Jewish Feast of Pentecost), and if the Gentile believers identified with the Old Testament people of God to the point of rejecting their own natural ethnic and national identity, the picture becomes more clear.

At the beginning of verse 13 Paul inserts the second of two comments that form a bracket around the saying concerning the Cretans (the first being Paul's reference to the reputation of the saying's author as a "prophet"): "This testimony is true." The next words may be translated "for this reason" (NRSV) or perhaps "on account of this"; the NIV's "therefore" lacks the punch of the Greek expression. "Rebuke" is a strong word (cf. its use in v. 9; 2:15; also 1 Tim. 5:20; 2 Tim. 4:2). It is argued that Paul has in mind the deceived Cretan people rather than the false teachers.[9] However, the sentence structure does not demand this or even favor it. The rest of Titus 1:13 is similar to 2 Timothy 2:25–26, which offers the hope that those who opposed Timothy will come to the truth and be freed from Satan's trap.

Verse 14 states the two aspects of the teachings of the "circumcision group" that must be rejected. (1) One is "Jewish myths" (1 Tim. 1:4 and comments; 2 Tim. 4:4; Titus 3:9, which picks up the "endless genealogies" of 1 Tim. 1:4). The presence of Jews throughout the ancient world provided a network through which those who promulgated nonbiblical deviant stories could circulate their errors. It is not surprising that they appeared both in Ephesus and in Crete.

(2) The other aspect of the heretics' teachings has to do with daily life: "the commands of those [lit., of human beings] who reject the truth." Contemporary translations that do not bring out the modifying term *anthropon* (i.e., "of mere human beings") miss the opportunity to show the connection with Isaiah 29:13: "Their worship of me is made up only of rules taught by men." This passage was cited by Jesus (Matt. 15:9; Mark. 7:7) and is reflected in Colossians 2:22.[10] Thus, the substitution of human commands for those of God was apparently even more pervasive than the following of myths and genealogies.

Basic to both aspects of error is the rejection of "the truth." It is especially regrettable that this is done by those who allegedly support Judaism, because the Jews had the heritage of the Old Testament, which embodies

---

9. See, for example, Knight, *Pastoral Epistles*, 299–300, and, less vigorously, Fee, *1 and 2 Timothy, Titus*, 180.

10. Note that the NIV and NRSV clearly bring out the human factor in the Isaiah passage, but not here in Titus 1:14. The NKJV and REB have "of men" and "human" respectively, but the NIV and NRSV have only "those."

truth. The false teachers are to be rebuked "sharply" (v. 13; or "harshly," see 2 Cor. 13:10). Apparently there is hope that the false teachers will repent, since the purpose of this rebuke is that they may become "sound in the faith" and reject error. (For Paul's use of the verb "be sound, healthy" in the Pastoral Letters see comments on 1 Tim. 1:10; cf. 6:3; 2 Tim. 1:13; 4:3; Titus 1:9; 2:1–2.) "The faith" refers to the doctrine of the Christian faith.

Paul's response in verse 15 to the commands of the circumcision group, which apparently have to do with ritual purity and food laws, is not theological but aphoristic. We might have expected a Galatians-like statement about freedom from the law. Instead, there is a proverbial statement expressed in the form of a chiasm (lit. trans. below):

A   all things [are] pure
   B   to the pure
   B′   but to the corrupted and unbelieving
A′   nothing [is] pure.

The verb represented in the participle "corrupted" (*miaino*) is then repeated at the beginning (in the Greek order) of the next clause (lit. trans.): "However, corrupted are both their minds and consciences." This is a turn of argument that is unexpected. It places responsibility directly on the apparently super-religious people, who carefully trace back the myths and rigorously seek purity by following their reconstruction of the ancient food laws. But in fact if they were truly pure, they would not be so obsessed with the need for such laws. Through their impure minds and consciences[11] everything appears impure and so needs legalistic regulation.

The assault on the false teachers reaches a climax in verse 16. The contrast is damning: Those who claim they know God not only fail to match their actions to their words but by those actions actually deny him (cf. Rom. 1:28–32). This is linked to the fact just stated at the end of verse 15 that both their minds and consciences are "corrupted." The strong word translated "detestable" occurs only here in the New Testament (though cf. the noun form in Luke 16:15 about hypocrites: "What is highly valued among men is detestable in God's sight"). Not surprisingly the heretics at Crete are also "disobedient" (cf. 3:3; also Rom. 1:30; 2 Tim. 3:2). "Unfit" (*adokimos*) refers to something that is not approved, with stronger meanings of disreputable and reprobate (cf. "depraved" in Rom. 1:28; see also 2 Tim. 3:8).[12]

---

11. For the word "conscience" see comments on 1 Tim. 1:5, 19. For sayings similar to these see Lock, *Pastoral Epistles*, 135–36.

12. In such passages as 1 Cor. 9:27; 2 Cor. 13:5–6; Heb. 6:8 this word carries more the idea of being rejected as useless or as not genuine.

ADDRESSING THE SOCIETY of Crete. The opening of Titus takes on particular significance when we reflect on the society in which Titus is minister-ing. The social commentary on the people of Crete in Titus 1:12 is well known: "Cretans are always liars, evil brutes, lazy gluttons." With Titus involved in the church situated in a society like that, there is a pressing need for a strong, unambiguous gospel. The opening of Paul's letter achieves just that. God's people are his "elect" (1:1), who can have a sense of security as the object of God's purpose in even the most depraved and hostile society. Their faith is coupled with "knowledge" and its basis is "the hope of eternal life" (1:2). As in other Pauline literature, hope is not a subjective feeling but a certainty (see esp. Rom. 5:1–11; 8:18–39). In contrast to the mendacious Cretans, "God . . . does not lie" (Titus 1:2), and therefore the eternal life "promised before the beginning of time" is a firm object of the Christian's hope.

God is working according to his schedule, "his appointed season" (1:3), and so at the right time he "brought his word to light" (we might say into open view) through the proclamation he "entrusted" to Paul. This "open view" is a characteristic teaching of the Pastoral Letters.[13] It is important from two perspectives. (1) In the ongoing history of salvation, God pro-gressively revealed truths and accomplished his will in a sequence of events, climaxed in the "appearing" of his grace through his Son. (2) In the compe-tition with contemporary religions, the idea of the appearances of one or another god were celebrated. No doubt in this "conflict of religions in the early Roman Empire"[14] it was important to demonstrate that Christianity also had its *epiphanies*.

Paul's ministry is carried on "by the command of God our Savior" (1:3), language familiar from Paul's correspondence with Timothy.[15] The command involves a trust or stewardship, also a Pastorals theme. In 1 Timothy 1:11 Paul wrote of "the glorious gospel of the blessed God, which he entrusted to me."[16] In this way Paul writes with firmness, as he does at the beginning of

---

13. Words in the *epiphaneia/epiphaino* ("appearance, appear") group occur in 1 Tim. 6:14; 2 Tim. 1:10; 4:1, 8; Titus 2:11, 13; 3:4. The verb *phaneroo* ("manifest") is found in 1 Tim. 3:16; 2 Tim. 1:10; and here. The idea is revelation, manifestation, coming to light. See esp. the repeated mention in Titus 2–3.

14. This is the title of a classic work on the subject by T. R. Glover (London: Methuen, 1909).

15. So far in the Pastoral Letters such command language has appeared in 1 Tim. 1:1, 3, 5, 18; 4:11; 5:7; 6:13, 17; and will recur in Titus 2:15. Words about "convicting" are in 2 Tim. 3:16; 4:2; Titus 2:15.

16. Cf. 1 Thess. 2:4, where Paul said he was "entrusted with the gospel."

1 Timothy, against false teaching. Paul's authority is now resident in what he wrote along with the personal gifting. Whatever theological training a servant of God may have, his or her authority lies in neither gifts nor training; it resides in God's Word.

A society where there is mutual distrust, skepticism about religious claims, or fearful uncertainty about the future needs the kind of solid foundation and clear direction the revealed Word of God provides. But that truth needs to be heard and understood if it is to be accepted and appropriated as truth. One step in this is Bible translation. Another step, over which missionaries and theologians have labored especially during the last half of the twentieth century, has been the task of contextualization and indigenization. The Word of God needs to be applied meaningfully to each culture. While it is true that the gospel is appropriate and sufficient for all people of all cultures, it is now generally agreed that it needs to be "contextualized" to be understandable.

The means and extent of each contextualization have been discussed a lot. But more than communication is involved. Basic differences in worldview, understanding of the spiritual world, concept of life beyond death, standards of ethics, and so on call for different aspects of biblical truth. Near the beginning of the twentieth century A. Paget Wilkes, a missionary to Japan, became convinced that the gospel he was preaching, truth though it was, was not winning converts. He tried harder to listen to the Japanese people as they expressed their own thoughts, fears, and needs. Among these were uncertainty and apprehension about what lies after death. Wilkes thus began especially to emphasize those Scriptures dealing with resurrection and eternal life. A strong indigenous church in Japan is testimony of his ministry.[17]

There are common hopes and fears in societies around the world, but there are also particular belief systems, values, and popular philosophies that have generated different worldviews. Europeans and Quechuas, Wall Street brokers and hockey players, medieval serfs and sixteenth-century explorers, Chinese diplomats and computer programmers—each subculture or people group has had its own distinct failings and values. We are more accustomed today to preaching and to writing with a view to these, but so was Paul as he attempted to reach Jews, barbarians, the wise, slaves, and Cretans. Christians in all times and in all places have been entrusted with a gospel that must be meaningfully explained and applied if it is to communicate. Otherwise, the authority that we rightly ascribe to Scripture is muted.

---

17. Alphacus Nelson Paget Wilkes, *The Dynamic of Service* (London: Japan Evangelistic Band, 1931; also Kansas City, Mo.: Beacon Hill, n.d.).

The importance of order and leadership in the church. Day Runners and other so-called "organizers" appeal not only to highly organized people but also to disorganized people obsessed with the need for organization. Stephen R. Covey's work, *The Seven Habits of Highly Effective People*, and other books have had immense success in helping people put their lives in order. There apparently was a measure of disorder in Crete in the form of unfinished business. While it is possible for zealous Christians to be overly dogmatic about church government, chaos and anarchy are worse. Some years ago an independent church in the eastern United States seemed to be functioning well with a loose form of decision by consensus, without designated elders. Therefore, when a need arose for the church to discipline a particular individual, that man claimed no one in the church had authority to do so. It was not long before the church established an eldership.

Elders are to be "successful" people not so much in business but in self-discipline and character. To be sure, such people often *are* successful in business, but moral qualities are more important than that. Among the personal qualities mentioned in Titus 1:6–8 only one—"entrusted with God's work"—has to do with spiritual ministry. But in verse 9 the overseer "must hold firmly to the trustworthy message as it has been taught" so that he can "encourage others by sound doctrine" as well as "refute those who oppose it." This is a direct response to the degenerate state of the society in which the church functioned and to the attacks of the false teachers who threatened that church.

To meet such attacks, the elders must have the respect of the believers. We have already seen in 1 Timothy 3:1–7 that the elders' reputation in the surrounding community is important. But also these leaders must be well established and honored in the church if their handling of false teachers is to have the church's support. Personal dynamics inevitably enter into such circumstances. Those whom the elders consider culpable in a matter often have friends and supporters who esteem them more highly than they esteem elders. That situation can cause a weakening of the elders' perceived authority and eventually result in a church split or the triumph of the dissidents over the elders.

The saying "to the pure, all things are pure" has often been quoted out of context. It can easily be misconstrued to mean that good people never have to worry about thinking evil, or that somehow even impure things or thoughts are transformed into good. The point of the section in which this occurs is that those with evil thoughts and motives, who mentally transform even what is good into evil, often compensate by external ritual. But those whose minds are pure see the inherent good in God's world and need no such alchemy. We have already met this mentality in the ascetic practices described in 1 Timothy 4:1–5.

PROCLAIMING TRUTH IN a pluralistic society. Our pluralistic and postmodern society lies exposed to doubts and despair over whether it is possible that a system of truth is at all possible. Strange and unexpected messages grasp the attention of people looking for certainty. Sometimes these messages contain elements of truth. The early 1990s, for example, saw an increased interest in angels. By 1996 this interest was embodied in a television series *Touched by an Angel*, which hovered at or near the top of the Nielsen ratings.

An example of a different sort is the immense growth of the Mormon church since the 1950s. Although the alleged circumstances of its origins falter when probed historically, and although their doctrines run counter to those of orthodox Christianity, the "family values" and other moralistic practices of this religion (as well as its interest in the angel Moroni) have immense appeal around the world. The approach of a new millennium has brought with it an almost cultlike interest in things mystical. The last years of the 1900s and the opening years of the 2000s may be looked back on as an extraordinary opportunity for the proclamation of the certainties expressed in the opening verses of Titus.

Christianity has often been viewed in isolation from or even in competition with Judaism. But we should never forget that Christianity belongs to the ongoing revelation and historical activity of God among his special people that began with the call of Abraham about two millennia before Christ. Christ did not come in a historical vacuum, but as the culmination of God's work, his inspiration of the Hebrew Scriptures, and the specific predictions about the Messiah. This, in turn, is set in the history of humankind, which resides within the work of God from eternity past. The eternal life proclaimed in the gospel was "promised before the beginning of time" (v. 2) and was brought to light in that gospel.

All this should be of great help in stating the case for the truth claims of Christ. The history of Israel and the messianic prophecies provide a solid foundation for the gospel and should be involved more than they are in our witnessing. It is common, and right, for those who bring the good news to Jewish people to refer to this, but it can also be a strong element in our Christian apologetic (i.e., the logical support for Christianity). The theme of truth in this passage is linked to the fact that God "does not lie" (v. 2).

Another apologetic element is that knowledge of this truth "leads to godliness" (v. 1). We often use changed lives as evidence of the truth of the gospel, and that is right. But this claim must be made with the honest acknowledgment that sincere adherents of other religions also often lead upright lives in conscious obedience to the ethical teachings of their faith. Moreover, the claim can be weakened by the failure of some Christians to be consistent with what they have been taught. Nevertheless, this letter, like the two to Timothy, insists that the Christian gospel should be backed up by Christian living, that is, by "godliness." This was important in Crete, and it is equally imperative for our day, whether in Seattle, Atlanta, or Toronto, or in a football game, boardroom, or seminary chapel. As I write, yet another pastor has been arrested in the Chicago area—this time for planning, for sexual purposes, to meet with a girl he came to know on the Internet. His "date" turned out to be a law officer.

Must all the details of church order be followed today? The Contemporary Significance section for 1 Timothy 3:1–7 already has offered some suggestions for application on church order issues. The qualifications for elders given here in Titus are almost identical to the ones listed for overseers there. This similarity enforces the probability that they are important for churches anywhere. But are they uniformly applicable? Do they have any connection with specific cases? Do they arise out of conditions that, if they vary, call for other qualifications?

By way of comparison, some of the great doctrines of the church have themselves been articulated in the context of doctrinal strife. The various councils that produced these doctrinal statements were called to deal with particular circumstances, and therefore doctrines were shaped because of those circumstances. In spite of some of the political elements involved in their framing, the church has generally respected the doctrines thus formulated as being at the core of the Christian faith, especially those that deal with Christology. Likewise, the beginnings of various denominations were occasioned by circumstances that led the new churches to emphasize certain doctrines, practices, or values. Sometimes these have been idiosyncratic, reflecting the personalities and experiences of the founders, but insofar as they may have recovered and brought to public attention neglected truths, these should be acknowledged.

What, then, about matters of church order? Here the church has embodied different perspectives and practices. As to sacraments and ordinances, almost all Christians believe that baptism and the Lord's Supper were intended by the Lord Jesus for the church in every age and circumstance, though their meaning and practices differ. As to church leadership, forms also differ, though some leadership is generally acknowledged as biblical and necessary. In Paul's churches there was usually some structure, even in the charismatic climate of Corinth. Spiritual leadership is preferable to both bureaucracy and anarchy, though most Christians would not put the form of leadership on the same level of importance as the essential doctrines.

As to the qualifications for overseers, we can probably agree that what is listed in Titus 1 and 1 Timothy 3 describe a kind of moral character that is desirable among all believers and that should be required in any age. But are some qualifications more important than others in different circumstances? After we give due considerations to the original meaning and matters of bridging contexts discussed above and in connection with 1 Timothy 3, what principles can be applied specifically in a contemporary church?

The stipulation of being the husband of one wife, even if understood to mean the heart attitude of faithfulness, will be applied differently in different cultures today—from those where multiple marriage is common to an American church with mainly new Christians, who may have few capable persons who have not been divorced. While there is often no simple, clear-cut way of determining an "innocent party" in a divorce, some churches are trying to weigh the factors in a divorce. Was there marital infidelity on the part of one but not the other? What other factors eroded the marriage? Who initiated the divorce? Did the person being considered for eldership become a Christian after the divorce? If there was a remarriage, is the present marriage healthy? The answers to such questions *may* justify admitting the person to eldership.

And does the fact that these Pastoral Letters were written at a time when female leadership would have been unthinkable and offensive to their society affect how we apply the reference to elders as husbands today? Some think that the reference to the elder being a husband was not intended as a requirement, but was simply circumstantial. This issue calls for careful consideration. Are deacons required because there are directions concerning them in 1 Timothy, or are they optional because they are not mentioned in Titus? Some suggestions were made in the sections on 1 Timothy 3, so the most appropriate comment here may be a plea for thoughtfulness, common sense, and humble acknowledgment that sincere, spiritually minded Christians have differed. As in other matters, the unity of the Spirit must be maintained (Eph. 4:3).

Strong discipline is sometimes required. Verses 10–16 require strong application. Although Paul's counsel, especially to Timothy, is to be gentle in correction, there are times when firm disciplinary action and public rebuke are called for, particularly those who are "rebellious" and "deceivers" (v. 10), "ruining whole households" for "dishonest gain" (v. 11), "corrupted" (v. 15), denying God, "detestable," and "disobedient" (v. 16). It is hard to deal with such people if there is no strong, recognized leadership in the church.

This is a case where plural leadership is important. In one situation (referred to earlier), in a small church blessed with a mature, wise congregation, there had seemed no need for elders. But when one member abused his wife and said (correctly) that no one had the authority to confront him, the church decided elders were needed. In time he threatened to kill one of the elders, and the church was at that point able to deal with him. The message of Titus 1:1–16 for today is that not only leadership, but also leadership vested with authority is needed to handle any situation and any personal hostility that may arise.

The elders must have a good reputation themselves if they are to be qualified to address sin. They must be doctrinally sound in order to deal with error, and they must be known as those whose children are responsive to their parenting so they can be expected to be evenhanded, just, and competent in their discipline of those who, if not silenced, would destroy the church. In all of this, the goal today, as always, must be restoration. In this case it means acknowledging error, being sound in the faith, and deliberately rejecting all who teach falsehood (v. 14).

If these false teachers see everything through impure eyes, their assessment of what is pure will be affected. As with those who search the Internet for sexually impure websites, they will take into their "minds and consciences" what is impure (v. 15). Their relationship to God and society will be distorted and corrupted. Since this is all a matter of the inner person and since such individuals claim to know God (v. 16), no one will realize what is taking place. Paul Little, the popular InterVarsity evangelist of the 1950s and 1960s, said that a Christian who seems suddenly to have a moral blowout has probably experienced an unobserved slow leak. This passage should serve as a wake-up call to all who are becoming attracted by impure sights and thoughts, who are entertaining offbeat ideas about life and doctrine, and whose profession of God is greater than the reality.

Sadly, it is sometimes the person who seems most spiritual who is farthest from God. Spirituality is not to be measured in terms of Bible knowledge, pious prayers, or attendance at religious gatherings. Every reader of this commentary knows that, but we value spirituality so highly that we pursue the appearance even when the reality is lacking. Spirituality is a matter of the extent to which the *Holy Spirit* is motivating, empowering, and changing our lives. He is holy and he is spirit, so no unholiness or fleshly, carnal motives are compatible with his work in our lives. The Holy Spirit produces holy people. Holiness plus obedience, faith, and love for God and other people produce Christian character as Christ is "formed" in us (Gal. 4:19). Today's church is so activist, program-oriented, and overt in its worship that the character of the participants easily slips to a lower level of priority.

Doing good. We have seen again and again in the Pastoral Letters that doing good (v. 16) is of primary importance. Clearly a major distinction between true and false teachers is behavior. Morals and ethics count. It is common to compare Romans and Galatians with James, the latter being seen as teaching the evidential and practical side of good works. The Pastorals far outstrip James in the number of references to the goodness and good works expected in a true believer.

The preceding comments have pointed out the importance of holiness and Christian character. The truly spiritual person will not seek to display her or his inner holiness, but the inner self will nevertheless be seen, and rightly so, in the doing of good works. "By their fruit you will recognize them" (Matt. 7:20) is still good advice.

Titus 2:1–10

YOU MUST TEACH what is in accord with sound doctrine. ²Teach the older men to be temperate, worthy of respect, self-controlled, and sound in faith, in love and in endurance.

³Likewise, teach the older women to be reverent in the way they live, not to be slanderers or addicted to much wine, but to teach what is good. ⁴Then they can train the younger women to love their husbands and children, ⁵to be self-controlled and pure, to be busy at home, to be kind, and to be subject to their husbands, so that no one will malign the word of God.

⁶Similarly, encourage the young men to be self-controlled. ⁷In everything set them an example by doing what is good. In your teaching show integrity, seriousness ⁸and soundness of speech that cannot be condemned, so that those who oppose you may be ashamed because they have nothing bad to say about us.

⁹Teach slaves to be subject to their masters in everything, to try to please them, not to talk back to them, ¹⁰and not to steal from them, but to show that they can be fully trusted, so that in every way they will make the teaching about God our Savior attractive.

Original Meaning

THE COMMAND THAT opens chapter 2, "You must teach what is in accord with sound doctrine," indicates that what follows will deal specifically with the expectation, characteristic of the Pastoral Letters, that those who embrace the true faith will demonstrate a certain type of behavior in their lives.

"Teach" translates the Greek *laleo*. While this word commonly refers to the simple act of speaking, in the Pastorals it assumes the status of teaching (see 2:15). The teaching must be "in accord with" (i.e., appropriate to or "consistent with," NRSV) the "sound doctrine" that Paul has been advocating throughout the Pastorals. (On the use of "sound" see comments on 1 Tim. 1:10; 6:3; see also 2 Tim. 1:13; 4:3; Titus 1:9, 13). The teaching here is not in itself doctrinal; it is practical instruction that is based on doctrine.

In the list of instructions that follows, the "household" image is once again invoked in the household codes (see comments on 1 Tim. 5:1–16).[1] It is more than an image because in the Pastoral Letters the Christian assembly *is* a household in its function, though probably not with the same degree of intense realism as in the Pauline concept of the church as the body of Christ.

The older men in this household are not only to be venerated because of their age, as is common in many societies, but because of their character. The following chart cites the desired characteristics, compared with the description of the overseers and deacons in 1 Timothy 3 and the elders in Titus 1:

Greek word	Titus 2	1 Timothy 3	Titus 1
nephalious	"temperate"	verses 2, 11	[cf. v. 7]
semnous	"worthy of respect"	verses 4, 8, 11	
sophronas	"self-controlled"	verse 2	verse 8
hygiainontas	"sound		
te pistei	in faith	verses 9, 13	
te agape	in love		
te hypomone	in endurance"		

In a similar comparison, the older women are to be:

Greek word	Titus 2	1 Timothy 3	Titus 1
hieroprepeis	"reverent ..."		
me diabolous	"not ... slanderers	verse 11	
mede oino pollo dedoulomenas	"not ... addicted to much wine"	verses 3, 8	verse 7
kalodidaskalous	"teach[ing] what is good"	verse 2	verse 9

In addition to these specific parallels, the general demeanor described for older men and women has several points of general similarity with the character of elders even where specific words are not identical. The characteristic terminology of soundness or health appears in verse 2 (see comments above). This time, however, it is love and endurance that must be healthy, not only doctrine (assuming that the "faith" here means the body of Christian truth).

---

1. "The author of the Pastorals never addresses the subject of the household life of church members as a topic in its own right. Rather, whenever he introduces the topic of household life, he does so in the course of discussing one aspect or another of life in the household of God" (David C. Verner, *The Household of God*, 128). See also Robert Banks, *Paul's Idea of Community: The Early House Churches in Their Historical Setting* (Grand Rapids: Eerdmans, 1980).

The older women have a similar responsibility ("likewise" in v. 3), though the specific traits are different. As to how they are to live (i.e., their demeanor or behavior), these women should act "in a reverent way,"[2] the way a person should act in a holy place. Two potential failings are nasty gossiping and addiction to alcohol. Presumably these women have high moral standards and might tend to be overly critical of others, using their leisure time to find fault and scold. The Greek word translated "addicted" can sadly describe even a pious older woman. In contrast to such behavior, these women should draw on their mature wisdom and use their time to teach "what is good," especially to the younger women.

The word "train" (v. 4) is worth noting, especially since the Greek word is related to the word for "self-control" in verse 5. This word group has to do with such virtues as being reasonable, sober, moderate, and self-controlled. In classical Greek the specific verb used here meant to bring a person to his or her senses. It subsequently came to mean to give good advice or encourage. The NIV's "train" may raise some questions about why young women need training to love their families. But the Greek word can imply a need to be reminded of something, in this case of the dimensions and implications of their original love for husbands and children, a love that can be diminished by circumstances or lack of response from others. The phrase "younger women" may refer not only to young adults but to any women not thought of as old. Possibly the need of such training or encouragement is not so much the love itself as the realization of what that love should produce.

The further content of the teaching of older women for younger women (v. 4) is an interesting complex of subjects, but not unexpected in a Christian household code in that society. "Self-control" is related etymologically to the verb "to encourage" (cf. comments above). It implies thoughtful moderation in behavior. Between the words "pure" and "kind" is a word variously translated as "keepers at home" (KJV, which is too quaint), "workers at home" (NASB, which today could imply having a home office), "good managers of the household" (NRSV, an over-translation, as though it were *oikodespotein* in 1 Tim. 5:14), or "to take care of their homes" (NLT, a reasonable rendering). The NIV's "busy at home" is a literal translation. The term *homemaker* common a few decades ago would probably convey best what was meant in the society of Paul's day.

---

2. The Greek word used here conveys the idea of reverence such as one would show in a pagan temple (or, in our religious context, the kind of hushed awe one might feel in a great cathedral; see LSJ, 822). BAGD (372) cautiously suggests that the "more specialized [meaning] *like a priestess*" may "perhaps" be "possible" here. This has to do with attitude; these women were not considered priestesses. Kroeger and Kroeger's calling these women "female elders" who are required to be "worthy of the priesthood" reads too much into the evidence (*I Suffer Not a Woman*, 91).

Wives' being subject to their husbands is consistent with Ephesians 5:22 and Colossians 3:18. The reason given here for such submission and the other virtues is "so that no one will malign the word of God." Paul knows that for a Christian woman to step out of line in these matters will bring serious criticism on the Christian gospel and consequently on the Lord himself. Potential converts who are morally sensitive and aware of the standards expressed in ancient household codes will be turned away. That does not mean that this is the only reason for the virtues Paul lists. But we cannot ignore the proximity between the injunction regarding the submission of wives to the expressed purpose to avoid causing any to malign God's word.

Paul goes on to tell Titus to instruct "the young men" (v. 6), but, after repeating (from v. 5) the injunction to be self-controlled, instead of issuing further instructions for them, the apostle tells Titus how *he* can be an example *to them*. "Doing what is good" reflects a repeated command in the Pastoral Letters (1 Tim. 2:10; 5:10, 25; 6:18; 2 Tim. 2:21; 3:17; Titus 1:8; 2:3, 14; 3:1, 8, 14). No one can understand the message of these letters without grasping this emphasis.

The rest of the list emphasizes the kind of character Paul has urged throughout these letters. Titus's teaching should show "integrity," a word that functions as a mirror image of the familiar idea of "soundness."[3] "Seriousness" is a quality that elicits respect and is used for deacons and their wives (1 Tim. 3:8, 11) and for the older women (Titus 2:2). One does not always think of this as characterizing younger men. Once again we encounter the word "sound/soundness," now applied to speech. This may be related to Paul's cautions against getting involved in the quarrels spawned by the false teachers (2 Tim. 2:14), but may also have more to do with Titus's inner holiness as expressed in "healthy" speech (see also Eph. 5:4). These qualities, like those of the younger women, while important in themselves, are also a means of warding off possible criticism from unbelievers.

The instructions to slaves (v. 9) are similar to those in Ephesians 6:5 and Colossians 3:22. In addition to being submissive in every area of the relationship, Paul urges integrity in word and deed. Slaves are not to "talk back" to their masters. This idiom has to do with disputing what someone says, directly contradicting, or, even worse, opposing to the point of refusing to do what one is supposed to (Rom. 10:21). This would be a terrible attitude for Christian slaves to have instead of trying to please their masters (v. 9). The worst action is to steal from one's masters. By showing instead that a slave can be "fully trusted," he or she will "make the teaching about God . . . attractive." A third time, then (along with vv. 5, 8), Paul's

---

3. See comments on "sound doctrine" in verse 1.

instructions show Titus and Cretan Christians how character and good deeds can help win others to Christ.

SOUND DOCTRINE AND moral character. Verses 2–10 unpack the command of verse 1, which expresses a major theme, arguably *the* major theme, of the Pastoral Letters: A Christian's moral character should be consistent with sound doctrine. God should be glorified not only verbally, as in the several doxologies of the Pastorals, but also in the good works of those who profess faith in Christ (see Introduction). While the importance of moral character and good works have been repeatedly applied to Timothy, Titus, and the church leaders, it is expected of every believer. The good works urged here are both important in themselves and as a segue for the missionary message of the gospel.

It is noteworthy that many of the characteristics of ordinary Christian men and women in verses 1–5 are similar to those expected of elders (1 Tim. 3:1–7; Titus 1:6–9). This fortifies the teaching of the Pastorals on the importance of integrity of character for church leaders. They are not people nominated by friends and voted on to serve a term or two routinely as a mere tour of duty. Far beyond that, they are people already honored in the church and known to embody with a high degree of consistency the qualities expected of all believers. Those who desire the "noble task" of overseer (1 Tim. 3:1) should be among those following the teachings of this passage.

Principles for bridging significantly different cultures. It is not enough to recognize that the people of Paul's day were familiar with the so-called household codes—that is, the lists of duties expected of various levels of society in relationship to each other. Rather, we should ask whether the examples given are to be followed precisely or whether principles should be drawn without cloning the specific directions.

The obviously easy example to discuss in this regard is slavery. That is, it is easy *to us;* it was not so in the America of the 1800s. The Scriptures, both Old and New Testaments, have clear instructions that presume and continue the practice of slavery. If Paul told slaves to be subject to their masters, should not a slave in, say, 1780 or 1850 do the same? Much has been written on this issue, with theologians and Bible scholars in that period taking opposite sides. A fascinating work on such matters by Willard M. Swartley[4] is helpful in sorting out the issues and applying them to another difficult

---

4. *Slavery, Sabbath, War and Women: Case Studies in Biblical Application* (Scottdale, Pa.: Herald, 1983).

issue, the "place" of women. It is instructive to learn that there is some similarity between the way biblical texts were used to support slavery and the way certain texts are used in the discussion about women today.

But is it also legitimate to ask the following, as some do: If a prevailing arrangement that is now seen to be temporary (i.e., slavery) received such accommodation, if not actual support, from Paul, to the extent that he gave instructions to govern it, could some aspects of the marital relationship of wifely subjection also legitimately be considered temporary? However such matters may be decided—and they require more hermeneutical attention than can be given here—eventually some application has to be worked out. Fortunately in this case there are clear principles that can instruct us if we are thoughtful and responsive enough.

These principles are found in the three clauses at the end of verses 5, 8, and 10. (1) Verse 5 suggests that the wise Christian in any age and culture will evaluate the way contemporaries with moral integrity view the relationship of men and women. If we are going to be good missionaries and seek to win others to Christ, our standards of morality and of personal relations should be at least as high as those of unbelievers.

Paul had a missionary heart and missionary principles. He wrote (1 Cor. 9:19–23):

> Though I am free and belong to no man, I make myself a slave to everyone, to win as many as possible. To the Jews I became like a Jew, to win the Jews. To those under the law I became like one under the law (though I myself am not under the law), so as to win those under the law. To those not having the law I became like one not having the law (though I am not free from God's law but am under Christ's law), so as to win those not having the law. To the weak I became weak, to win the weak. I have become all things to all men so that by all possible means I might save some. I do all this for the sake of the gospel, that I may share in its blessings.

If the apostle was willing to interact with others in his society on their terms in order to accommodate for missionary purposes to their viewpoints, even with regard to the law (on which he had clear, firm convictions), we should be able to avoid alienating our contemporaries in the matter of gender relationships. This does not mean giving up our convictions, but it does mean softening the rhetoric. To go beyond this is to move not only into contemporary significance, but into further matters this commentary is not intended to pursue.

The result of Paul's principle as stated in verse 5 is that "no one will malign the word of God." He will proceed to show how to prevent Christians from being maligned, but here Paul is concerned that the gospel itself be vindicated by the lives of those who proclaim it.

(2) The principle in verse 8 suggests that our behavior should be unimpeachable so that even opponents of the gospel will have no ground for accusing us of evil. Like the first principle, this one echoes the concern seen throughout the Pastorals. It also reflects Paul's missionary principles. But the difference is significant. Not only should the integrity of the Christian be clear, the opponents should be ashamed. In 2 Timothy 2:15 Paul says the *Christian* workman should *not* be ashamed. Here the contrast between the critic and those the critic might accuse is obvious. The former incurs shame.

(3) Verse 10 also cites a good missionary principle. The practice of "lifestyle evangelism," which has been popular in recent years, accords with this. Unfortunately, that has sometimes been wrongly thought of as a *substitute* for "giving the gospel." Its intention, however, is to facilitate presentation of that gospel The assumption in the text is that the believers are declaring the "teaching about God our Savior." Our behavior should not only not alienate others; it should *attract* people to the gospel. The gospel will only be as attractive to the world as the behavior of those who profess it.

CURVES AND ANGLES. If there is any passage in the Pastorals that needs to be applied today, it is this one. Christians must work hard to live so that they give no cause to unbelievers to "malign the word of God," have anything "bad to say about us," or find Christian doctrine unattractive.

What may seem like straightforward advice that can easily be applied, however, turns out to have some curves and angles to negotiate. Older men and women today are trying hard to be contemporary and be "pals" with their grandchildren, rather than seem pious and remote. The old image of a grandmother knitting in her rocking chair, hair in a bun, humming hymns is long gone. Young women are not usually only "busy at home" in the sense here, but are more likely to be found on the judge's bench, in the executive suite of a downtown office, or skillfully using the latest computer program and searching out the newest exciting website. Ambition has overtaken them and many young men, who have little spare time for moral or religious concerns after rising early to hit the gym for a workout, catch the 6:44 train or battle the expressway, have a power lunch between long hours at the office, and perhaps squeeze an occasional flight to and from New York, to say nothing of watching football, basketball, or baseball on the tube in seasonal rotation. And slaves? How can that paragraph possibly be relevant?

What *is* relevant is the fact that like people of the first and every other century, we must work hard at character, spirituality, and communication of biblical truths to children, grandchildren, and neighbors. Great-grandfather may have shown his piety in how he put up with hot, sweaty hours on a farm without tractors or in a steel mill, working for low wages and without unions. We today may show our piety in putting in a full day at the office while suffering jet lag, in maintaining our peace when the stock market goes south, or, far worse, in maintaining our dignity and hopes while undergoing chemotherapy that makes us sick and causes us to lose our hair.

Christianity for the contemporary elderly. Older men and women should not be obsessed with their age or distressed the first time the salesperson offers a senior discount without being asked. But they should recognize that their time is definitely more limited than it seemed (at least) before age fifty-five. There is a growth of character that usually only comes with time, even if some mature faster than others. Faith and obedience can characterize even a new believer whenever that believer responds to one of God's commands positively. We can be filled with the Spirit at any age. Spirituality, however, is our habitual response to the Spirit, which takes time. Walking with God requires a sequence of steps. Endurance (v. 2) by definition is measured by time or distance. Love deepens. Wisdom requires the context of experience in which to come to know God as he wants to be known.

Old age is, therefore, an opportunity in itself. One does not have to have the same activities and ministries of youth to have challenges and usefulness. Arthritis may limit action, but it does not limit prayer. Neither does failing vision or hearing. The greatest opportunity for cheerfulness and witnessing may come not in a corporate jet but in a nursing home. While one's grandchildren may not enjoy being a captive congregation hearing repeated advice and moralistic stories from grandpa's younger years, they can be blessed when we go to their games and concerts, listen with interest to their joys and woes, and receive (perhaps without their realizing it) the benefit of our prayers.

The "Friends' Forum" is a group of older men in a northern Illinois church. They came together initially to help men who had difficulty finding meaningful relationships with other men in a church composed mainly of young adults. They have now taken initiative not only to know and enjoy one another, but to help others as well. During their initial years one of their number was a university professor from Ghana, who then returned to continue teaching and to serve as pastor of a church. They have had continued fellowship with him, sending books he can use with younger Christians. Another of the "Friends" is showing the group how to die. He is already past the time the doctors predicted. Roland shares openly and without complaint the progress of his disease and his feelings about it. This group takes aging and dying seriously, seeing them as opportunities to apply their faith.[5]

Most important in view of this passage, these older men are seeking ways to have fellowship with younger men, sharing with them (without "preaching" *at* them) what they have learned along the way from the Lord. There is a willingness among the men of the church to work cross-generationally, even though they would naturally tend to be with men of their own age. Together these men, younger and older but all Caucasian, also have fellowship across racial and denominational lines with the men in a black church. In these ways the "Friends" actively seek to fulfill the Lord's expectations of older men and are becoming good examples of Titus 2:2.

Young women and men. Young women are often turned off by the repeated criticisms of older women because they go to work, have their children in day care, and share decision-making with their husbands. They may already feel sad and even guilty for having to work and letting others care for their children; they need understanding and encouragement rather than criticism. Older women may have little concept of how much a mortgage, food, and taxes take out of even two regular paychecks. And if mother or grandmother thinks that daughter Michelle's payments on two cars and a large screen TV are unwise or unnecessary, perhaps more prayer and loving help in learning about caring for a family will bring Michelle to new spiritual perspectives and values.

It is true that in Paul's day women were expected to be subject to their husbands in a way and to an extent that is virtually unthinkable today. But some phases of secular feminism in the twentieth century involved so much hostility to men that many men and women also feel it went too far. Men have sometimes felt demeaned and far from equal (getting, some would say, a taste of what women have experienced). The instruction in Ephesians 5:33 that a wife should respect her husband is worth noting today. An equal, mutually loving, and respectful relationship can be a testimony that will keep people from maligning the word of God.

Young men today live in a world that can easily bring out the worst in a person. Temptations and pressures are intense. Competition is always present, whether in sports, sales, or popularity. Such issues hardly need to be specified here. In this environment phrases such as "self-controlled" and "doing what is good" are important. The example of a leader such as Titus with respect to "integrity," "seriousness," and "soundness of speech" can be a great encouragement and may help to counter shady practices and dirty jokes.

---

5. Since I wrote this Roland has died. His memorial service was a testimony to his openness and faith.

If slaves were to refrain from talking back to their masters, how much more should freely employed people rise above office slander. The Dilbert cartoon is funny because it is so true to life. Likewise, a Christian can see the funny side of work, can analyze it, can see through the boss, but still act with integrity, respect, and healthy ambition. Every day at work offers ways to "make the teaching about God our Savior attractive."

Preaching some of the ethical injunctions we find here and elsewhere in the Pastorals requires awareness of the audience. The days are long past when a Sunday morning congregation was familiar with and supportive of them all. Now not only has society at large moved far away from ethical standards against lying and cheating, but it is also far from moral standards of purity—as seen in the public reaction to an American president's extramarital affairs. Agreement can no longer be assumed—not even among church attendees.

The preacher needs to call for obedience to ethical injunctions on the part of the congregation, but he or she also needs to have a more nuanced approach to those who do not share these values. Their meaning and legitimacy need to be established, and we must trust the Holy Spirit to convict the world of sin. The parabolic approach of Nathan to David concerning Bathsheba (2 Sam. 12:1–14) may be one example of how to bring people today to a recognition of their own sin, a recognition that brings repentance rather than resentment.

Titus 2:11–15

OR THE GRACE of God that brings salvation has appeared to all men. ¹²It teaches us to say "No" to ungodliness and worldly passions, and to live self-controlled, upright and godly lives in this present age, ¹³while we wait for the blessed hope—the glorious appearing of our great God and Savior, Jesus Christ, ¹⁴who gave himself for us to redeem us from all wickedness and to purify for himself a people that are his very own, eager to do what is good.

¹⁵These, then, are the things you should teach. Encourage and rebuke with all authority. Do not let anyone despise you.

THIS SECTION DEALS with two "appearings." The first is the appearing of God's grace, an allusion to the first coming of Christ (v. 11), when God's grace was revealed "through the appearing of our Savior, Christ Jesus" (2 Tim. 1:10). Titus 2:13 cites the second "appearing," the second coming of Christ, described as the "blessed hope." Together these two references continue the theme that first appeared in 1 Timothy 3:16 of the vindication and public disclosure of Jesus as to his true nature and accomplishments.

The fact of Christ's first and second comings underlies the instructions in 2:1–10 (cf. the word "for" [*gar*], which introduces the basis for what precedes). This continues the pattern of alternation in the Pastoral Letters, where, instead of the more typical Pauline section on doctrine followed by a section on practical application, the Pastorals move frequently from one to the other.

This basis is not only the *fact* of the two comings of Christ, but (1) the first appearing is an appearing of "the grace of God," which both brings salvation and teaches self-discipline, while (2) the second appearing constitutes a great hope, to be realized in the return of him who is not only the Savior, but actually "our great God" (v. 13). The language of verse 11 contains an ambiguity, however. The key question is whether the indirect object in the phrase "to all [people]" depends (1) on the verb "has appeared" (i.e., "the grace of God . . . has *appeared* to [all people]"), or (2) on the verbal idea in the adjective *soterios*, "bringing salvation" or "that which brings salvation" (i.e., "the grace of God that brings *salvation* to all [people] . . ."). This can be clarified in the following diagram (the first and third lines show the order of the Greek words and the numbers in the second and fourth lines show two different sequences to read them):

has appeared	for	the grace of God	bringing salvation	to all people
4	1	2	3	5
has appeared	for	the grace of God	bringing salvation	to all people
3	1	2	4	5

A strong argument *for* associating "to all [people]" with "bringing salvation" rather than with "appeared" is that of proximity, while "appeared" occurs seven words away from "to all people," at the beginning of the Greek sentence. But the strongest reason *against* that connection is theological. God's grace does not save everyone (universalism), as the second option seems to teach. But if "bringing salvation to all [people]" were to be rejected because it is not true in a literal, all-inclusive sense, so should "appeared to all [people]," because, it may be argued, two thousand years later the gospel has still not reached every person.

There are, however, other possibilities. (1) "All [people]" can be understood to refer to all *believers*. The word "all" can be used in that sense when used alone (e.g., see Rom. 5:18b; 1 Cor. 15:22), but see further below. (2) "All" can be understood instead as *distributive*, that is, "all people without distinction."

The way the sentence *continues* must also be considered in making our decision. Verse 12 opens with a participle (rendered as the finite verb "teaches" in NIV, relating grammatically to the noun *charis*, "grace" (v. 11). Its object is "us," which in the context must mean believers. The sentence has its climax in "the glorious appearing of our great God and *Savior* ... who gave himself for us to *redeem* us" (emphasis added). Thus it is "grace ... teach[ing] us ... while we wait [for the one who redeemed us]." This emphasis on salvation and its redemptive effect on our lives points to a grace that brings salvation to all believers and teaches them, once saved, how to live for our coming Savior.

If this is the meaning, however, it is hard to explain why *anthropois* ("human beings, people") was used in the preceding verse rather than some word like *laos*, which often designates the people of God. Moreover, the use of "appearing" at the end of this section (v. 13) can (assuming that the second appearing of Christ is to *all* humanity) provide some ground for understanding "appearing," rather than "bringing salvation," as referring to "all [people]." It has also been suggested that "bringing salvation" can have a potential rather than realized sense, that is, "*offering* salvation." It must be noted, however, that in classical Greek the phrase conveys the sense of actually bringing deliverance or safety to someone, not merely trying to do so.[1]

Nevertheless, in the present context, while many have *not* accepted deliverance, many *have* (as the next clause makes clear). Probably the best way to understand the clause is to let "bringing salvation" stand together with the following words "all [people]" and to understand "all" as distributive, with the sense that God's grace brings salvation to *all* people for them to *accept*. That leads to the verse 12 as a contrast: *We* are the ones who are *taught* by it.[2]

In summary, the choices are as follows:

1. Grace has appeared to all people.	Not true in a literal sense, but would fit the contextual emphasis on "appearing."
2. Grace has appeared to all kinds of people.	A possible meaning, but not the emphasis here; stretches the meaning of "all."
3. Grace has appeared to all believers.	Possible and meaningful, especially if the emphasis is on *appearance* rather than salvation, though the use of *anthropois* is a problem.
4. Grace brings salvation to all people.	Not true theologically.
5. Grace brings salvation to all kinds of people.	Same as # 2.
6. Grace brings salvation to all believers.	Possible and meaningful, especially if the emphasis of the passage is on *salvation* rather than appearance, though the use of *anthropois* is a problem.
7. Grace brings the *potential of* salvation to an unrestricted number of people, many of whom accept it.	Possible, fits the contextual emphasis and is a possible extension of the classical usage cited.[3]

---

1. See LSJ, 1751.

2. In whatever way this particular exegetical issue may be solved, the importance of the gospel of God's grace in the Pastoral Letters is without question and must not be lost in the exegetical discussion. It is important to note that the "Savior" is also mentioned in verse 10, immediately before this section.

3. Peterson's paraphrase, "Salvation is for everyone!" communicates this option well (*The Message*).

The grace of God not only saves, it "teaches" (v. 12; perhaps better "trains," as in NRSV. The *paideia*-word group used here is the comprehensive Greek term for education. It connotes a disciplined kind of formation or training for life. But even "training" fails to communicate all that is in the Greek word. The description that follows in verse 12 of what this training should accomplish demonstrates the meaning of the verb better than any single English word. There are two goals: a negative one, to renounce two specified undesirable habits of life; and a positive one, to adopt in their place three desirable habits.

(1) The negative goals are introduced by the words "to say 'No.'"[4] What one should renounce or reject is not a person but "a godless, indulgent life."[5] The specific pair mentioned is "ungodliness" and "worldly passions." (a) The first of these (*asebeia*, cf. 2 Tim. 2:16) is the opposite of that highly desirable character trait *eusebeia*, "godliness, piety" (see later in this verse). It is the object of God's wrath (Rom. 1:18) and describes the objects of his judgment in Jude 15, 18. (b) The other trait combines the idea of desires, which can be good or (more usually) bad, with the modifying word "worldly," which characterizes them as belonging to the human society that ignores or despises God.

(2) God's grace also trains us positively to embrace the Christian life in a way that is "self-controlled, upright [or just] and godly." The last word is the adverbial form of *eusebeia*, which appears frequently in the Pastoral Letters as an important component in the life that pleases God (1 Tim. 2:2; 3:16; 4:7, 8; 6:3, 5, 6, 11; Titus 1:1, see esp. comments on 1 Tim. 2:2; 3:16). Knight suggests that these three adverbs refer to one's self, relationships with other people, and relationship with God.[6] Whether or not that was conscious intention on Paul's part, they probably overlap somewhat, and together they are comprehensive.

It is significant that Paul neither centers on the future consummation of our hope in the return of Christ to the neglect of our character and way of life here and now, nor centers on matters of conduct without setting these in the context of the Christian hope. The introduction of that "hope" in verse 13 is, in fact, joined to the ethical instructions grammatically by the use of a modifying participle (translated "while we wait" in NIV). All of this—manner of life and expectation of heart—is the content of the training that grace gives us.

In other words, before Paul addresses that "blessed hope," he mentions the virtues that grace teaches us to adopt and live out "in this present age."

---

4. On this verb, see Peter's denials of Christ (Matt. 10:33; 26:70, 72) and Titus 1:15 (regarding those who claim to know God but deny him by their actions; cf. also 2 Tim. 2:12–13 and comments).

5. *The Message.*

6. Knight, *Pastoral Epistles*, 320.

This exact phrase does not occur elsewhere in Paul's writings, but he often uses the word "present."[7] Paul is adopting the Jewish concept of two ages—the present age (sometimes translated "world")[8] stands in contrast to the age to come.

"Wait" in verse 13 (which connotes "waiting in expectation") appears elsewhere in the New Testament with other noteworthy objects, including the kingdom of God (Mark 15:43; Luke 23:51), the "consolation" of Israel (Luke 2:25), and the redemption of Israel (Luke 2:38). All these express the hope of pious Jews in the time of Jesus. Note especially Jude 21, which (like Titus 2:12–13) contrasts those who are godless with those who are "waiting" for the mercy of God. The object of the waiting here in Titus is "hope." Our hope rests in God (1 Tim. 4:10; 5:5; 6:17), Christ himself is our hope (1 Tim. 1:1), and our hope is in eternal life (Titus 1:2; 3:7).

The hope is called "blessed." Normally in Scripture, it is people, not things that are called "blessed." Nevertheless, at creation "God blessed the seventh day and made it holy" (Gen. 2:3). This made it a unique, sacred day. Also the Lord blessed a field (Gen. 27:27) and a kneading trough (Deut. 28:5), apparently prospering them for the benefit of the owners. By analogy the hope may be blessed because it is sacred or, though less likely, because it brings us benefit.

Although the object of our waiting is twofold, "the blessed hope and glorious appearing," it is a conceptual unity, with the two nouns joined in the Greek by one article. The NIV nicely expresses this by the use of a dash between them rather than with an "and." There are several options for assessing the grammatical structure of the content of the "blessed hope." To help view their distinctives they may be paraphrased and diagrammed as follows:

1. the *glorious* appearing of our great God and Savior, Jesus Christ
2. the *glorious* appearing of the great God and of our Savior Jesus Christ
3. the appearing *of the glory* of our great God and Savior, Jesus Christ
4. the appearing *of the glory* of the great God and of our Savior Jesus Christ

There are two issues here. Should the genitive "of the glory" be translated like a Hebraic genitive of description (i.e., "glorious"; cf. 1 and 2) or simply "of the glory" (cf. 3 and 4)? What about the grouping of the words that follow "appearing"? Does the single article after "glory" belong with both "God" and "Savior" (i.e., "the-great-God-and-our-Savior-Jesus Christ"; cf. 1 and 3), or only with "God" (i.e., "the-great-God and of-our-Savior-Jesus-Christ"; cf. 2 and 4).[9]

---

7. See Rom. 3:26; 8:18, 22; Gal. 4:25; Eph. 2:2; 1 Tim. 4:8; 6:17.

8. See Rom. 12:2; 1 Cor. 1:20; 2:6, 8; 3:18; 2 Cor. 4:4; Eph. 1:21; cf. Gal. 1:4.

9. An excellent discussion of this, combined with an appendix on "The Definite Article in the Greek New Testament," is in the important work *Jesus As God* by Murray J. Harris (Grand Rapids: Baker, 1992), 173–85, 301–13. Harris structures his discussion on several

As regards the first issue, while "glorious appearing" is possible, "the appearing *of the glory of God*" corresponds, perhaps intentionally, to the appearing "*of the grace of God*" in verse 11 and is therefore more likely. On the second issue, the use of the definite article in Greek to link together words constituting a conceptual unity (e.g., a single article with "hope" and "appearing" earlier in v. 13) enables us to see "God" and "Savior" as together. In the Pastoral Letters God is repeatedly called "Savior" (1 Tim. 1:1; 2:3; 4:10; Titus 1:3; 2:10; 3:4). By calling him the "great" God and Savior, Paul affirms this truth against those Greco-Roman cults who honored their gods as saviors.[10] If Paul had wanted to separate God and Christ in this sentence and avoid any attribution of deity to Christ, that could easily have been done with grammatical precision.

"Who gave himself" in verse 14 points to the voluntary offering of Christ on the cross for us (Mark 10:45; Gal. 1:4; Eph. 5:25; cf. Heb. 10:5–10). It is also true that God gave him to us and gave him up for us (John 3:16; Rom. 8:32). Earlier, Paul noted that the training that grace gives us is in both a positive and a negative form. Here the same pairing is the result of our Lord's sacrifice: negatively, to "redeem us from all wickedness," and positively, "to purify for himself a people that are his very own, eager to do what is good." These last words remind one of 1 Peter 2:9, especially "a people belonging to God." In Titus the people of God, taught by grace, are to do good works (cf. Eph. 2:10); in 1 Peter God's chosen are to declare his praises.

In verse 15 "these . . . things" occurs first for emphasis. Titus is to "teach" these things (cf. comments on "teaching" in 2:1). Two verbs follow: "encourage" (NRSV "exhort," which may be more appropriate in this context) and "rebuke." This continues the tone of the Pastorals (cf. 1 Tim. 4:11; 5:1, 20; 6:2; 2 Tim. 4:2; Titus 1:9; 2:6). These three verbs can have "these things" as its object (as Knight argues).[11] However, the grammar of Titus 1:9, in which Titus was instructed to encourage by sound doctrine and to rebuke those who opposed it, suggests that here in 2:15 "teach," "encourage," and "rebuke" all have people as their object.

Timothy was to do this "with all authority." Timothy needs authority in order to "command" (or "charge") the heretics to stop their teaching (see comments on 1 Tim. 1:3; cf. also 4:11; 5:7; 6:17), just as Paul charged Timothy to keep his command (6:13–14). The word for authority here in Titus

---

different grammatical options, four of which I have synthesized above (he also cites a fifth, more complex, option).

10. See comments on 1 Tim. 1:1; also Bridging Contexts section there about "God our Savior."

11. Knight, *Pastoral Epistles*, 329.

2:15 is *epitage*, a specific command. The use of this word in 1:3 is helpful in understanding the kind of authority Titus has. There Paul writes of the preaching (or "proclamation") entrusted to him by the "command" (*epitage*) of God our Savior. Just as this proclamation was entrusted to Paul, so Paul entrusts it to Titus. And just as Paul functioned under the command of God, so Titus is to function under the apostolic command of Paul, though there is no indication that Titus had broad apostolic authority as Paul did.

LEARNING HOW TO live. In verses 1–10 Titus was to tell several specific social groups to demonstrate the truth of God's Word in the way they lived. Now we see an important reason why they, and we, are able to do that: The same grace that saves us from the penalty of sin reorganizes our lives by "training" us how to live. The ancient Greeks, although encompassing different modes of education, had a word that came to characterize Greek education. The word was *paideia*: training the individual for life as a mature, wise person. It was a high ideal.

However, certain aspects of Greek education forfeited idealism in favor of pragmatism. While their study of language and the widespread training in rhetoric or oratory had a positive side, this could degenerate into mere platform performances of rhetorical ability and legal debate. One comic playwright caricatured Sophists as those who make the better argument sound worse and the poorer argument sound better. Sophistry reappeared in what we call the Second Sophistic (roughly second century A.D.), when its "chief characteristic [was] its irrelevance to life."[12] Thus even the highest ideals, whether of Greek *paideia* or of Christian education, can degenerate into arguments about words and opinions and into mere performance.

But Hebrew education both antedated and surpassed the Greek. Memorizing facts, learning history, and mastering the teachings of the Law were all intended to provide the means to live for the God who delivered their ancestors from Egypt. This had immediate implications in obedience to the Law God had taught them. Behavior was the necessary fruit of knowledge. The goal was not to be an educated person, even in the best Greek sense, but to be a good son or daughter of the covenant. Wisdom was not the ability to solve philosophical or mathematical problems or to win debates, but to understand the transcendent yet personal God of both their corporate and individual salvation. Jewish education at its best was in the context of the Exo-

---

12. Moses Hadas, *A History of Greek Literature* (New York: Columbia Univ. Press, 1950), 244.

dus, and the grace that saved them, so to speak, also instructed them. Psalm 119 was a magnificent reminder that God's Word should be active in every realm of life.

Thus, God's saving grace does not end at the crucial point of salvation, but accompanies us on the further journey of our new life, providing the wisdom and direction needed to remake our now-redeemed lives. The contrast of verse 12 in itself has a teaching function, as contrasts often do. A "Yes" to one choice requires a "No" to another. Paul opted here for the advantage of using a pair of similar sounding familiar words (*eusebeia* and *aseibeia*) that contrast a way of life that is godly and wholesome with a life totally opposite to that. The other expressions Paul uses, both positive and negative, flesh out the picture.

The reference to "this present age" was familiar (as noted above) to Jewish readers, who were used to the idea of the present age in contrast to the age to come. However, non-Jewish readers in any culture can recognize that if there is a "present" age during which we "wait" for the realization of a "hope," there must be a future "age" of some sort, however long or short it may be, in which that hope is fulfilled. The present age is also a time of opportunity for Christians to live a life of high moral quality that is appropriate between Christ's two "appearings," the one of God's saving grace (i.e., the first coming of Christ), the other his second coming. That kind of life is both possible and required because we have been "redeemed" (or "liberated") from wickedness and "purified" for doing good (v. 14). Thus, we have the two assertions, the "No" and the "Yes," the two ways of life, the two ages, the two appearings, and the two divine actions, redeemed and purified—all true of the one "people that are his very own."

The description in verse 13 of hope as an objective reality for which we wait accords with the fact that in Christianity hope is not merely a subjective feeling. Romans 5:1–11 demonstrates that the Christian hope is based on the fact that God has already accomplished the harder part of our redemption, in that while we were still helpless sinners and enemies of God, Christ died for us. That we "rejoice in the hope of the glory of God" (Rom. 5:2) is, in content, comparable to Titus 2:13. In Romans 8:22–25 even in the context of suffering Christians are given strong hope.

This section continues the all-important theme in the Pastoral Letters of the character that God expects to be found in his people, especially church leaders. Again, therefore, we must observe that both the *fact* of frequent repetition of this theme and the *manner* in which it is inextricably entwined with doctrinal matters is a distinctive feature of the Pastoral Letters. We affirm again that the pervasive theme of these letters is not church order, which appears only at certain points, or the refuting of heresy, even though it is the occasion for the letters and an urgent theme in them, but the importance of orthodoxy-plus-character.

The issue of authority. One of the most persistent and universal issues among churches and parachurch organizations is that of authority. Is authority passed down in apostolic succession or some equivalent mode of transmission (such as from the founder of a mission to his or her hand-picked successor), or is such a process restrictive and susceptible to unspiritual influences? Is church leadership best chosen by democratic voting, or is that a flawed method, especially in a church too large for the people to know the candidates and their qualifications? Should elders be self-perpetuating, or does that spawn nepotism and inbreeding? Is it right that a person who occupies the pulpit be accorded, or be *perceived* as possessing, an authority that others do not have? And who should make the decision as to where a pastor should serve and when it is time to leave—the church elders, the congregation, the bishop, or the pastor?

It is clear by now that while the Pastoral Letters do not address the specific means of perpetuating leadership in the church, they do (1) prescribe doctrinal correctness for the health of the church and (2) demonstrate the need for morally upright teachers to communicate God's commands. While Timothy and Titus were to convey these commands, it was neither a single individual, such as Timothy at Ephesus or Titus at Crete, or a successor to each of them who was to exercise authority in the continuing church, but the overseers or elders whom they were to see installed. This explains why the other Pauline letters (except for the personal one to Philemon) are not addressed to some individual church leader but to the "saints" in general, with Philippians specifically addressing a plurality of leadership ("the overseers and deacons," Phil. 1:1).

In other words, the ongoing ideal was plural leadership, with warnings on hand for any Diotrephes, who "loves to be first" (3 John 9). This, however, does not lessen the importance of authority; on the contrary, it emphasizes it. Paul's address to the elders from Ephesus showed that elders must be able to maintain doctrinal purity and guard the flock from heretics (Acts 20:25–31). That is a function of authority, and it is similar to the concerns of the Pastoral Letters.

LIVING IN THIS **present age.** The wide availability of the Christian gospel today is an amazing reality. Although there are many of the earth's inhabitants who still have never heard the name of Christ, the grace of God has "appeared" to an immense number of people worldwide, with unexpected responsiveness even among those traditionally opposed and hostile. Ralph Winter, to cite one mission authority, has repeatedly shown the progress of the gospel among the "people groups" of the world. Wycliffe Bible Translators and other lesser known translators have opened the Word of God to ever smaller groups of people in the languages they understand best. In spite of flaws and misunderstandings in our presentations, God's grace has powerfully brought the saving word of the gospel to billions of people.

In megacities, rural lands, tribal domains, universities, offices, hospitals, and other locations beyond imagination, this gospel message has been brought by earnest witnesses whose lives have commended their words. Martyrs and kings have represented the Lord with clear consciences. But more often than we know or want to know, the communicators of God's grace have failed to be taught by that grace.[13] And even if their failures have not been discovered, their effectiveness may have been lessened by spiritual battles in the unseen world. It is easy for a pastor to say "No!" to the twice-divorced visitor to the church office who wants a third marriage without counseling. It is harder for a missionary to deal with the recently converted tribal chieftain with multiple wives who seeks church membership. But it is harder still to say "No!" to our own passions and undisciplined use of time and money. True believers are "eager to do what is good."

Some years ago, several of my maternal uncles and an aunt were employed by a Christian publishing house and its associated printing firm in New York. One item this firm published found its way into many homes, especially in the 1940s. It was called the "Perhaps Today Calendar." Those who used it were of the eschatological persuasion that no biblical event needed to take place before the rapture of the church to heaven. We were to wait for what was understood to be the "blessed hope," focused and ready for the coming of our Savior. There have been many, of course, who have not looked for a "secret rapture," but for a glorious appearing of Christ to the whole world. In either case, such intense hope and eager waiting for the Lord's return is both commendable and all too easily lost.

The two world wars and a depression that made Christ and heaven more desirable have been succeeded by decades of changing world history and corresponding moods. Such recent competitors for our attention as the Internet, video games, video disks, and interactive TV seem to make waiting for the "blessed hope" less attractive. Those deeply involved in corporate life, trying earnestly to maintain performance standards and focused on seeking

---

13. For a significant and challenging treatment of grace and its many implications for Christian life see Philip Yancey, *What's So Amazing About Grace* (Grand Rapids: Zondervan, 1997).

promotions, will naturally find it harder to value a supernatural eschatological event than those who struggle with life's basic necessities. No doubt, if we could probe our inner dispositions honestly, some of us would like time to accomplish further personal goals on earth before every eye stares in wonder at that "glorious appearing" as a headline event on our TV screens.

Authority and its limits. We have seen that Timothy and Titus were given a clear mandate by Paul that is restated and interspersed throughout the Pastoral Letters. But the authority Timothy and Titus had was not autonomous. It was the authority inherent in the commission and message they received from Paul. Today the preacher's authority comes from the Word that is being preached. Timothy and Titus had that Word directly from the apostle Paul; we have it in the Scriptures. This is a warning regarding pastors who have an unhealthy sense of personal authority. Such pastors may, if they feel their authority waning, try to control a hostile congregation by taking illegitimate recourse to apostolic claims to authority. That apostolic language must not be detached from the circumstances of its legitimate authoritative use in its original context.

To combine the teaching, encouraging, and rebuking mentioned in verse 15 without feeling "despised" requires maturity and confidence in the Lord's commission. As one who has devoted many years to preaching as well as to academic teaching, I can testify that preachers can become very sensitive to criticism and discouraged if a congregation does not seem to respond to exhortation. (We should note here that the teaching, encouraging, and rebuking of individuals should take place in private rather than in public. Too often a rebuke from the pulpit is a thinly veiled criticism of individuals in the congregation.) With the Reformed emphasis on preaching, pastors can feel inadequate or even as failures if they lack in this aspect of ministry, even though they may be effective in other areas.

At the same time, however, skill in preaching can easily bring pride and neglect of other responsibilities. Further a so-called "bully pulpit" (Theodore Roosevelt's phrase is still used today) can become a bullying pulpit. Therefore it requires the "great patience and careful instruction" mentioned in 2 Timothy 4:2, rather than a domineering attitude. In this connection, the attitude of Ezra the scribe is instructive. He set his heart (1) to study the law of the Lord and (2) to do it; and then, as an obedient student, (3) to teach the statutes and ordinances in Israel (Ezra 7:10, NRSV). In recent years the practice of expository preaching has been much discussed and highly praised. We must remember, however, that expository preaching is not validated only by the truth conveyed, but by the life of the preacher.

Moreover, preaching is not a matter of mere sequential comments on a text, but the explanation *and application* of a portion of Scripture with due attention to its place *and function* in its context.[14] The contemporary significance of verse 15 is complex and of immense importance. The principles must be derived carefully, with due regard for the differences between the unique commission of Titus as an apostolic delegate to a threatened congregation and the commission of those who care for churches today with a broader and less authoritative range of responsibilities. Yet this passage, like other passages in the Pastoral Letters, teaches the importance of transmitting sound doctrine, and that doctrine carries divine authority. It is right for us to say, "Thus says the Lord" or, "The Bible says," making sure that we are properly teaching and applying Scripture.

14. See the Contemporary Significance section on 2 Tim. 4:2. See also Sidney Greidanus, *The Modern Preacher and the Ancient Text: Interpreting and Preaching Biblical Literature* (Grand Rapids: Eerdmans, 1988); Walter Liefeld, *New Testament Exposition;* D. Martyn Lloyd-Jones, *Preaching and Preachers* (Grand Rapids: Zondervan, 1971).

Titus 3:1–11

REMIND THE PEOPLE to be subject to rulers and authorities, to be obedient, to be ready to do whatever is good, ²to slander no one, to be peaceable and considerate, and to show true humility toward all men.

³At one time we too were foolish, disobedient, deceived and enslaved by all kinds of passions and pleasures. We lived in malice and envy, being hated and hating one another. ⁴But when the kindness and love of God our Savior appeared, ⁵he saved us, not because of righteous things we had done, but because of his mercy. He saved us through the washing of rebirth and renewal by the Holy Spirit, ⁶whom he poured out on us generously through Jesus Christ our Savior, ⁷so that, having been justified by his grace, we might become heirs having the hope of eternal life. ⁸This is a trustworthy saying. And I want you to stress these things, so that those who have trusted in God may be careful to devote themselves to doing what is good. These things are excellent and profitable for everyone.

⁹But avoid foolish controversies and genealogies and arguments and quarrels about the law, because these are unprofitable and useless. ¹⁰Warn a divisive person once, and then warn him a second time. After that, have nothing to do with him. ¹¹You may be sure that such a man is warped and sinful; he is self-condemned.

Original Meaning

CHAPTER 3 CONTAINS what appears at first glance to be, *in structure*, a repeat of chapter 2. Verses 1–2 contain another modified form of the household code, in the familiar style of a list of virtues. This adds the topic of submission to authorities to the instructions to various groups in 2:2–10. Then verses 3–8 portray the transition from the state of unbelief to new life by the grace of God (cf. 2:11–14); the latter part of which focuses on the importance of doing "what is good". Verses 9–11 contain instructions to Titus about his teaching mission (cf. 2:15).

True Conversion Should Make a Difference (3:1–8)

VERSE 1 OPENS with the word "remind," a gracious but insistent way in which Titus can reinforce teaching that the Cretans have already heard. It may also serve as a marker between chapters 2 and 3, with the teachings on personal relationships in chapter 2 possibly being newer to the church. Paul's "reminder section" deals with the theme of good works with a particular focus on the world of unbelievers. Note verse 3, where he not only affirms the grace of God in our conversion, but labors to identify our pre-Christian state with that of others yet unconverted.

The proper attitude toward the secular "rulers and authorities" is submission, obedience, and readiness "to do whatever is good." The fact that obedience is mentioned separately from submission indicates that not all submission requires obedience (Eph. 5:22 may be an example of this). One's civic obligations to secular authority are a staple in ancient "household codes." Being "ready to do whatever is good," Hanson observes, "almost a cliché"[1] (note the importance of this theme in the Pastorals: 1 Tim. 2:10; 5:10, 25; 6:18; 2 Tim. 2:21; Titus 2:7, 14; 3:8, 14).

The examples that follow in verse 2 include refraining from slandering others, being peaceful (lit., "not fighting"), being considerate (a requirement of elders in 1 Tim. 3:3; see also Phil. 4:5), and showing genuine "humility" to all people. The noun for "humility" (*praütes*) conveys the idea of gentleness as well as humbleness. This is a characteristic worth attention because it is both taught by and embodied in our Lord Jesus (Matt. 5:5; 11:29; 21:5; 2 Cor. 10:1) and is urged in such passages as Galatians 5:23; Ephesians 4:2; Colossians 3:12.

Verse 3 is joined to the preceding by the word *gar* ("for," untranslated in NIV). In other words, this section provides foundational or exemplary information pertinent to verses 1–2. The reason for this may not immediately be apparent, since verses 1–2 simply give instructions about functioning well in society. Underneath, however, is the fact that a first-generation Christian, like those still not Christians, can live disfunctionally. These instructions are, therefore, far from being mere moral platitudes. They indicate a contrasting life to that in society around them.

The next word in verse 3 is *pote* ("once"; NIV, "at one time"); it is paired with *hote* ("when") in verse 4. This is a before-and-after pattern (cf. also Eph. 2:11, 13; 5:8; Col. 1:21–22). The next words, "we too," serve to identify the Christians' preconversion experience with that of those around them in Crete. The effect of all this is to keep the Christians humble (cf. Titus 3:2), to offer

---

1. Hanson, *Pastoral Epistles*, 189, cites one example. It is not clear how frequently he has found this "cliché" use.

hope to the present unbelievers, and to allow the use of strong words describing the unbelievers, since these characteristics had at one time been true of the converts: "foolish" (see Rom. 1:14), "disobedient" (see "obedient" in Titus 3:1), "deceived" (see 1 Tim. 4:1; 2 Tim. 3:13), and "enslaved." The reference to slavery directs attention to the identity of the masters, which are "all kinds of passions and pleasures," as well as to the character degeneration that this involved: "malice," "envy," "hated," and "hating."

Fee observes that while grammatically verse 3 provides a reason for the appeal made in verses 1–2, it is like a "vice" list in its form.[2] Likewise in its form verses 1–2 look like a "virtue" list.[3] Given this structure, it is natural to look for corresponding positive and negative characteristics. This cannot be demonstrated at each point, but certainly the good attitude to others that verses 1–2 encourage has a terrible counterpart in the last part of verse 3.

The descriptive words in verse 3 reveal several facts about unbelievers. Being "foolish" is being without understanding, in a state of folly—a deliberate, rebellious choice, and not the state of a person merely lacking intelligence. This not only recalls the unbelieving fool of Psalm 14:1; 53:1, the people who lack the wisdom of God throughout Proverbs and Ecclesiastes, and those whom God calls "fool" in Luke 12:20, but also those described in Romans 1:21 and its context. The "disobedient" likewise reject God's sovereignty over them. Those who are "deceived" are led astray by Satan (cf. 2 Tim. 3:13; cf. 1 Tim. 4:1 ["deceiving spirits"]). We know from 2 Corinthians 4:4 and 11:2 that Satan is active in blinding people and deceiving Christians (2 Cor. 11:3). Thus, these unbelievers reject God's wisdom and lordship, deceived by Satan and enslaved by their own passions and pleasures. Their attitude toward others is an natural outcome of this spirit.

Verse 4 provides the kind of gracious interruption found in Ephesians 2:4: "But God, being rich in mercies, because of his great love with which he loved us" (lit. trans.). In Ephesians 2 the great operative words are mercy, love, grace, and kindness. They reappear here in a different order: kindness, love, mercy, and grace. In both passages God "saved" us. In Ephesians he raised us up and seated us with Christ in the heavenly realms; here he washes us, renews us, justifies us, and gives us "the hope of eternal life" (Titus 3:7). The Ephesians passage concludes with the call to good works—the same emphasis that concludes this passage in (v. 8).

The following diagram may be useful in conceptualizing the relationships of the clauses and phrases in this section:

---

2. Fee, *1 and 2 Timothy, Titus*, 202.
3. See C. G. Kruse, "Virtues and Vices," in *DPL*, 962–63, for a brief survey of New Testament ethical lists and alleged backgrounds, along with a bibliography.

Conjunction	But
Time (= circumstance) of salvation	when the kindness and love of God our Savior appeared
False grounds of salvation	not from (i.e., because of) things which, in righteousness, *we* had done
True grounds of salvation	but according to his mercy
Affirmation	**he saved us**
Means (of salvation)	through washing
Genitive (modifying "washing")	of regeneration
Means (of salvation)	and [through] renewing
Agency (of renewal)	[by the] Holy Spirit
	{**or:**
{*Means of salvation*	*through washing*
{*Genitive (modifying "washing")*	*of regeneration*
{*Genitive (modifying "washing")*	*and [of] renewing*
{*Agency (of renewal)*	*[by the] Holy Spirit}*
Relative clause (= manner of bestowal of the Spirit)	whom he poured out on us generously
Agency (of bestowal of the Spirit)	through Jesus Christ our Savior
Conjunction	so that
Circumstance (= basis)	having been justified by his grace
Purpose	we might become heirs
Concordance	according to the hope of eternal life.

The first clause in verses 4–7 is, as noted above, temporal. Using the distinctive terminology of the Pastoral Letters, the verb used in this clause is *epiphaino* (trans. "appeared"). And like 2:11, where the same verb occurs, it does not directly feature Christ as the subject, but rather refers to him obliquely. Thus, what has appeared is "the kindness and love of God our Savior," just as in 2:11 it was "the grace of God that brings salvation." In the previous passage the appearing motif occurs again with "our God and Savior, Jesus Christ" as the subject. Paul's emphasis is not only on the coming of Christ as Savior but also

(1) on the merciful, gracious work of salvation and (2) on the fact that this was *God's* work, using once again the characteristic reference to God as Savior (see also 1 Tim. 1:1; 2:3; 4:10; Titus 1:3; 2:10). The word for "kindness" conveys more than just goodness; it includes the idea of benevolence.

The next two phrases in the Greek structure are prepositional phrases modifying the main verb of the sentence, "he saved." The first phrase expresses what we may call *false* grounds. The basis on which God saved us is not the good things we have done (lit., "not out of works that we did in righteousness"). An emphatic "we" appears at the end of that phrase, stressing that it is not *our* doing (compare Eph. 2:8–9). The second prepositional phrase stands in strong contrast to the first, introduced by the strong adversative conjunction *alla*; it indicates the *true* grounds on which God saves us: "his mercy."

The next word is the main verb, "saved," in the simple aorist tense, indicating the basic fact of that completed work. Paul then cites the means by which God has accomplished this. The use of the Greek genitive after the preposition *dia* ("through") is significant here and not entirely easy to understand. Illustrating this by grouping the English words together by hyphens, one can read it "through-washing-of-regeneration and renewal-of-Holy-Spirit." In this reading, the washing is characterized by regeneration or perhaps produces it, and the renewal is accomplished *by* the Holy Spirit or perhaps comes *from* the Holy Spirit as a source.

These phrases can also, however, be understood as "through washing of regeneration-and-renewal of-the-Holy-Spirit." In this reading the regeneration and renewing are both functions of the washing. In either case it is difficult to separate the regeneration (a word used more in the Greco-Roman world than in Scripture, though see Matt. 19:28, NIV "renewal") from the washing.

The theological question is whether this teaches baptismal regeneration. On the one hand, on reading this from a Christian point of view it is hard not to think of baptism, and this was true especially in the early centuries, when ritual was a larger part of church life than it is now. On the other hand, it is *not* necessary to take the word "washing" as identical to and solely referring to baptism. Baptism can be understood as the visible form of washing without removing the fact that the Spirit and the Word cleanse us on the basis of the blood of Christ shed on the cross. If one takes the two genitive nouns ("rebirth" and "renewal") along with the "washing," this is grammatically and theologically permissible, but must not be allowed to minimize the fact of the further modifying genitive phrase ("by the Holy Spirit"). We might say that the means of salvation are: the washing (represented by but not identical to baptism), the regeneration, and the renewing, while the agents of the renewing are the Holy Spirit and Jesus Christ our Savior, through whom the Spirit has been so generously poured out on us.

The purpose of this process includes one further circumstance that can be considered as further modifying "saved" (in sense although not grammatically) or else as modifying "we might become heirs" (v. 7), namely, "having been justified by his grace." The overall point is clear: The purpose of God's mercy, grace, and kindness in our lives is "so that" we may be heirs of God, a concept closely linked to our having the "hope of eternal life" (cf. Rom. 8:16–17 and context).

The "trustworthy saying" referred to in verse 8 is one of the so-called "faithful sayings" in the Pastoral Letters.[4] It is not always easy to tell which words in the context are the "faithful saying" that Paul is quoting. In this case it is probably verses 4–7. Normally, the trustworthy sayings contain expressions uncharacteristic of the works attributed to Paul.[5] In this case such language is sprinkled throughout verses 4–7. Note too that what follows (vv. 8–11) does not have the structure of a quotation.

As noted earlier, the latter part of verse 8, in common with Ephesians 2:8–10, sets out the importance of good works for those who have experienced God's grace. One may have expected that Paul would then state that these things are to the glory of God or to the benefit of believers, but instead he makes the broad statement that they are excellent (cf. Titus 2:7, 14; 3:14) and profitable for everyone. Once again the apostle shows a concern for the world around him.

Several emphatic words are worth noting in verse 8: "to stress" (i.e., to strongly maintain, an exercise of Titus authority), "be careful," and "devote themselves to" (denoting being concerned about or caring for something).

Final Words About Controversies (3:9–11)

AS IN 2:11–14 Paul's exhortation here has a negative as well as positive side. In contrast to this strong affirmation of doctrine and life, there are things to be avoided (v. 9). The handling of controversies is an important matter in the Pastoral Letters (see 1 Tim. 1:4, 7; 6:4; 2 Tim. 2:23 and comments). The reason given here for avoiding them is that they are "unprofitable and useless." In 2 Timothy 2:23 the reason is because stupid arguments produce quarrels, which are contrary to the attitude a servant of the Lord should have in trying to win others. Here in Titus the uselessness of controversy relates to its ineffectiveness in changing others. Therefore, after a couple of warnings (Titus 3:10), Titus is to have "nothing to do" with that person.

---

4. See 1 Tim. 1:15; 3:1; 4:9; 2 Tim. 2:11; see the comments on 1:15 and the major work on the subject, Knight, *The Faithful Sayings in the Pastoral Letters*.

5. See Knight, *Pastoral Epistles*, 347–49, for evidence.

The words "you may be sure" (v. 11) introduce the reason why this person should be rejected: the individual's own hopeless nature. This does not mean that grace is never extended, for the person has already had a second chance (v. 10; cf. Matt. 18:15–17). It has been established that this "divisive person" cannot be redeemed. He is not only "warped and sinful," but he has also condemned himself, so the responsibility is not on Titus.

REPEATED THEMES IN the Pastorals. Someone writing another commentary in this series mentioned to me how difficult it is when writing the Original Meaning, Bridging Contexts, and Contemporary Significance not to repeat the same things. That is, of course, natural to this format because in essence what is taught in the text is true both in principle across contexts and specifically in our own world. But when studying the Pastorals, this repetition is multiplied because of these three letters tend to repeat the same theme: In passage after passage sound doctrine must be accompanied by a godly life. Yet in this section Paul says, "I want you to stress these things, so that those who have trusted in God may be careful to devote themselves to doing what is good" (v. 8). If Paul stresses these themes, so should we.

The section begins with a reminder to be subject to and to obey rulers and authorities. That, of course, is not new to Paul's writings (see esp. Rom. 13:1–10). This little paragraph in Titus moves the reader from the requirements of specific governmental regulations to having a humble Christian attitude in all social relationships. The steps in between are not necessarily in any logical sequence, put rather pick up sample elements of Christian attitudes to others. Doing good, not slandering people, being peaceable in relationships, and being considerate to others keep us from self-congratulation for the mere observance of law.

There is an implied contrast between the Christian who seeks to express the love that is the goal of God's law and the person who cannot even be subject and obedient to secular authorities. One can perhaps picture a wealthy Scrooge conferring with his accountant and tax attorney, looking for loopholes in the law that will save him taxes, in contrast to a businessman or woman who gives away as much as possible to help those in need.

Looking to the mercy of God. Having said that, Paul launches into another list, this time describing life before Christianity in highly negative terms. He focuses on disobedience to regulations, enslavement by personal passions, and hostile behavior to other people. This list is easier to accept because Paul includes himself as an example of pre-Christian behavior, but it does raise the question as to how severely one should characterize those who are not yet believers. After all, while we know that "all have sinned and fall short of the glory of God" (Rom. 3:23), it is also true that God has not left humanity without standards or without the remnants of morality and kindness. Christians are not the only ones who volunteer for charitable service. While it can be said that there is at least a little selfishness even in the things people do for others, unbelievers are capable of heroic sacrifices for the good of others.

C. S. Lewis once dealt with the question as to why some non-Christians are nicer than Christians. Postulating a Christian woman he calls "Miss Bates," who "may have an unkinder tongue than unbelieving Dick Firkin," he says the question is "what Miss Bates's tongue would be like if she were not a Christian." Further, "Dick's placid temper and friendly disposition ... result from natural causes which God himself creates."[6] As regards behavior, this is the substance of verses 3–8, though Lewis was dealing more with character and personality. No one can be saved by natural goodness, and those who have "trusted in God" should do "what is good," and that includes "Miss Bates's" use of her tongue.

There is a touch of sarcasm, though probably not intended, in Paul's words in 3:5 that God saved us "not because of righteous things we had done." Since this immediately follows the description of the miserable behavior of non-Christians, it is clear that such people cannot claim "righteous things" as a basis for salvation. But in the larger context, and especially recalling such passages as Philippians 3:4–6, where Paul describes his own religious accomplishments before conversion, the significance of this passage becomes more clear. Religious people can do bad things, and evil people can do good things. For *any* of us to be saved requires the mercy of God.

Titus 3:3–8 and Ephesians 2:1–10 manifest a point-by-point similarity. Both deal with the sinful life before salvation (cf. Eph. 2:2–3), the intrusion of God's love (cf. 2:4–5), God's saving of us not by our good works (cf. 2:8–9), and our having been raised to new life and hope, with the desired result that we devote ourselves to "good works" (2:10) and do "what is good" (Titus 3:8). In Ephesians Paul shows us the heavenly perspective on the purposes of God in the church, in that the good works are related to that display of God's wisdom made known to supernatural beings (Eph. 3:10–11). In Titus doing good is related to the display of a changed life over against the character of opponents of the gospel.

Warnings about divisive people—again. A number of problems surface in the Pastoral Letters that we find difficult to understand today. These

---

6. C.S. Lewis, *Mere Christianity* (New York: Macmillan, 1943), 116–64.

include "genealogies" and "quarrels about the law" (Titus 3:9). But the lasting principle is not the nature of these controversies (though that is sometimes important) but the fact that they breed controversy and arise from divisive intentions. The point of verses 9–11 is not so much to identify and correct wrong doctrine as it is to silence the divisive person. Some churches have painfully come to the realization that a wrong-headed advocacy for truth can be as destructive as a sincerely held minor error. This is not to ignore the seriousness of heresy or the fact that the Pastorals are dealing with evil-minded heretics. But this passage in particular has to do with those who are divisive in their intentions, "warped and sinful."

We can gain some perspective on this by noticing that in 1 Corinthians 5:9–11, when Paul talks about the kinds of people with whom Christians must not associate in the church (e.g., the immoral, the greedy, idolaters, drunkards, and swindlers), he inserts the verbally abusive person (KJV "railer"; NRSV "reviler"; NIV "slanderer") into this list. Every pastor knows the threat that such people can be to the life of the church. Unfortunately, a pastor may tolerate such behavior, not facing it squarely until it is directed to the staff or perhaps directly to that pastor.

"DOING GOOD" IN our neighborhoods. Verses 1 and 8 both speak of doing good. It would be useful if Christians could periodically sit down together to discuss how they can do good and better represent the Lord in their own communities. While there will always be stock figures such as the town drunk, the heartless creditor, and the seductive prostitute, nuances of evil change from place to place and from generation to generation. Rather than the small neighborhood groups of a church simply praying for one another's problems or debating eschatology, they can make immense strides in their community witness if they talk together about the spiritual climate in their neighborhoods and how they may better implement the gospel of Christ in their lives.

Surely there are not only distinctive ways *to witness* in different communities, but distinctive ways in which to *be a* witness. The story of a changed life has immense power to turn people to Christ. But that life must be genuinely changed not only as regards the cessation of sin but also in the performance of good. Ephesians 4:28–29 tells us that the thief must not only stop stealing but must do "something useful with his own hands, that he may have something to share with those in need." The person with a foul mouth should not only stop saying such things but must say what is "helpful for building others up according to their needs, that it may benefit those who listen." It is this kind of good that is going to make for an effective witness (cf. Titus 3:8). Every community has its own set of needs, problems, crises, and opportunities that call for specific Christian responses; "these things are excellent and profitable for everyone."

Dealing with the dark side. Every pastor dreads certain aspects of ministry. Grieving with those in the valley of death and those recently bereaved is often both a precious privilege and a heavy experience. But one of the most difficult tasks is working with church leaders in the confrontation of strong-headed divisiveness (v. 10). This sometimes occurs low key, gradually grinding away at love and unity. But sometimes it is open to the view of the whole community.

A 1998 segment on the CBS TV program *48 Hours* focused on the conflict between a gospel-preaching minister and a fundamentalist preacher who was having an affair with the evangelist's wife. The hiring of a hit man (who was actually an undercover agent) to kill the fundamentalist resulted in the imprisonment of the other minister. What impressed this viewer (along with sadness and embarrassment) was the intransigence of the adversaries and the apparent disregard by allegedly Christian ministers of the very theme we have been observing in the Pastorals: sound doctrine blended with godly living before the outside community. Intransigence can characterize anyone—from heretic to minister. The godly pastor must face such people with all the wisdom, patience, and boldness described in verses 9–11. Freedom from heresy does not mean freedom from controversy. How a church and its pastors handle this may affect the church's witness for years to come.

The controversies and divisiveness that call for strong action on the part of Christian leaders (vv. 9–10) require a rare blend of humility and authority, of love and uncompromising admonition. The stronger the reputation of a church and its leaders for expansive love, integrity, and civility in demeanor, the more effective will be their vigorous insistence on doctrinal purity. If Jesus had had a reputation as a hard-liner devoid of compassion, his resolute opposition to error and sin would have seemed more like the outburst of a pathological faultfinder than the justified outrage of a holy prophet and compassionate Savior.

Titus 3:12–15

A S SOON AS I send Artemas or Tychicus to you, do your best to come to me at Nicopolis, because I have decided to winter there. ¹³Do everything you can to help Zenas the lawyer and Apollos on their way and see that they have everything they need. ¹⁴Our people must learn to devote themselves to doing what is good, in order that they may provide for daily necessities and not live unproductive lives.

¹⁵Everyone with me sends you greetings. Greet those who love us in the faith.

Grace be with you all.

Original Meaning

PAUL'S FINAL REMARKS in verses 12–15 include personal requests (vv. 12–13), a reprise of the latter part of 3:8 (which repeats the emphasis on doing good, v. 14), and finally greetings and a benediction (v. 15). The Pastoral Letters are full of personal instructions, but the closing allows for the kind of specific instructions contained in Ephesians 6:21–22 and Colossians 4:7–9.

In comparing the conclusions of the three Pastoral Letters, Fee sees 1 Timothy and Titus more "all business," with 2 Timothy "more personal in every way."[1] This is certainly true and reflects the nature of each of these letters. Paul intends to send either Artemas or Tychicus to substitute for Titus (Titus 3:12), whom the apostle wants to meet him at Nicopolis. This was a good place for Paul to go for the winter. It was on the western edge of Greece on the Adriatic Sea, a little over fifty miles south of the present border of Albania and Greece.

Nothing more is known about Artemas, though Tychicus is well known (Acts 20:4; Eph. 6:21; Col. 4:7). Since we know from 2 Timothy 4:12 that Tychicus had gone to Ephesus (and by that time Titus had gone to Dalmatia, 4:10), we can assume that Artemas was the one who continued the necessary work on Crete. At this time Paul was apparently still ministering in Macedonia (1 Tim. 1:3).

In 3:13 Titus is instructed to do all he can to help Zenas and Apollos on their way. There is some difference of opinion as to whether "Zenas the

---

1. Fee, *1 and 2 Timothy, Titus*, 213.

lawyer" was an expert in Jewish law or Roman law. It is unlikely that Paul would have cited him as an expert in the former, and given the importance of Roman law, to be an expert in that field would have been a distinction. Apollos is well known in the New Testament (Acts 18:24–19:1; 1 Cor. 1:12; 3:4–22; 16:12).

Regarding the verb *propempo* ("to send someone on one's way"), in ancient times wandering preachers were supported in various ways, frequently begging or in other ways trying to raise money. Paul was determined not to do this, but preferred to work with his own hands to support himself (1 Thess. 2:5–9). Early Christian evangelists depended on those in churches already established to provide for their needs rather than on those to whom they were preaching. When a servant of the Lord went from one place to another, Christians in the location of origin would provide something for their journey. The word *propempo* originally meant to go partway along with someone as they started out their journey. It later came to signify providing for someone's needs (without actually starting out with them). This is especially important in 3 John 6, where it shows the contrast between Christian and non-Christian itinerant preachers.[2] This meaning of *propempo* is supported by the words "and see that they have everything they need."

Verse 14 picks up the latter part of verse 8, repeating the same words in the same order: "to devote themselves to doing what is good." This means believers not only providing for themselves in order to avoid being a burden to others, but, it may be assumed, also being fruitful in providing for others.

The closing greetings of verse 15 are warm and all-inclusive as both senders and recipients. The simple words "grace be with you all" conclude the letter—one final reminder of the saving grace of God.

EVERYBODY LIKES STORIES about people. *Reader's Digest* discovered this fact many years ago. The popular books in Christian bookstores often are those that are full of illustrations about people. The Gospels contain narratives and parables about people. Thus, one almost has a feeling of relief when, after the heavy instruction in this letter to Titus, Paul also talks about people.

This closing section stirs the imagination. We like to think about the busy apostle preparing for where he will spend the winter. Did he plan to take any time for vacation? We wonder what Zenas the lawyer was like and why he and Apollos were the special objects of Paul's loving care. It is in this

---

2. See also Acts 15:3; 20:38; 21:5; Rom. 15:24; 1 Cor. 16:6, 11; 2 Cor. 1:16.

paragraph that we find Paul spelling out what it means to do good, that is, to "provide for daily necessities" (or "urgent needs," NRSV). We always like to read his greetings to friends (v. 15).

Every instruction about doctrine, every warning about heresy, and every encouragement to holiness and good works is effective only as it is realized in the lives of real people. Surely one of the joys of heaven will be to meet first-century slaves and their masters, medieval peasants and their lords, pilgrims, business people from India, school teachers from the Czech Republic, and computer scientists from Asia—all testifying to the grace of the Lord in their lives. The Christian's joy in any age is to bring the love of Christ to people.

MOST MISSIONARY LETTERS and magazines today contain vivid pictures or descriptions of the people whom that particular mission or missionary is reaching for Christ. Christian agencies make pictorial appeals to provide Bibles for the Chinese, to send missionaries to the remaining unreached people groups, and to support orphans. All this is good and can be facilitated by contemporary means of production and communication. Charitable organizations, such as those caring for children in deprived areas, must be sure to channel all the money possible from the donations received to those in need.

The conclusion to Titus also reminds us of the people right around us, people like Zenas and Apollos, who need encouragement along the way. It serves as a reminder to make that phone call or send e-mail to brighten someone's day. All this may sound folksy and trite in a commentary but it was not trite to the great apostle Paul.

Scripture Index

Scripture Index

Scripture Index

Scripture Index

Subject Index

Subject Index

Christology, hymnology and, 144–47
church, the: ecclesiology of, 31, 126; establishment of, 126; growth in, 61; in history, 303–4; leadership in, 320; missionary task of, 30; models of service in, 135; relationships in, 174; role of, 229; sin and purity in, 195–96, 274
circumcision group, 316–17
Claudia, 302
Clement, 27
coming, of Christ, 149, 336–38. *See also* appearance, Second Coming
command: of God, 45–46; false teachers, 52; Paul functioned under, 48; to refer to the law, 55; teaching of, 164; Timothy is to, 220; vocabulary of, 36; what to, 77
communion, 125, 169
confession: of faith, 215–17; Timothy's good, 210
conscience, 38; is a God-given ability, 59; that produce love, 78; word for, 56–58
consecration, by the Word of God, 152, 154
contentment, and true godliness, 204–7
context, importance of, 105
contextualization, 319
controversies, 54–55, 58; final words about, 353; handling, 260–63; obsession with, 204
conversion, 349
Conzelmann, Hans, 42
creation, God's, 107, 155
creed, reliability of the, 141–42
Crescens, 302
Crete, 20–21, 23–24, 33, 312; the church on, 314–15; society of, 318; Titus at, 309
crown, idea of, 289–90
cultural background, 108. *See also* background
culture, interpreting Scripture by, 107
Cynic philosophers, 28

Dalmatia, 20, 24
date, matter of, 33

deacons: dignity of, 34; qualifications of, 132–39; and their wives, 329
Dead Sea Scrolls, 54
death: destruction of, 239; facing, 306
deconstruction, process of, 82
defection, among leaders, 200
deity, of Christ, 30–31
Demas, 297, 302
diakonos, 32, 71, 133, 135
Dibelius, Martin, 42
disciple, called as, 46
discipline, in the church, 323
discipling, 229, 253–55
divorce: and children, 189; factors in, 323; increase in the Roman empire, 181; remarriage after, 128–29; suffered through, 228
doctrine: and behavior, 143; blended with holy living, 37; called "sound," 65–67; in connection with deacons, 133; and life, 161, 169; is not sound, 61; into practice, 185–86; of Scripture, 242; of succession, 247. *See also* instruction, sound doctrine, sound teaching, teaching
Donelson, L. R., 43
doxology, 35, 73–74, 76, 212–13, 217–18, 300
drinking: dangers of excess, 196, 199; moderation in, 133. *See also* abstinence, alcohol, wine

ecclesiastical background, 104. *See also* background
ecclesiology, 31–33, 126. *See also* church, deacons, elders, leadership, overseers
education, modes of, 342
eirene, 47
elderly, 333; feel unable to manage, 190; needs of, 185–90; respect for, 198; support groups for the, 189
elders: able to teach, 127, 130–31; accused of sinning, 193; character of, 121, 320, 324; definition of, 121; and divorce, 129; at Ephesus, 115–31, 193; honoring, 194–95; need for, 311; and overseer, 31–32;

Subject Index

Bring ancient truth to modern life with the
NIV Application Commentary *series*

Covering both the Old and New Testaments, the **NIV Application Commentary** series is a staple reference for pastors seeking to bring the Bible's timeless message into a modern context. It explains not only what the Bible means but also how that meaning impacts the lives of believers today.

Genesis
This commentary demonstrates how the text charts a course of theological affirmation that results in a simple but majestic account of an ordered, purposeful cosmos with God at the helm, masterfully guiding it, and what this means to us today.

John H. Walton
ISBN: 978-0-310-20617-0

Exodus
The truth of Christ's resurrection and its resulting impact on our lives mean that to Christians, the application of Exodus is less about how to act than it is about what God has done and what it means to be his children.

Peter Enns
ISBN: 978-0-310-20607-1

Judges, Ruth

This commentary helps readers learn how the messages of Judges and Ruth can have the same powerful impact today that they did when they were first written. Judges reveals a God who employs very human deliverers but refuses to gloss over their sins and the consequences of those sins. Ruth demonstrates the far-reaching impact of a righteous character.

K. Lawson Younger Jr.
ISBN: 978-0-310-20636-1

1&2 Chronicles
First and Second Chronicles are a narrative steeped in the best and worst of the human heart — but they are also a revelation of Yahweh at work, forwarding his purposes in the midst of fallible people, but a people who trust in the Lord and his word through the prophets. God has a plan to which he is committed.

Andrew E. Hill
ISBN: 978-0-310-20610-1

Psalms Volume 1

Gerald Wilson examines Books 1 and 2 of the Psalter. His seminal work on the shaping of the Hebrew Psalter has opened a new avenue of psalms research by shifting focus from exclusive attention to individual psalms to the arrangement of the psalms into groups.

Gerald H. Wilson
ISBN: 978-0-310-20635-4

Ecclesiastes, Song of Songs

Ecclesiastes and Song of Songs have always presented particular challenges to their readers, especially if those readers are seeking to understand them as part of Christian Scripture. Revealing the links between the Scriptures and our own times, Iain Provan shows how these wisdom books speak to us today with relevance and conviction.

Iain Provan
ISBN: 978-0-310-21372-7

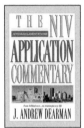

Jeremiah, Lamentations

These two books cannot be separated from the political conditions of ancient Judah. Beginning with the time of King Josiah, who introduced religious reform, Jeremiah reflects the close link between spiritual and political prosperity or disaster for the nation as a whole.

J. Andrew Dearman
ISBN: 978-0-310-20616-3

Ezekiel

Discover how, properly understood, this mysterious book with its obscure images offers profound comfort to us today.

Iain M. Duguid
ISBN: 978-0-310-21047-4

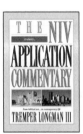

Daniel

Tremper Longman III reveals how the practical stories and spellbinding apocalyptic imagery of Daniel contain principles that are as relevant now as they were in the days of the Babylonian Captivity.

Tremper Longman III
ISBN: 978-0-310-20608-8

Hosea, Amos, Micah
Scratch beneath the surface of today's culture and you'll find we're not so different from ancient Israel. Revealing the links between Israel eight centuries B.C. and our own times, Gary V. Smith shows how the prophetic writings of Hosea, Amos, and Micah speak to us today with relevance and conviction.

Gary V. Smith
ISBN: 978-0-310-20614-9

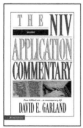

Mark
Learn how the challenging Gospel of Mark can leave recipients with the same powerful questions and answers it did when it was written.

David E. Garland
ISBN: 978-0-310-49350-1

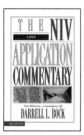

Luke
Focus on the most important application of all: "the person of Jesus and the nature of God's work through him to deliver humanity."

Darrell L. Bock
ISBN: 978-0-310-49330-3

John
Learn both halves of the interpretive task. Gary M. Burge shows readers how to bring the ancient message of John into a modern context. He also explains not only what the book of John meant to its original readers but also how it can speak powerfully today.

Gary M. Burge
ISBN: 978-0-310-49750-9

Acts
Study the first portraits of the church in action around the world with someone whose ministry mirrors many of the events in Acts. Biblical scholar and worldwide evangelist Ajith Fernando applies the story of the church's early development to the global mission of believers today.

Ajith Fernando
ISBN: 978-0-310-49410-2

Romans

Paul's letter to the Romans remains one of the most important expressions of Christian truth ever written. Douglas Moo comments on the text and then explores issues in Paul's culture and in ours that help us understand the ultimate meaning of each paragraph.

Douglas J. Moo
ISBN: 978-0-310-49400-3

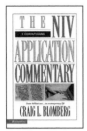

1 Corinthians

Is your church struggling with the problem of divisiveness and fragmentation? See the solution Paul gave the Corinthian Christians over 2,000 years ago. It still works today!

Craig Blomberg
ISBN: 978-0-310-48490-5

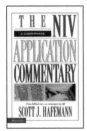

2 Corinthians

Often recognized as the most difficult of Paul's letters to understand, 2 Corinthians can have the same powerful impact today that it did when it was first written.

Scott J. Hafemann
ISBN: 978-0-310-49420-1

Galatians

A pastor's message is true not because of his preaching or people-management skills, but because of Christ. Learn how to apply Paul's example of visionary church leadership to your own congregation.

Scot McKnight
ISBN: 978-0-310-48470-7

Ephesians

Explore what the author calls "a surprisingly comprehensive statement about God and his work, about Christ and the gospel, about life with God's Spirit, and about the right way to live."

Klyne Snodgrass
ISBN: 978-0-310-49340-2

383Philippians

The best lesson Philippians provides is how to encourage people who actually are doing quite well. Learn why not all the New Testament letters are reactions to theological crises.

Frank Thielman
ISBN: 978-0-310-49300-6

Colossians, Philemon

The temptation to trust in the wrong things has always been strong. Use this commentary to learn the importance of trusting only in Jesus, God's Son, in whom all the fullness of God lives. No message is more important for our postmodern culture.

David E. Garland
ISBN: 978-0-310-48480-6

1&2 Thessalonians

Paul's letters to the Thessalonians say as much to us today about Christ's return and our resurrection as they did in the early church. This volume skillfully reveals Paul's answers to these questions and how they address the needs of contemporary Christians.

Michael W. Holmes
ISBN: 978-0-310-49380-8

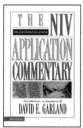

1&2 Timothy, Titus

Reveals the context and meanings of Paul's letters to two leaders in the early Christian Church and explores their present-day implications to help you to accurately apply the principles they contain to contemporary issues.

Walter L. Liefeld
ISBN: 978-0-310-50110-7

Hebrews

The message of Hebrews can be summed up in a single phrase: "God speaks effectively to us through Jesus." Unpack the theological meaning of those seven words and learn why the gospel still demands a hearing today.

George H. Guthrie
ISBN: 978-0-310-49390-7

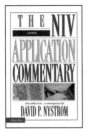

James

Give your church the best antidote for a culture of people who say they believe one thing but act in ways that either ignore or contradict their belief. More than just saying, "Practice what you preach," James gives solid reasons why faith and action must coexist.

David P. Nystrom
ISBN: 978-0-310-49360-0

1 Peter

The issue of the church's relationship to the state hits the news media in some form nearly every day. Learn how Peter answered the question for Christians surviving under Roman rule and how it applies similarly to believers living amid the secular institutions of the modern world.

Scot McKnight
ISBN: 978-0-310-49290-0

2 Peter, Jude

Introduce your modern audience to letters they may not be familiar with and show why they'll want to get to know them.

Douglas J. Moo
ISBN: 978-0-310-20104-5

Letters of John

Like the community in John's time, which faced disputes over erroneous "secret knowledge," today's church needs discernment in affirming new ideas supported by Scripture and weeding out harmful notions. This volume will help you show today's Christians how to use John's example.

Gary M. Burge
ISBN: 978-0-310-48620-6

Revelation

Craig Keener offers a "new" approach to the book of Revelation by focusing on the "old." He stresses the need for believers to prepare for the possibility of suffering for the sake of Jesus.

Craig S. Keener
ISBN: 978-0-310-23192-9